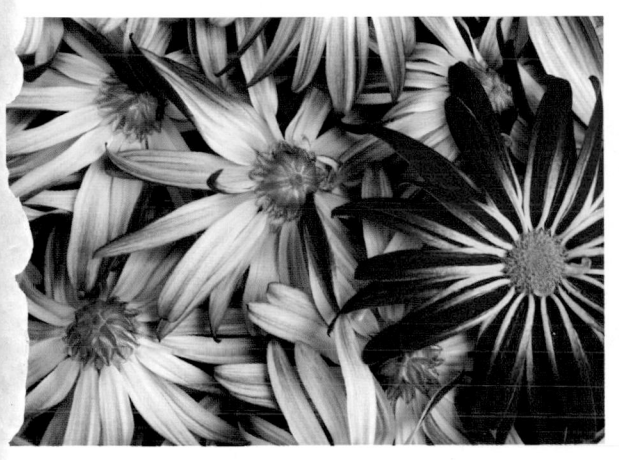

BRYAN PETERSON'S

UNDERSTANDING
COMPOSITION
FIELD GUIDE

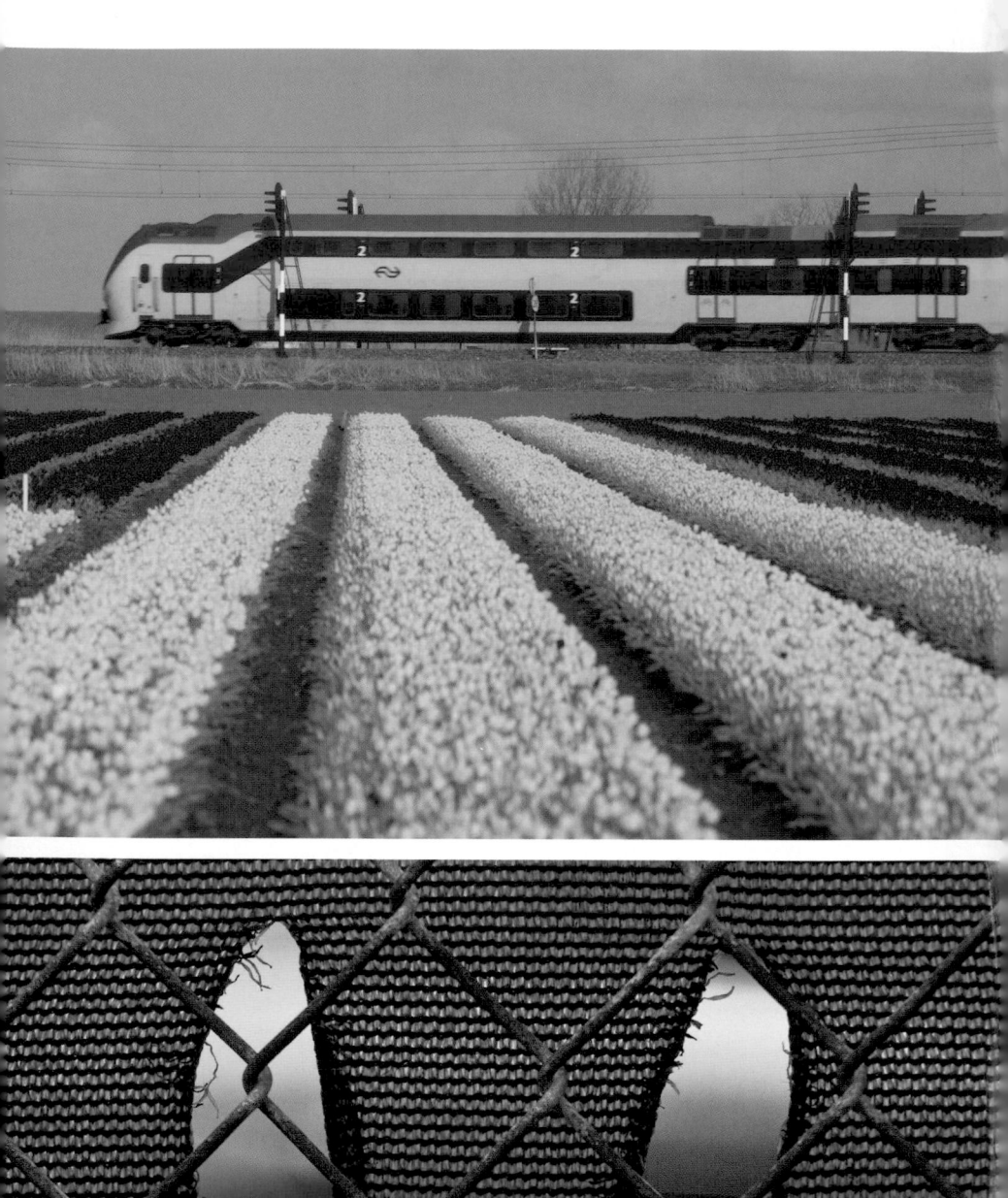

BRYAN PETERSON'S

UNDERSTANDING
COMPOSITION
FIELD GUIDE

HOW TO SEE AND PHOTOGRAPH
IMAGES WITH IMPACT

AMPHOTO BOOKS

an imprint of the Crown Publishing Group / New York

Published in the United States by Amphoto Books, an imprint of the Crown Publishing Group, a division of Random House, Inc., New York.
www.crownpublishing.com
www.amphotobooks.com

AMPHOTO BOOKS and the Amphoto Books logo are trademarks of Random House, Inc.

Some of the photographs in this book originally appeared in previous Bryan Peterson publications.

Library of Congress Cataloging-in-Publication Data
Peterson, Bryan,
  Bryan Peterson's understanding composition field guide / Bryan F. Peterson.
    p. cm.
  Includes bibliographical references and index.

1. Composition (Photography) I. Title.
II. Title: Understanding composition field guide.
  TR179.P466 2012
  770—dc23
            2012007279

ISBN 978-0-7704-3307-9
eISBN 978-0-7704-3308-6

Printed in China

Design by: Karla Baker

10 9 8 7 6 5 4 3 2 1

First Edition

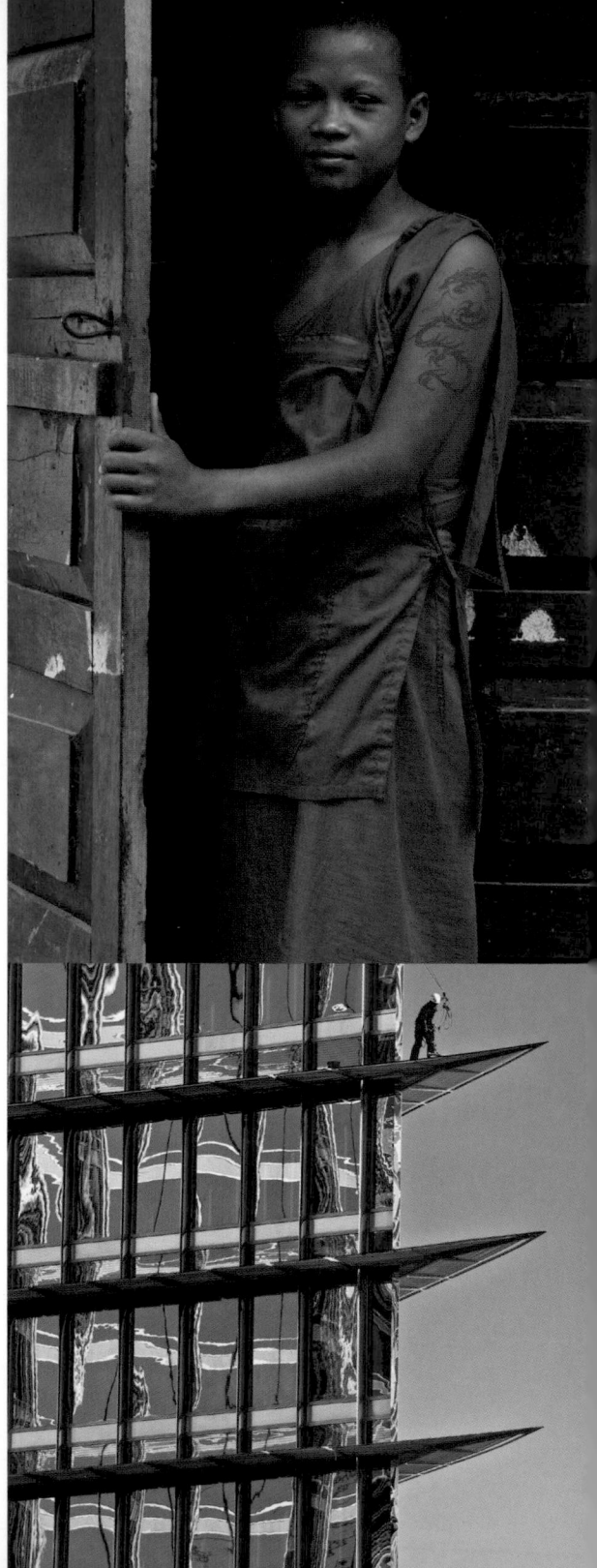

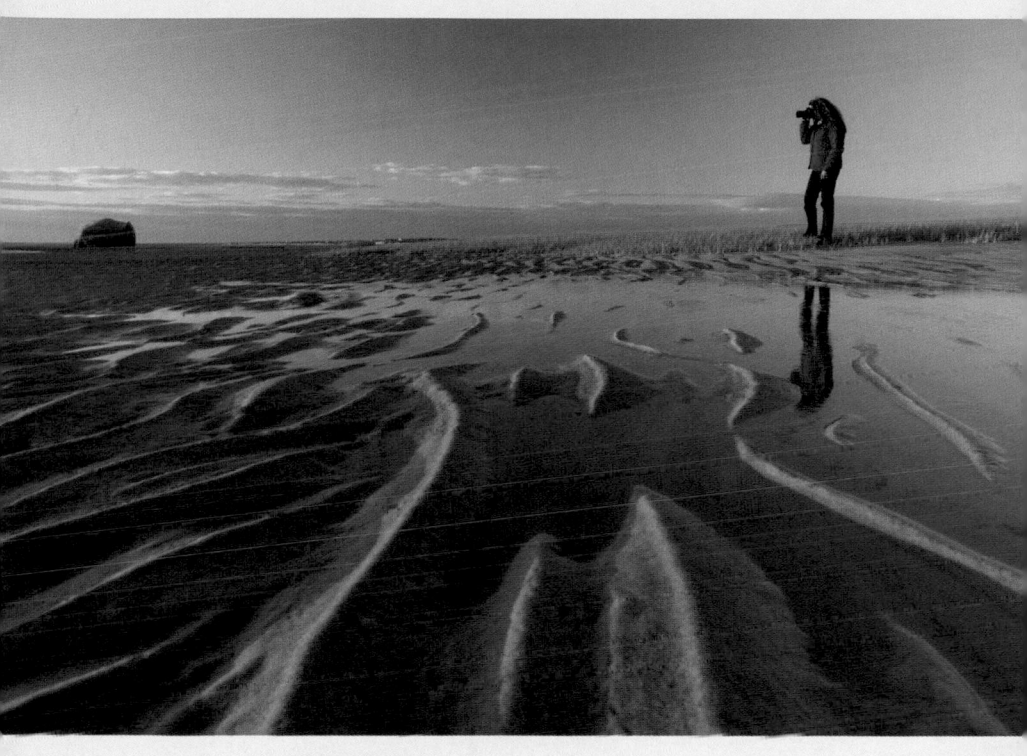

Put fear aside, allow yourself to be blinded by your passion, and soon you will see!

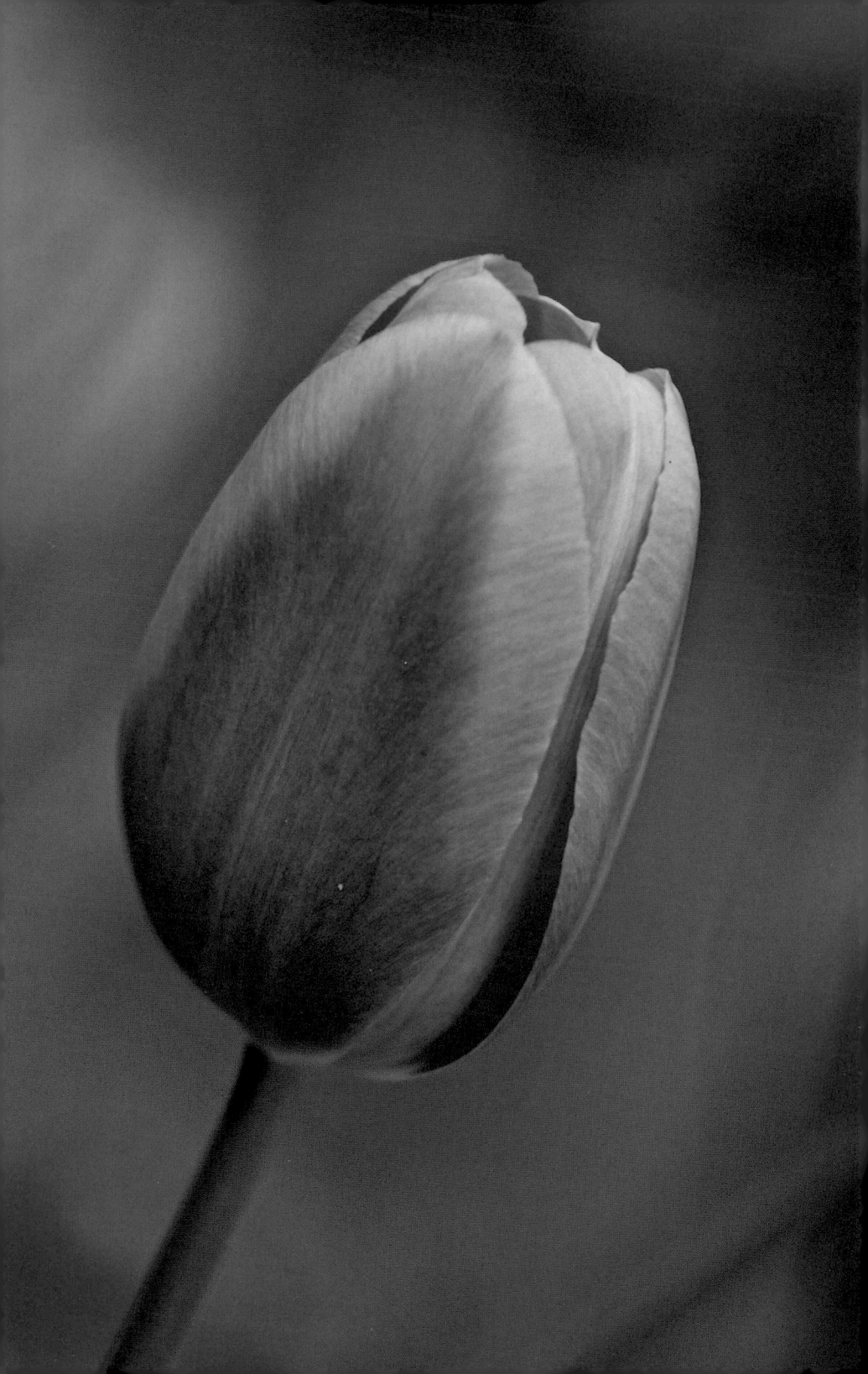

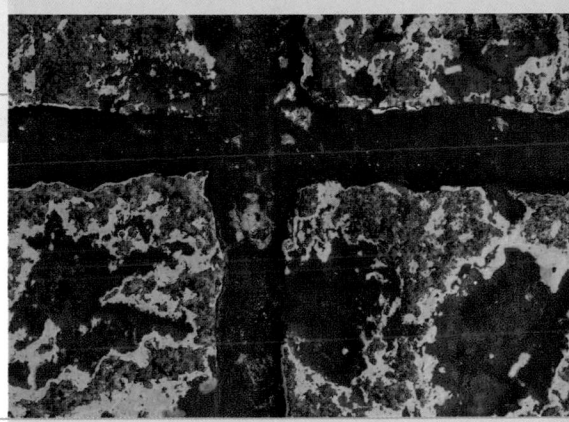

CONTENTS

INTRODUCTION

What constitutes an amazing image? If you ask nature photographers, they might describe an image of Half Dome at Yosemite shot in inclement weather when, as luck would have it, the clouds parted just enough to allow several shafts of low-angled, late-afternoon light to cast an incredible glow across its face. If you ask fashion photographers, they might describe an image of a model who, while running on a sandy beach, leapt into the air at exactly the same moment that a large ocean wave crashed into a rock behind her. If you ask newspaper photographers, they might describe an image of a family whose tearstained faces encompass a large part of the foreground, while over their shoulders you can see the remnants of their house, reduced to smoldering ashes.

All three of these images *do* sound amazing, and yet without the actual photographs in front of us, we can only trust that they are as incredible as described. Or maybe they aren't! Although the *content* of all three images suggests "amazing," it is entirely possible that they are far from compelling, without impact, without emotion. How could that be, when clearly what I have described sounds like three amazing images? Because compelling photography is, first and foremost, not about the *content*! Compelling photography is about the *arrangement* of content.

This is a book about the language of that arrangement and how that language also speaks volumes about you, since I am firmly convinced that every image you will ever take is a revealing self-portrait of the inner you and all that goes on inside you. As you frame each and every image you take, each individual arrangement reveals a snippet of the inner you; the you that is driven or indecisive, passive, sorrowful, ambitious, elusive, impulsive, spontaneous, balanced, warm, integrated, angry, and so on. Photographic

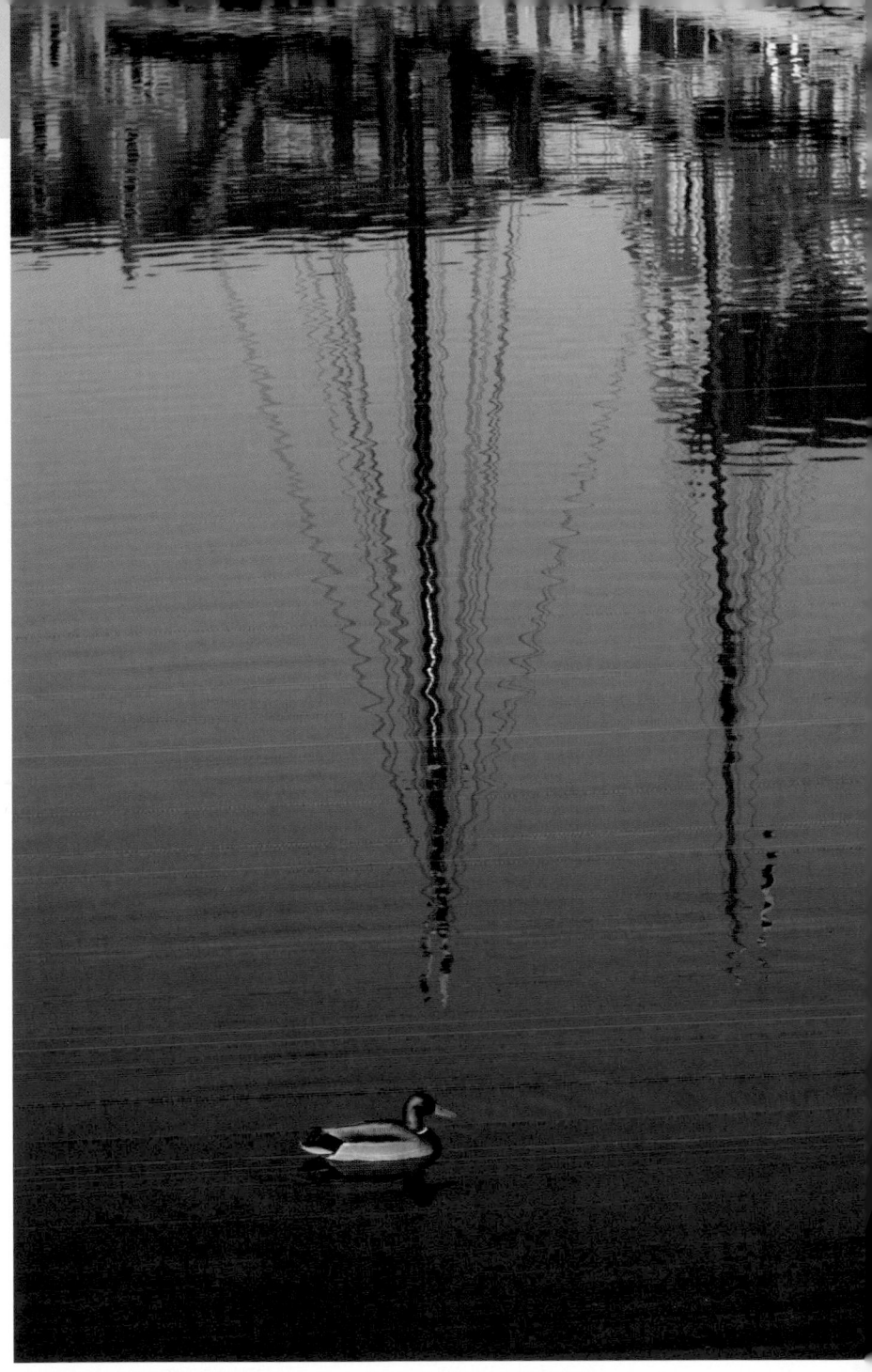

Nikon D3X with Nikkor 70-300mm lens, f/11 for 1/100 sec., ISO 200

composition is a lifelong journey that reflects various passages over time *if* you know where and how to find the clues—clues that I will share with you in this book.

Technical know-how is good but far from liberating. True photographic freedom comes from a willingness to look at the world through a "virgin eye." I can't stress those two words enough: *willingness* and *virgin*. Each one of us is born with virgin eyes, though it isn't long before well-meaning parents and teachers have shaped our vision: what's good, what's bad, what's pretty, what's ugly, what is a turnoff, what is compelling. The aim of this book is simple: no matter how mundane or "ugly" the *content* of an image might be, it is the *arrangement* of that content—what is known as composition—that makes for compelling imagery.

Whether you are shooting garbage, Half-Dome in Yosemite, a fashion model, or a stricken family, a compelling image awaits *if* you understand the "rules" and nuances that every successful arrangement relies on. Sometimes it is a simple matter of filling the frame. As I have often said when viewing a student's work, "You are two feet short of a compelling image!" Put another way: walk closer to the subject to better the fill the frame, and don't ever forget that the cheapest and most reliable zoom lens is your feet! Other times you will call on the Rule of Thirds, or simply switch the camera from its more comfortable horizontal position to a vertical position. Maybe your subject will benefit from tilting the camera at a 45-degree angle; then again, maybe the prob-

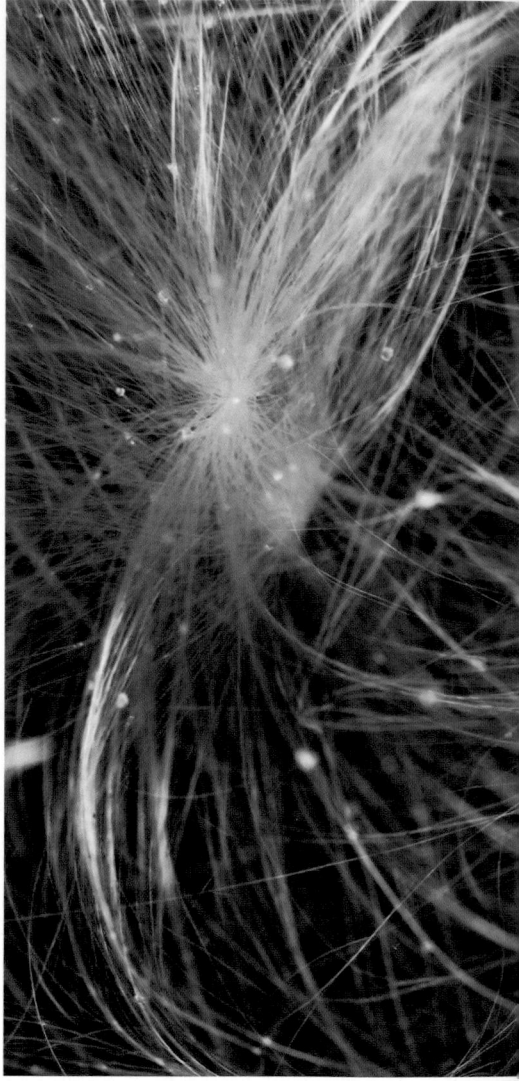

lem is all that distracting contrast, a wrong choice in aperture, a stale point of view, or an image that is a wee bit "soft."

Additionally, there are a number of visual exercises in this book—"alarm clocks," if you will—designed to train even the most untrainable eye not only to "see" but to successfully arrange content in a compelling

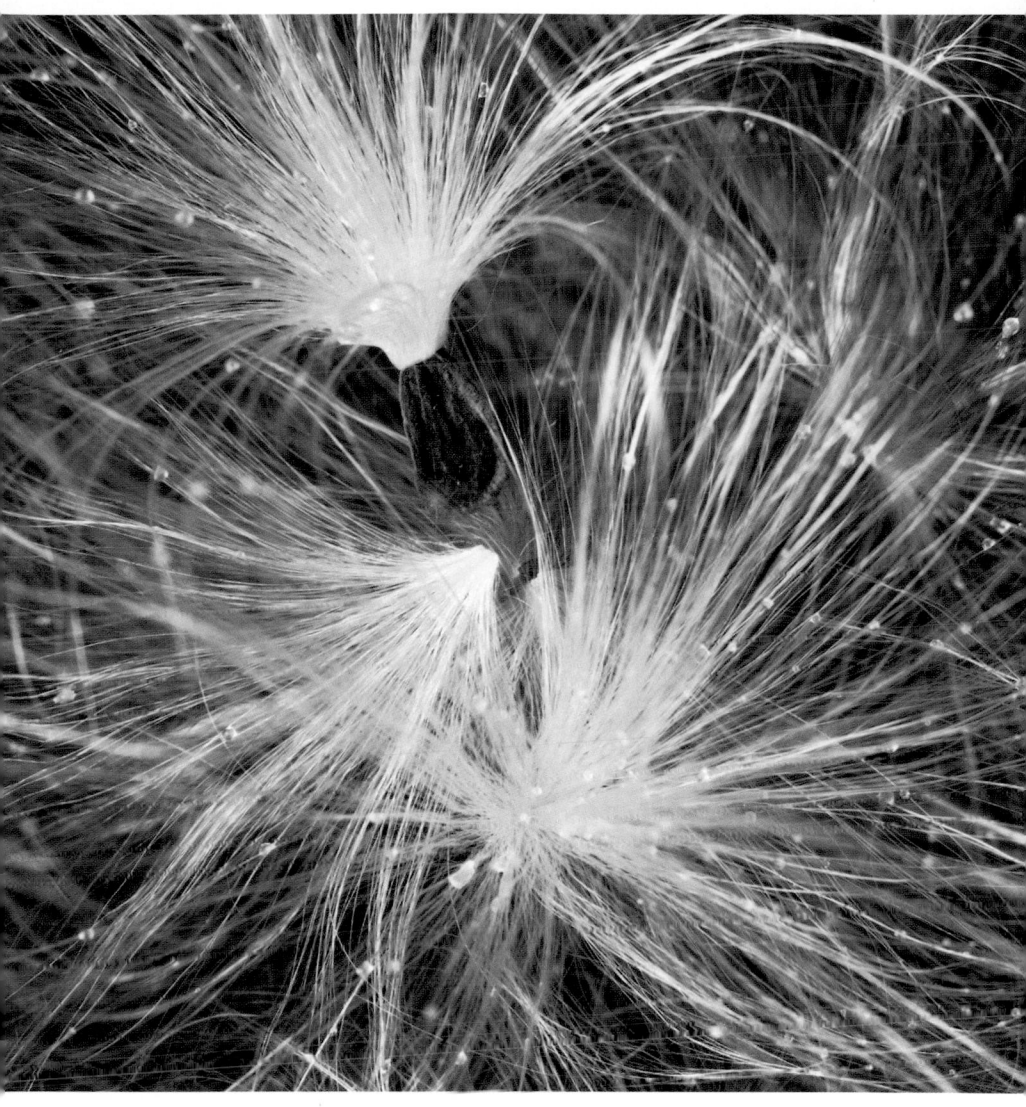

manner each and every time. These alarm clocks will awaken the creative vision that lies within each of us, even those who claim to be the deepest sleepers among us all!

Nikon D3X with 24–85mm lens, f/16 for 1/125 sec., ISO 100

TAKING CONTROL OF YOUR IMAGES

Most of us are familiar with the software Photoshop and perhaps even the term *layers*. Layers is a Photoshop feature that allows you to stack two or more images atop one another and, by using a "mask," blend elements from one image onto another to create an all-new image. It is a technique called on more and more by amateurs and professionals alike in their quest to create the ultimate image.

Perhaps if I were starting my career today, I would be a diehard Photoshop layers kind of guy, if only because the possibilities are truly endless. But I have been doing my thing for so long now that my ideas and approach are firmly entrenched in the "get it done in camera" mentality. This means a careful and sometimes methodical approach to seeing "layers," from the background to the foreground, along with choices about lens, point of view, time of day, and the addition of or subtraction of objects or props, into a final arrangement in camera.

I believe I save time using the "get it done in camera" approach. In addition, there is something else, something that remains important to me when creating visual records of the world I live in: the physical experience. In recalling most, if not all, of the images I have recorded, I notice how quickly my "emotional reminders" rise to the surface. It might be the texture of a subject, the way it felt if I touched it. It might be the smell of salt spray in the air, or the sound of distant thunder and the flash of lightning, or the memory of a dog that almost took a bite out of my face had I not jumped up from his food dish just after shooting a wide-angle close-up. Each image is a reminder of a period in my life, both good and bad, and I prefer to preserve that reminder unchanged. I have always done, and will continue to do, just about anything necessary to get the shot in camera, whether that means waiting for a car or a person to get out of the way, placing a leaf on a rock, or asking my subject to move inside the doorway rather than sit on the porch steps. I'll ask the model to wear a certain piece of clothing or walk in a certain direction, place a chair where a chair would not normally be, wait for a hoped-for rainbow, or for the sun to make an appearance and flood the eastern sky with low-angled, warm light as the sun sets to the west, even spray "dewdrops" on blades of grass because the hoped-for morning dew from Mother

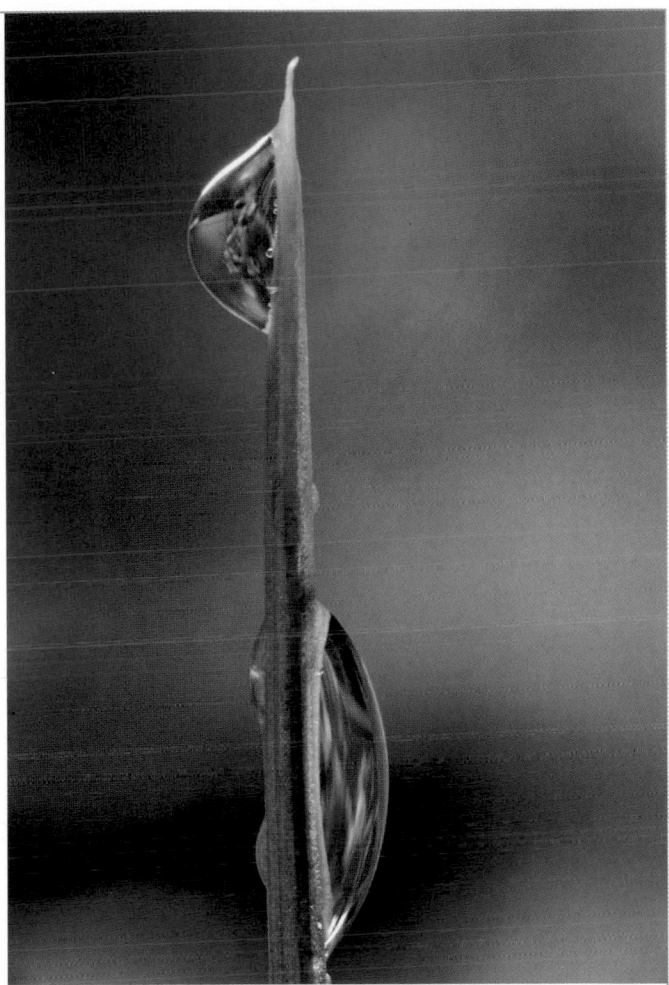

Why wait until spring to shoot in your garden when you can just as easily bring a flower garden inside your house? After a quick trip to the grocery store in the cold month of February, I was soon immersed in a "garden" that I had set up in a large vase. In this image, the flowers are an out-of-focus background behind the stem of a Dutch iris that I had sprayed with water moments before. The stem was about 6 inches in front of the vase of flowers. In the world of macro photography, a background 6 inches away is akin to a normal background 30 feet away, which explains why the flowers record as nothing more than out-of-focus tones.

Nikon D3X with Micro-Nikkor 105mm lens, f/22 for 1/15 sec., ISO 100

Nature was nothing short of a bust. This is me; this is my approach. It is about "feeling" a very organic experience. To me, getting the shot in camera is akin to eating a sumptuous meal, while the mechanical and sterile approach of Photoshop is more like watching a cooking show on television. It seems that every generation has its own approach to life. It's the same with photography.

The lesson here is simple: *You* are the artist, so take full responsibility for the outcome of your images, including the experience of designing and creating each and every image, even if that means moving objects in the scene. Some will argue against this, but how often do you approach a subject and change your point of view by getting down low, climbing stairs, or lying on your back to shoot up? How often have you changed lenses, added a filter, or used your flash for fill light? Since you *have* repeatedly embraced these kinds of changes, why do you find it difficult to embrace the idea of getting rid of an object or moving the subject, such as picking up a leaf from the ground and placing it on a tree stump? How do you know that leaf was not on the stump earlier, only to get blown off by a breeze just before you arrived? Can you imagine a painter being chastised for "adding" something to a scene?

Some photographers (and many camera clubs) hold dear the notion that truly compelling imagery requires nothing more than persistence and luck. If that were true, the history book of compelling photographic images would be well under a hundred pages. Take Robert Doisneau's *Le basier de l'hôtel de ville (Kiss by the Town Hall*, for example, one of the world's best-known images. This image fooled most of the world for decades as a lucky shot until it was discovered in the late 1990s that the couple were models directed by Doisneau to walk back and forth in front of a French café until he got the shot. The real tragedy is that Doisneau could not tell the truth about the image, because, at that time, photography could only be "art" if the image was spontaneous, not altered or invented in any way.

In my mind, the measure of a photograph's success is its ability to evoke an emotional response; to cause us to feel joy, discomfort, elation, disgust, sadness. To that end, I encourage you to use all your skills and talents, including the courage to be creative.

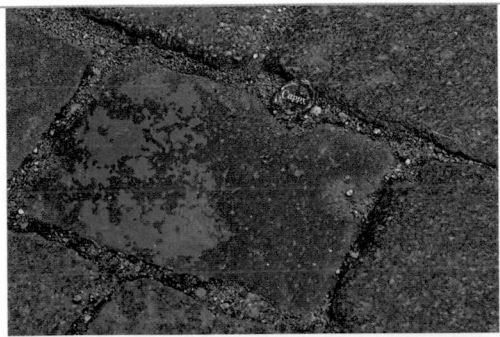

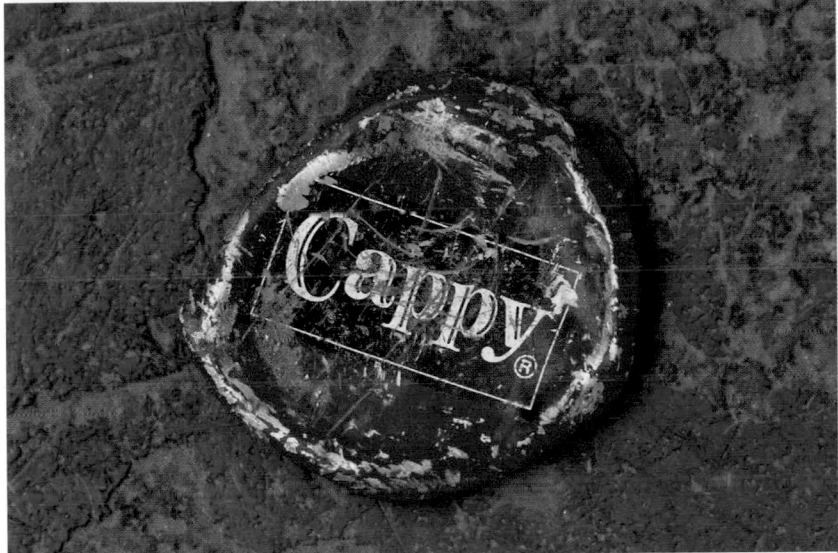

When was the last time you shot a bottle cap? In terms of a subject, a bottle cap sounds about as interesting as your big toe, *after* a five-mile hike. But what if it's a red bottle cap lying on top of blue painted bricks? And what if you exercised the same rights as a painter, beginning with the idea of a blank "canvas" on which *you* decide not only what elements to add but also how to arrange those elements? You, too, might be quick to pick up the bottle cap, place it on a cleaner portion of a blue brick, and proceed to shoot a frame-filling image of red and blue.

Nikon D300 with Micro-Nikkor 105mm lens, f/11 for 1/30 sec., ISO 200

1

LEARNING TO SEE: MINING THE MUNDANE

During the mid-1980s and the 1990s, I found myself shooting a number of annual reports for both Fortune 500 companies and not-so-fortunate companies. Much of my work back then focused on what I affectionately called "Hard Hats with Soft Hearts," or what is commonly known as the blue-collar industries: oil, gas, coal, hydro, ship repair, construction, steel plants, foundries, lumber mills, and silver and gold mining.

Shooting silver and gold mines took me to some fairly remote and often harsh locations. The gold mines of Colorado, Idaho, Nevada, and California didn't look very different than the gold mine atop the 14,000-foot mountain in Bolivia, or the 2,400-foot underground gold mine in Santa Bárbara, Brazil. *Mundane* would be the best word to describe most gold mines, at least on the surface. Since most of us are drawn to landscapes teeming with life, the rocky, sparse, dry, desertlike landscape where most gold is found gets little of our attention, unless, of course, we are prospecting for gold.

Leica D-Lux 4 with 24mm lens, f/8 for 1/250 sec., ISO 100

And just as when we're mining for real gold, mining for gold images requires effort, as these images remain buried, hidden from view in some truly mundane locations. The terrain where you can find these golden opportunities is often composed of broken-down cars, scarred sheet metal, retired crab pots, broken glass, banged-up bicycles, rusty old water heaters—in other words, terrain normally described as an eyesore!

I believe that every junkyard, secondhand store, and wrecking yard is teeming with "flora and fauna" and that the path toward successful composition *must* include several trips to the mundane—preferably early in your photographic career. No other location as adequately affirms my belief that every successful image is first and foremost about the arrangement of the content and not the content itself.

Most of my photography workshops include several hours (or, if the students are lucky, an entire day) spent shooting garbage, such as in a junkyard, an auto wrecking yard, a 40-yard Dumpster, or an alleyway with no shortage of plastic trash bags. During the entire time spent at these locations, the students are strongly encouraged to use their macro lenses, a close-up filter such as the Canon 500D, or extension tubes. The sole goal is to create compelling arrangements, and because of this, the eye and the brain are freed from the often constraining need to know what you are looking at so you can photograph it the "right way." (Remember, it is not about the content, it's about the arrangement!)

It is in these mundane locations where the two most common "rules" in all of photography can be learned and applied time and time again: the Rule of Thirds and the need to fill the frame. It is here where the eye/brain is awakened, liberated from the prejudice of what constitutes a "beautiful" image. It is here where the repetition of these two most basic of fundamentals is applied and affirmed. And once your eye and brain have been awakened, they will have an insatiable appetite for the mundane. You, too, will soon be saying, "Successful image making is all about the arrangement and not the content!"

Over the next few pages, we'll explore some examples of shooting the eyesores—those subjects that are often passed by, overlooked, or even avoided because they couldn't possibly be interesting. If my hunch is correct, by the end you will share the same reaction as Danielle, a student who took a workshop with me in Provence during the summer of 2011. Danielle was dreading the trip to the junkyard. After all, it was her first time in France and she was about to spend several hours in a junkyard! But when it was over, she didn't want to leave. Not until then did she realize how much beauty there was in the mundane.

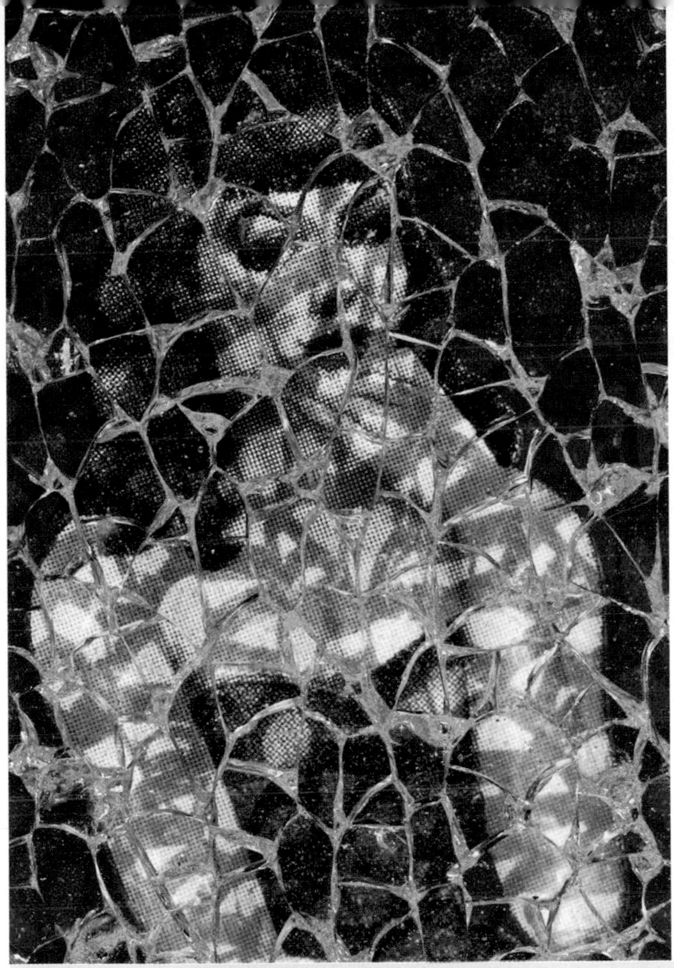

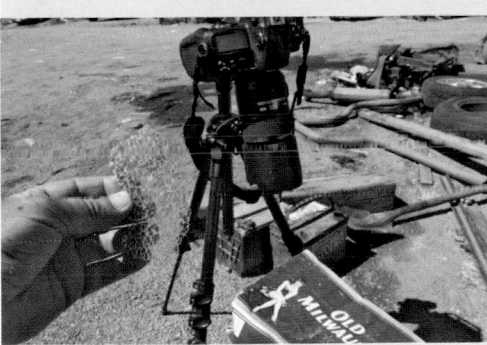

While standing in a small pile of trash, I noticed at my feet several small pieces of broken glass from what I gather was once the windshield of a car. Just a few feet away was an empty half-case of Old Milwaukee beer, emblazoned with an Illustration of the Old Milwaukee girl. I placed the broken glass over the Old Milwaukee girl, and as you can see above, this simple idea of marrying two pieces of discarded waste became one mighty interesting composition! It is an image of lines, color, and shape, culminating in an unusual "portrait."

Nikon D3X with Micro-Nikkor 105mm lens, f/16 for 1/125 sec., ISO 100

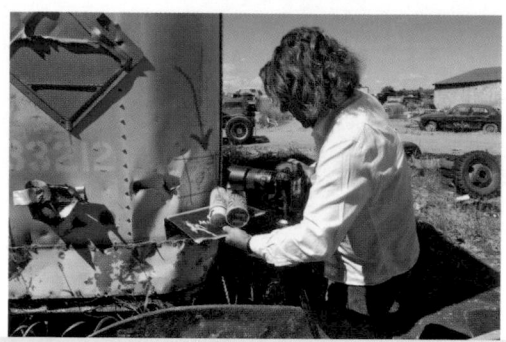

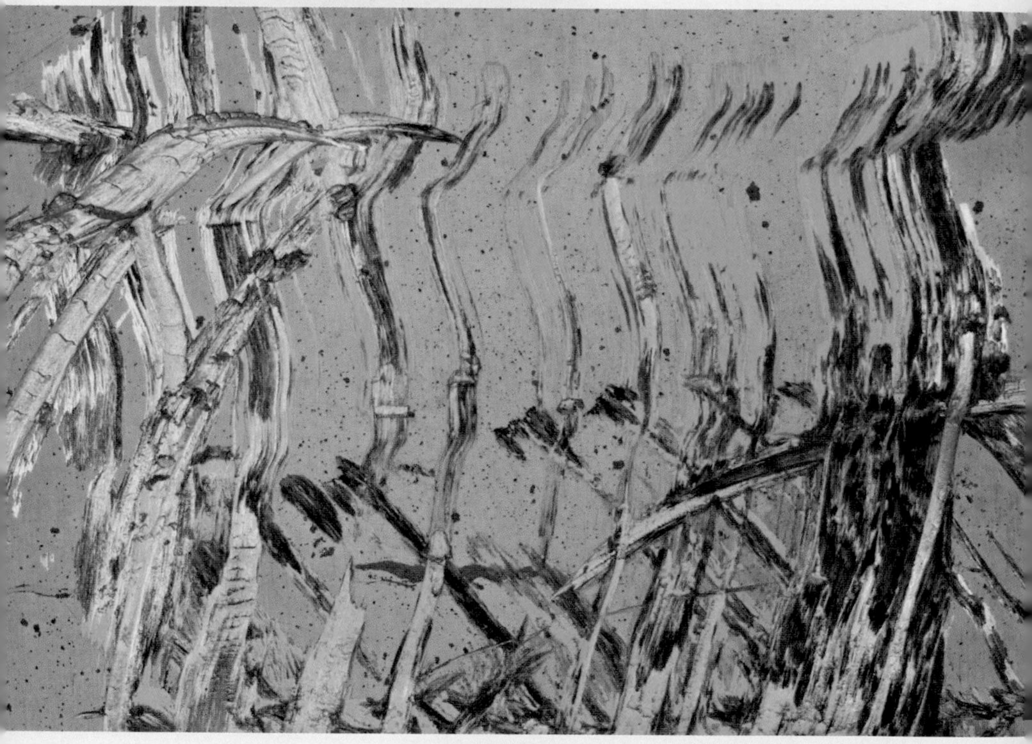

What do you get when you hold various brightly colored pieces of waste against the side of a deeply scratched refrigerated trailer? A color-filled "landscape," that's what! Finding a refrigerated trailer with deep scratches and colorful garbage was the easy part. The harder part was balancing the garbage in one hand while tripping the camera's shutter with the other. The solution was to use the camera's self-timer, set here to a 10-second delay.

Nikon D3X, Micro-Nikkor 105mm lens, f/16 for 1/125 sec., ISO 100

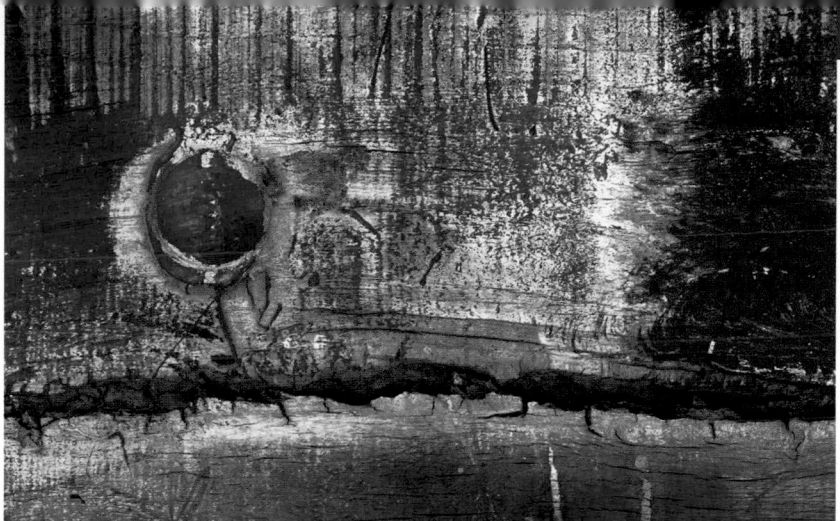

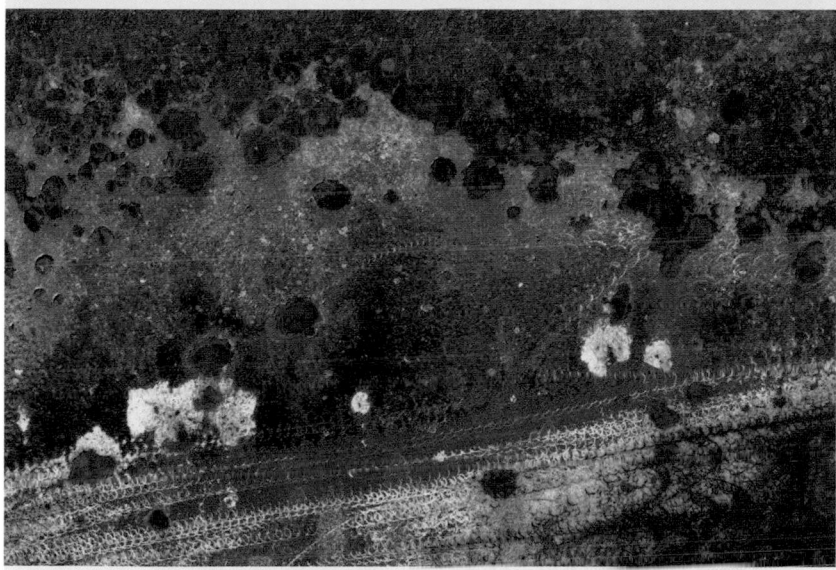

These two images are clear examples of how the Rule of Thirds can contribute to a compelling image, even when the subject matter is a piece of broken wood pulled from the trash or a detail from the sidewall of an old wheelbarrow. In both these "landscapes," we clearly see the implied horizon and the small and narrow landscape below. In the piece of wood at top, we see a blue "moon" and remnants of a sunset sky; in the rusty wheelbarrow below that, we see a dusky blue sky with a fading red sunset. If you are having trouble seeing what I am describing in these two photos, describe it to a few children. Chances are their imagination is still very much alive and they can help you see what I see.

Both images: Nikon D300S with Micro-Nikkor 105mm lens, f/16 for 1/125 sec., ISO 200

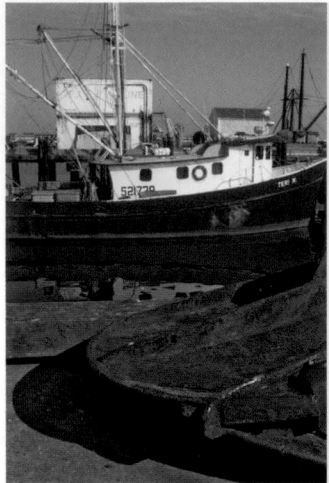

Small fishing ports are "gold mines," too, and you don't have to look far to find the most commonly found "gold" of all: rust. When I found this rusty propeller, someone had been grinding on it earlier, revealing a wonderful contrast between old and new. I set up my camera and tripod, making certain to position the camera so it was parallel to the overall composition to record the sharpest image in conjunction with my small aperture choice of f/22. When shooting "abstract" images like this, always try rotating the image on your computer later. Often, this simple rotation gives the image a whole different look and/or meaning. Although I shot this image as a horizontal, I actually prefer it as a vertical.

Below and opposite: Nikon D300S with Micro-Nikkor 105mm lens, f/22 for 1/125 sec., ISO 200

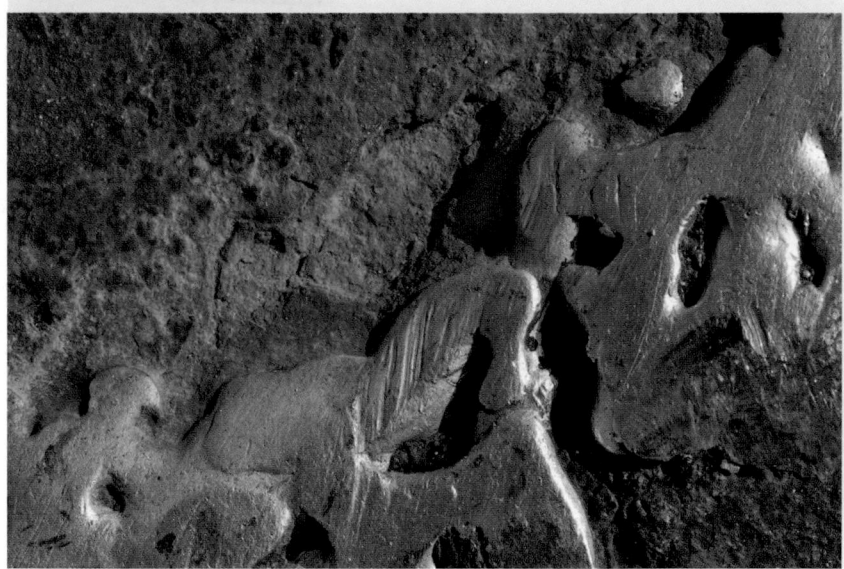

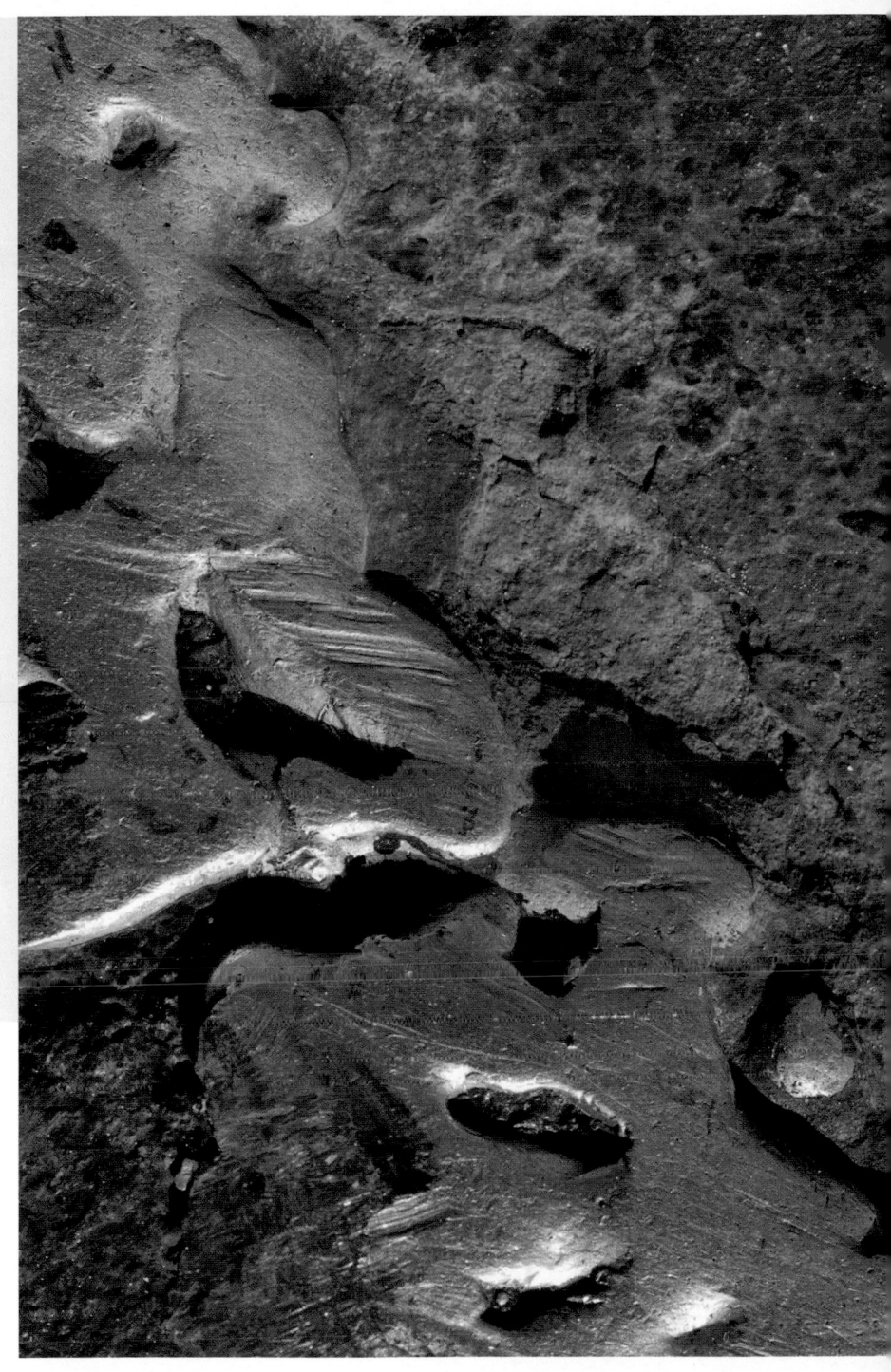

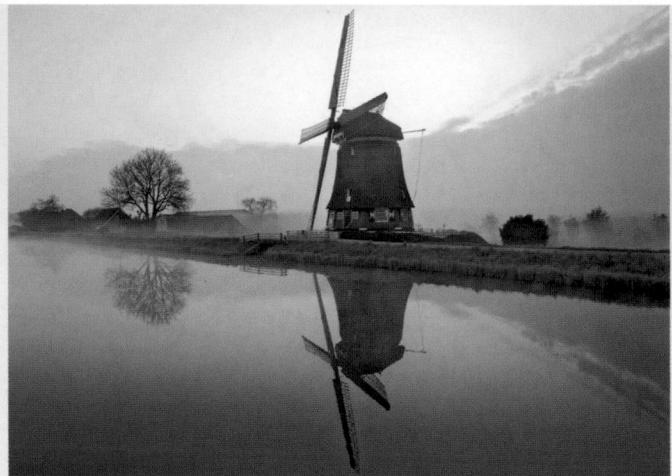
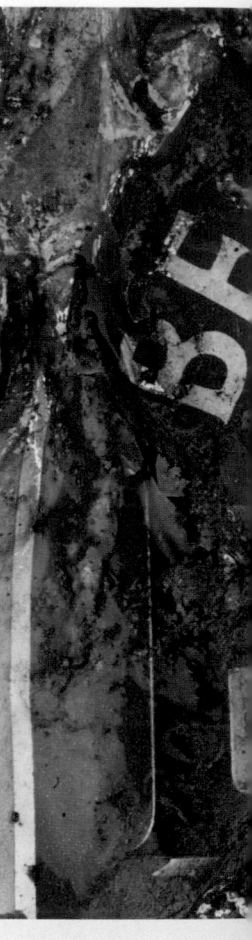

This is undoubtedly the "best" image of trash I've ever taken! I took this image shortly after dawn during an April workshop in West Friesland, Holland. Our intended subject was actually the windmill shown above. As one might expect, all the students took similar shots of the windmill that morning and were quite happy with their results. As we stood on the edge of this dike shooting this scene with our wide-angle lenses, I felt a small "lump" under my foot and noticed a smashed and very rusted Best beer can. As I bent down and picked it up, I felt a growing excitement—the same type of excitement I felt watching my son and two daughters as they were born. Hard to believe, but true!

I proceeded to photograph the beer can over the next few minutes and, once finished, was quick to offer it to all my students, but every one of them refused politely, choosing to relish their windmill shots instead. It was not until our critique the next afternoon that they saw my beer can image on the computer screen—and every one of them lamented not taking the shot after all!

Why is this image so compelling? In part, it's due to the contradiction. It might say "Best," but that is one of the worst Bests I have ever seen. The arrangement of what is clearly a chaotic Best, makes for the "best Best" of all. As I said, I love the contradiction!

Above: Nikon D3X with Nikkor 16–35mm lens at 16mm, f/11 for 1/15 sec., ISO 100; Right: Nikon D3X with Micro-Nikkor 105mm lens, f/22 for 1/4 sec., ISO 100

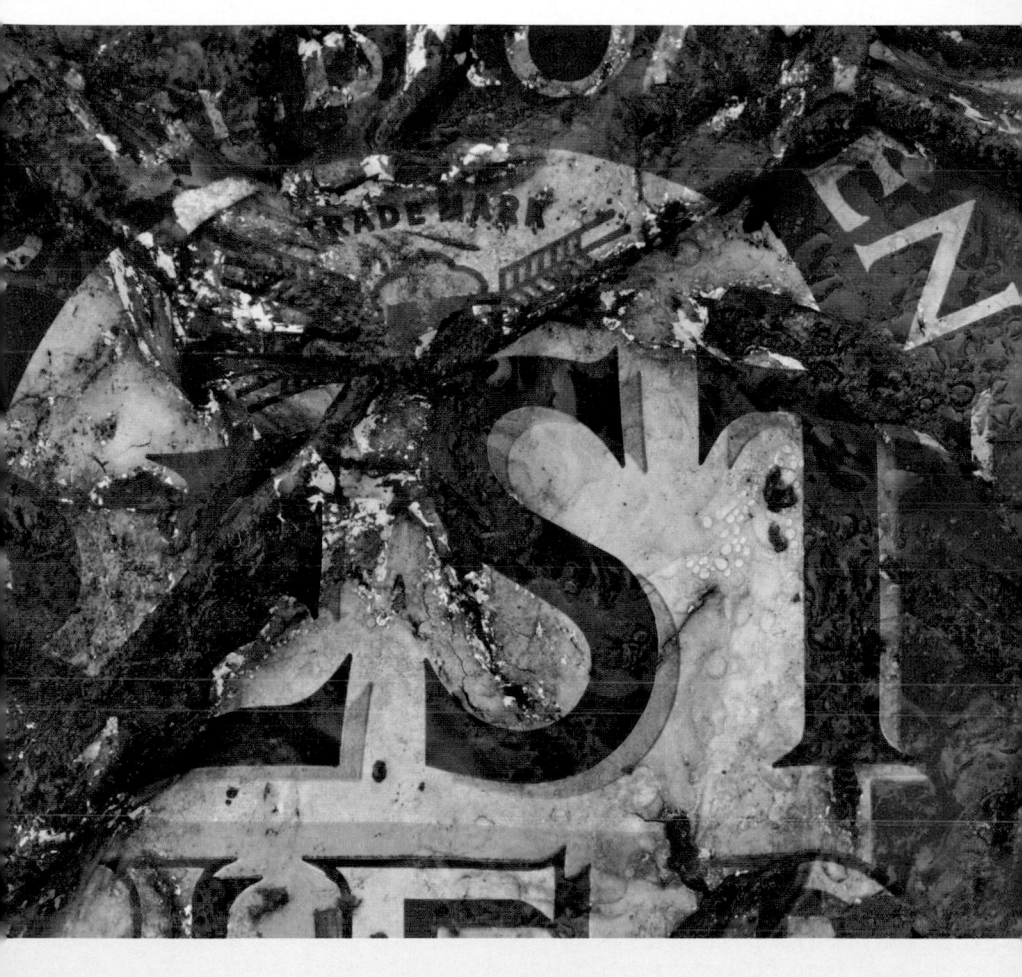

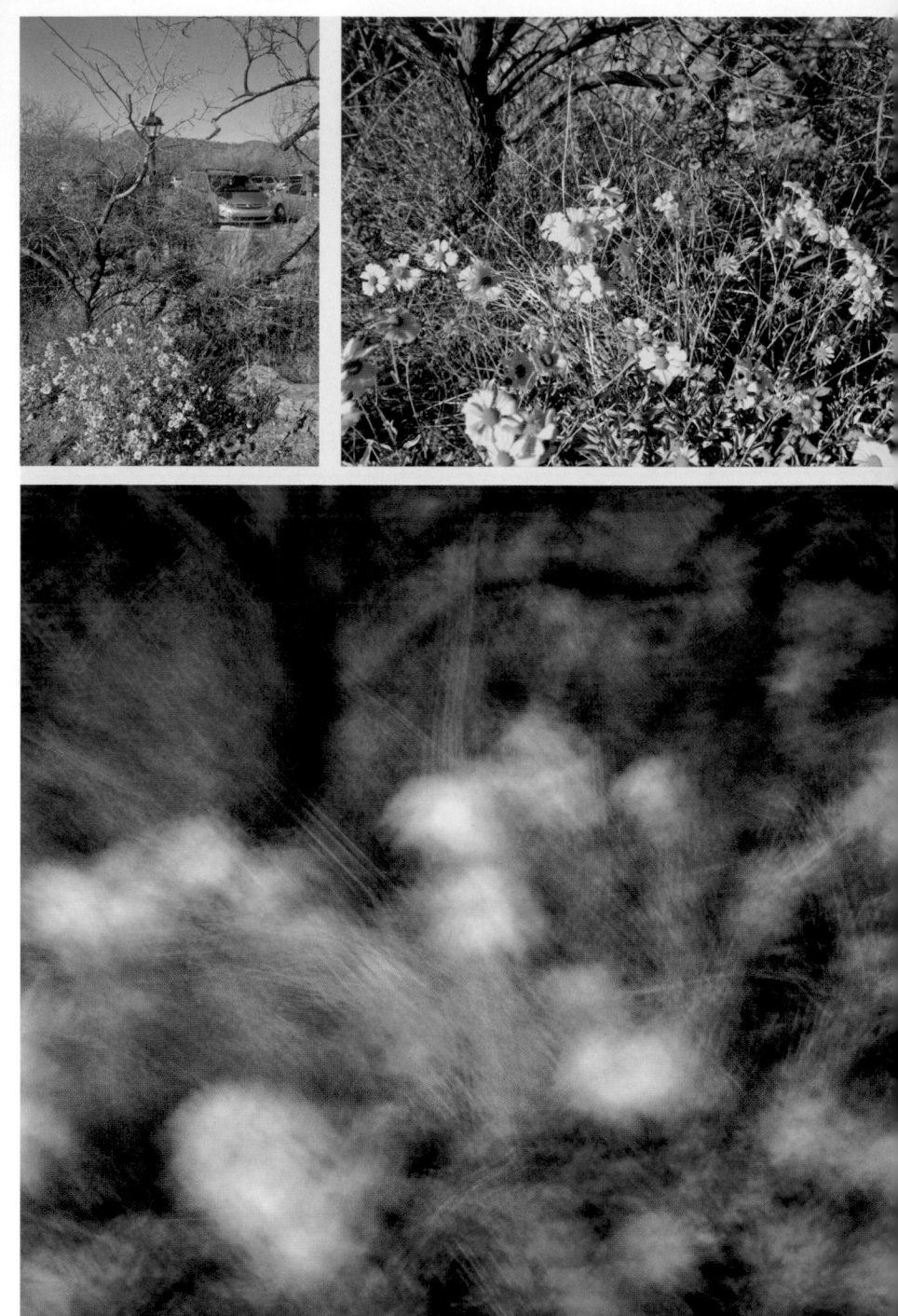

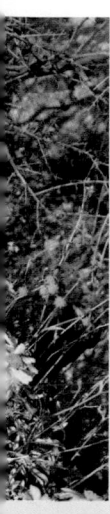

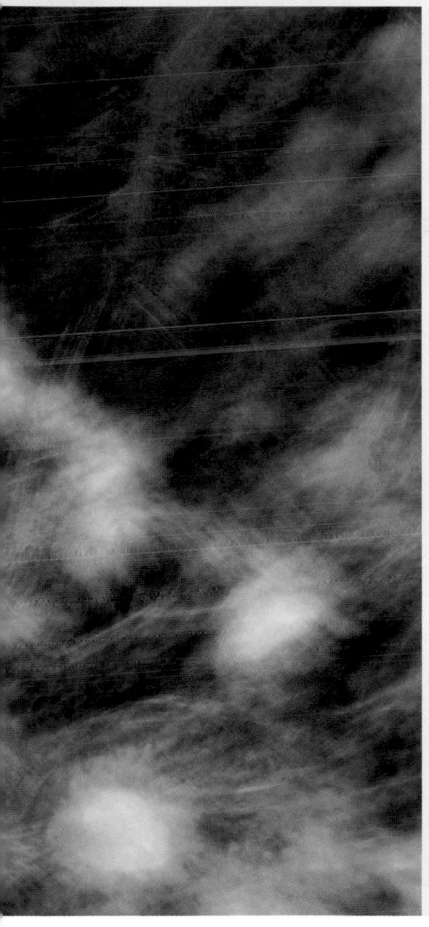

Several years ago, I was in Tucson, Arizona, and stopped by one of the desert museums during a mid-day break. As I returned to my car, my eyes caught sight of the arrangement shown above. (My eyes are constantly searching for "arrangements," otherwise known as pleasing compositions.) As is clear to see in the image at top left, my arrangement is in a parking lot, of all places. Many of you might be quick to turn off that search engine inside your brain when you come upon a location or area that you deem uninteresting or unphotographable or boring. And, let's face it, parking lots aren't usually where most of us look for compelling photographic opportunities. (As an aside, I know of no place that is boring or uninteresting, at least in photographic terms. Sure, some locations have proved remarkably challenging, as in "pulling my hair out" challenging—and if you know my hair, that *is* serious—but once I surrendered my vision to the elements of design and used my go-to lens, the Micro-Nikkor 105mm, I have always found something to shoot—always!)

Within seconds, I was shooting a multiple-exposure image with Nikon's Multiple Exposure feature—nine exposures, in fact, all shot at f/11 for 1/100 sec., though each taken at a slightly different angle. All nine exposures were then magically and automatically blended *in camera* thanks to Nikon's onboard computer, and as we can see in the final arrangement, we have a completely out of focus yet quite compelling arrangement! Multiple exposures like this are possible with most Nikon digital SLRs (DSLRs), a few of the Pentax models, and, as of this writing, one Canon (the 1DX).

All nine exposures: Nikon D300S with 70-300mm lens, f/11 for 1/100 sec., ISO 200

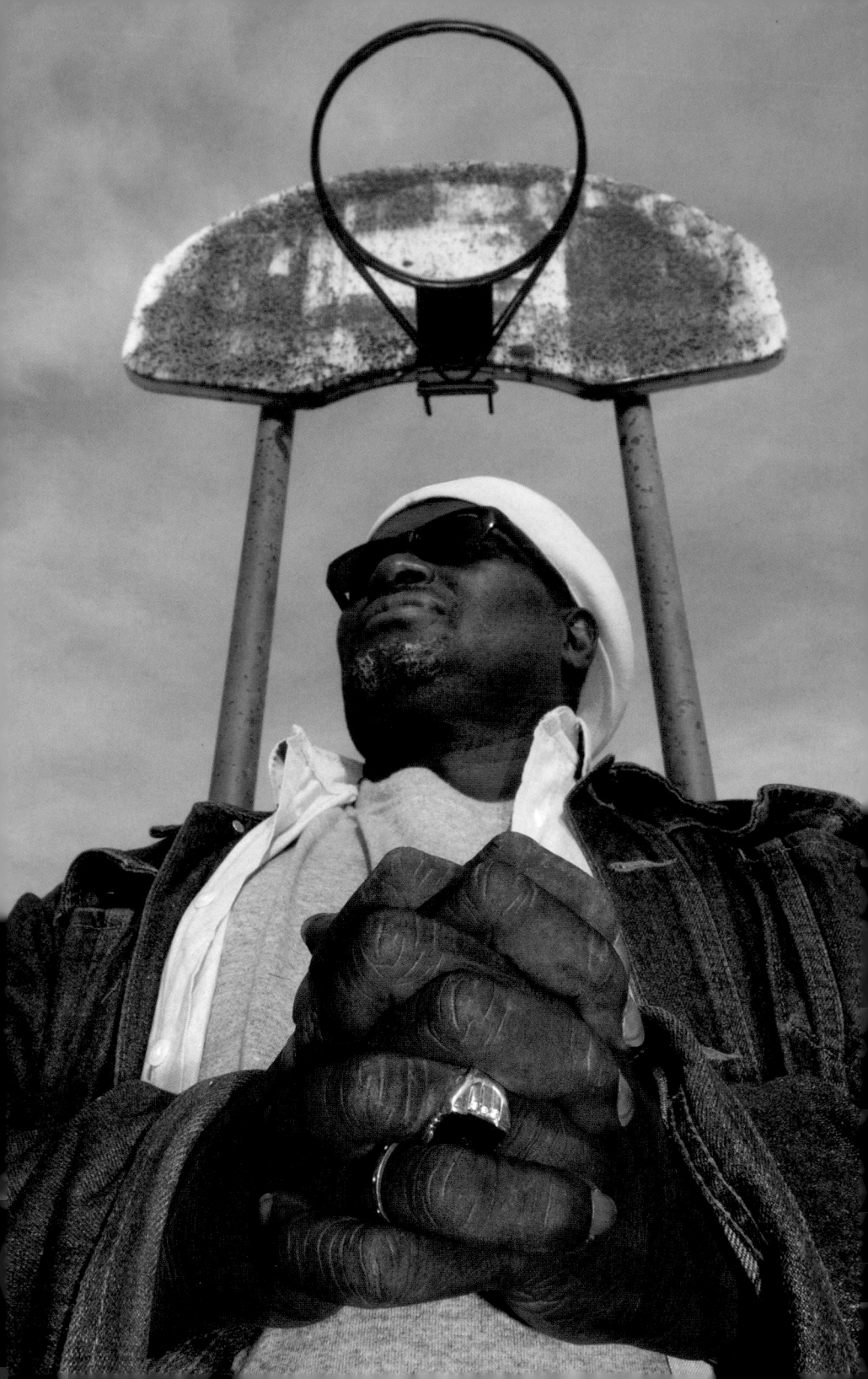

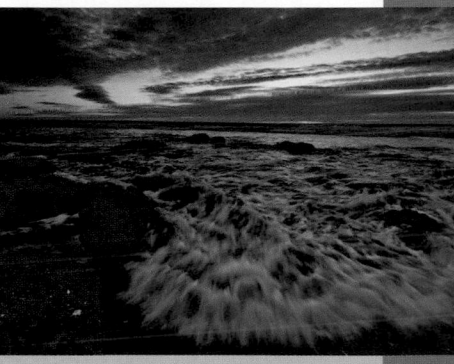

2

THE ROLE OF APERTURE AND SHUTTER SPEED

Many photographers are under the impression that aperture and shutter speed only have to do with correct exposure and little, if anything, to do with composition. However, a wrong aperture or shutter speed can literally destroy an otherwise successful composition.

How is that possible? Let's begin with one of the biggest truths about photographic composition: the fundamental rule of *visual weight*. Visual weight can be described as the contrast between what is in focus and what is not in focus. Clearly, a difference exists. If something is in focus, it's important; if it's not in focus, then it's not as important. That sounds simple enough, yet the lack of attention given this basic law of composition is evident every week at my online photography school—even in the advanced classes. So the obvious question is this: How do you control the visual weight of any given composition? It's all about lens, focus, and aperture.

Nikon D3X with Nikkor 24–85mm lens, f/16 for 1/100 sec., ISO 200

APERTURE

If you wish to compose a grand landscape with everything in focus, from the immediate foreground to the infinite horizon, there is but *one* aperture that can do that for you. If, on the other hand, what you're after is a portrait against a blurry background so that only your subject is sharp, there are only *two* apertures capable of rendering that background to the blur that you need. And if you're looking to isolate a butterfly sipping nectar from a purple coneflower, are you confident that your aperture choice will render the butterfly in exacting sharpness from front to back?

As we are about to discover on the following pages, the right aperture (and/or shutter speed) *does* play a powerful role in dictating the visual weight and overall balance of a given composition. Because aperture controls what is commonly referred to as depth of field (a.k.a. sharpness), it defines which part of the image has the "visual weight," or emphasis—a serious tool of photographic composition.

Once you embrace aperture as a sharpening tool, able to "sculpt" the point of emphasis, you will quickly realize that the *right* aperture is behind any successful composition. Although covered in more detail in later chapters, the right lens choice and the distance the subject is from its surroundings also play roles in an image's overall sharpness, but again, it is first and foremost the right aperture that leads the way toward effective visual weight. And when the visual weight is executed to perfection, a major component of compositional excellence has been achieved.

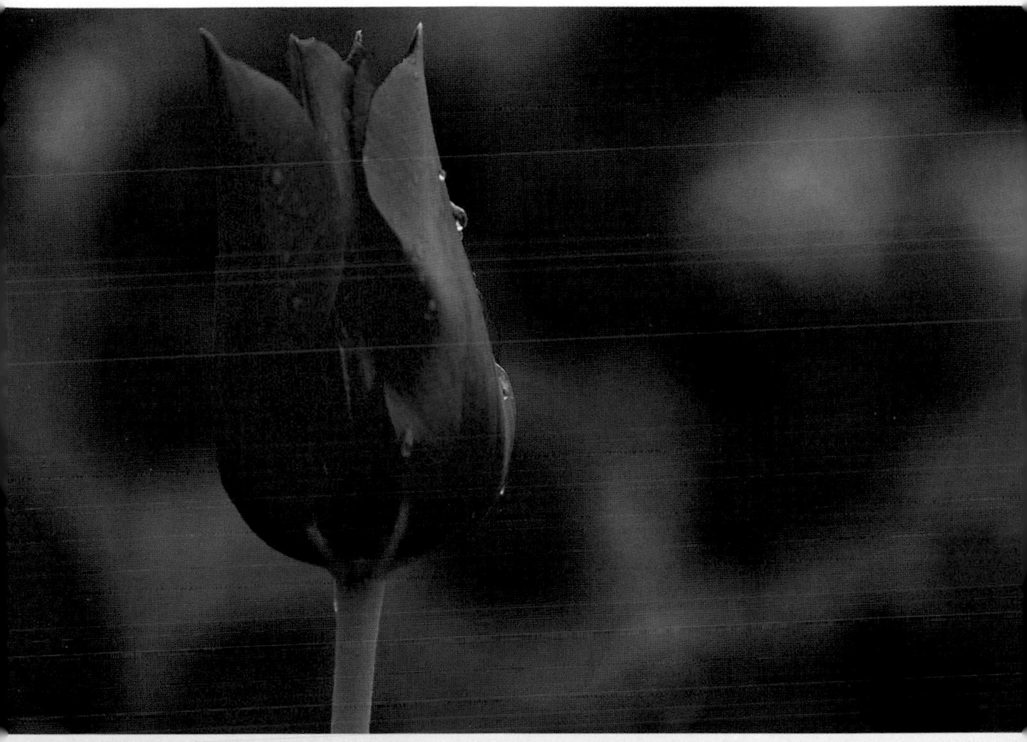

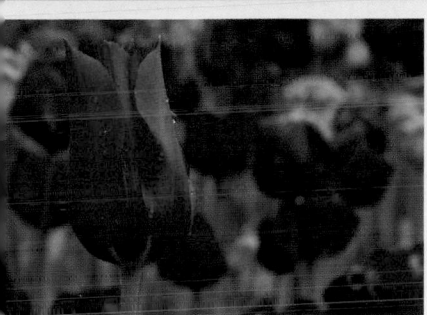

If there's one bit of advice that bears constant repeating, it is this: Pay close attention to your aperture choice, because many times, the wrong aperture choice ruins an otherwise wonderful composition!

Take a look at the image above. It's a wonderful image of a lone tulip against a background of out-of-focus tones, shapes, and colors. This is what each and every one of us would see if we all stood in this spot and shot with our 70–200mm zoom lens using a 200mm focal length and with the aid of a small extension tube. But just because this is what we all would see as we looked through the viewfinder is no guarantee that this is what we will record on our image sensors. If, in your excitement over framing a shot like this, you fail to notice that you are, in fact, at an aperture of f/16, you will record the tulip with a much busier background. As the image to the left clearly shows, we no longer have a background of out-of-focus tones, shapes, and colors but rather a defined background of other tulips, creating a much busier background.

Above: Nikon D300S with 70–200mm lens, f/5.6 for 1/1000 sec., ISO 200; Left: Nikon D300S with 70–200mm lens, f/16 for 1/125 sec., ISO 200

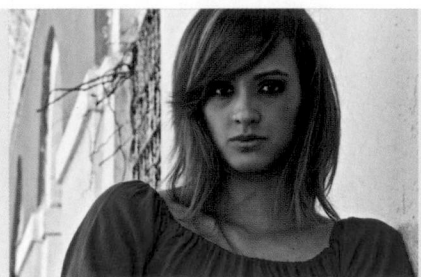

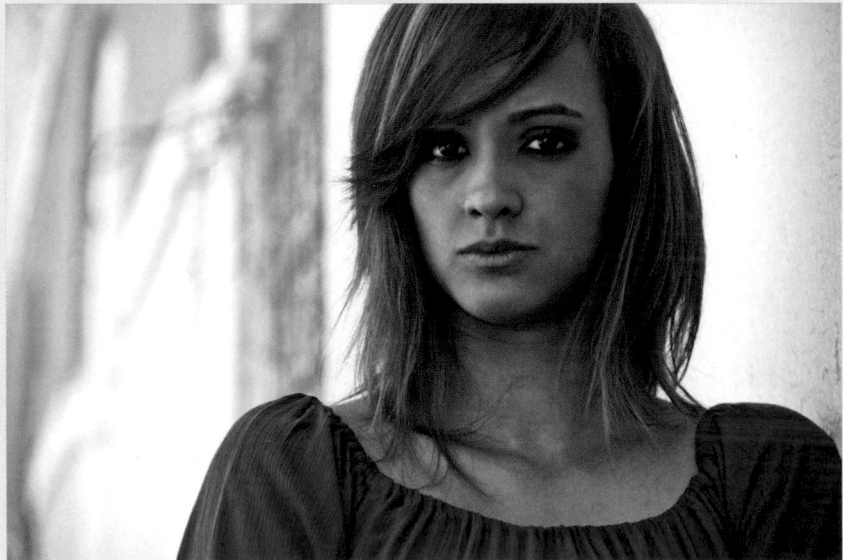

The wrong aperture has ruined many "singular theme" compositions, including the portrait shown here. Do you notice the difference between these two "identical" portraits? One has a clean background while the other has a cluttered, and thus distracting, background. The smaller the aperture, the greater the detail beyond the subject. When it comes to singular-theme compositions, you will want to use a larger aperture to limit detail in the background and focus attention on the main subject.

Top: Nikon D3X with Nikkor 70–300mm lens at 240mm, f/16 for 1/60 sec., ISO 200;
Bottom: Nikon D3X with Nikkor 70–300mm lens at 240mm, f/4 for 1/1000 sec., ISO 200

WHERE TO FOCUS

Once you start focusing your attention on storytelling compositions, you may wonder, Where the heck do I focus? In a pastoral scene of a barn in a wheat field, for example, focusing on the foreground stalks of wheat will cause both the barn in the middle ground and the sky in the background to go out of focus. If you focus on the barn and the sky, however, the foreground wheat stalks will be out of focus. The solution? Don't focus the lens at all. That's right: don't focus. Instead, preset the focus via a predetermined distance setting.

Single-focal-length lenses have a depth-of-field scale that makes it very easy to preset your focus for a given scene, but few are the photographers today who use single-focal-length wide-angle lenses. Wide-angle zooms are the norm, but there is a trade-off: no depth-of-field scales! However, they do have distance settings, and knowing how to set the distance is key.

Distance settings are similar to depth-of-field scales in that they allow you to preset the depth of field before you take your shot. And since every storytelling composition relies on the maximum depth of field, first set your aperture to f/22 and then align a specific distance—3 feet (1 meter) or 6 feet (2 meters), depending on what focal length you are using—directly above the distance marker.

So, when shooting storytelling compositions in which you want as much front-to-back sharpness as possible, try my fool-proof formula:

1 Turn autofocus off.

2 If you're using a camera with a "crop factor" and a lens with a 75-degree angle of view (18mm on the digital 18–55mm zoom), set the aperture to f/22 and then focus on something approximately 6 feet (2 meters) from the lens.

3 If you're in manual exposure mode, adjust your shutter speed until a correct exposure is indicated, then shoot. If you're in Aperture Priority mode, simply shoot, since the camera will set the shutter speed for you. Your resulting depth of field will extend from about 3 feet (1 meter) to infinity.

4 If you're using a 12–24mm digital wide-angle zoom, again on a crop-factor camera and with a focal length between 12mm and 16mm, set the lens to f/22 and then focus on something 3 feet (1 meter) away, then repeat step 3. Your resulting depth of field will be from approximately 14 inches to infinity.

5 Those of you shooting with a full-frame digital sensor and using focal lengths between 14mm and 24mm would simply focus at 3 feet (1 meter). When combined with an aperture of f/22, the resulting depth of field will again be from 14 inches to infinity. If you're shooting with a focal length between 25mm and 28mm on a full-frame camera, set the focus distance to 6 feet (2 meters) and you'll record a depth of field from 3 feet to infinity.

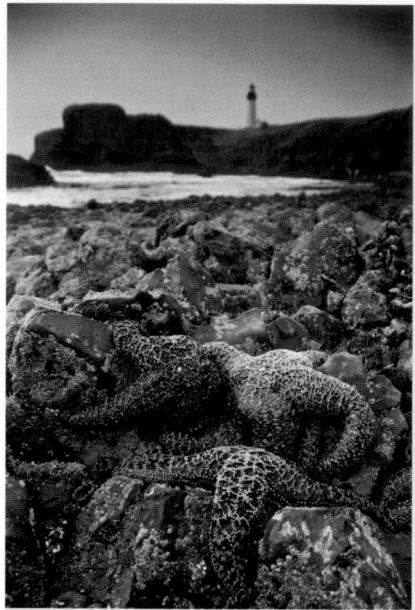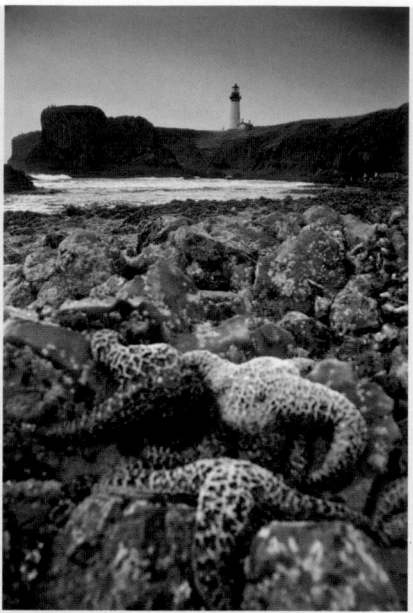

When it comes to storytelling compositions, nothing works better than the really small apertures of f/22, or even f/32, if you are lucky enough to have it. Naysayers will have you believe that when you shoot at these small apertures you will lose sharpness, contrast, even color. But I—and an army of other shooters—insist that you turn a deaf ear to this advice. If you do, you will create some of the most intimate landscapes and cityscapes you could ever hope to achieve, and enjoy sharpness from the up-close-and-personal distance of 14 inches all the way to infinity.

If you take storytelling compositions without a small enough aperture, your image will miss the vital "opening paragraph" of your story, due to a blurry foreground. You cannot record a depth of field from 14 inches to infinity at f/8 or f/11 when using your 12–16mm crop factor wide-angle lenses or your 17–24mm full-frame wide-angle lenses. For example, compare the three images shown here—all are shot with the same lens from the same point of view, and at the same exposure in terms of quantitative value, yet at different apertures and focusing distances.

The first image, shown top left, was shot at f/11 with the focus on the starfish and does not render the background acceptably sharp; the lighthouse is out focus. In the second image, shown top right, shot at f/11 with the focus on the lighthouse, the starfish in the foreground are now out of focus. Only the third image, shown opposite, shot at f/22 with the focus preset to 3 feet, renders both the starfish and the lighthouse in acceptable sharpness.

Top left: Canon 5D Mark II with 17–35mm lens at 20mm, f/11 for 1/125 sec., ISO 200, focused at 2 feet; Top right: f/11 for 1/125 sec., ISO 200, focused at infinity; Opposite: f/22 for 1/30 sec., ISO 200, focused at 3 feet

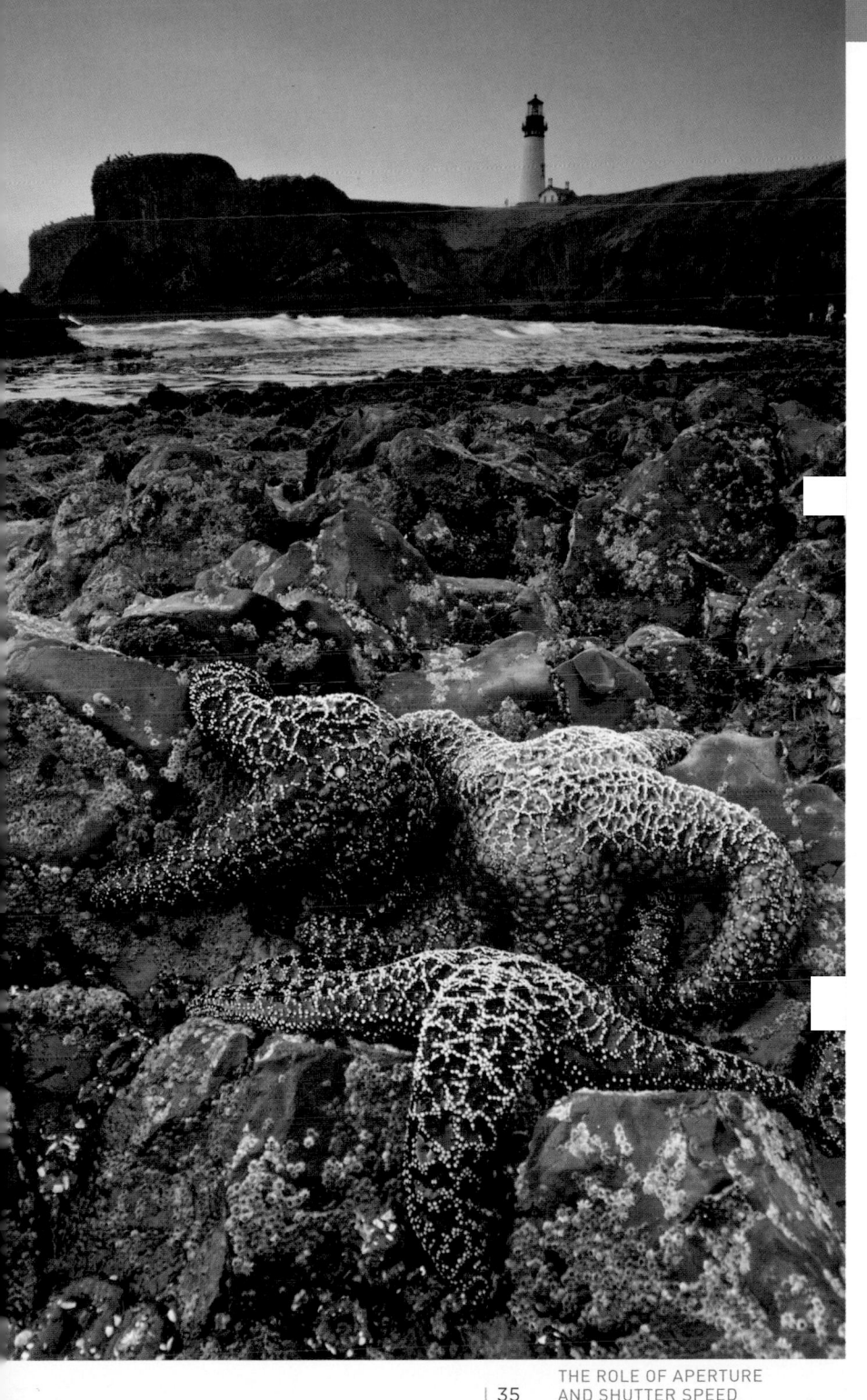

THE ROLE OF APERTURE
AND SHUTTER SPEED

SHUTTER SPEED

When it comes to shutter speed, it might seem elementary, but a 1/3-stop difference can dramatically alter the viewer's response to an otherwise successful arrangement.

For example, when action is moving up and down in front of you or side to side, it is a safe bet to use a shutter speed of 1/500 sec. or faster. So what happens if, after reviewing several quick frames on the digital monitor, you decide the images are a wee bit dark? Since you are already using a wide-open aperture, you decrease your shutter speed by 1/3 of a stop, to 1/400 sec. You take a quick snap and check your exposure again, and you are much happier. It isn't until you get home that you are confronted with an ugly truth: a 1/400 sec. exposure looks great in terms of light but is just slow enough to render most of the images with a subtle blur. Unlike grilling a steak, there is no such thing as a rare or medium-sharp image when freezing action is your goal. When it comes to image sharpness, anything short of "well done" must be thrown out!

Of course, *deliberate* blurring, whether via panning, zooming, or the motion of moving traffic or a waterfall while shooting at a very slow shutter speed, can be a highly effective way to deflect visual weight. A slow shutter speed, such as 1/2 sec., will substantially increase the visual weight of the subject in focus, such as a person standing perfectly still at the edge of a busy intersection surrounded by the blurred movement of cars and other pedestrians.

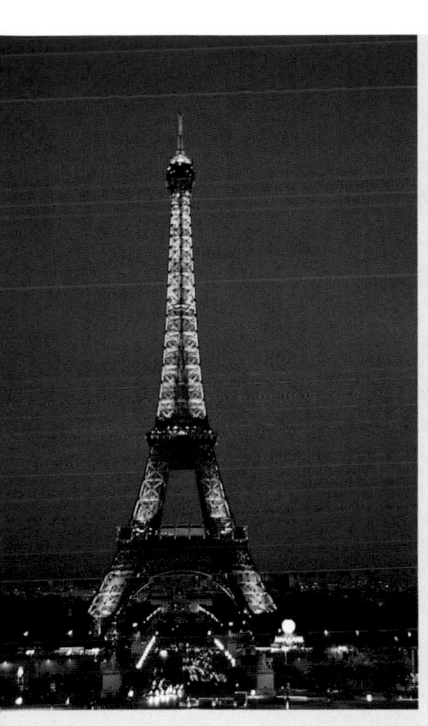
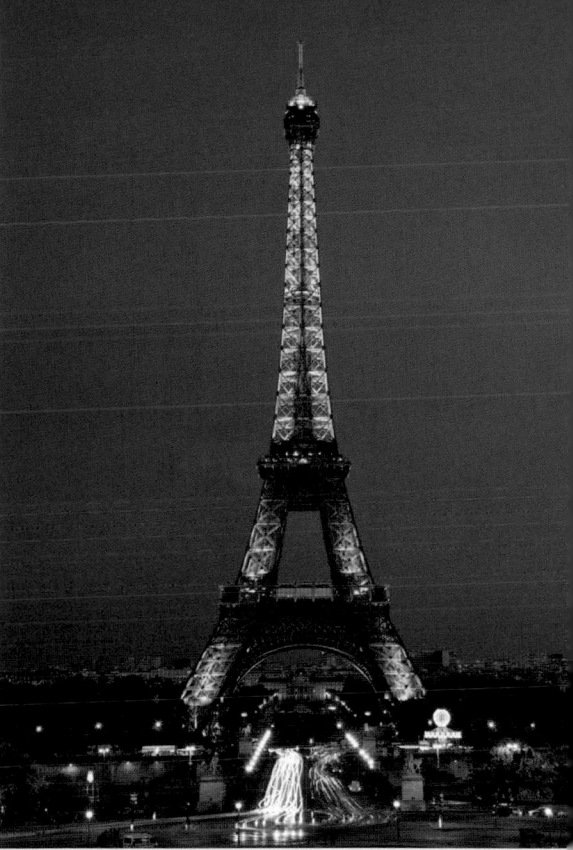

The Eiffel Tower may be the most photographed monument in all of Europe, if not the world. Paris is among the world's most popular travel destinations, and for many, that trip is a once-in-a-lifetime experience, so all the more reason to come back with the most compelling compositions possible. And what's a surefire way to do just that? Pay attention to your shutter speed! In this case, the longer the better, and I am talking *full* seconds, not fractions of seconds. That also means the need for a tripod.

Compare the two photos shown here. The traffic flow in the first image (left) is cut short by a "fast" shutter speed of 1/2 sec. In photography, a half-second is a really long time, especially when compared to 1/8000 sec. Yet in this case, 1/2 sec. is actually too fast to create a flowing river of headlights and taillights. One needs no fewer than 8 seconds, as in the second photograph (right). You be the judge, but I would be very surprised if you were more fond of the first image. The lesson is a simple one: the amount of motion you record in a given scene is 100 percent dependent on the duration of time your shutter is allowed to remain open. The longer your shutter stays open, the greater the flow of motion. Trial and error are important parts of photographic excellence, so don't be afraid to experiment with various combinations of apertures and shutter speeds. Over time, you will learn what shutter speeds to apply for the most effective compositions.

Above left: Nikon D3X with Nikkor 70–300mm lens at 100mm, f/5.6 for 1/2 sec., ISO 100; Above right: Nikon D3X with Nikkor 70–300mm lens at 100mm, f/22 for 8 seconds, ISO 100

THE ROLE OF APERTURE
AND SHUTTER SPEED

THE TRIPOD SOLUTION

All of us have had the experience of recording tilted or split horizons, unexpected mergers, too dark or too bright exposures and soft, out-of-focus images. More often than not, the solution to these common problems is to use a tripod, one of the most vitally important pieces of photo gear. A tripod by its very design forces us to slow down, take the time to set up our shots, and check and double-check that our horizons are straight, that our subject(s) are placed where we want them, and that we have no unsightly mergers or contrast issues and no unwanted softness or blurring. Tripods also open the door to hundreds, if not thousands, of motion-filled compositions and just as many dusk or dawn or star-filled landscapes and cityscapes. And of course, exacting sharpness is almost assured, assuming you use a cable release or the camera's self-timer when shooting long exposures.

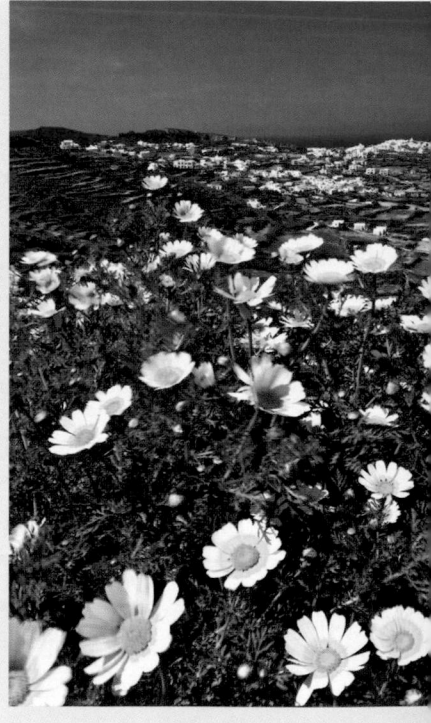

It was a windy morning a few years back and I was shooting on the Greek island of Santorini. As I have learned from numerous other experiences, cursing the wind does little to make it stop, so instead I found reasons to embrace it. With my camera and 12–24mm lens mounted securely on a tripod, I moved close to these windblown daisies, intent on shooting a storytelling composition while at the same time making it clear that this was a windy morning (opposite). My goal was to use a slow shutter speed to emphasize the wind, combined with the small storytelling aperture of f/22 to record exacting sharpness from front to back of any subject *not* being blown by the wind. The slow shutter speed allows the flowers to blur, calling attention to the windy conditions and providing, at least initially, an anxious moment for the eye/brain, which then quickly searches for something safe and stable—meaning, something in focus. The other sharp and stable objects serve as compositional anchors, allowing the eye to enter and latch onto a "safe" object while it then feels the windy day that it is. Compare the first windblown image with the second, shown at right, where, for a brief moment, the wind died down considerably. Which image creates the most visual anxiety and is thus the most compelling?

Right: Nikon D300 with 12–24mm lens, f/22 for 1/2 sec., ISO 200; Opposite: Nikon D300 with 12–24mm lens, f/22 for 1/2 sec., ISO 200, 3-stop ND filter

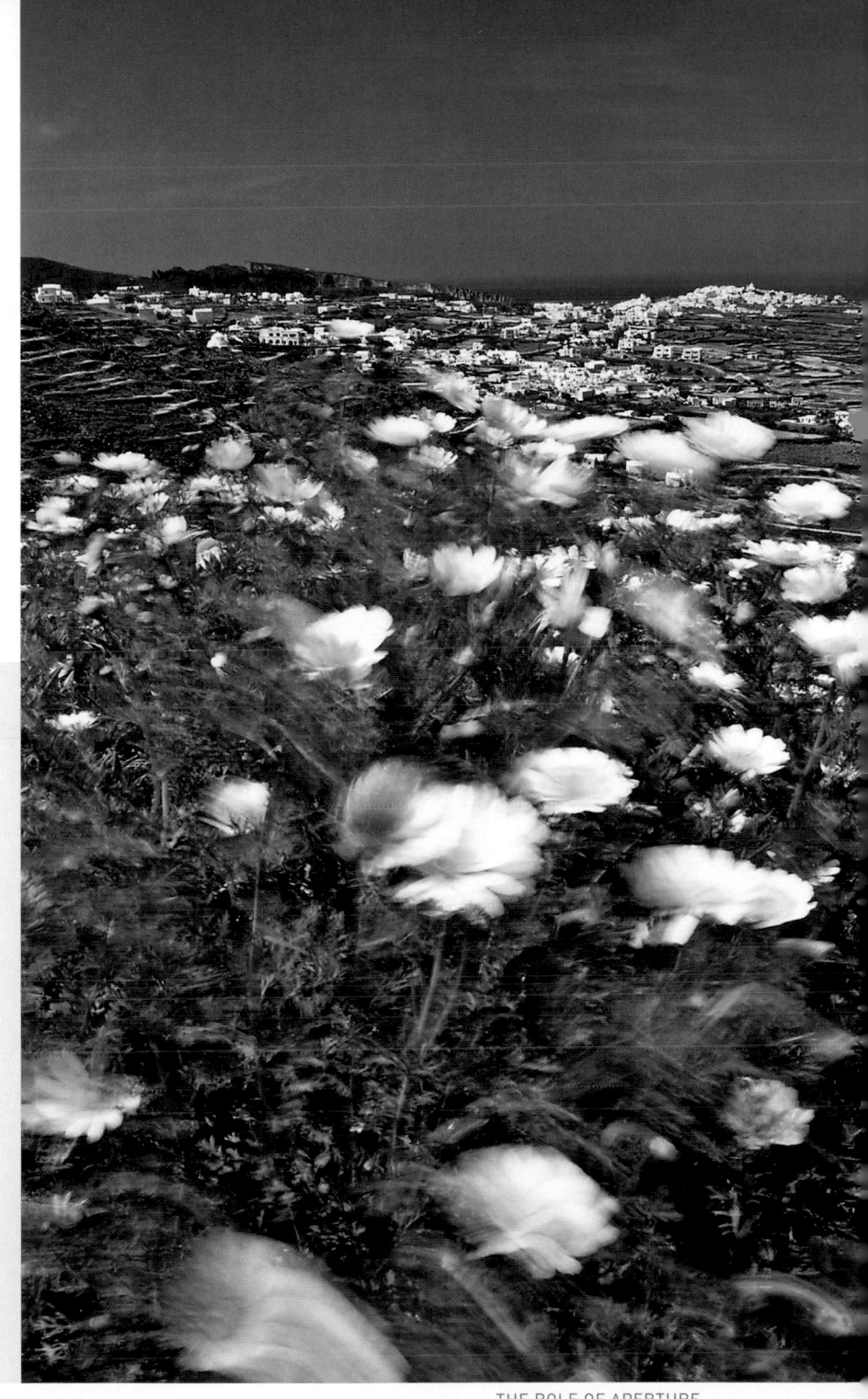

39

THE ROLE OF APERTURE
AND SHUTTER SPEED

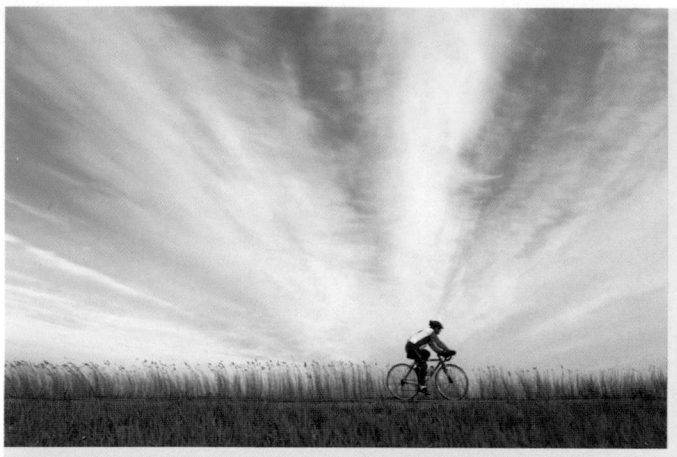

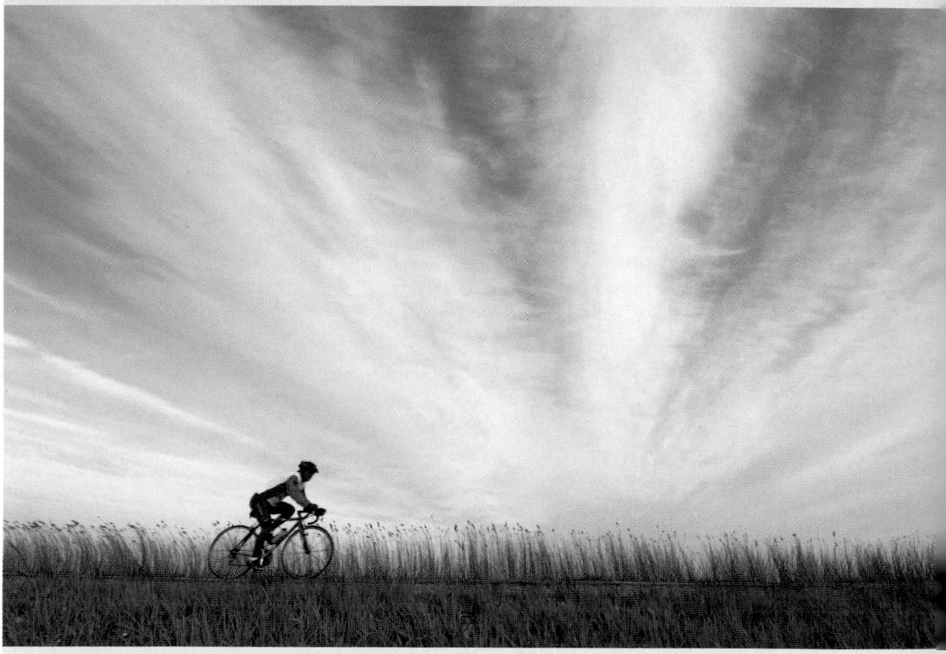

In looking at these two photos, notice how the motion of the rider coming in from the left is preferable to the top image, in which the rider has gone beyond the middle of the frame and is working his way toward the right edge. The second example allows the eye and brain to "fill up" the empty space with the implied and continued movement of the biker.

Both images: Nikon D3X with Nikkor 16–35mm lens at 16mm, f/11 for 1/400 sec., ISO 200

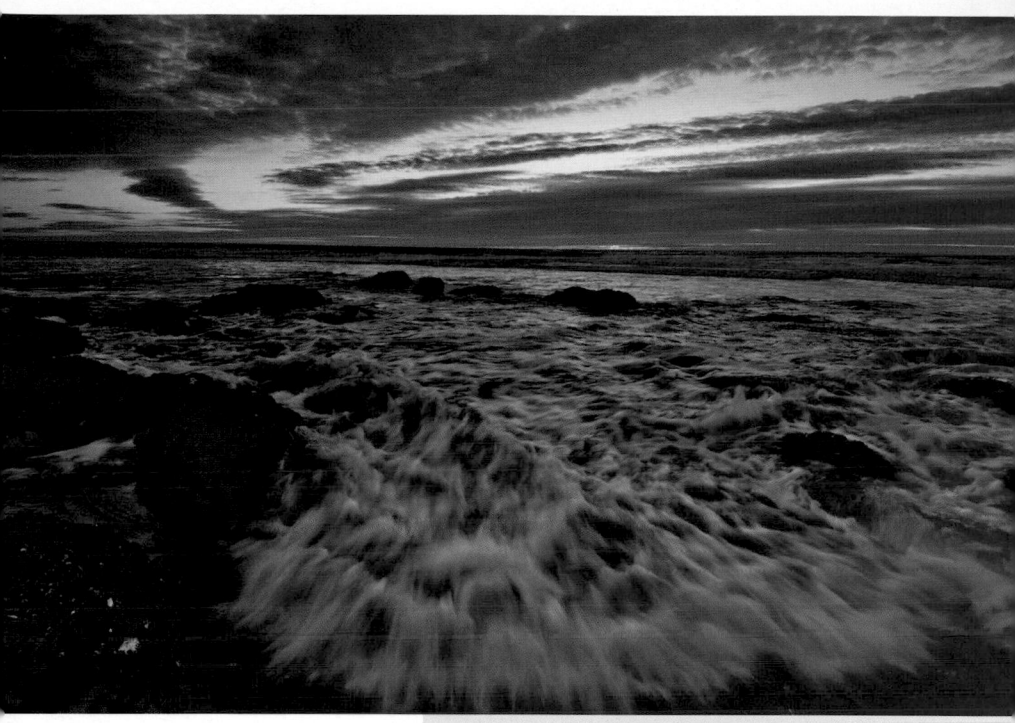

I found myself shooting near dusk in Lincoln City, along Oregon's beautiful coastline. Fortunately, a low tide coincided with sunset, so I had no trouble finding some exposed rocks to climb up on to work from an elevated position. I wanted to convey the energy of the powerful incoming surf, and the only way to do that was with the right shutter speed.

With my camera and 12-24mm lens mounted on a tripod, I selected a shutter speed of a 1/15 sec. and then adjusted my aperture until f/8 indicated a correct exposure for the scene before me. I then played the waiting game, waiting for a wave with enough energy to flow into the entire frame, top to bottom.

Within a few seconds of recording the exposure shown above, I shifted gears, choosing now to convey the mighty ocean as the somewhat calm and tranquil landscape it seldom (if ever) is. With the aid of my Tiffen variable 2-8 stop neutral-density (ND) filter set at a 5-stop reduction, and then reducing my aperture to f/22, I was able to create another correct exposure for this same scene: f/22 at 15 seconds (shown on pages 42-43). The message is now radically altered, as we have gone from a "force to be reckoned with" to one that is far more docile.

Above: Nikon D300S with Nikkor 12-24mm lens, f/8 for 1/15 sec., ISO 200; Pages 42-43: Nikon D300S with Nikkor 12-24mm lens, f/22 for 15 seconds with ND filter set to 5-stop reduction, ISO 200

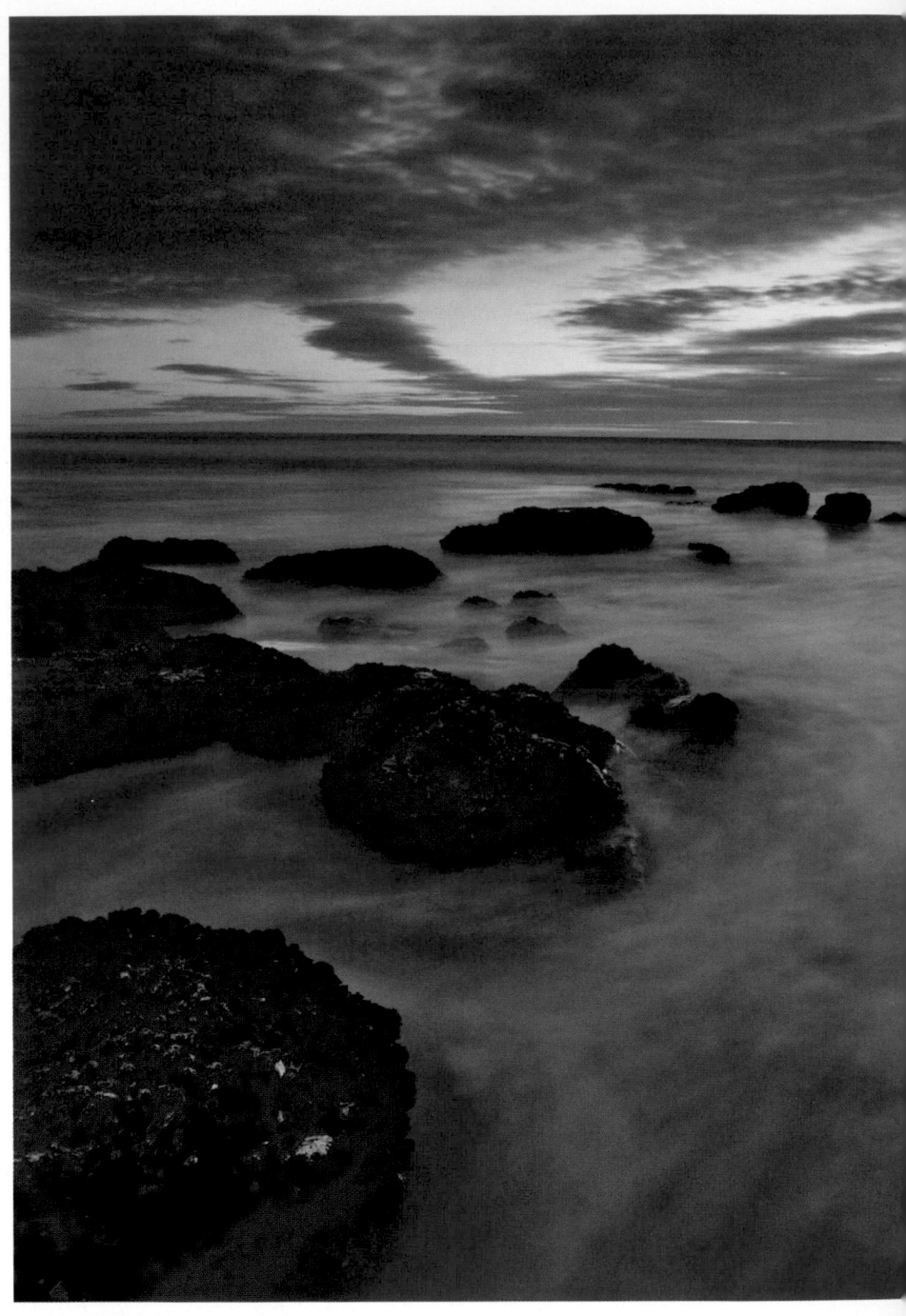

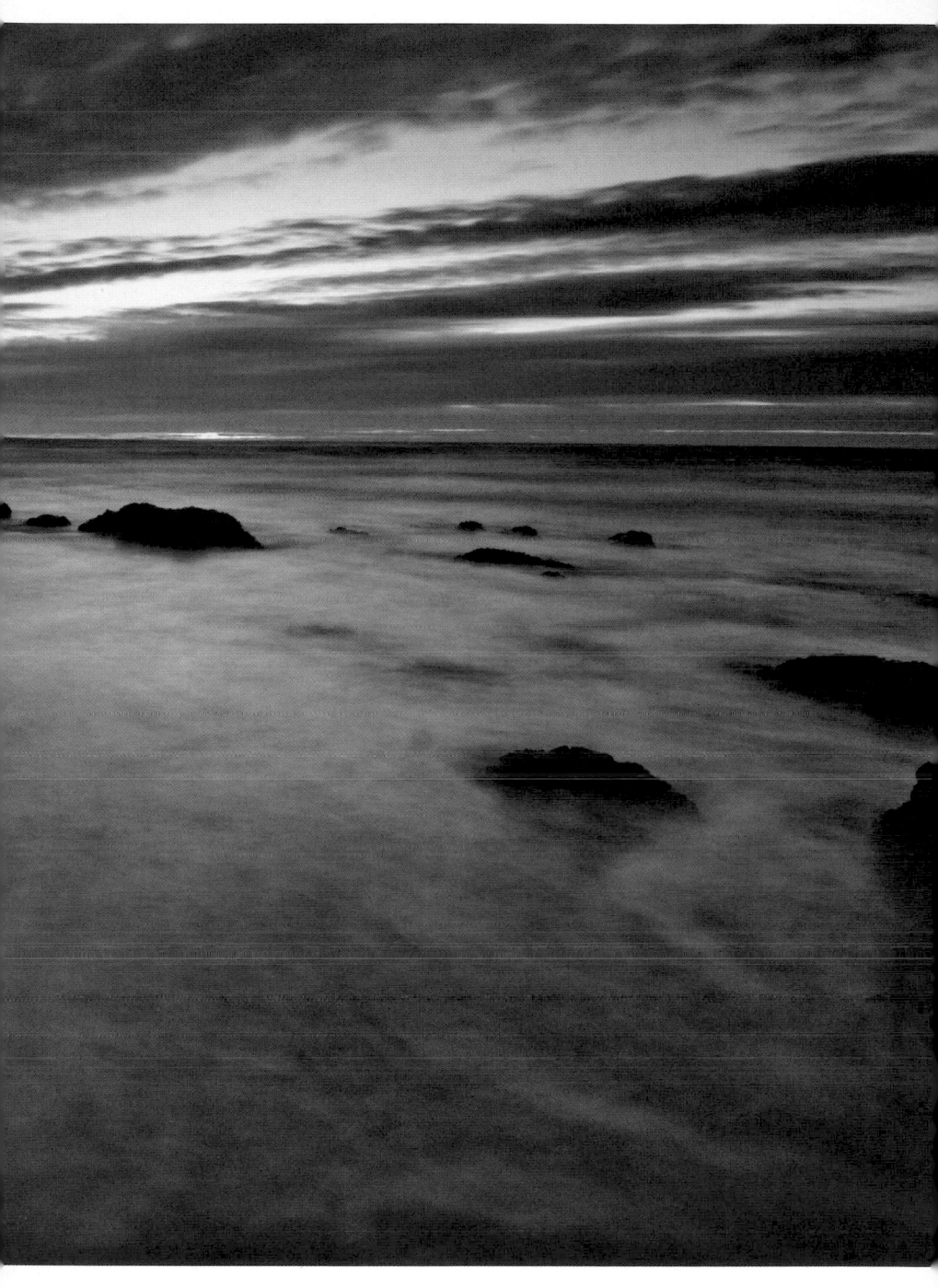

THE ROLE OF APERTURE
AND SHUTTER SPEED

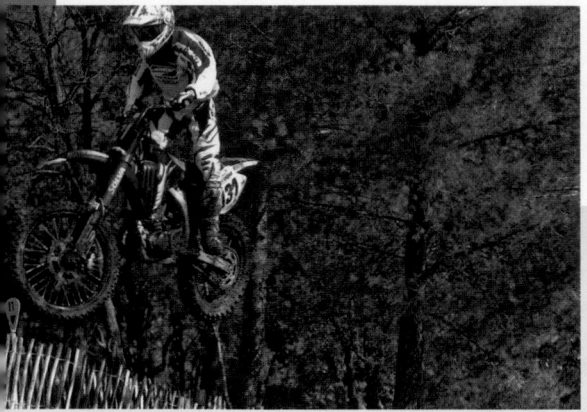

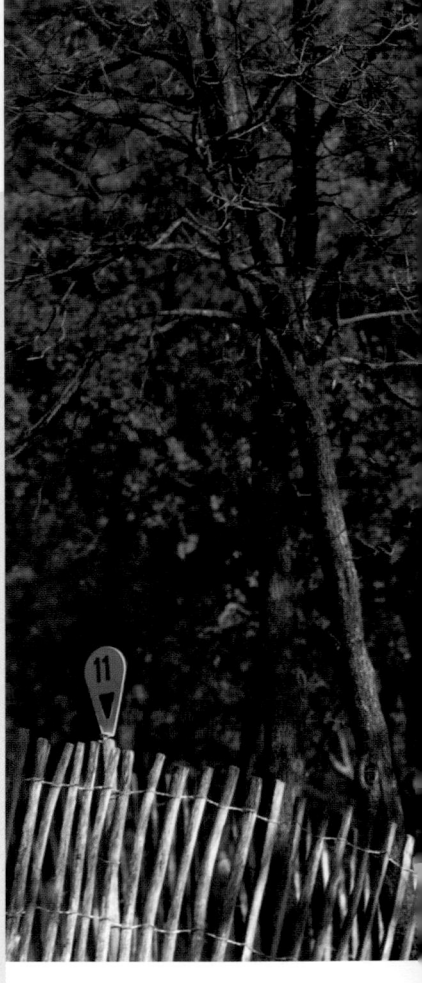

When we use motion in a given composition, it is often understood that we are using it as the primary subject, making the placement of that motion in the frame of vital importance to an effective composition.

In Western society, we have been "trained" since kindergarten to feel more comfortable with motion that enters from the left, partly because we read from left to right. So conventional wisdom would suggest that you should have moving subjects coming in from the left, with enough "empty space" to the right for the subject to move into. And indeed, this practice is recommended quite often in photographic circles—yet one that I would suggest not be adhered to. Sometimes motion does work best if composed and seen moving left to right, yet other times it can only be photographed moving right to left. Plus, as you may know, not everyone reads from left to right. In Middle Eastern and Asian cultures, such as in the UAE, Iraq, Saudi Arabia, Israel, Japan, and China, they read from right to left.

It is also understood that we must not bring the motion more than one-third of the way into the composition. This ensures that the subject is given ample room to continue moving across the frame and isn't smashed up against the side. Having everything "weighted" to one side creates a feeling of imbalance, as if everyone moved to the front of the bus as it sped down the highway. This one I agree with. Left to right, right to left—my only real preference is that the moving subject is not centered or moving much beyond that first third of the frame. Any time I see an action-filled image that is almost out of the frame, I experience a sense of loss, the loss of not fully experiencing the action-filled moment. As with the images shown here, most of us prefer the one at right, with the biker entering the frame with ample space for him to move through.

Both images: Nikon D300 with Nikkor 70–300mm lens, f/5.6 for 1/1000 sec., ISO 200

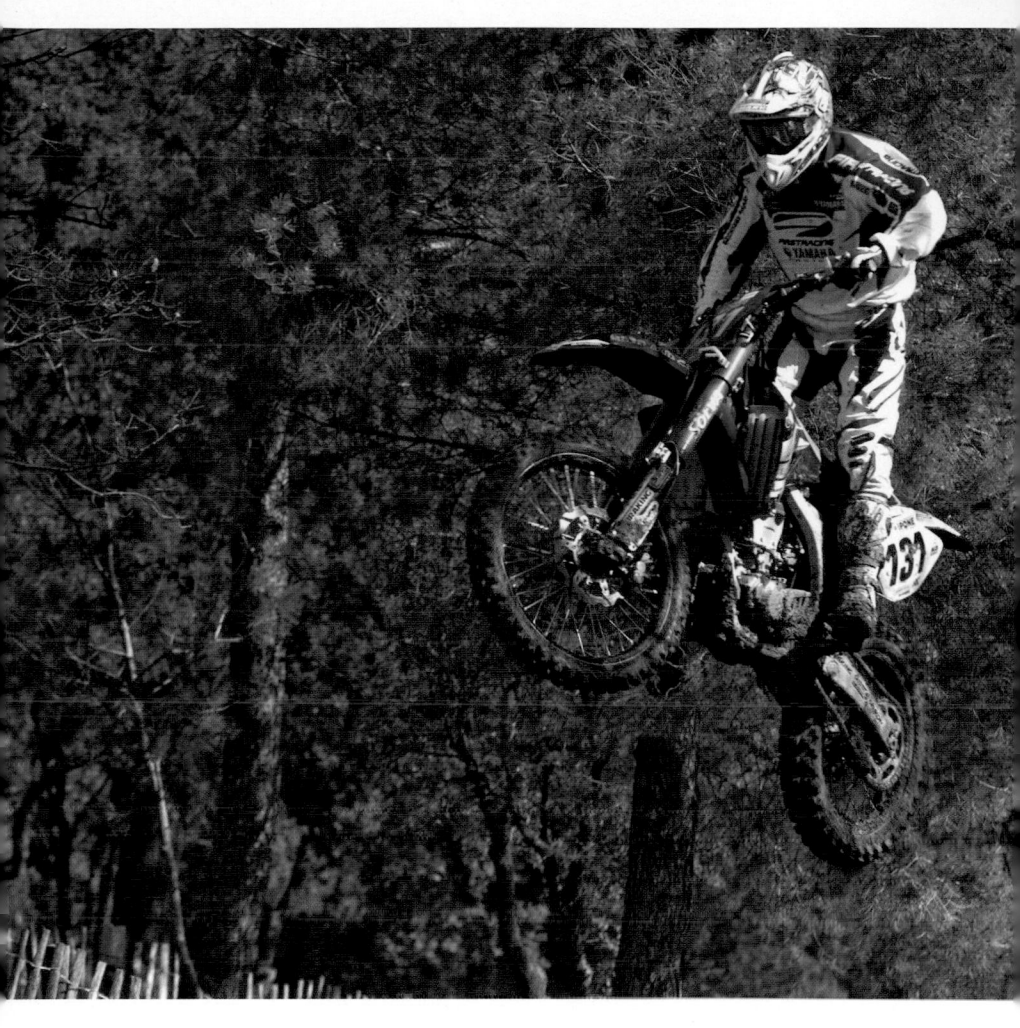

THE ROLE OF APERTURE
AND SHUTTER SPEED

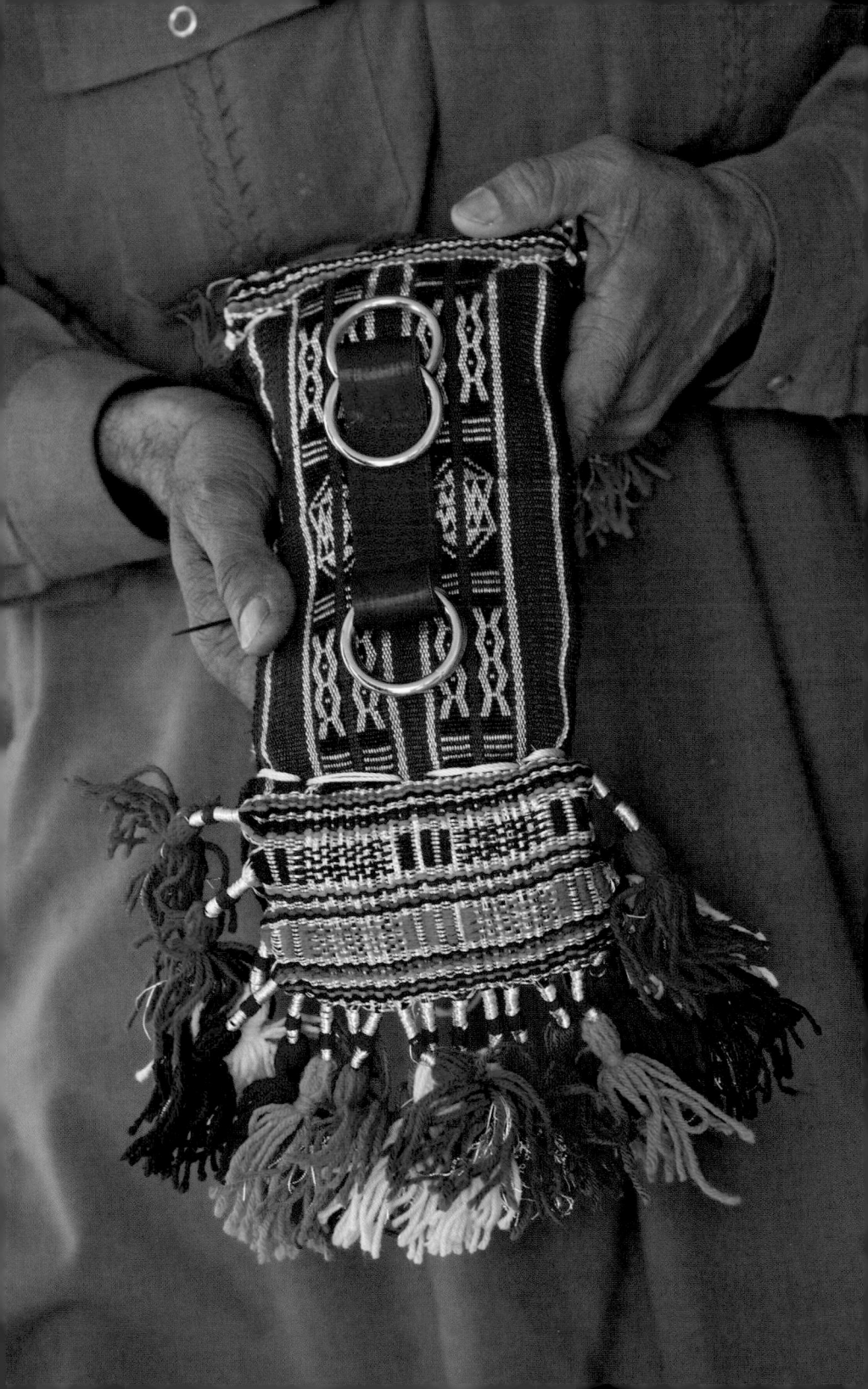

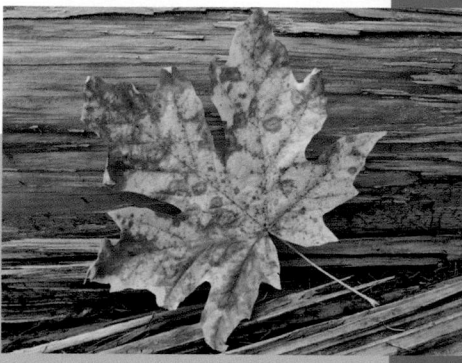

3

FILLING THE FRAME: TWO STEPS FROM A COMPELLING COMPOSITION

Of the many hurdles that await you on your way to the finish line of a compelling composition, none is easier to overcome than the simple act of filling the frame—assuming, of course, that you are able to place one foot in front of the other to take about two steps, on average.

Whether you have your images on display on Flickr, SmugMug, Facebook, or your very own website, you may have heard from other well-meaning photographers that a picture could have been improved had you simply gotten closer. Not getting close enough is perhaps the largest, tallest, and biggest compositional hurdle to overcome yet also one of the easiest! All you have to do is stop blowing things out of proportion and walk, on average, 2 feet closer to the subject.

Nikon D3X with Nikkor 70–300mm lens, f/8 for 1/60 sec., ISO 400

TWO STEPS TO SUCCESS

You may not have realized it, but it's possible that you blow things out of proportion just about every time you step up to your camera's viewfinder. And so do I, I might add. But there is most likely a difference between what I blow out of proportion and what you blow out of proportion.

As you approach that one flower in the garden, your eye/brain is quick to zero in on it, quick to give that one flower 110 percent of your visual attention. That flower becomes the only thing you see, and in a matter of seconds, you press the shutter release. Not until you return to the computer and look at your image do you even begin to see all that other "stuff" surrounding your lone flower, stuff that you and I both know is nothing short of distracting! Why did you not see all that other stuff when you were out in the garden composing your image?

The psychology of "blowing things out of proportion" is, in many respects, a kind of survival mechanism. It allows us to eliminate the infinite and constant distractions around us so we can focus exclusively on whatever threatens or pleases us. So even though you *think* you are focusing exclusively on that one flower, you may be doing so more with your brain than with your camera. Luckily, there is a proven solution that I have used with students in my workshops and online classes for years now.

Once you think you have filled the frame with that flower or portrait of your friend, spouse, lover, neighbor, or stranger, ask yourself the following questions: Are the flower petals touching the edges of the frame inside your camera's viewfinder? Is the person's forehead cut off a bit at the top of your frame? If the answer to either question is "Nope!" then you are not yet close enough—so get closer!

If every shooter made it a point to get in so close that the main subject(s) was touching the edges of the frame, compositional success would increase tenfold. I am not advocating that every shot you take should be one with the subject(s) touching the edges of the frame. But at least initially, it is a great habit to get into, since in a few short months, you will be taking those two steps closer without hesitation and making the consistent discovery that your compositions are far more intimate than ever before. Such is the psychological impact of filling the frame!

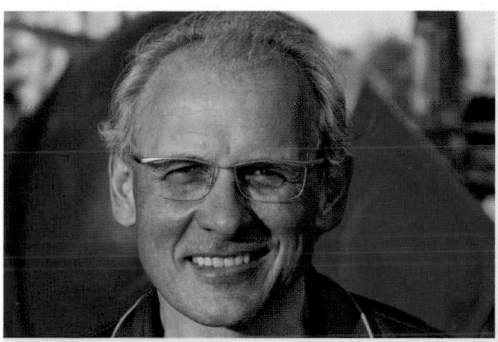

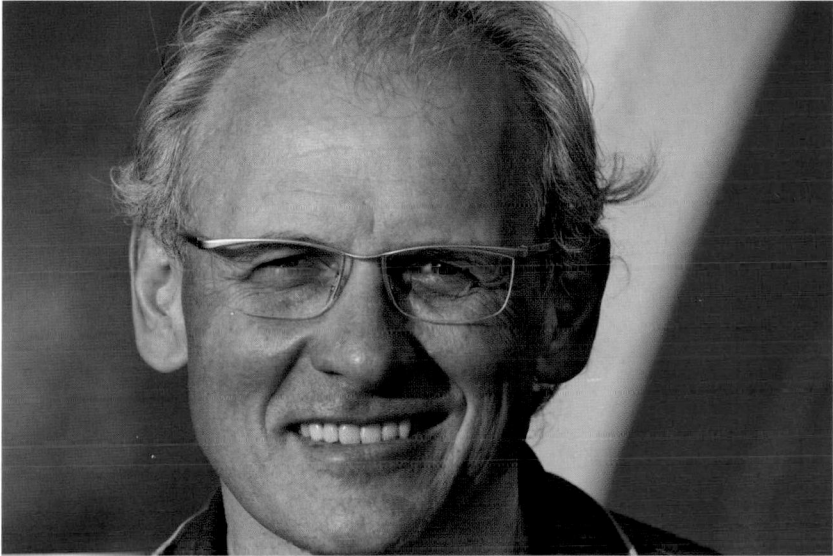

The first morning outing of my Vancouver workshop found us on Granville Island, where I was quick to call on one of the students to serve as a model. With my camera and lens on a tripod, I set up the top shot you see here and asked the students, one by one, to look through my camera's viewfinder and tell me what they thought. Each one said how much they liked the composition, especially the out-of-focus colors behind the subject. (The colors are from a large beach ball–like sculpture about 20 feet behind the subject.) I then took the photo and immediately afterward asked each of the students to review the shot on my camera's monitor. Four of them still liked it, but three others now noticed that the colorful balloonlike sculpture did *not*, in fact, fill all the background. I was thrilled for these three students but was also quick to ask why they hadn't noticed this before I took the photo. The reason, as mentioned earlier, has much to do with our mind's tendency to blow things out of proportion. By moving two small steps forward, I was quick to fix the problem and took the second image, a colorful and frame-filling portrait.

Both images: Nikon D300S with 70–300mm lens at 300mm, f/6.3 for 1/500 sec., ISO 200

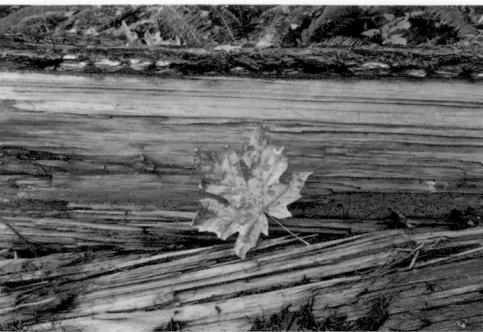
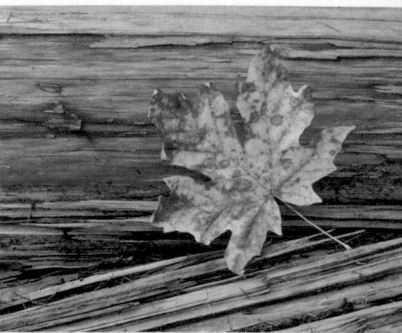

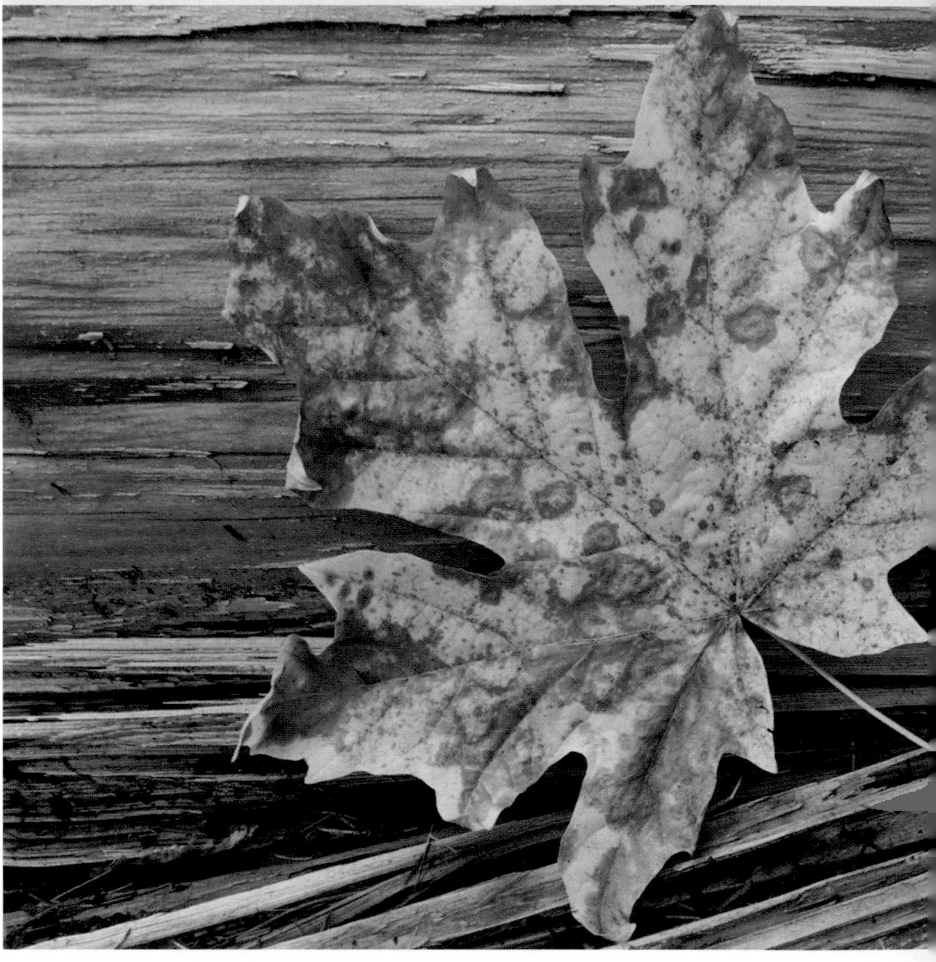

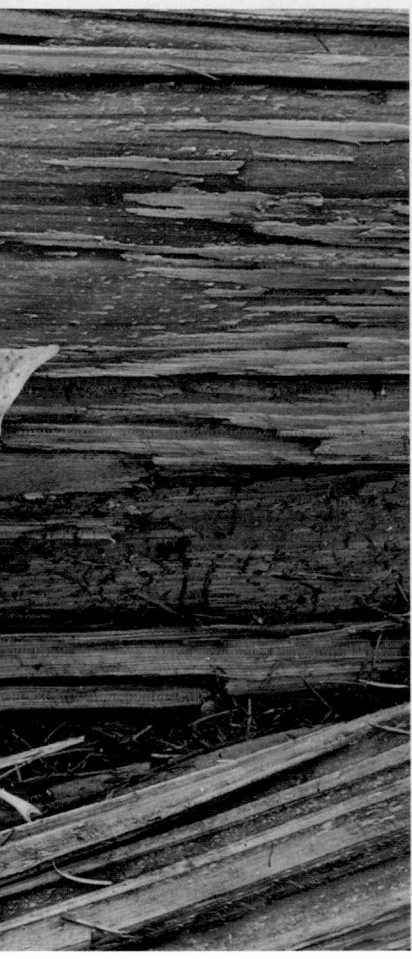

Silver Falls State Park continues to be a favorite haunt of mine when visiting Oregon. I spent much of my first five years as an amateur photographer honing my skills in this park, especially during spring and fall. I returned to the park a few months ago with a fresh group of workshop students, one of whom was determined to get a composition of a lone maple leaf lying atop a Douglas fir. I have duplicated here her first, second, and final attempts at composing this photo.

With her camera and lens mounted on a tripod, she asked me to look through her viewfinder. Before I did, I asked if she felt good about the composition and she said yes. I took a look and told her to take the shot. The top left image you see here is very close to what she composed. I suggested she move a bit closer, explaining that my eye was bothered by all the "empty" space and the shift in contrast toward the green ferns at the top of the frame, which, not surprisingly, she hadn't noticed. She moved in closer and said, "Okay, the ferns are gone and I like it much better," and took the top right shot. I asked her to get even closer, close enough that she could see the edges of the leaf touching the edges of her frame, then backing off just a wee bit so they are *almost* touching the edges. About 2 hours later, back in the parking lot, she was reviewing her images when another student, who was looking over her shoulder, remarked, "Wow, that's a nice leaf shot!" He was, of course, referring to the final image you see here.

All images: Nikon D300S with Nikkor 70–300mm lens at 100mm, f/11 for 1/45 sec., ISO 200

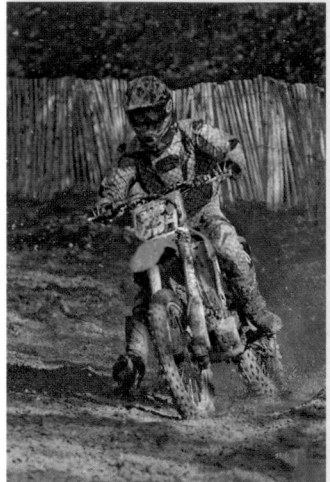

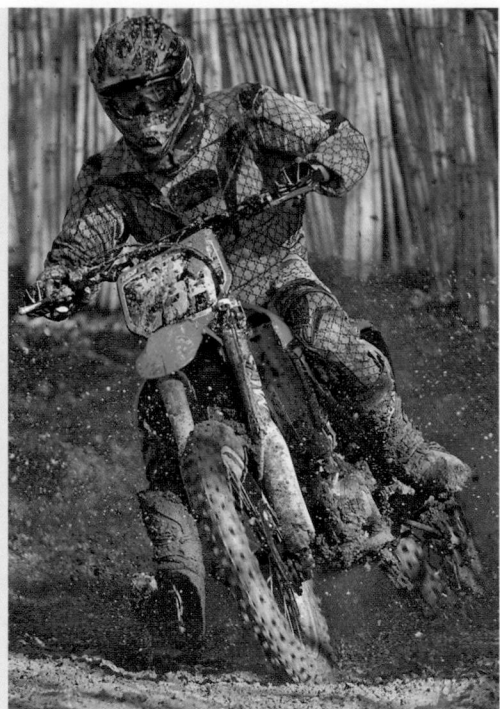

I have only been to one motocross race, and it's safe to say it won't be my last! I don't know if it's the norm at all motocross events, but I was able to get ridiculously close to these guys. I hadn't been that near the action of a sporting event since shooting an NFL game in Pittsburgh back in 1997. Granted, I walked away quite dirty, but it was worth all the mud that came flying my way.

On one part of the track, the bikers would come around a corner and hit a straightaway before making another turn that sent them flying over one of the many hills. Each rider seemed to follow the same deep ruts in the dirt track, which made it extra easy for me—all I had to do was focus on that spot and fire away as each rider came through. But I was also quick to realize that my point of view would not allow me to frame the riders against the solid backdrop of a fence, but rather against both the fence and the contrasting trees, as you see top left. I didn't like the trees, as they reminded me of "crying babies"—in other words, a distraction. Nearby I spotted a solution: a large plastic box, about 18 inches high, sitting behind one of the vendors' tables. I asked if I could borrow it for a few minutes and was soon taking "two steps" up to tower over the other photographers and fill the frame without the background distraction.

With my camera and lens mounted on a monopod, I chose an action-stopping speed of 1/250 sec., since the riders were coming toward me (see box opposite). I then adjusted my aperture until f/11 indicated a correct exposure, and over the course of only 5 minutes, recorded more than fifteen mud-caked motocross riders, one of which you see here.

Both images: Nikon D300 with 70–200mm lens at 200mm, f/11 for 1/250 sec., ISO 100

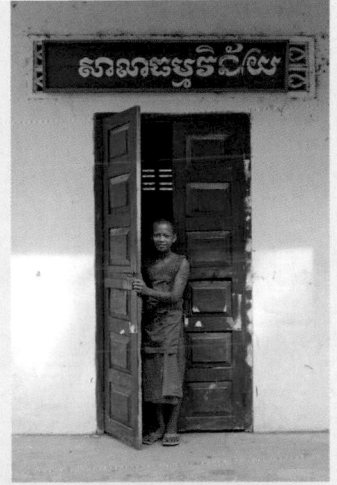

HERE THEY COME

No matter what type of action you're photographing, if that action is coming directly at you, you can safely shoot at 1/250 sec. This is especially true with regard to sports. The hundred-yard dash at a track-and-field event, cars on the straightaway at a NASCAR race, the lone swimmer nearing the end of the pool, the tight end running toward the end zone, the number four greyhound crossing the finish line—these are just a few examples of the many subjects that await the use of 1/250 sec. when they are moving straight toward you.

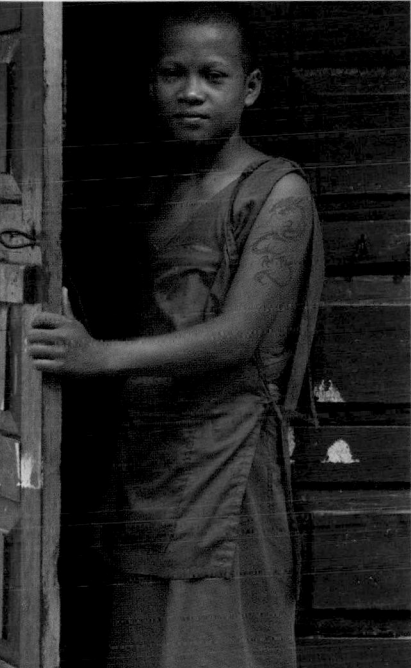

My first trip to Angkor Wat and its surrounding temples will surely be my last. When the local vendors and their trinkets far outnumber the tourists, a long day of waving off enthusiastic sales pitches is in store! On the other hand, I have every intention of returning to Siem Reap and the nearby villages you see featured here and throughout this book. The Cambodian people are truly a hardy and optimistic lot.

I met this boy, a young monk in training, near the Angkor Wat temple as he exited the small white building you see in the top image. I was immediately struck by the contrast between the blue door and his orange clothing, as was one of my workshop students.

The student was quick to ask the boy to pose in the open doorway. Upon seeing her image, I asked if she thought it was necessary to include much of the white building surrounding the doorway. She answered, "Well, isn't that part of the story? I mean, I am guessing this is where he lives." Let's assume he does live here. Does that mean we must include the white walls of the building? If the image was about the architect who designed the building, or the guy who painted the building white, then, sure, it should be included. But if the intent is simply to come away with a colorful and compelling composition of a young Buddhist monk in training, then perhaps the composition should be *all* about him and the contrast that surrounds him. By moving in closer, we limit the composition to two very complementary colors and offer the audience a far more intimate encounter.

Both images: Nikon D300S with 70–300mm lens at 135mm, f/11 for 1/160 sec., ISO 200

AVOID THE CROP

Now that you have returned home from your photo adventure, why are you sitting in front of the computer calling on the crop tool? Obviously, the need to crop on the computer is a direct result of *not* getting close enough to your subjects. Oh, how I wish I could eliminate your need for the crop tool! With each and every use, you are providing evidence that you were incapable of filling the frame. If the world of art had an actual court where trials took place, you would be charged with the crime of falling short of your creative potential!

Oh, I am fully aware of new technologies that will allow us to stretch pixels without losing quality, including the Nikon D800 with its 36-megapixel sensor. Should that come to pass, will many shooters become lazy in their compositional approach, knowing that they can fix things in Photoshop or with an app on their iPhone? I am usually the first in line to embrace new technologies—but only if they *free up* time to do what I love most: create images in camera. For me, the experience of creating an image is about clicking a shutter release, not a mouse. It is about the wind on my face, the smell in the air, and the taste in my mouth. It is about hearing the roar of the ocean or the music or the voices—and, of course, the texture of whatever I am about to shoot. It is also about an opportunity to watch amazing light. Call me "old school," but it is this very organic experience that has provided the motivation for me to get up early and stay out late for many years. It is my wish that when Father Time comes a-knocking, I will be found in the great outdoors with camera in hand and a tripod at my side—not slumped over the computer desk with a mouse in my hand!

I am all too familiar with the defense for cropping: most photo frames available at the chain retail outlets are 8 x 10, while the dimension of the digital sensor produces images that are 8 x 12. I also know that some of you shoot subjects that do not allow you to truly fill the frame, such as family portraits. However, my guess is that most of you are hobbyists who migrate toward landscapes, flowers, travel, people, and vacation photography—subjects that look better when the frame is filled, edge to edge, top to bottom.

Successful painters paint all the way to the edges—side to side, top to bottom—of the predetermined boundaries of their canvas. Dancers dance—side to side, front to back—within the predetermined boundaries of the stage. Just like successful painters and dancers, photographers need to use the full canvas, the entire stage, if you will, and claim it as their territory. Commit your eye to taking your subject(s) up to, if not over, the edges—top to bottom, side to side—and, not surprisingly, you will hear that elusive "Wow!" much more often.

WHEN IT'S OKAY TO CROP

There are, of course, situations that fully justify cropping. For example, when you are prevented from walking closer to your subject by a raging river, a deep canyon, or a protective fence. Or when you don't have a long enough lens; your telephoto zoom only goes to 200mm and the shot before you calls for at least a 300mm. I would never suggest that you should walk away and not take a shot. Take the shot, but let it serve as a reminder *why* you need that longer lens or the full-frame DSLR with that much bigger sensor!

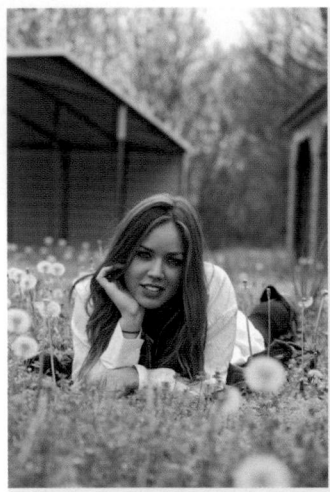

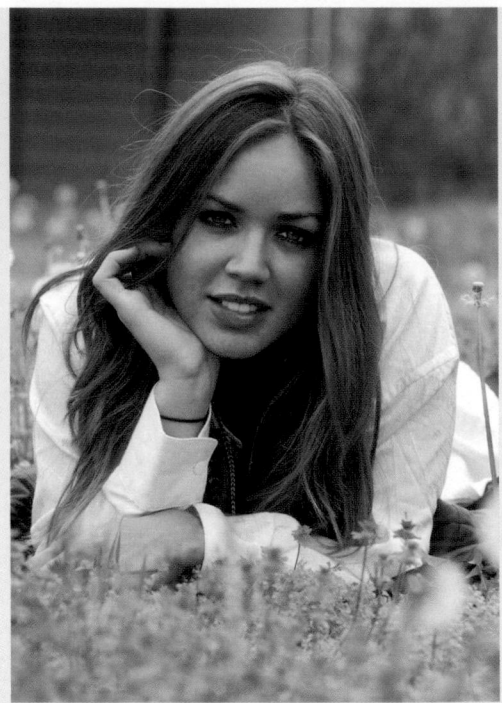

Meet Jill Sipkins, a recent art major and journalism graduate of Wisconsin University and one of our esteemed instructors at the Picture Perfect School of Photography (PPSOP). In the first image, shown top left, I deliberately composed the type of composition we commonly see in beginner classes at the school. By now I am sure the problem is obvious to all of you: Jill does not even come close to filling the frame. If I just crop it in Photoshop, as shown in the second photo, above, the composition is better, but the image is severely limited as to how large it can be, since you have now cropped away about 60 percent of your pixels. You might be able to salvage a print size up to 5 x 7 but no larger.

Alternatively, I can simply pick myself up and walk a few steps closer to Jill, as shown in the shot opposite. This way I end up with the same frame-filling composition but with 100 percent of my pixels, and I can easily generate a 16 x 24–inch (poster-size) print if desired.

Both images above: Nikon D3X with 70–300mm lens at 70mm, f/6.3 for 1/400 sec., ISO 100; Opposite: Nikon D3X with 70–300mm lens at 280mm, f/6.3 for 1/400 sec., ISO 100

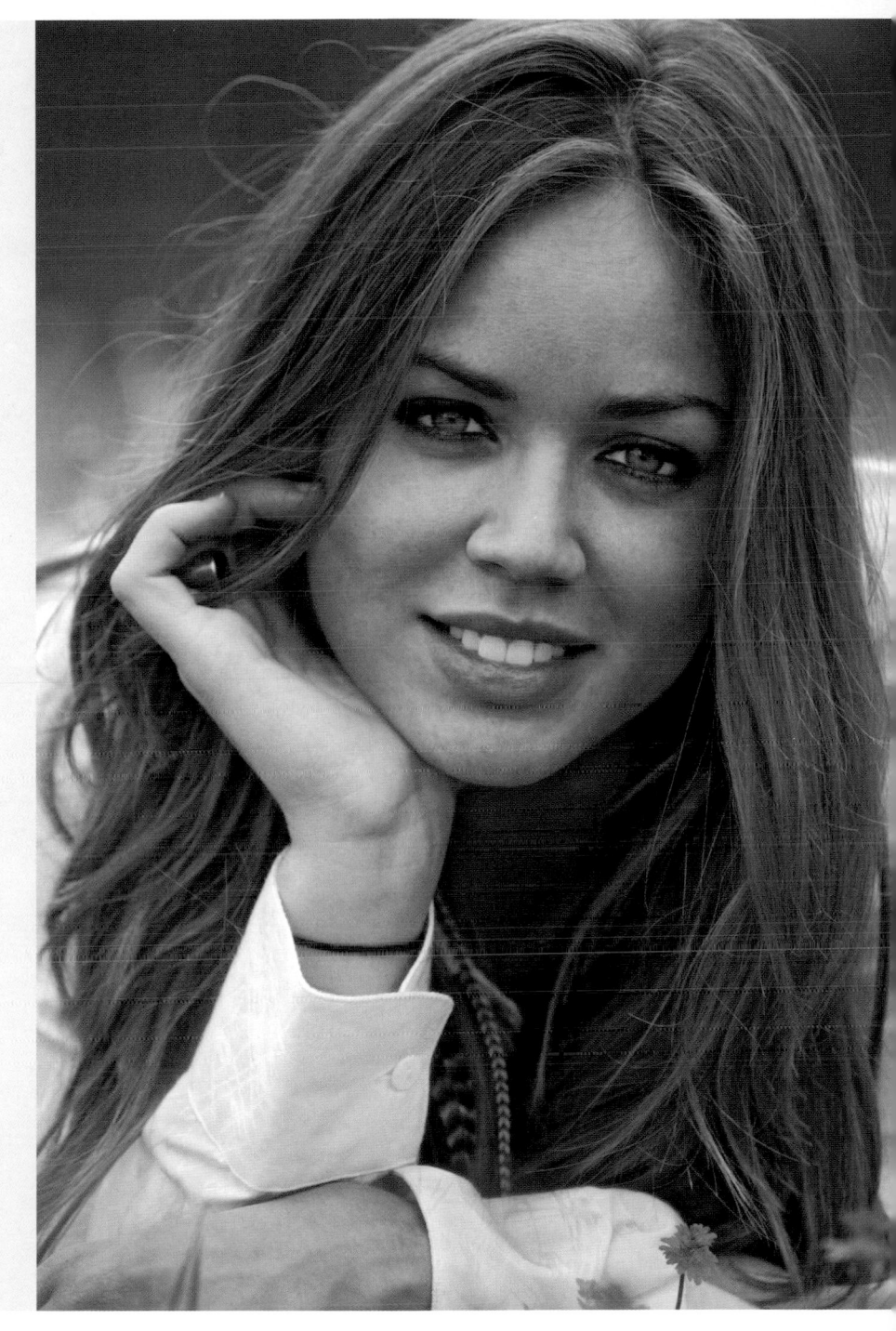

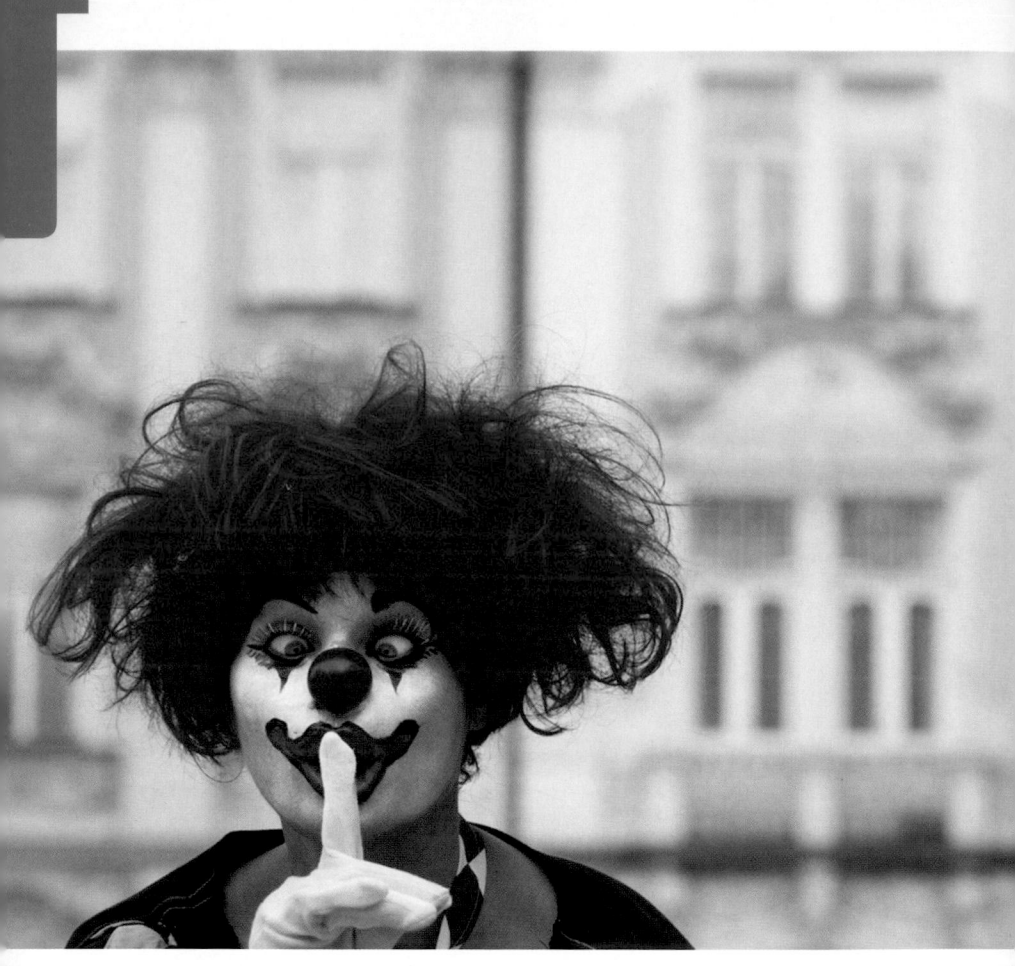

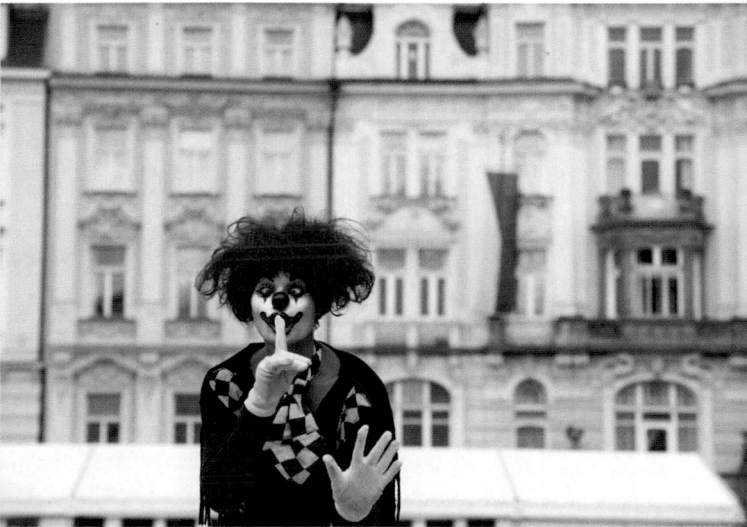

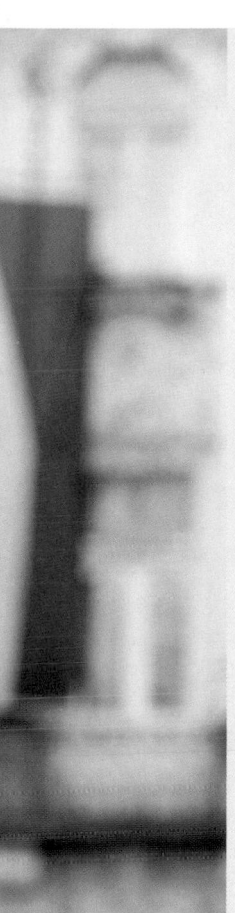

While in Prague, we had the pleasure of working with Lucie the Clown (the wife of one of the students). In an effort to "prove" that I'm a fair guy, let's look at two examples that were taken during one of the morning shoots. In my first example, shown above and shot with my Nikon D3X and Nikkor 70–300mm at 100mm, it is clear that I am too far away and I need to get closer. The white rooftops at the bottom of the frame are distracting, and there is too much background. I have two options: I can walk closer or simply zoom the lens out farther toward the 300mm range. I opted to zoom the lens, and as you can see in the image shown at left, at 230mm Lucie fills up more of the frame and the background is much cleaner. The once-distracting visual weight of the white rooftops no longer pulls our eyes down.

If all you were able to record was a composition similar to the first shot, you would probably find yourself, upon your return home, calling on the crop tool. Unfortunately, your shot would quickly diminish in quality if you tried to make it any larger than 8 x 12 inches. When you cropped into your composition, you threw away almost half your pixels; needless to say, the remaining pixels can only "stretch" so far before they begin to rip and tear. The bottom line is to do your best to fill the frame while you're there!

Above: Nikon D3X with 70–300mm lens at 95mm, f/6.3 for 1/250 sec., ISO 100, Left: Nikon D3X with 70–300mm lens at 210mm, f/6.3 for 1/250 sec., ISO 100

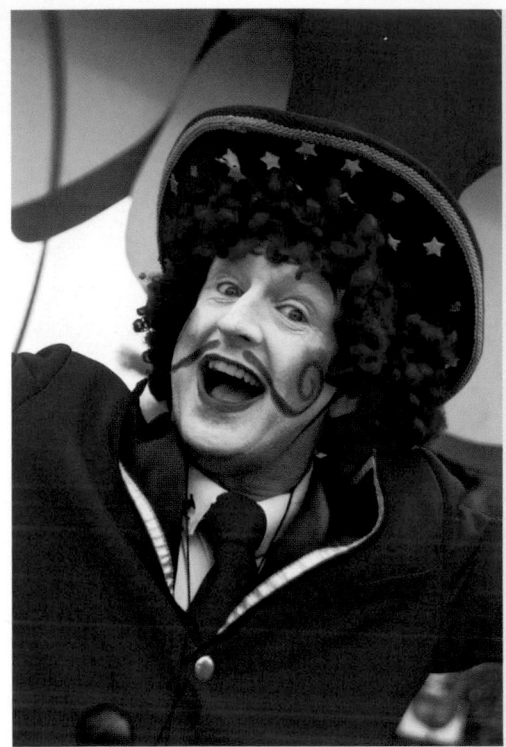
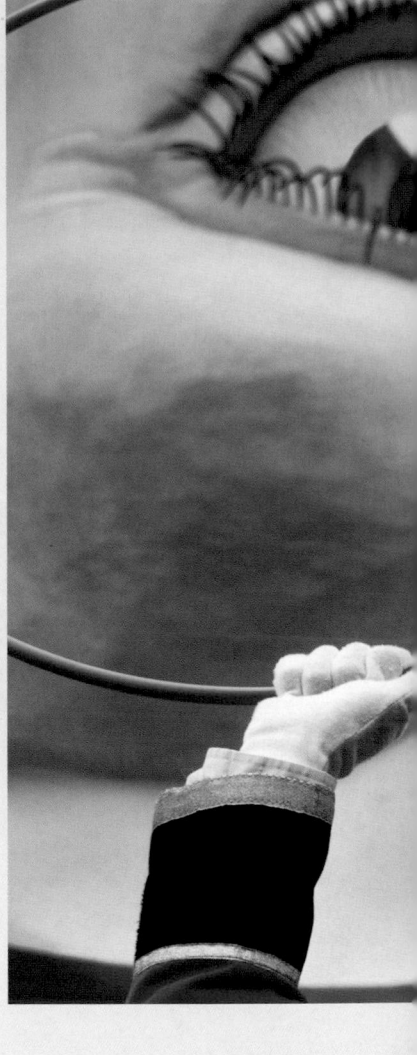

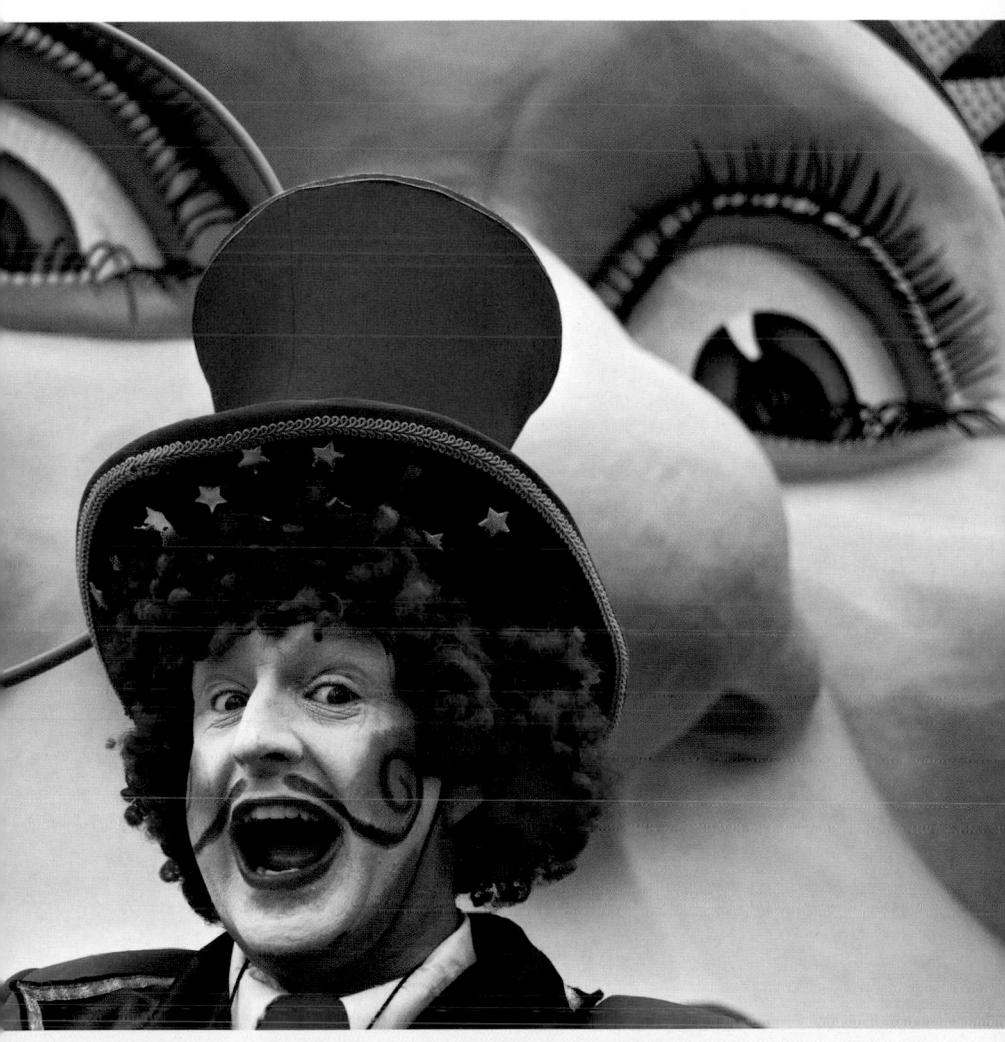

Before closing this chapter, I want to mention that it is also a good idea to take the occasional two steps back. I remember with great fondness several years ago shooting under the Sydney Harbour Bridge in Sunrise Park. Just as the park opened in the early evening, several characters began showing up, including this jovial door greeter. I was so fixated on getting a frame-filling shot of his gleeful expressions and contrasting colors (shown at left) that I almost failed to get what turned out to be my favorite shot of the evening: the image shown above, contrasted against a much larger cartoonlike backdrop of a young child—fantasy atop fantasy. Luckily, he was kind enough to wait while I changed lenses before moving on to another group anxious to have their picture taken with him.

Opposite: Nikon D300S with 70–300mm lens at 120mm, f/6.3 for 1/200 sec., ISO 200; Above: Nikon D300S with Nikkor 24–85mm lens, f/8 for 1/80 sec., ISO 200

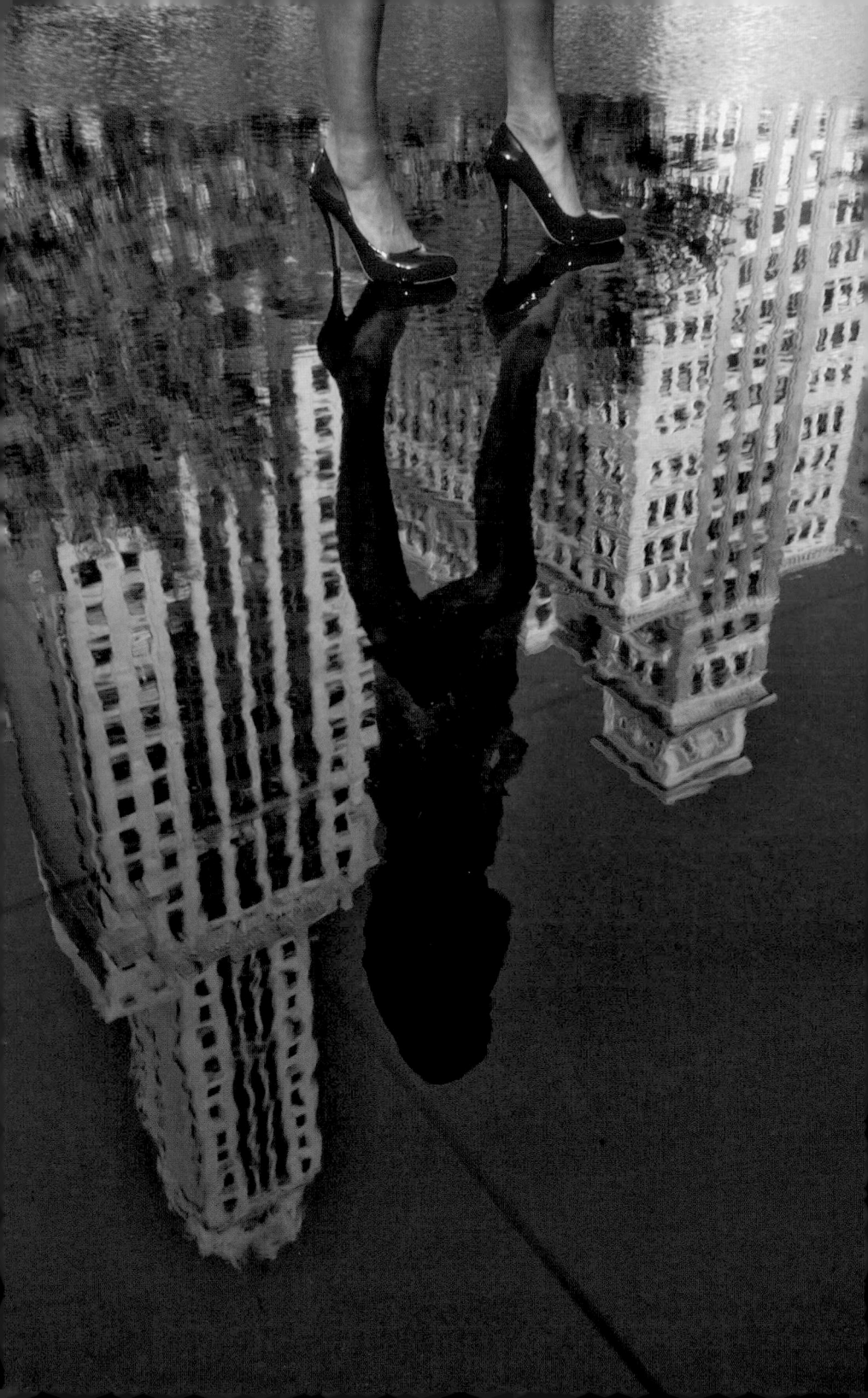

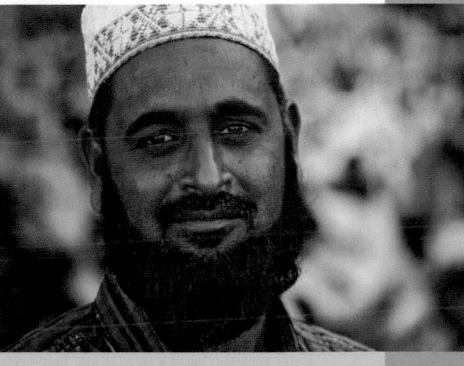

4

CHOOSING YOUR BACKGROUND

If there is one area inside the viewfinder that I wish more photographers would give their full attention to, it is the background. I have said on multiple occasions that it's more important to spend time looking at your background than at the subject who is sitting, standing, hanging, lying, walking, running, tripping, or jumping in front of it. Clean backgrounds are like a clean dinner plate. And if you have ever been served food on a dirty plate, well, you know what you did . . . and just like a dirty plate, a dirty background is a turnoff, too.

Nikon D3X with Nikkor 24–85mm lens, f/16 for 1/60 sec., ISO 100

HOW TO QUIET THE "CRYING BABIES"

When you are watching the final episode of your favorite television show, all your attention is on the TV—at least until crying is heard from the baby's room in the "background." Many times—and, oh my, do I mean *many* times—I have seen potentially great compositions get compromised by that "baby crying in the background," which, of course, distracts the viewer from focusing on the main subject.

So how do you quiet the crying baby in the background? There are several ways. The first is so obvious that it reminds me of the guy who can't find his reading glasses even though he has looked everywhere—except on top of his head. *Do not shoot any composition where babies are crying in the background.*

If you cannot avoid crying babies, then make sure they are fed and have a clean diaper. In other words, move your foreground subject, if possible, so it hides or covers up the distracting element, or change your point of view or lens. Background distractions are found just about everywhere between you and the finish line of a perfect arrangement, but with practice will come an astute eye. Sooner than you think, you will be quick to "hear" the cry and when you do, you will be just as quick to silence it.

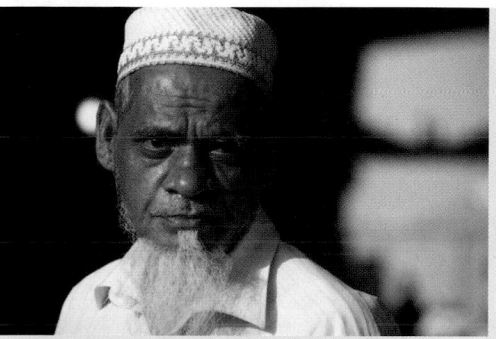
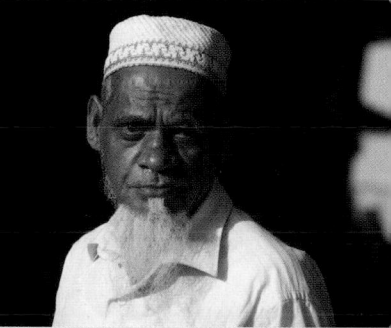

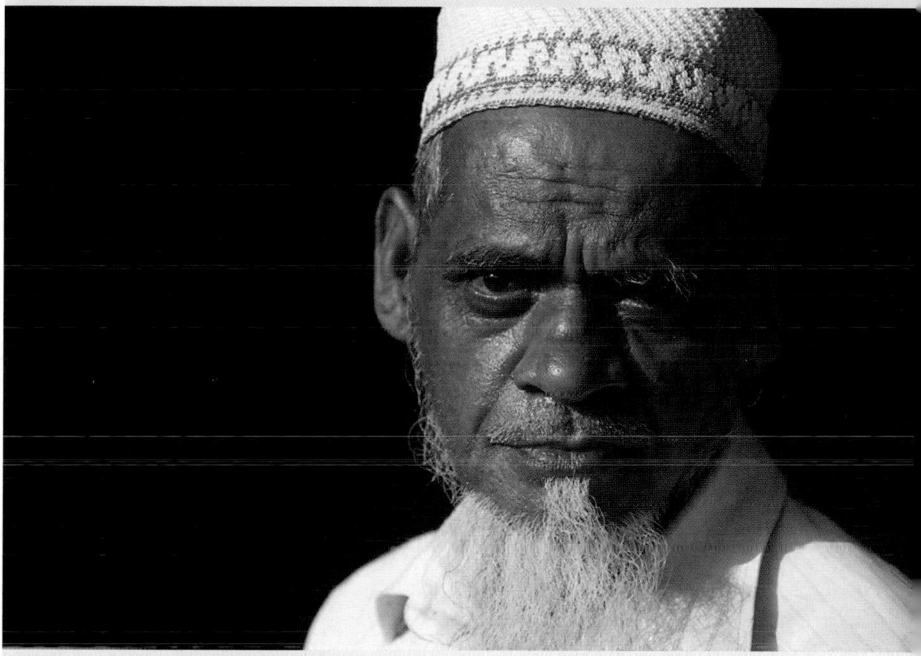

Late-afternoon sidelight opens the door to a host of wonderful photographic opportunities. The light is not only warmer and thus more inviting, but strong sidelight intensifies the contrast between light and dark, emphasizing form, depth, and a sense of mystery. While conducting a workshop in Kuwait, I met this man at an aluminum-fabrication plant. He was quick to pose for me, but as you can see in the first example, top left, I started with a background full of crying babies. By moving to my left, I was able to "hide" one of the distracting elements behind the subject's head, as shown in the second image (top right). Finally, I moved a bit closer and farther to the right to get a completely clean background (above). Black backgrounds, like the one shown here, are the result of setting your exposure for the much brighter sunlight on the subject's face. Any resulting shadow areas, which in this case include the left side of his face and the background, are then severely underexposed.

All images: Nikon D3X with Nikkor 70–300mm lens at 240mm, f/8 for 1/500 sec., ISO 100

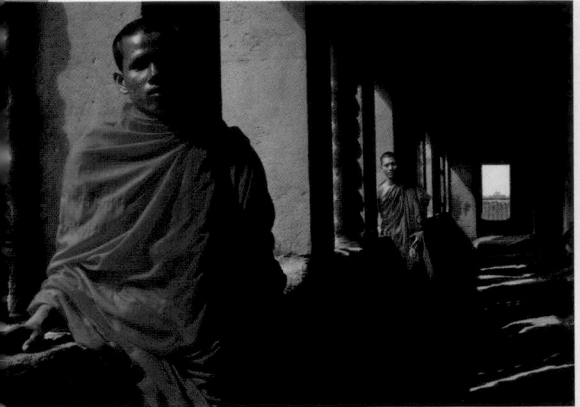

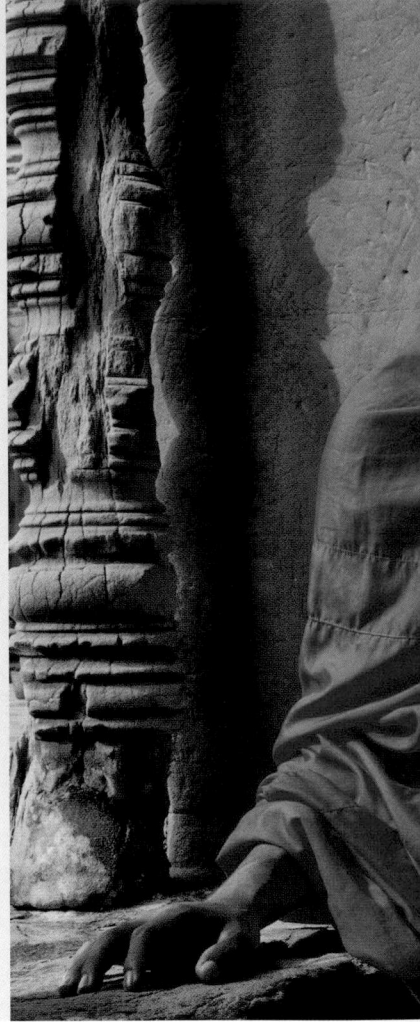

It was my student Arno's idea to pool some of our money and offer it to a few of the monks at Angkor Wat in exchange for 15 minutes of their time in front of the camera. Although I rarely pay people to take their picture, this is one time when it proved to be a wise decision. In a matter of minutes, we were able to photograph these two monks in a number of exciting compositional arrangements around the Temple Angkor Wat, including the one shown here. However, note the "crying baby" in the background of the first image (above): the extreme contrast shift from dark to white, much as we saw in the first image on the previous page. The solution was a simple one-two step to my right, and just like that, my two monks were now composed for all to see and without any background distractions (right).

As an aside, I am often asked where I take my meter reading in situations like this, with strong sidelight. I wanted a lot of depth of field for this composition, so I opted for f/16 and then moved in close until my lens was filled with the first monk's orange robe. I then adjusted my shutter speed until 1/100 sec. indicated a correct exposure for the light reflecting off his robe.

Both images: Nikon D3X with 16–35mm lens at 30mm, f/16 for 1/100 sec., ISO 100

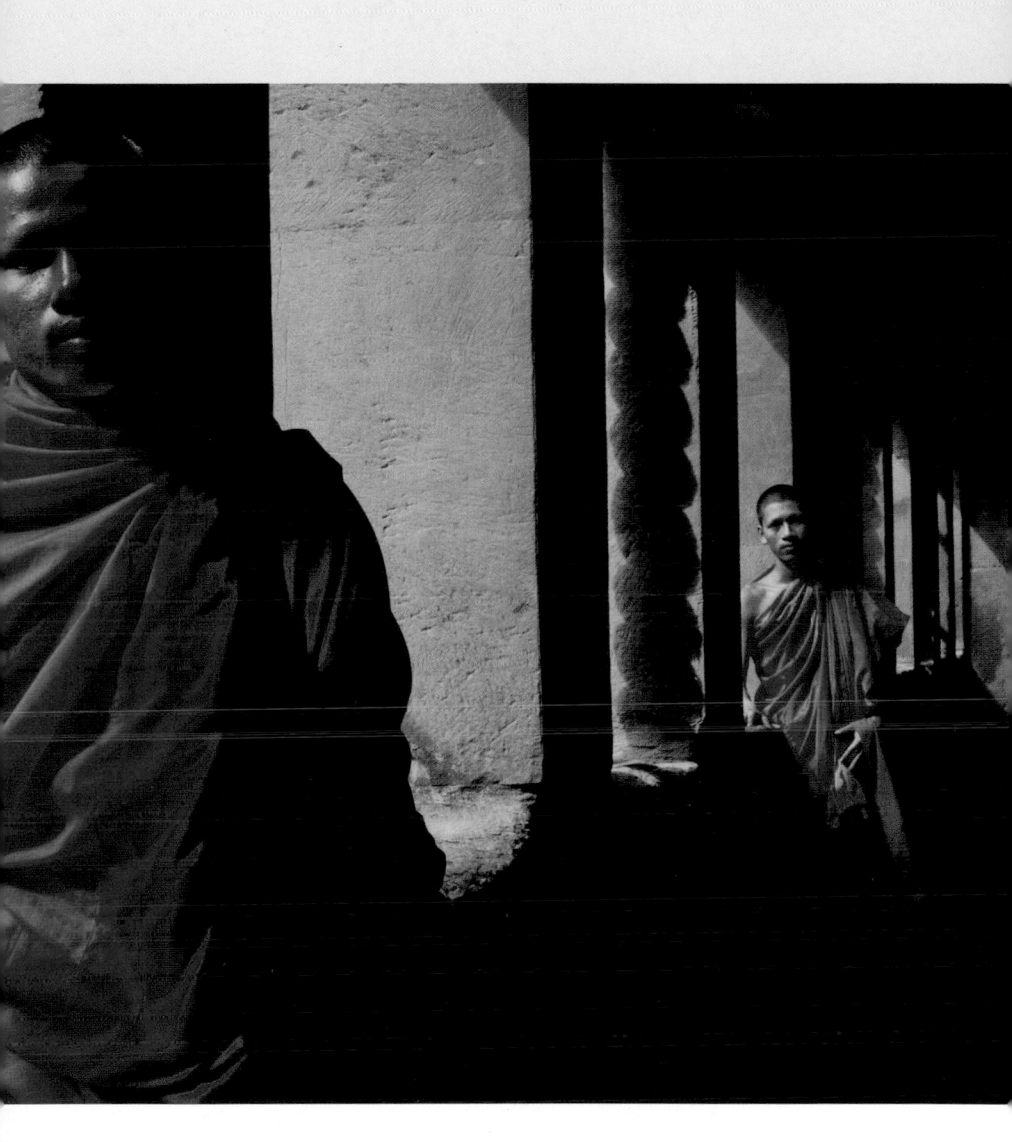

67

CHOOSING YOUR
BACKGROUND

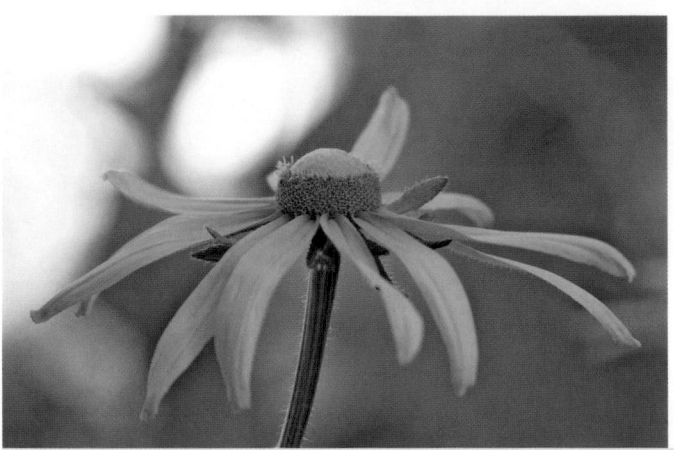

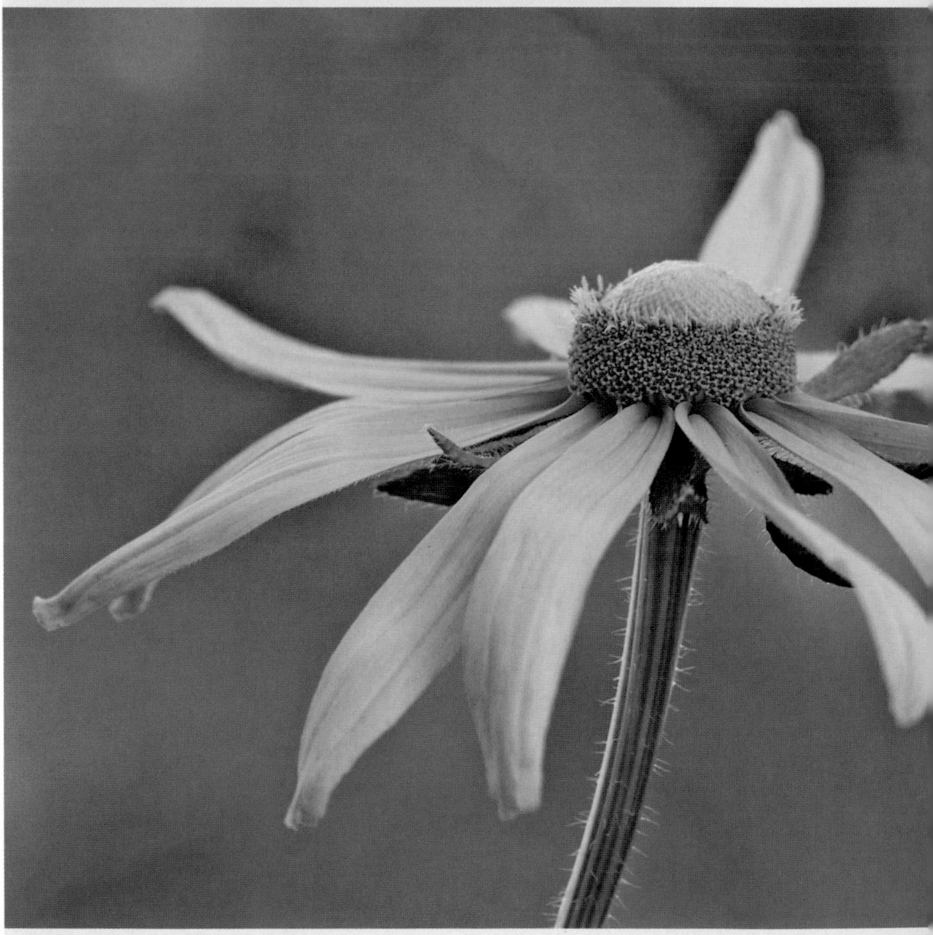

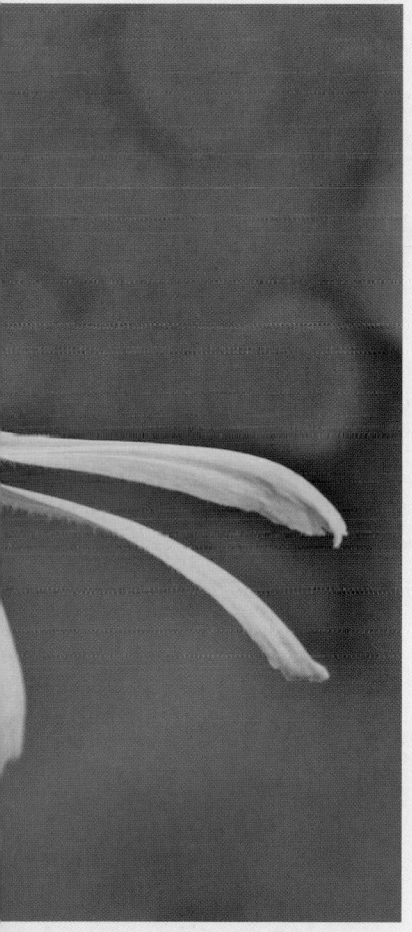

Who doesn't like to shoot flowers? If I were paid a penny for every flower photograph I have critiqued at my online school . . . And what is the biggest problem I have found in most flower compositions? That's right: crying babies in the background!

Amateur photographers are often so taken by what they see inside the viewfinder, so blinded by their passion for their main subject, that they fail to look at—let alone think about—what's going on in the background. They cannot see the problems with the background, even when they look in the LCD screen—and, in some cases, even after processing the image on the computer.

As you look at this first photograph (opposite, top), note the jarring shift in contrast as you scan from the soft green tones in the top right over to the loud, bright yellow-gold and white tones in the top left. Doesn't that bother you? The solution, once again, is to either move a wee bit or change lenses. In this case, the smallest of shift in my point of view quickly hid the bright background light behind distant foliage and I fired off the second, much "quieter" shot you see to the left.

Both images: Nikon D300S with Micro-Nikkor 105mm lens, f/8 for 1/30 sec., ISO 200

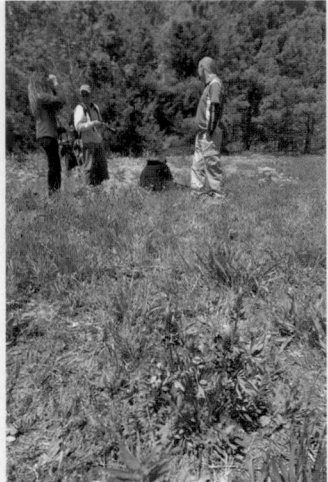

Sometimes the cries coming from the back room are so muffled that unless you have that baby monitor turned up full blast, you won't hear them at all. Such was the case with me last year while on a workshop in Cape Cod. My students and I were thrilled to find a small meadow of flowers across the road from a nearby cemetery and soon we were all immersed in the welcome color. As for me, I was lying down about 5 feet from the small clump of lupine shown in the first photograph (above), intent on photographing a single bloom against the somewhat distant yellow flowers of the background. I was happy with my result, shown to the right, until a student pointed out the contrast shift in the upper left corner. Obviously my baby monitor was set too low on this particular afternoon. Without hesitation, I returned to the scene and after moving a bit to the right, was able to create a much cleaner, distraction-free composition (opposite).

Both images: Nikon D300S with Nikkor 70–300mm lens at 300mm, f/6.3 for 1/500 sec., ISO 200

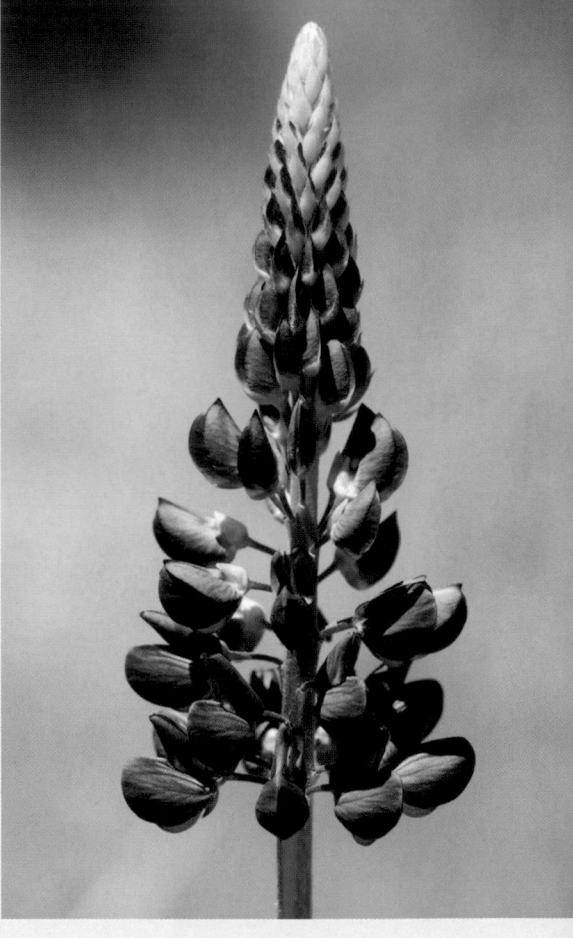

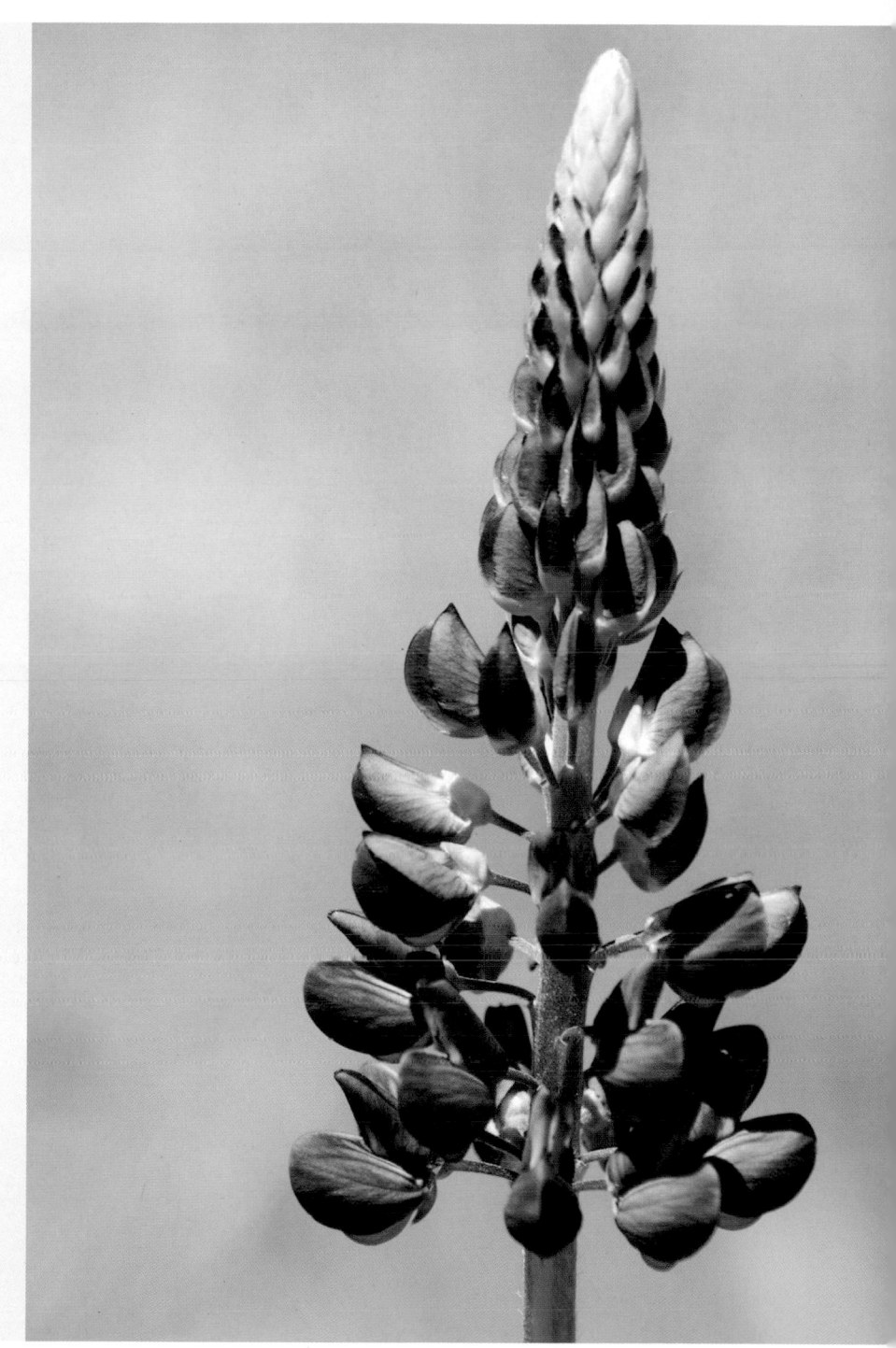

71 CHOOSING YOUR BACKGROUND

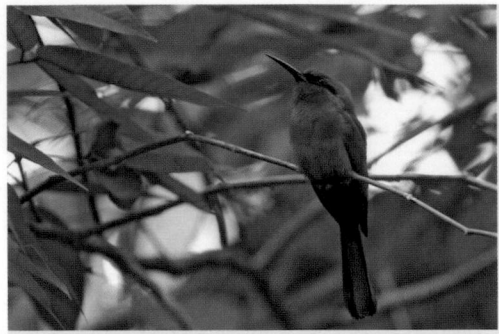

What causes background trouble? Several things. Sometimes it's the wrong aperture, resulting in too much depth of field. Other times it's the wrong point of view, resulting in that telephone pole sticking out of your daughter's head. And then there are those jarring tones and/or shapes in the background that distract from the focused subject, such as that out-of-focus background of purple flowers behind the lone bright red tulip. But of particular note are large shifts in tonal contrast of light and dark. The human eye can see a total of 16 stops, but your digital SLR can only record about a 7-stop range, so anything outside this range is recorded as very dark or very bright patches of light within your composition.

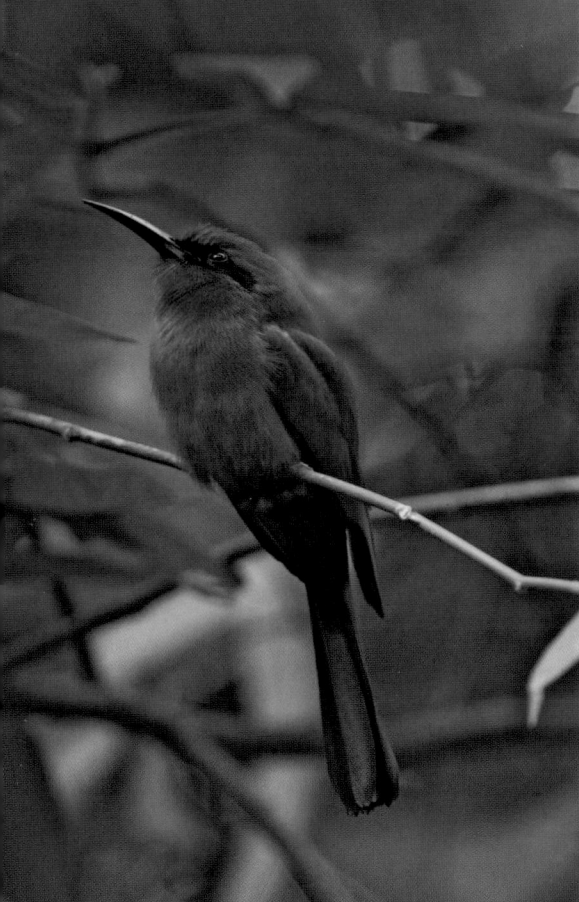

This was certainly the case with this shot of a flycatcher, taken in Singapore at the Jurong Bird Park. Try as I might, I could not find any position, left or right, that would allow me to get a clean shot with my Nikkor 200–400mm zoom lens. It wasn't until I rotated the tripod collar of my lens that I was able to get the much cleaner vertical composition you see here. Sometimes a vertical composition is the only way for you to clean up the background.

Both images: Nikon D2X with Nikkor 200–400mm lens, f/5.6 for 1/125 sec., ISO 200

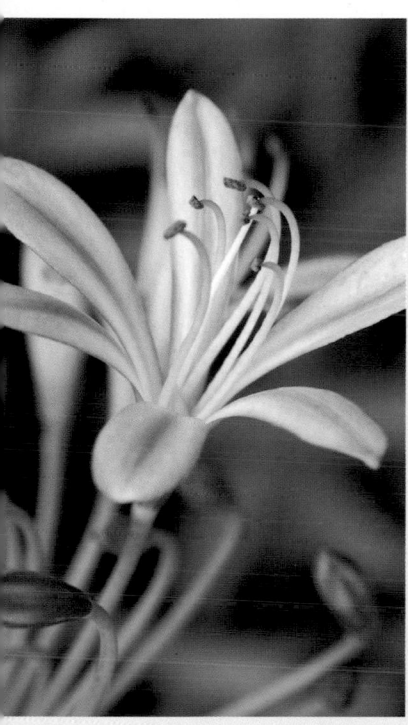

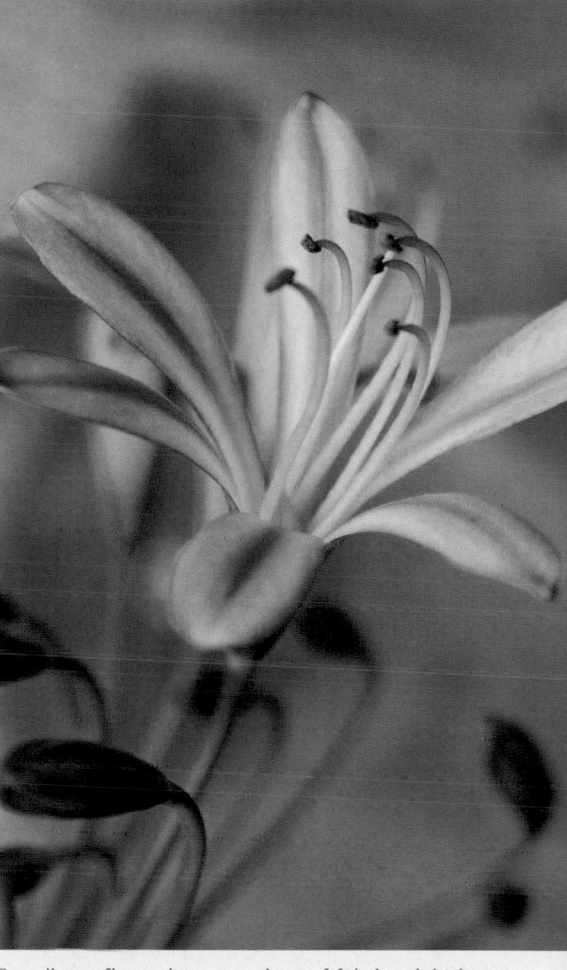

For all you flower lovers, a piece of fabric might be the only thing standing between you and a truly remarkable composition, as long as the fabric is not revealed as such. After shooting this agapanthus flower in its natural state (left), I took the orange ball cap off my head and placed it about 2 feet behind the flower, making sure to hold the surrounding background green stems gently "down" with the weight of the cap. As you can see in the second photo, I was now able to add another version of this one lone agapanthus flower to my collection.

Both images: Nikon D300S with Micro-Nikkor 105mm lens, f/6.7 for 1/250 sec., 100 ISO

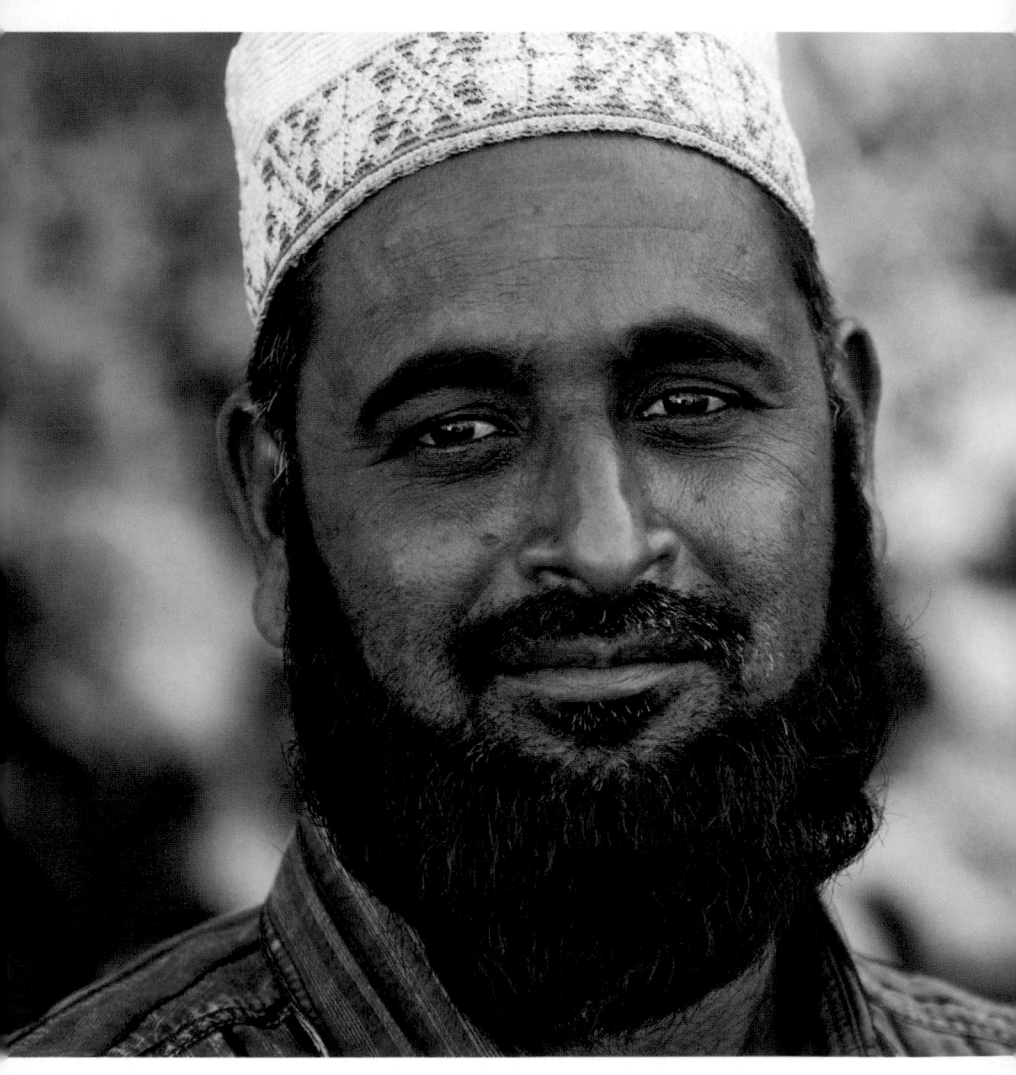

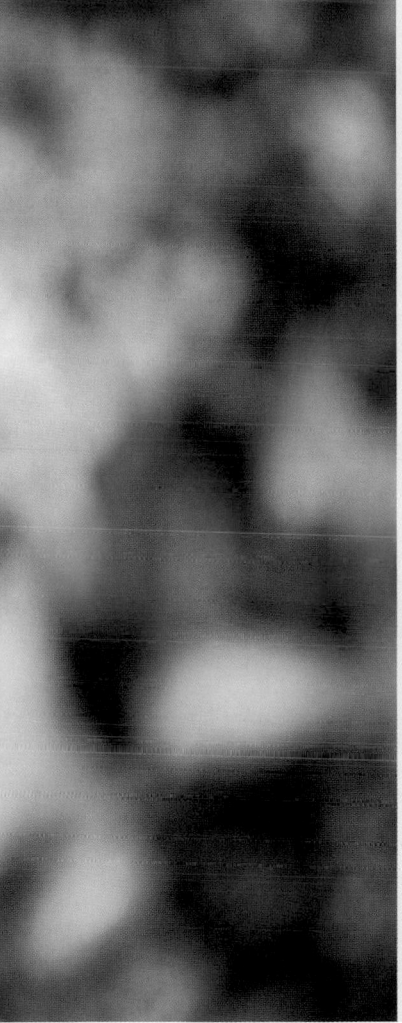

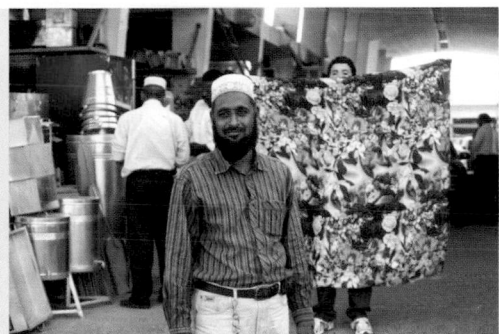

If there is one area in photography that photographers can fully control, it is their backgrounds. Any studio photographer will tell you that it's important to have a collection of backgrounds. You may not be a studio photographer, but that doesn't mean you can't maintain the same level of control in your outdoor pictures. One large piece of black fabric suspended behind your subject and, presto—a clean background! But don't limit yourself to black backgrounds; at any fabric store you can find a wide assortment of large and colorful patterns. Once you put them to work, your fellow photographer friends will be quick to say, "Wow!" upon seeing them in action.

I found myself in Kuwait at a small factory that was remarkably monochromatic in its offerings. Normally I have no trouble finding a wall or area around a factory that offers some degree of color, but that was not the case here. Thank goodness I had one of my colorful and large pieces of fabric with me. As my assistant held the fabric about 20 feet behind one of the workers, I fired off a few frames. The background here may be a bit too bright and cheerful, perhaps, but it's a far cry better than the choppy tones of light and dark that I was seeing behind the subject.

Nikon D300S with 70–300mm lens, f/8 for 1/160 sec., ISO 200

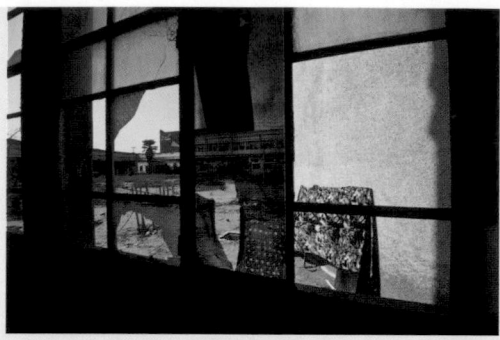

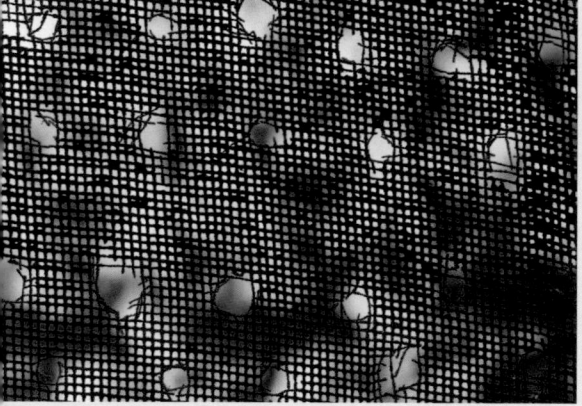

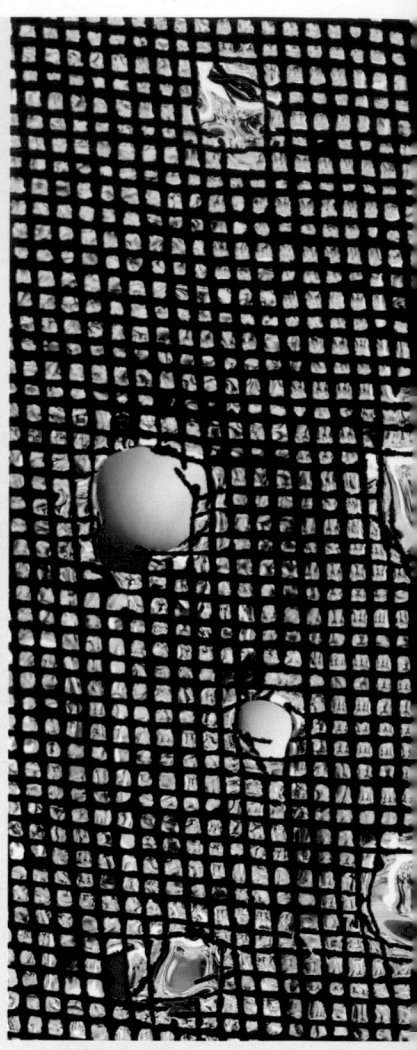

The next morning, I found myself in an old, abandoned hospital and I caught sight of an old window screen (top). After punching a number of holes in the screen with a pencil found on the ground nearby, I was ready to create some "fine art"—the only thing missing was color. I reached into my camera case and again pulled out the large piece of colorful fabric, folding it over a small piece of plywood found out in the hospital yard. I recorded the first image (above), then pondered the possibility of creating "drops of dew" on the screen. I walked to a nearby store and purchased a small bottle of cooking oil and several bottles of water, and was soon concocting a brew of "dewdrops," which I then poured on the screen and photographed (right). It's clear to me, and perhaps to you as well, that I also used a different aperture choice for each: the first was shot at f/22 and the second at f/11, which rendered a bit more blur in the background tones and shapes.

Above: Nikon D300S with Micro-Nikkor 105mm lens, f/22 for 1/30 sec., ISO 200; Right: Nikon D300S with Micro-Nikkor 105mm lens, f/11 for 1/125 sec., ISO 200

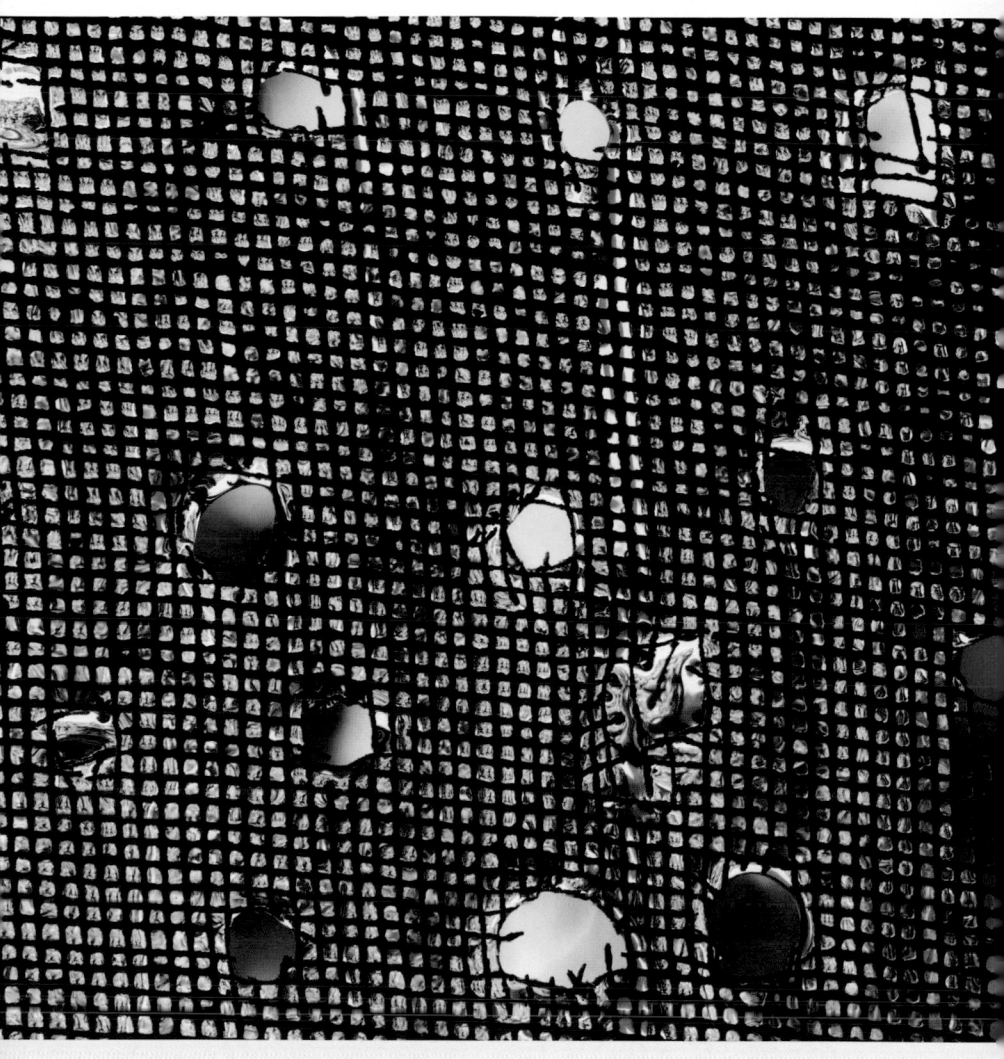

CHOOSING YOUR
BACKGROUND

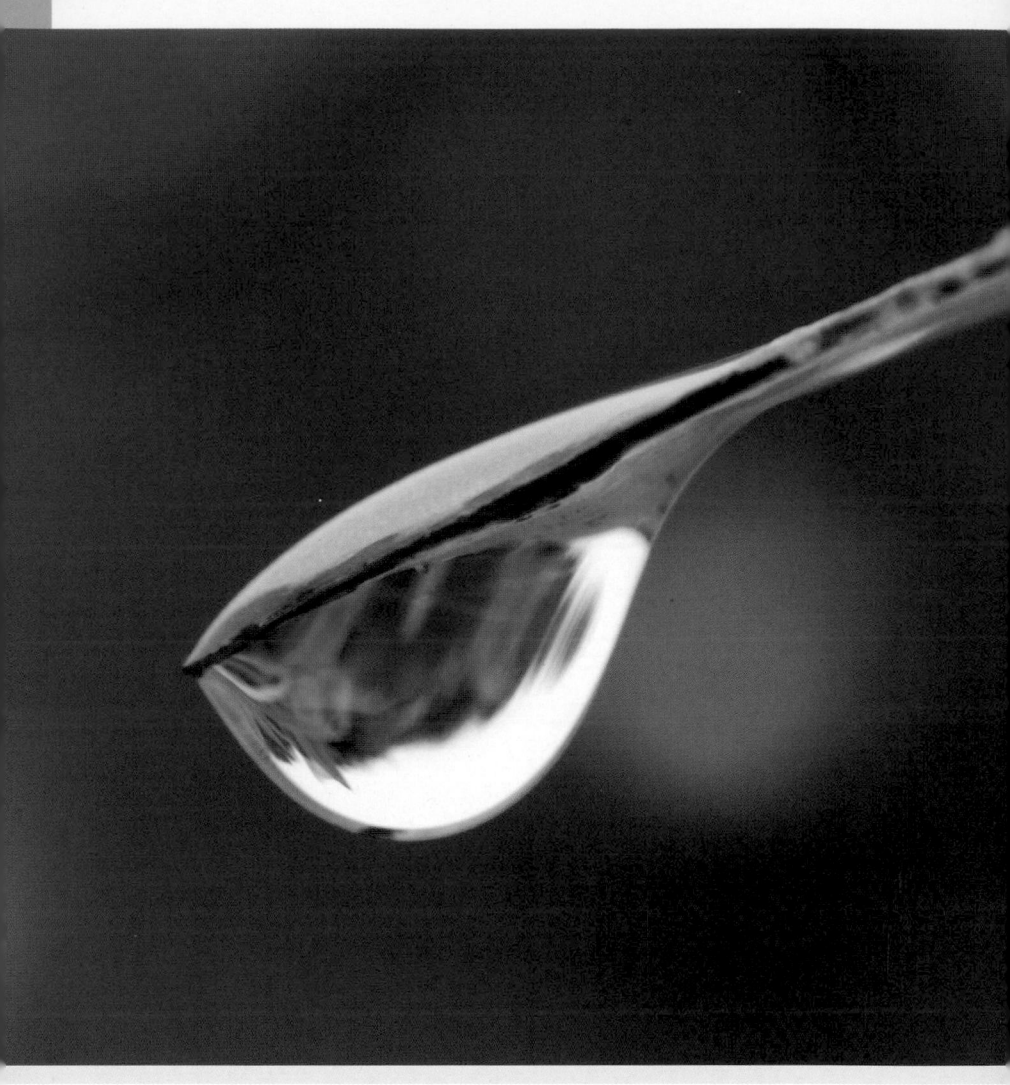

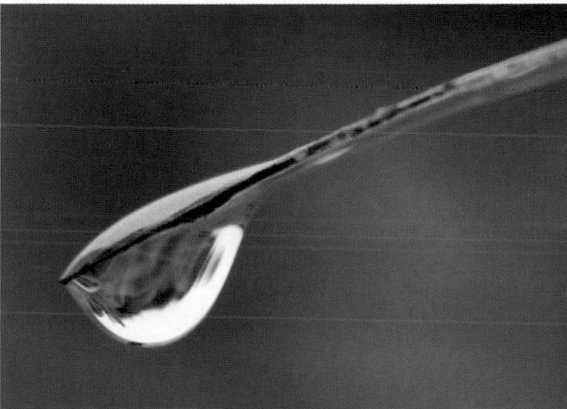

I am a fan of dewdrops, something that perhaps has its roots in my very first years as a photographer, when I would awaken on many mornings to heavy coastal fog in Oregon's Willamette Valley. As long as there is no wind present, I am quick to migrate toward large raindrops or dewdrops. The drops themselves are what I found most fascinating, since they are like tiny camera lenses, capturing a fish-eye view of the scene directly behind them. But after thirty-five-plus years of shooting dewdrops, I am less inclined to shoot the familiar (and monochromatic) drops on green grass against green grass, shown in the first image (above). Instead, I tend to borrow nearby flower blossoms and place them in the background, bringing welcome color to otherwise placid compositions. Today was no exception. I found a purple clematis nearby and there on the ground was a fallen blossom. After placing the blossom on top of some background fauna, I was ready to shoot the second shot (left). Perhaps the lesson here is that you can favorably alter the outcome of just about any background. Studio photographers have been controlling their backgrounds for years, so why not you?

Both images: Nikon D3X with Micro-Nikkor 105mm lens, f/18 for 1/30 sec., ISO 100

CHOOSING YOUR
BACKGROUND

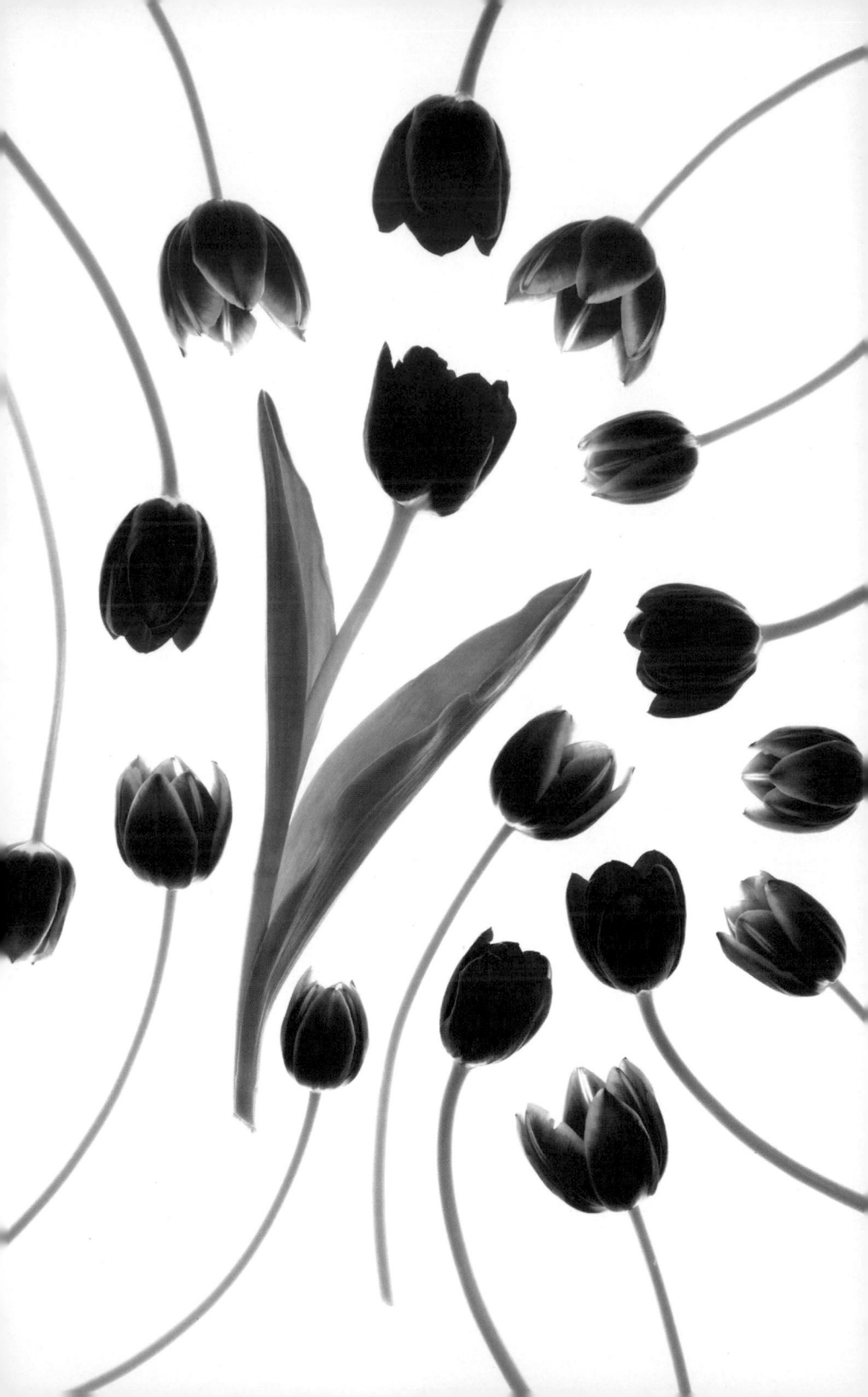

5

USING THE EMPTY CANVAS

The word *artful* refers to something that is pleasing to the eye, the ear, or to the touch. Although what is pleasing to one person is not necessarily pleasing to another, most of us find that life is most pleasurable when there is order and some measure of predictability, mixed with a slight degree of uncertainty. When life is erratic, chaotic, without focus or direction, trouble cannot be far behind. How many of us have sat through the speech of a drunk best man at a wedding? Unable to speak clearly or hold on to his thoughts long enough to string a meaningful sentence together, his speech is memorable, sure, but for all the wrong reasons.

The photographic compositions of many beginning photographers are akin to those drunken speeches—chaotic, without focus or direction; not surprisingly, the audience is quick to turn away. It is the clear and articulate composition that holds the audience's attention, so why—*why?*—is it so hard for so many, at least initially, to achieve "articulate compositions"?

Nikon D3X with Nikkor 35-70mm lens, f/11 for 1/250 sec., ISO 100

SEEING THE
EMPTY CANVAS

Earlier I spoke about the "blank canvas" that every painter faces—though perhaps painters actually have the unfair advantage, since their canvas really is blank. There is nothing to distract their attention, and they are free to place whatever they choose, wherever they choose. (Painters can also take their time, whereas photographers, faced with diminishing light or impatient subjects, must often create their masterpieces in a fraction of second.)

This is in marked contrast to the view that often confronts photographers when they look through the viewfinder: pure and utter chaos. Yes, we can move some objects out of the way or to a better place, but we must also learn to see an empty canvas before we begin. If not, the viewer will be forever tripping over and running into objects that have nothing to do with the intent of your photograph.

Throughout my more than thirty-five-year career, I have had my share of photographic critiques by my peers. The overall feedback has been that my overall style and composition are simple and clean, vibrant and colorful, bold and graphic, and profoundly stated. My eye has a *learned* ability to see my camera's viewfinder as a blank canvas, and to recognize and embrace with zeal my freedom to place whatever subjects I wish on that canvas. Just as a painter uses his brush, I use my eyes, letting them move across the canvas, placing color, lines, and shapes at will. I do not expect to see these photographs already composed in front of me but rather the *ingredients* to the image. My job is to arrange the ingredients in a pleasing and compelling manner. For example, by simply changing my point of view and/or my lens, I can alter not only *what* ends up on my canvas but *where* it ends up, too. If I am dealing with subjects that can be moved, or with animate subjects that respond to suggestions or commands, the exact placement of these same objects is further ensured. Of course, I cannot move mountains, trees, buildings, or spitting cobras, but in these situations, I often have the option of diminishing or emphasizing their importance by, again, just changing my point of view and/or lens.

How do you see the empty canvas before you? Training the eye to do this is actually rather easy. Begin with the most basic of blank canvases, such a brick wall free of posters or graffiti, or the side of a barn. Alternatively, point the camera down at that concrete slab you call a deck or the sidewalk in front of your house. Using your street zoom (meaning, your 24–105mm or 18-200mm lens), fill the frame with nothing more than the brick wall, the weathered wood of the barn, or the concrete of the sidewalk. And, to be clear, I am talking about filling the frame—edge to edge, top to bottom—with *just* a brick wall, the weathered wood of the barn, or the concrete deck or sidewalk. Now just stare at this empty canvas and ask yourself, "What can I now add to this canvas?" If you are shooting down on concrete or green grass, I suggest a single flower, a feather, a small piece of fruit like a strawberry, or a screw from your toolbox. If you're shooting against the wall of a barn or a brick wall, pose your spouse, child, or friend. After spending no more than a few days at this exercise, you will soon migrate toward other "simple canvases," such as a pebble-strewn shoreline, a sandy beach, large pieces of driftwood, or tree bark. Soon you will observe that on sunny days you can always turn your attention to the empty canvas of the sunset or blue sky above, and shoot any number of subjects against it. These are not complicated compositions at all, but rather simple and clear. Best of all, everyone will "hear" these compositions, since they present a singular message and have no distracting background interruptions.

A BLANK CANVAS IS LIKE A FOOD TRAY

In many ways, the background of our image is similar to a food tray in a cafeteria. Upon entering the cafeteria, we might place any number of food items on it, and in no particular order. The only thing that is certain when we get to the checkout is that the tray is full of food.

To be sure, it can be tempting to opt for fast food or get seduced by an "all you can eat" buffet. And it isn't until we experience a scare—a high cholesterol reading, a rapid weight gain—that we may feel motivated to change our behavior. In photography, the "scare" may come in the form of a classroom critique, a negative post on Flickr or Facebook, or the failure to come close to winning yet another photography contest. That might prompt some of us to take a class—in cooking, say, or photography—to help us learn how to make more careful decisions about the foods and portions we place on our tray, aka the canvas.

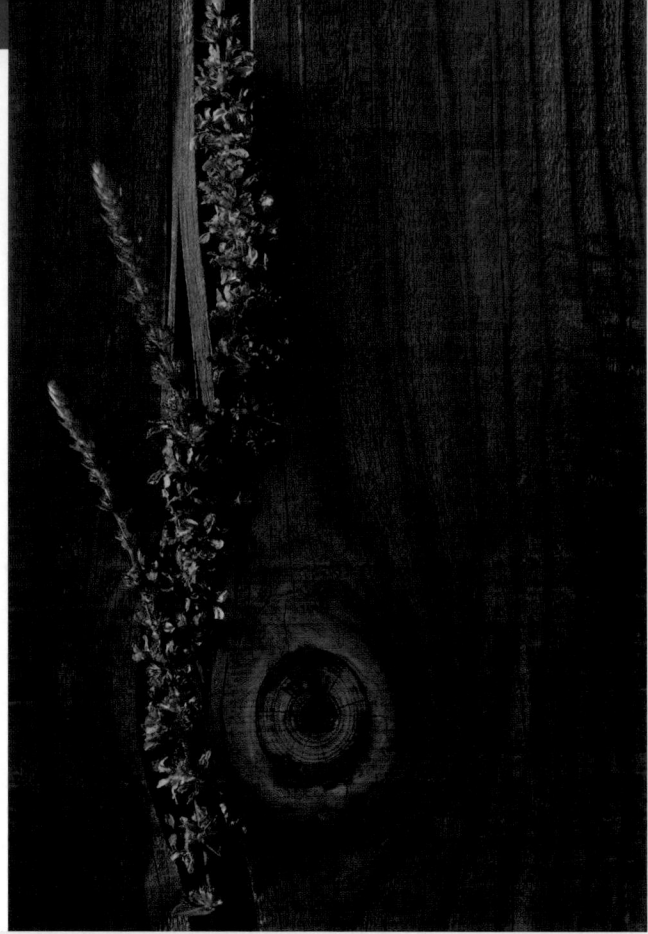

Two things are memorable about this shot: it was getting late in the day and the light was becoming nice and warm, but the location did not offer a wide variety of subject matter. It was then that I spotted this crack in the side of a weathered building and immediately scoured up a flower that was blooming in a nearby ditch. At this moment, one of my students exclaimed with surprise, "What are you doing?" I replied that I was making a picture of color and texture. I could tell by the student's reaction that she had qualms about how I was composing the photo. Finally, she asked, "It doesn't bother you that you put that flower in that crack?"

Obviously, it did not bother me to create that image back then—and it does not bother me to create similar images today. If you expect to shoot only shots that do not require any intervention on your part, you will be coming home each day or night with morsels rather than spoils from the hunt. Like you, I am an artist—or at least I like to think that I have flashes of artistic talent. As such, I can be expected to call on "artistic license" and do whatever I feel needs to be done in the name of art. When you are shooting a portrait and directing the person to stand in the doorway, are you not guilty of altering the scene before you? When you place that person against a particular background, are you not manipulating the outcome? So, when I shoot a portrait of a flower, why not place it in a crack, or against the background of my choice? Of course, I have limits to how far I will go. I won't cut down a tree, for example, no matter how much it might be getting in the way of my shot (unless I cut it down virtually in Photoshop, of course, and if I do that, I'll let you know). The bottom line is that if you are an artist, be an artist!

Nikon D300S with Nikkor 70–300mm lens at 200mm, tripod, f/11 for 1/60 sec., ISO 200

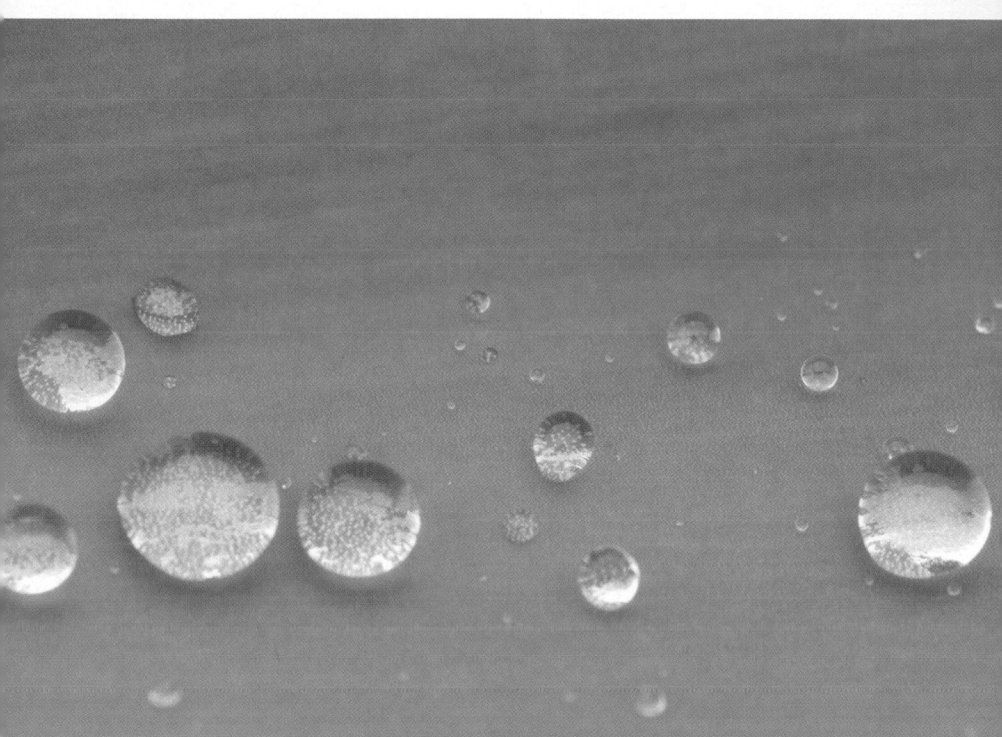

Perhaps no lens is better at producing an unlimited supply of blank canvases than the macro lens. At least, that has been my experience, and today was no exception as I found myself shooting in a park on a somewhat rainy morning in Sydney, Australia. There before me was a green leaf, which served as a perfect empty canvas of green with a random pattern of raindrops. All that was needed was a bit of color contrast. A quick "snip" of a nearby flowering plant and voilà—a clear, concise, remarkably simple composition (next page). With my camera and Micro-Nikkor 105mm lens firmly attached to a tripod, I chose a point of view that found the camera parallel to the green leaf, to ensure that my plane of focus was consistent top to bottom, side to side. I chose an aperture of f/16 to allow the added depth of field that my close-up point of view required, then I adjusted the shutter speed until 1/60 sec. indicated a -2/3 underexposure and fired away. (If you are familiar with my book *Understanding Exposure*, you'll know that when metering "Mr. Green Jeans," I always do so at -2/3.)

Above and pages 86–87: Nikon D300S with Micro-Nikkor 105mm lens on a tripod, f/16 for 1/60 sec., ISO 200

USING THE
EMPTY CANVAS

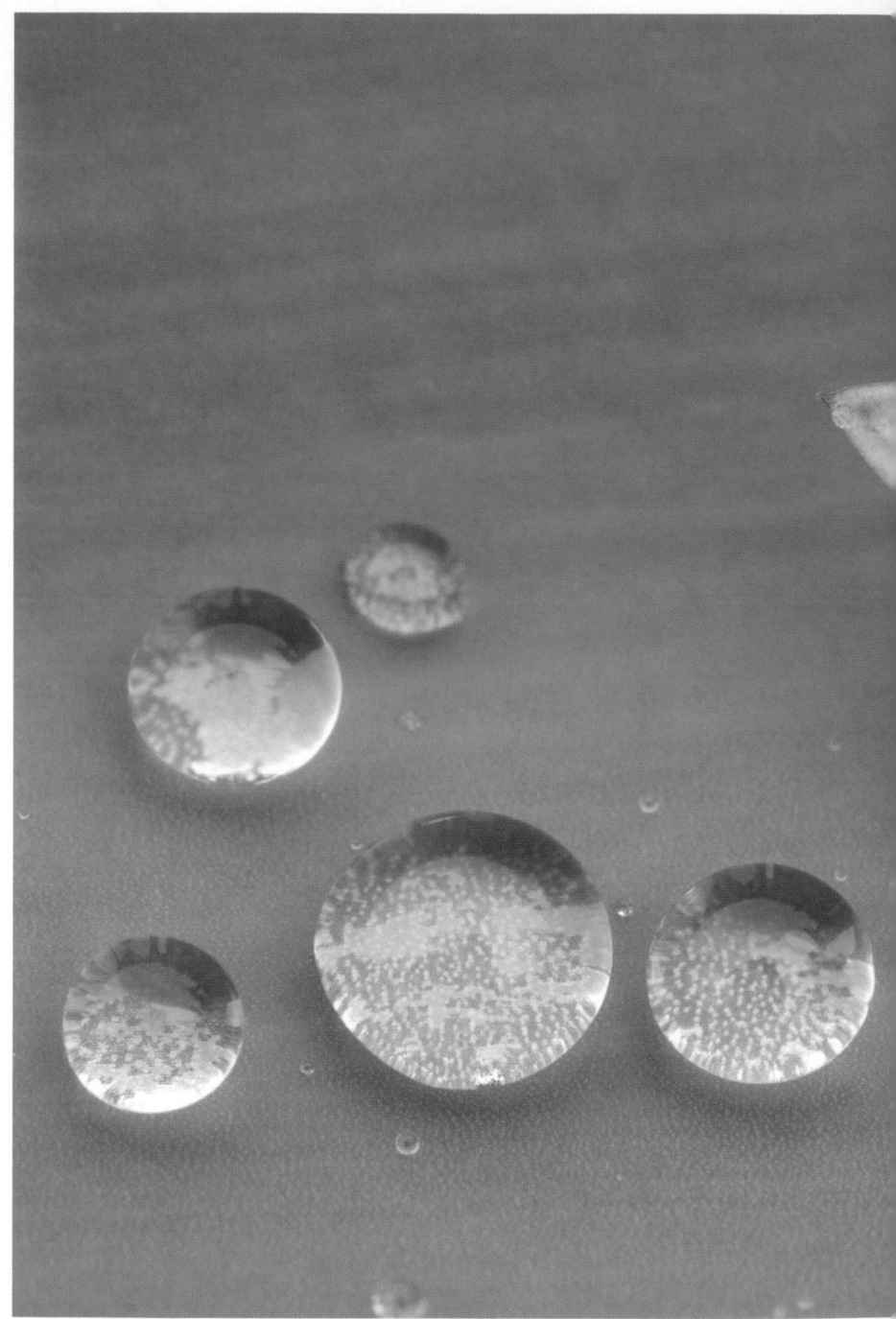

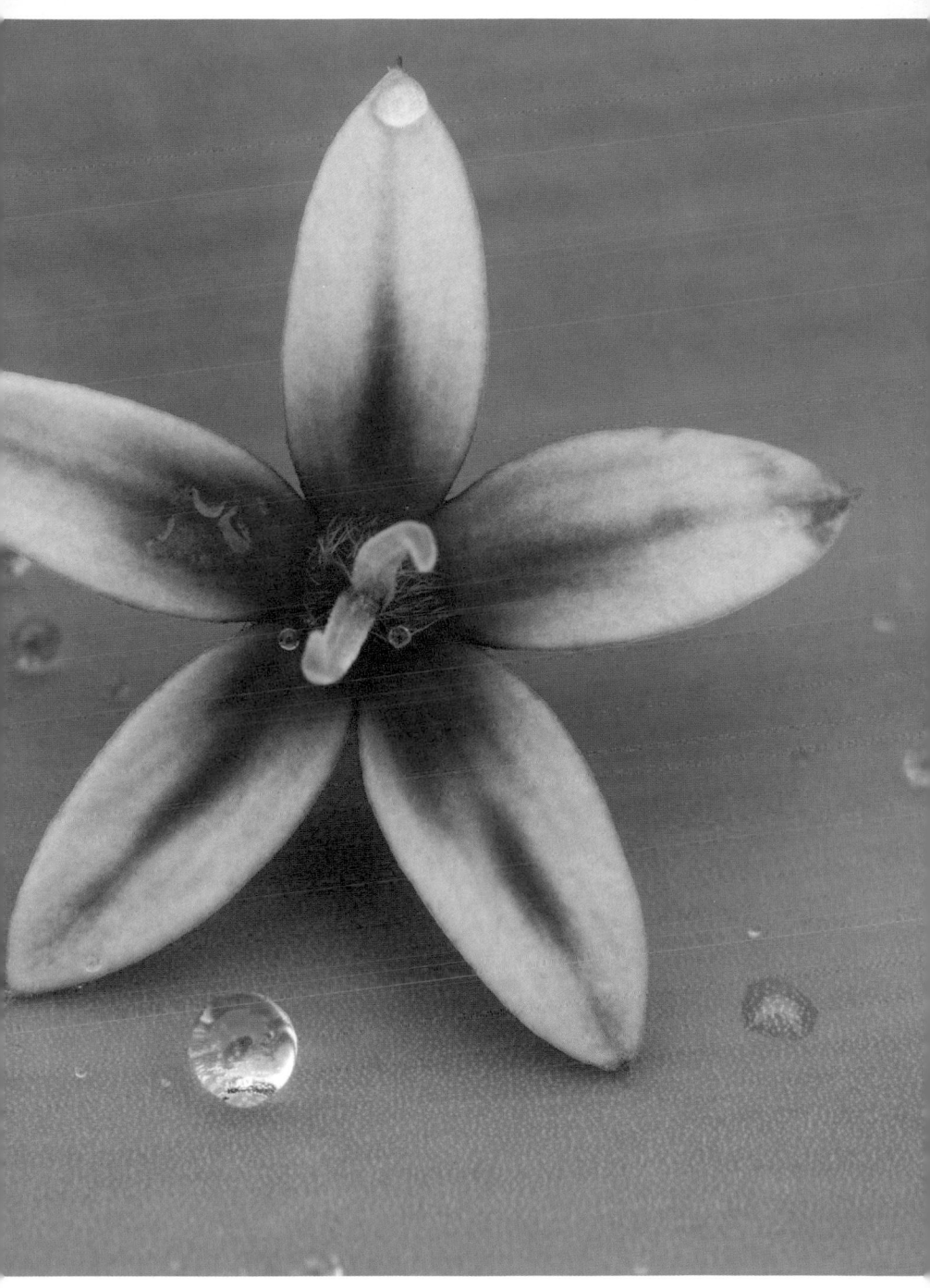

87   USING THE
EMPTY CANVAS

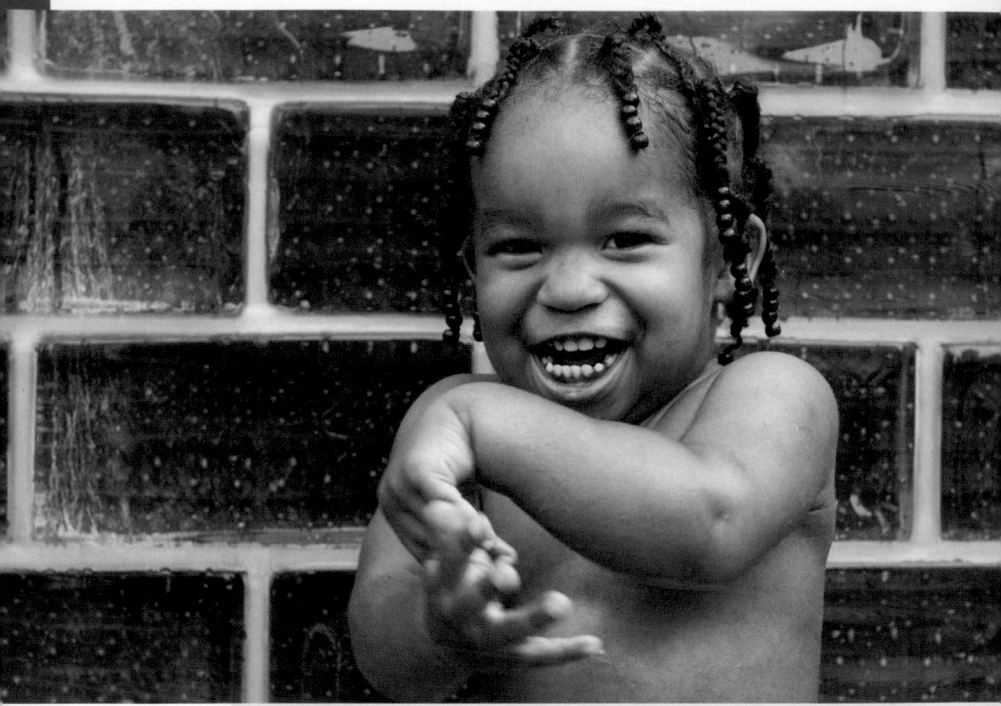

If you can't find a brick wall, then how about a glass wall? Such was the case when I was shooting in Chicago's Millennium Park in summer 2009. All the ingredients were there for compelling imagery: it was hot, there was a waterfall-like fountain nearby, and plenty of kids were playing without the slightest inhibition. To use a worn-out phrase, it was like shooting fish in a barrel. The bigger challenge on this day was finding the parents, both to share the results and to get signed model releases. This young boy was of particular interest to me because he seemed filled with joie de vivre. When I returned home and opened up the many images I took that day, there was not one bad one of this little guy; he was as expressive as this in all the photos I took.

Note the clean, concise, and simple composition. It is nothing more than a glass wall with a little boy in front of it. You will find no "crying babies" here!

Nikon D300S with Nikkor 24–85mm lens at 85mm, f/5.6 for 1/250 sec., ISO 200

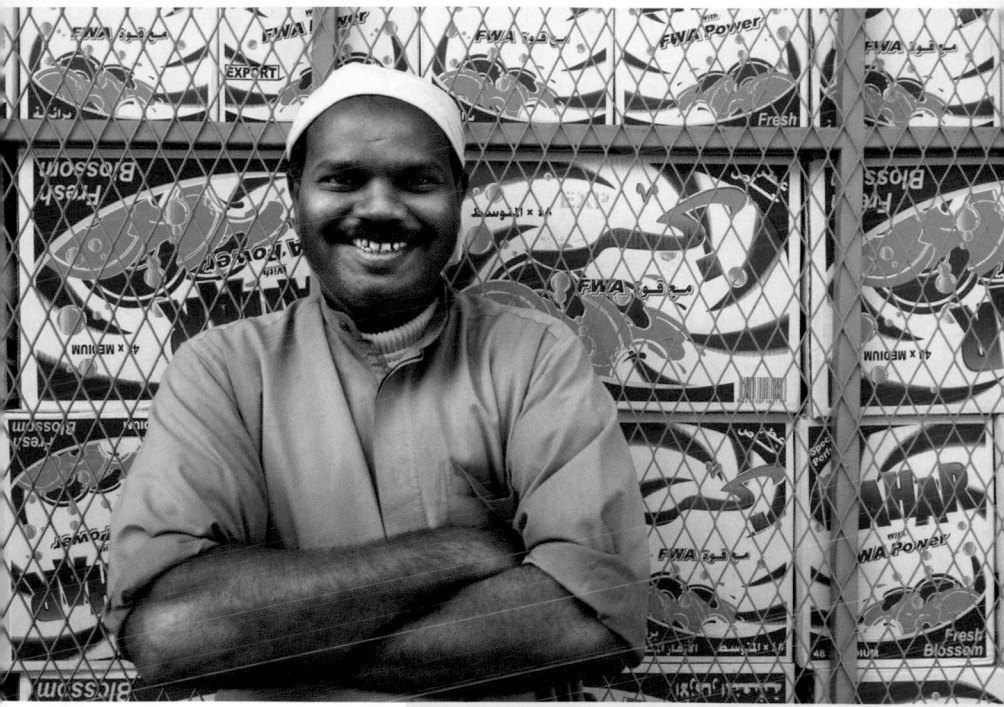

As I sipped my coffee in the city of Fallujah just two doors down from a fruit stand where this guy worked, I noticed across the street this wall of laundry detergent boxes—another "blank canvas." With some degree of prodding, the fruit seller agreed to pose for me. Fortunately for me, he got some ribbing from his buddies and as the laughter broke out, I got this shot.

Tripod, Nikon D300S with 24–85mm lens at 70mm, f/11 for 1/160 sec., ISO 200

USING THE
EMPTY CANVAS

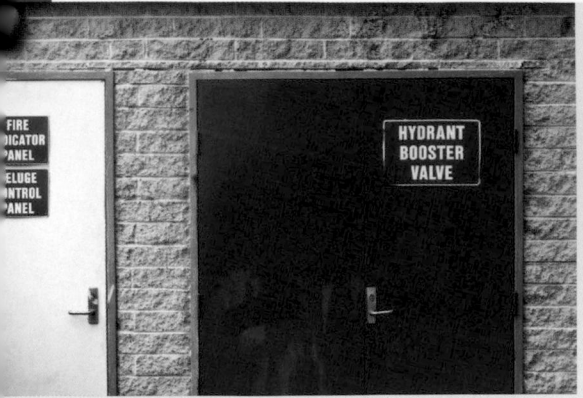

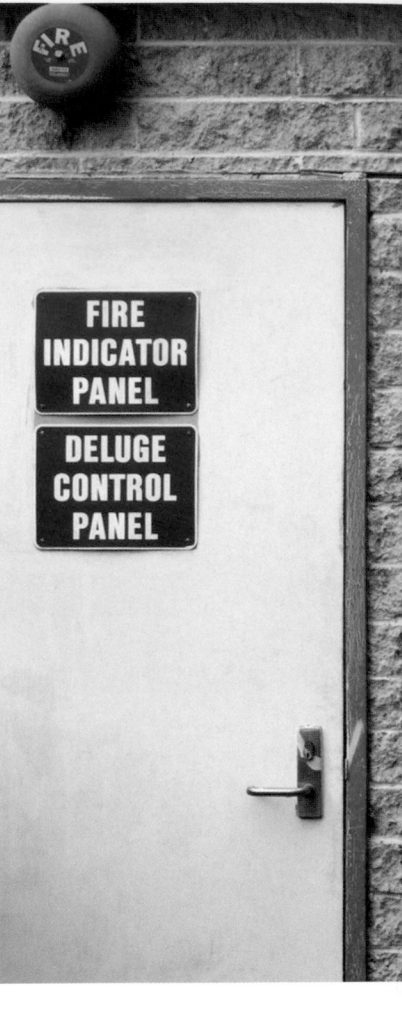

During one of my workshops, we started the day looking for blank canvases. When I suggested this wall of two doors to one of my students, he looked at me, stumped. "What can we possibly do here?" he asked. When I suggested we pop open the yellow umbrella in my bag and simply throw it into scene, shooting slow exposures as it fell through the air, his look changed from stumped to dumbfounded. Hey, I'm all about trying out anything if there is the possibility of coming away with a compelling image.

You decide. Perhaps you do not care for either of these photos, but if you do, you probably prefer the image with the "paranormal activity," as do most shooters when I share these images. We began with a blank canvas that was quite red, so it only stood to reason that if we were to throw an umbrella into the mix, it should be a complementary color, and yellow was it.

Both images: Nikon D300S with Nikkor 24–85mm lens at 50mm, tripod, f/22 for 1/8 sec., ISO 200

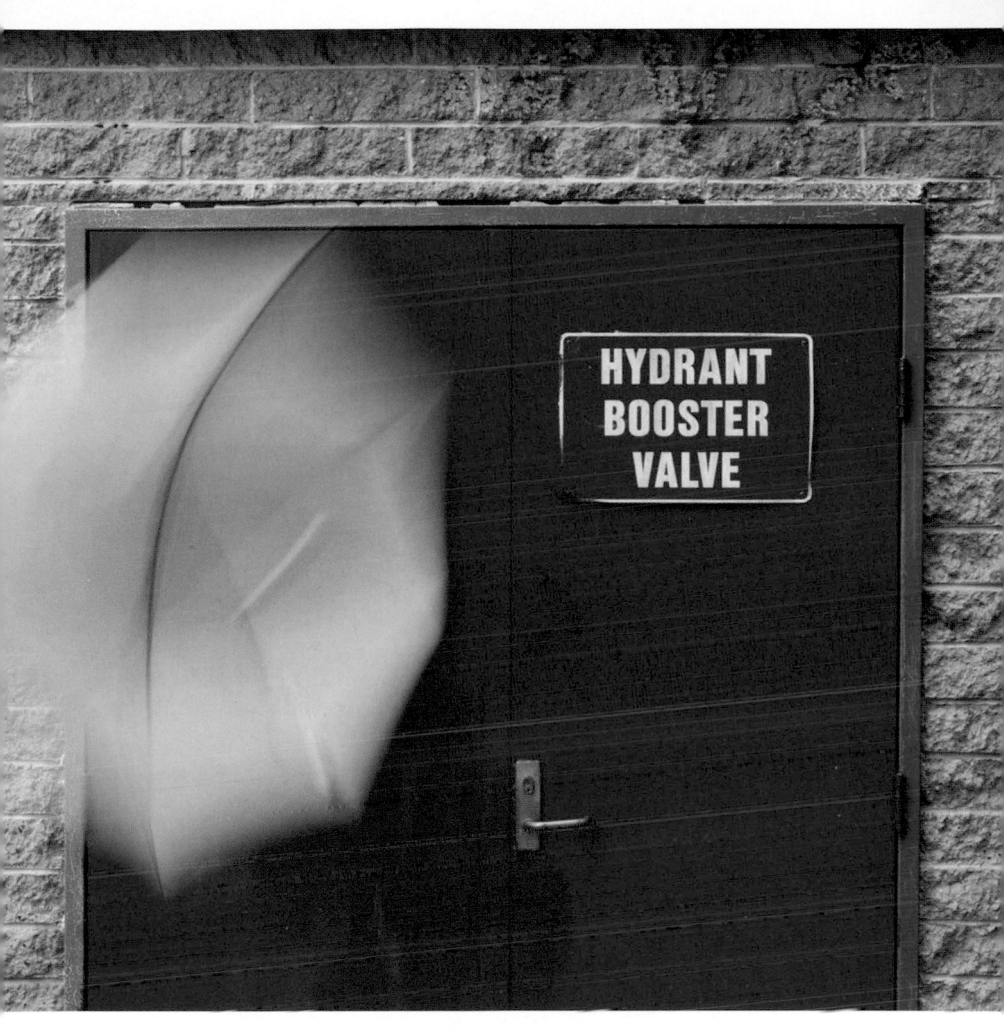

USING THE
EMPTY CANVAS

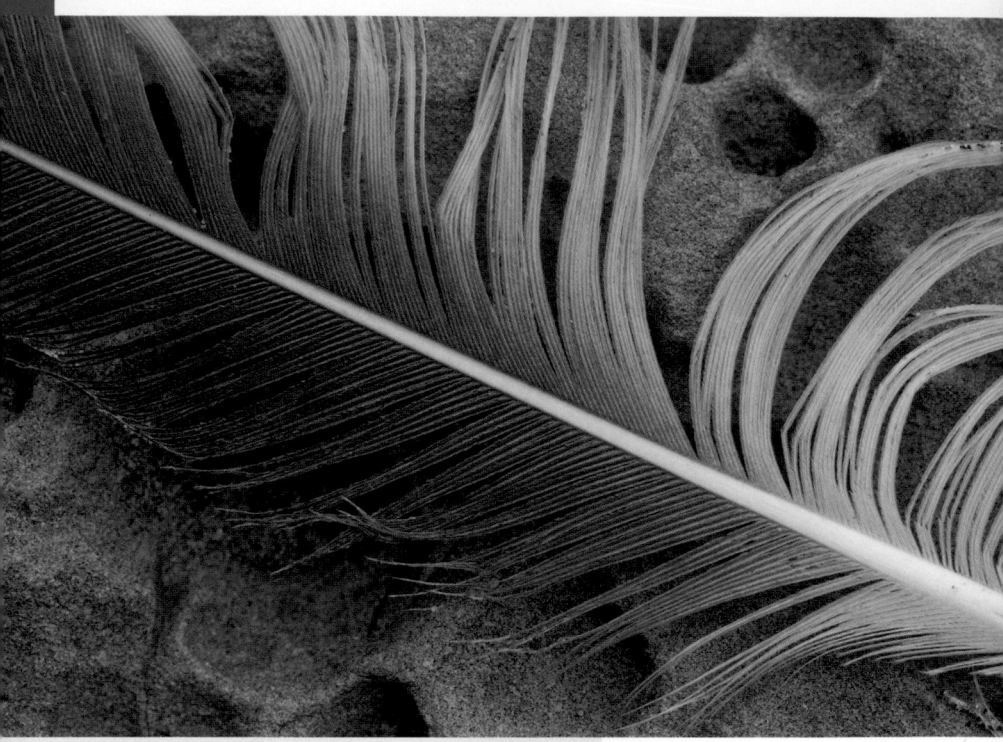

Sometimes I do just happen to be in the right place at the right time, and in all my years of shooting, no place has found me in the right place at the right time more than coastlines and roadside ditches.

Other than the wide-open sky, there is no larger or emptier canvas than a large stretch of sandy beach at low tide. There is room for hundreds to practice their craft, and no shortage of props, either. Feathers, seashells, pebbles, small rocks, and seaweed are yours for the arranging. And if not for a flat tire years ago, I would never have grown to appreciate the abundance of great material found in roadside ditches, where a smorgasbord of grasses and wildflowers, from minuscule to large blooms, are, again, yours for the making and taking. Best of all, the pressure to be quick with your shots rarely exists in sites like these, since they also offer tremendous quiet and solitude.

Here I placed a feather atop a large rock and then placed my camera and 105mm macro lens on my tripod. I set my aperture to f/16, then adjusted my shutter speed until 1/30 sec. indicated a correct exposure.

Nikon D300S with 105mm macro lens, tripod, f/16 for 1/30 sec., ISO 100

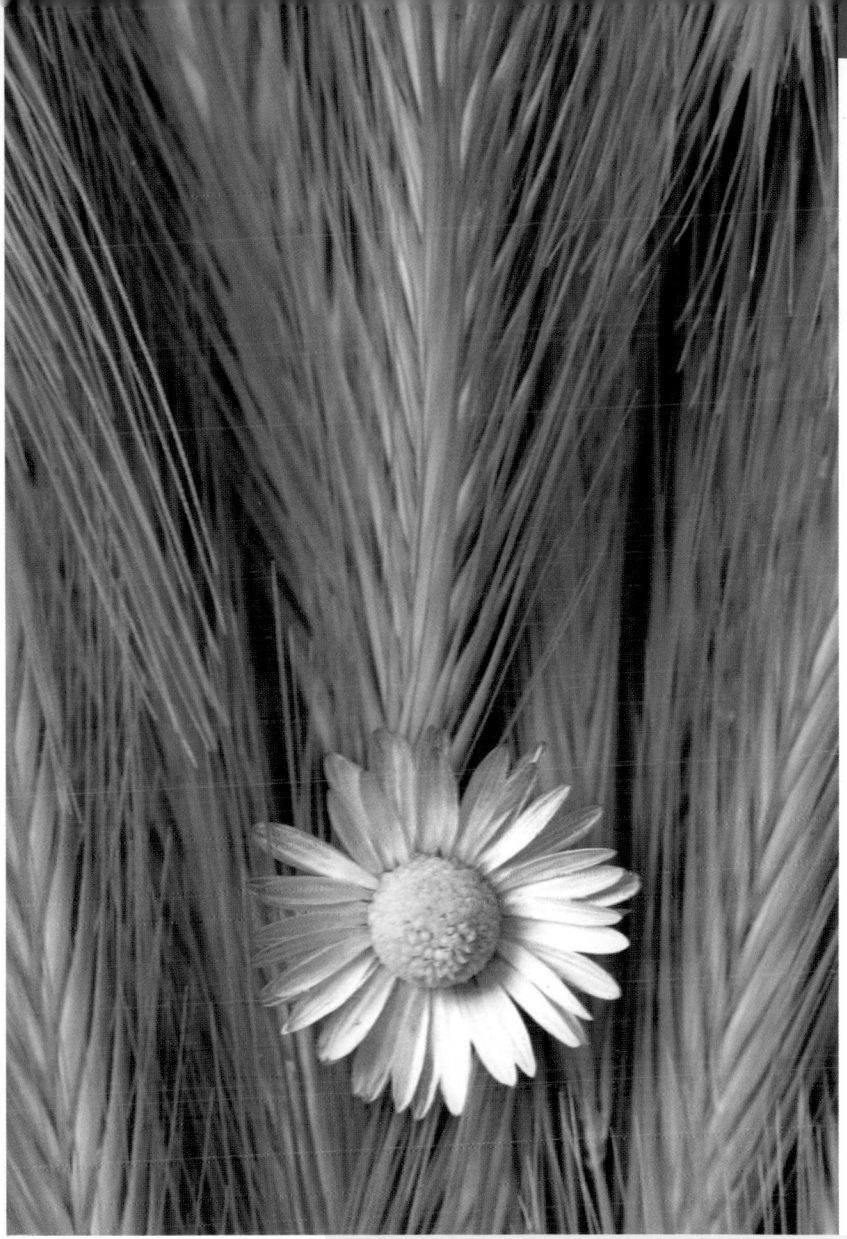

After picking some wild wheat in a roadside ditch near Kalispell, Montana, I arranged it on the ground next to me. I then found a little white daisy and placed it on the wheat. With my camera and 105mm macro lens on my tripod, I set my aperture to f/16 and adjusted my shutter speed until 1/125 sec. indicated a correct exposure.

Nikon D300S with 105mm macro lens, tripod, f/16 for 1/125 sec., ISO 200

USING THE
EMPTY CANVAS

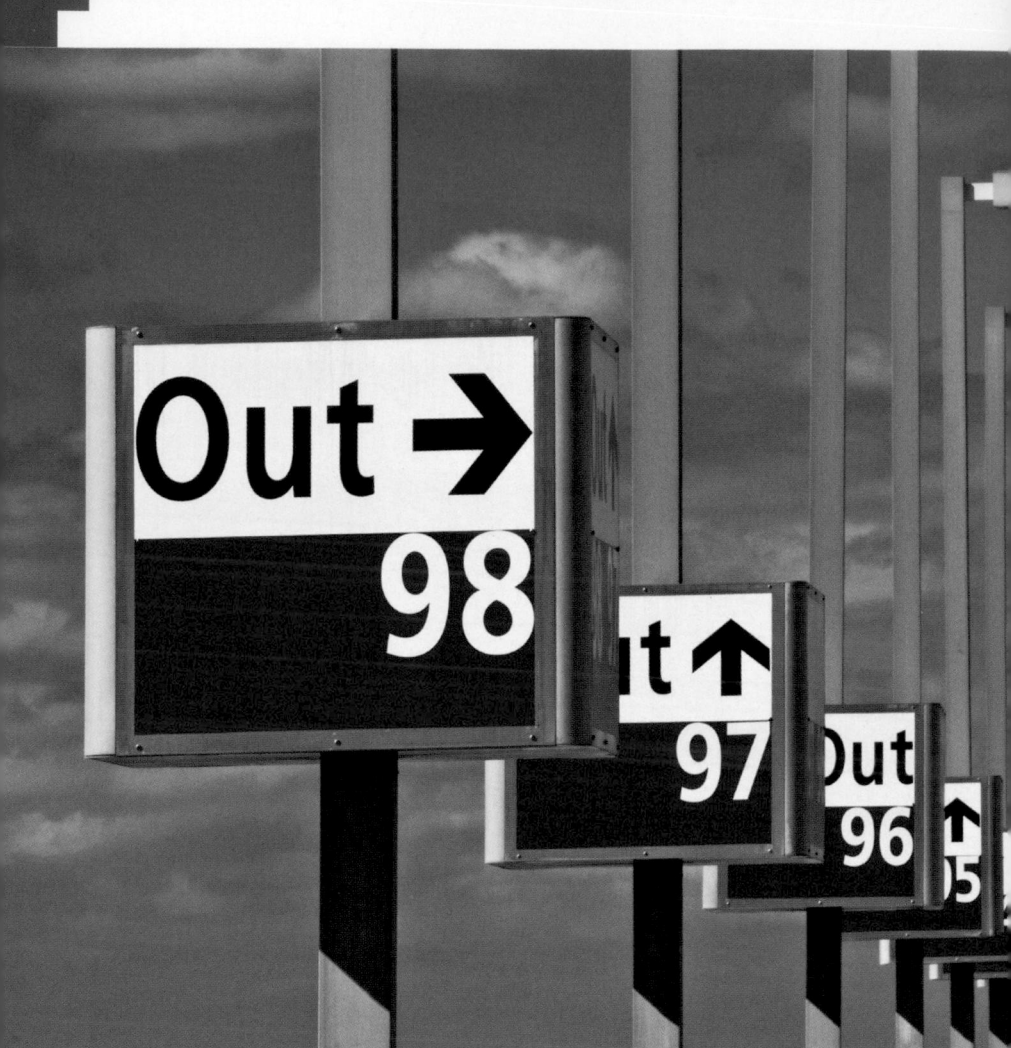

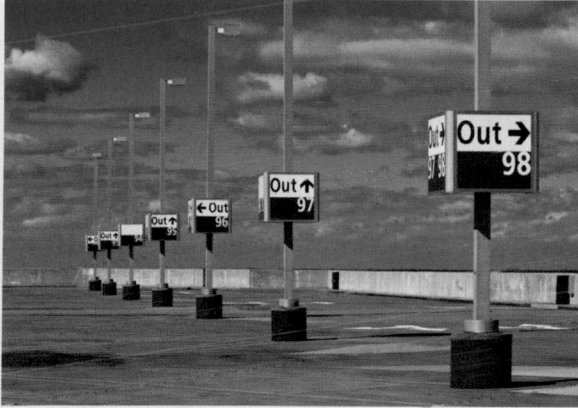

On top of the parking garage at the Tampa International Airport is a somewhat surreal landscape, which can be made even more surreal if you are willing to let go of any sense of "reality." By turning my attention to the blank canvas of the sky, and with my telephoto zoom lens, I was able to create a composition showing only numbered signs with arrows saying "Out." What is this place?

Nikon D300S with Nikkor 70–200mm lens at 200mm, tripod, f/22 for 1/60 sec., ISO 200

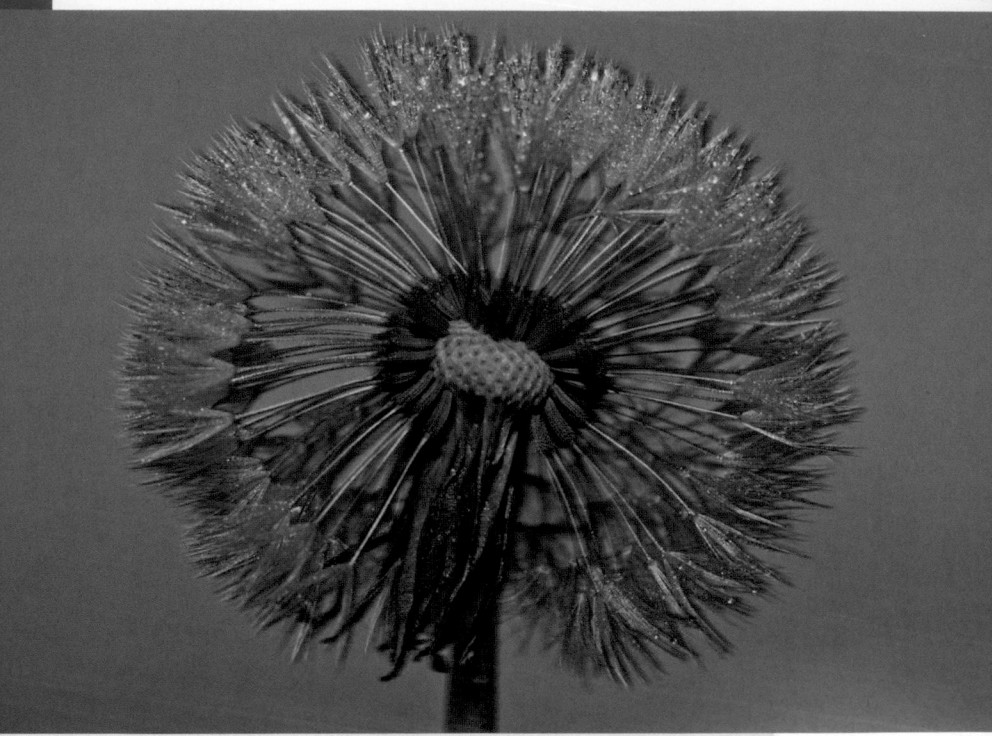

Arising about 45 minutes before sunrise, I was soon outside picking dew-laden dandelions that had gone to seed, holding them in front of my tripod-mounted camera and 105mm macro lens. After shooting several of them against the orange presunrise sky to create silhouetted shapes of dew-laden seed heads, I turned to my flash to extract some detail of the seed heads while maintaining the ambient exposure of the colorful sky, aka the empty canvas. I pulled out my SB-900 flash and called up Nikon's Commander mode feature, which allows me to fire my flash remotely, far from the camera's hot shoe. Holding the seed head in my left hand and the flash in my right, I triggered the shutter release with my self-timer engaged. Five seconds later, the shutter fired, along with the flash, and as you can see here, a backlit and front-lit seed head now fills the once-empty canvas.

Nikon D300S with Nikkor 105mm macro lens, tripod, f/22 for 1/8 sec., ISO 200

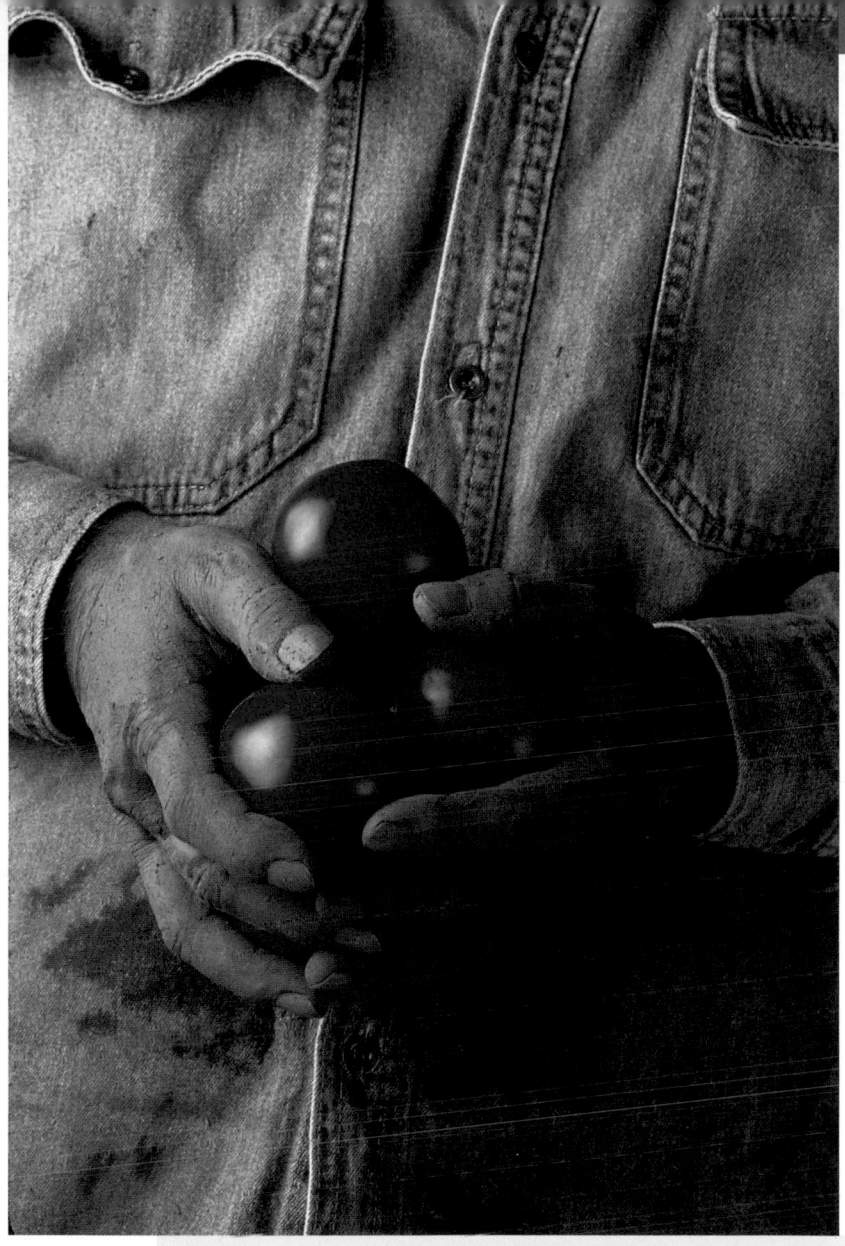

If it hasn't happened yet, it's about to! It's going to occur to you that the world is *full* of empty canvases, and each one is all yours for the taking and placing on it *whatever you wish*! Even a blue denim shirt qualifies as an empty canvas, and when we wipe a bit of dirt on the canvas and then place a pair of dirty hands in front of it, dirty hands that are holding tomatoes, we end up with a fairly compelling image!

Nikon FE2 with 35–70mm lens at 50mm, f/16 for 1/250 sec., one studio strobe inside a softbox, Ektachrome E100VS film

At some point it will also occur to you that most of the empty canvases you will find are composed of lines, textures, and color(s), often combined to create what are called *predictable patterns*. Sometimes these patterns make truly compelling imagery completely on their own. In fact, these background patterns, such as the strawberries shown here, are sought out and used a great deal by magazine art directors and graphic designers. I remember with great fondness a phone call I received years ago from a stock agency in New York. The agency's executives had seen some of my work and called to tell me that if I were to go out and shoot more compositions of patterns similar to what I had been doing, I would make lots of money. Over the next eighteen months, I must have shot more than two thousand patterns—and what an education that proved to be. Not only did I meet great people along the way, but I became even more aware of how most of us prefer to live in an orderly, predictable, patterned manner.

Nikon D300S with Nikkor 24–85mm lens, f/11 for 1/250 sec., ISO 200

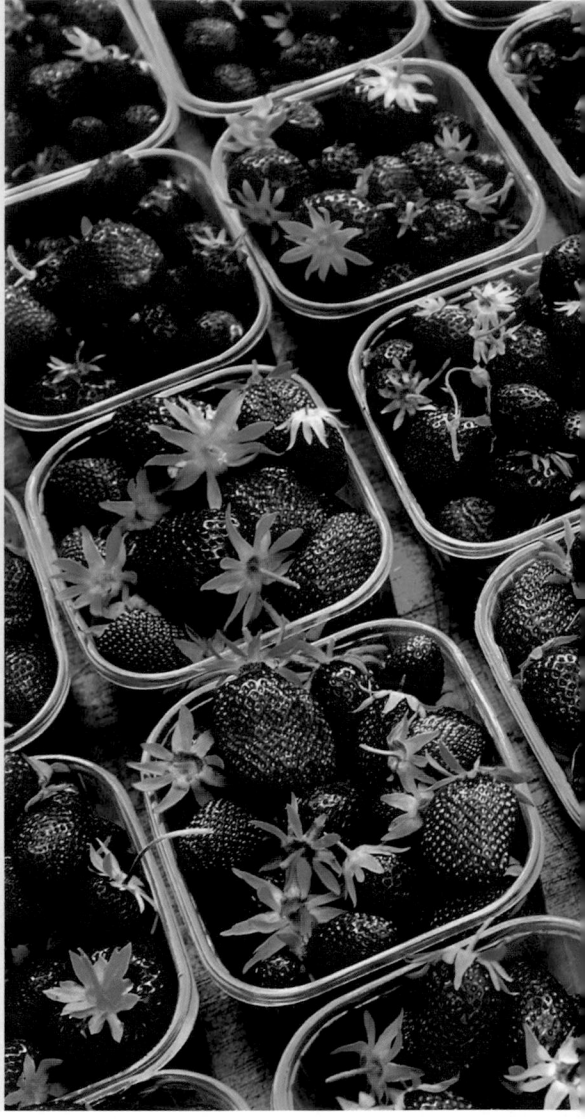

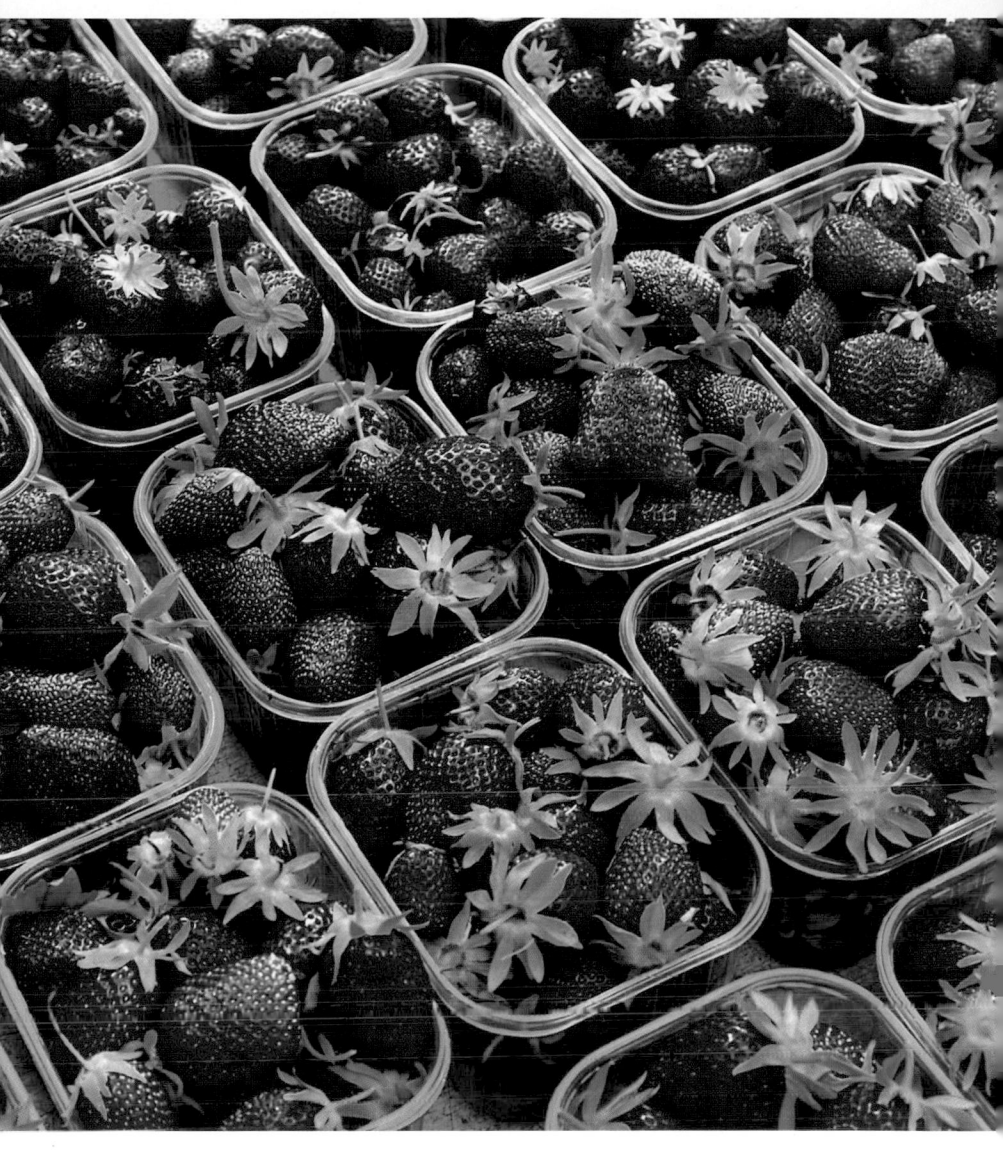

USING THE
EMPTY CANVAS

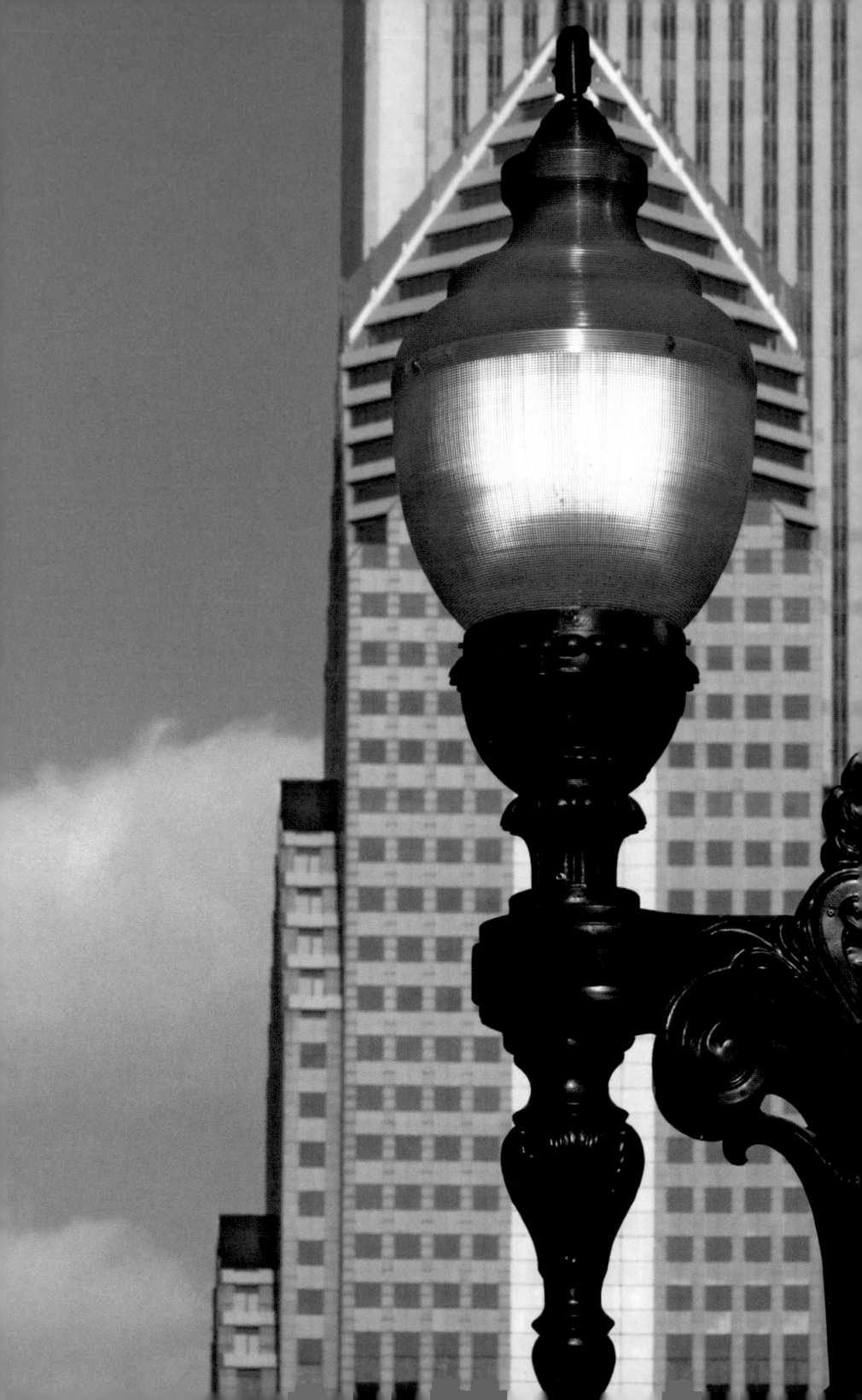

6

ADDING INTEREST IN THE FOREGROUND

Backgrounds, as we now know, form the foundation of every composition. A background can be as simple as a brick wall or as complicated as a rain-forest floor. In effect, the background is the first layer we "paint" on the canvas. It is a vital part of every composition, like the background singers who support the lead vocalist in a church choir. If the choir is singing a different tune than the lead vocalist, the song will never be heard.

But what about the foreground? With the foreground (what I call the *top layer*), we have the opportunity to create a far more intimate connection with the viewing audience. By simply dropping to your knees, or elbows and belly, or moving closer to the tree trunk, you are, in effect, moving your viewing audience closer to the stage, and in doing so, you have turned up the volume of the composition.

Nikon D3X with Nikkor 70–300mm lens, f/11 for 1/200 sec., ISO 200

USING TEXTURE

As you go on your search for the ultimate landscape, start by considering the number of compositional layers that are usually involved. More often than not, there are three: a foreground, a middle ground, and a background. And, not surprisingly, most experienced landscape shooters use an aperture of f/22, or even f/32, to render the necessary front-to-back sharpness that these compositions rely on.

More important, experienced landscape photographers make compositions that use texture in much of the foreground and middle ground because most of us react with a "feeling" when textures dominate. Our personal experience with texture goes way back to our earliest days, when we quickly learned to make assumptions about the soft blanket versus the hard concrete. Soft is good; hard is not.

When it comes to lens choice for capturing an all-encompassing foreground, the wide-angle lens is my go-to lens. Just how wide I go is determined in large measure by the foreground subject. Flora and fauna can be shot with a super–wide-angle lens and without the slightest concern of unwanted distortion. If only for effect, you can even reach for your full-frame fish-eye lens for the most intimate of encounters. Though be warned: Overuse of the fish-eye in your photography will soon produce a number of yawns.

When my subject is a person or persons, on the other hand, I seldom go much wider than 28mm. Anything wider opens the door to a face that is quickly distorted, Silly Putty–like. Unless it is your intent to embarrass or deliberately call attention to a large nose or chin, I would not use any wide-angle lens in the 12–16mm range on a cropped sensor DSLR or a 14–24mm on a full-frame sensor DSLR when shooting up-close-and-personal portraits. For those I resign myself to a moderate telephoto, or the now-popular fixed 50mm when using a small sensor DSLR.

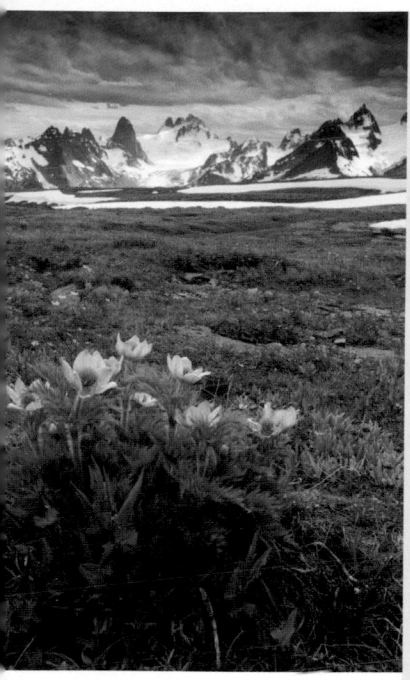

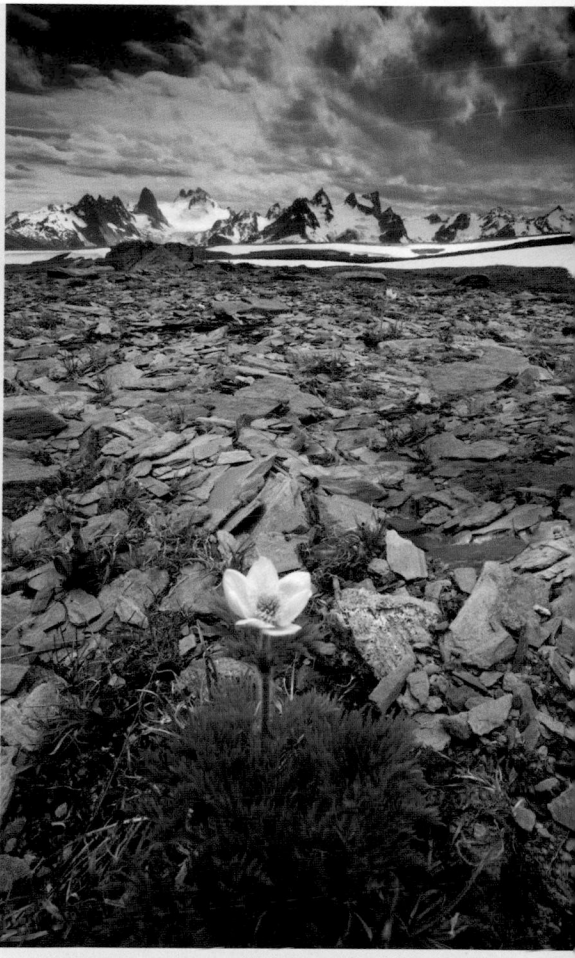

In both these compositions—taken less than 100 feet from each other—the immediate foreground and middle ground are filled with texture. Texture is "food" for an image. How much and what kind you include, and where you choose to place it on your "tray," are entirely within your control. These two images convey radically different messages, thanks to the texture shown in each. Which image looks more inviting, should you wish to walk barefoot? Which would make a better ad for a hiking boot brand?

Both images: Nikon D3X with Nikkor 16–35mm lens at 16mm, f/22 for 1/30 sec., ISO 100

ADDING INTEREST
IN THE FOREGROUND

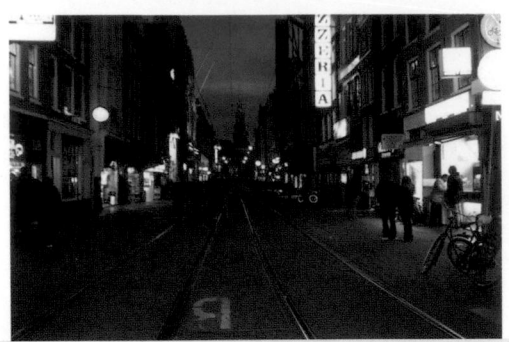

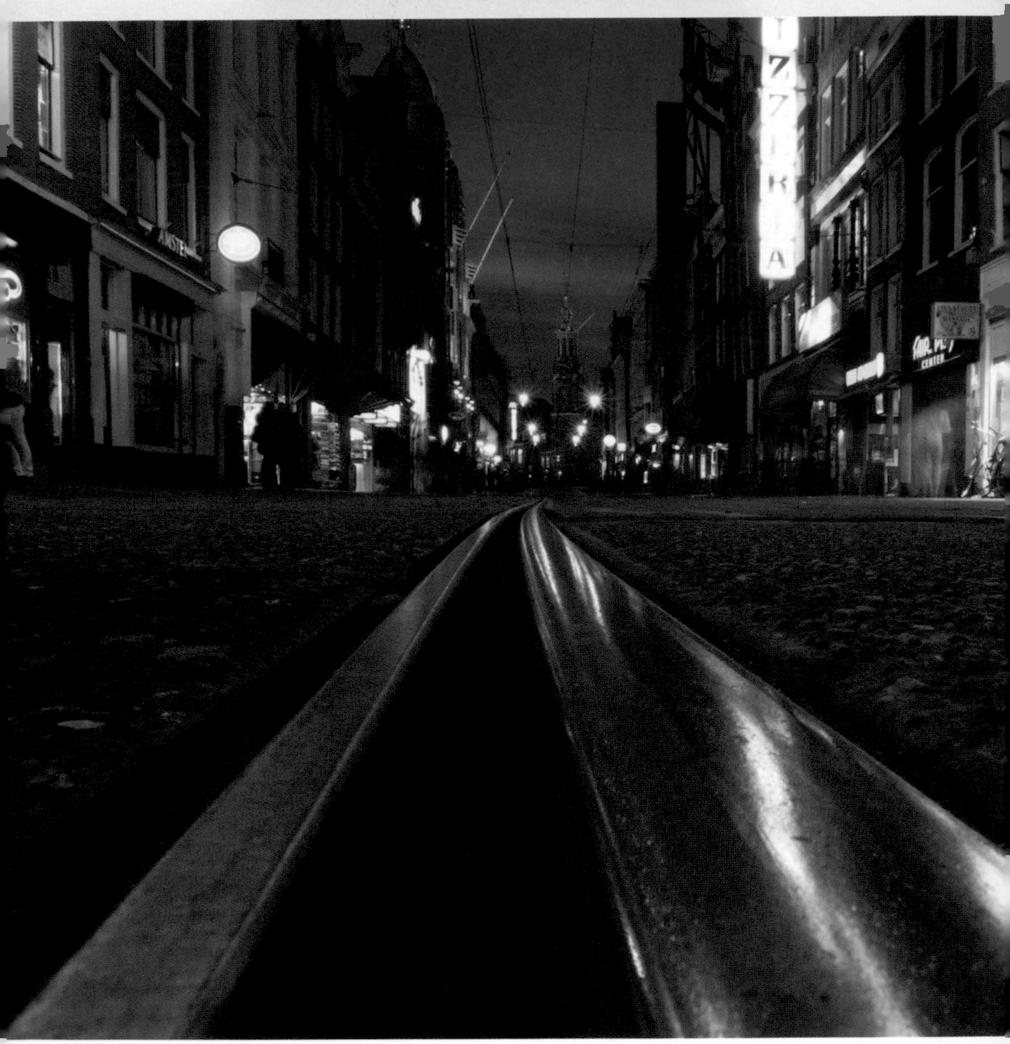

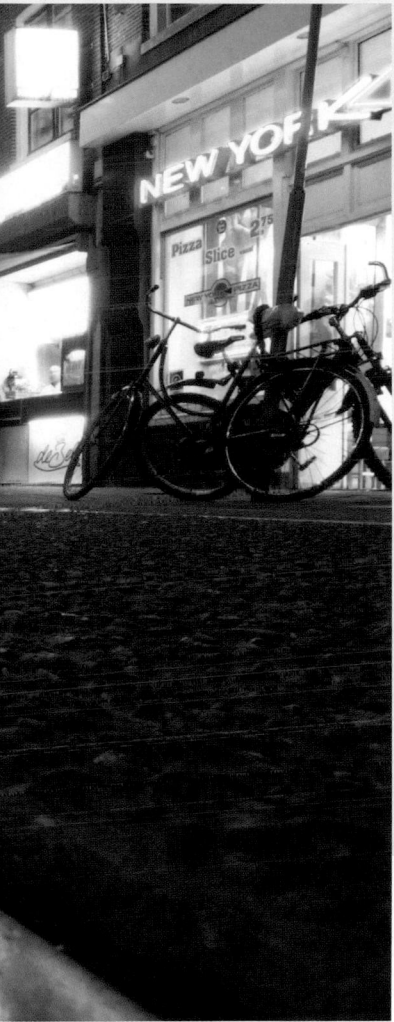

"[That is a] very dangerous thing to do!" said the policeman to me when I was making this photograph in Amsterdam (near Rembrandtplein, to be exact). You see, I was lying on top of the tram tracks, lining up the shot you see here, and his concern was that I would not hear or see a train coming from behind. However, I can assure you that I had several friends close by whose job was to yell if they saw a train coming so I could get off the tracks.

There is an obvious difference between the first image, a boring, pedestrian view shot at eye level, and the second one, which utilizes *line* in the foreground by taking a much lower point of view. (Please do not try this yourself without a spotter!)

Since I needed a great depth of field, I called on f/22. With the camera pointed up to the dusky blue sky, I adjusted the shutter speed until 2 seconds indicated a correct exposure. I then composed the scene you see here and with the camera and lens on a tripod, I used the self-timer to record the exposure.

By the way, I am often asked where I focus when shooting a scene like this and my answer is always the same: I don't focus at all. Rather, with the camera's autofocus turned off, I manually set the distance of 3 feet (1 meter) directly above the focus distance indicator. With the lens at f/22, I am assured that I will have sharpness from 14 inches to infinity.

To learn more about this simple technique, go to http://videos.ppsop.com/storytelling.html and see for yourself, from start to finish, just how easy it is to do.

Nikon D300S with 12-24mm lens, f/22 for 2 seconds, ISO 200

If there is one effective technique when composing with a wide-angle lens, it is to use line in the foreground to pull (or at the least, lead) the viewer into the scene. The use of line and the sense of depth that results, can also create a 3D feel in the two-dimensional image.

Seconds after arriving in the UAE desert near the Saudi Arabian border, I was quick to ask my friend Yousif to walk atop a large sand dune. I wanted to convey the feeling of humility, and what better canvas to express this than the enormity of the desert in contrast to the small, fragile form of man. Handholding the camera, I chose a low point of view on the sand to trigger the viewer's sense of touch as well as used lines in the foreground and middle ground to lead to and call attention to the struggle of man. As Thoreau said, most men lead lives of quiet desperation, and this photo tries to convey that same message. Regardless, it is safe to say that everyone who views this composition gets a very strong sense of the terrain and the main subject in the overall composition, which has much to do with the use of immediate foreground texture and the many lines.

Nikon D3X with Nikkor 16–35mm lens at 16mm, f/22 for 1/125 sec., ISO 200, with elbows firm on the sand

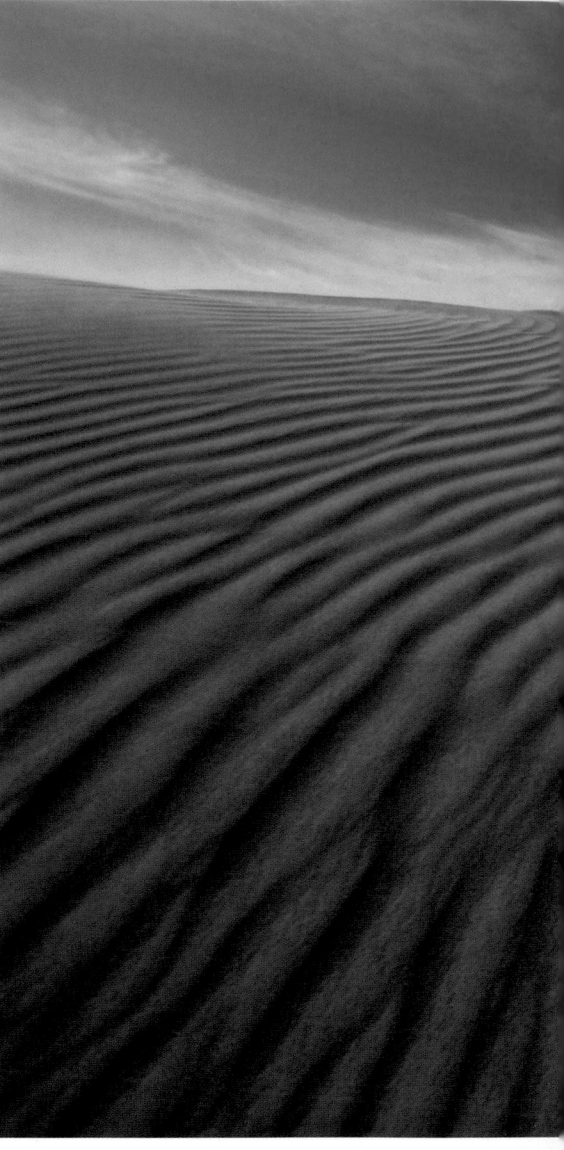

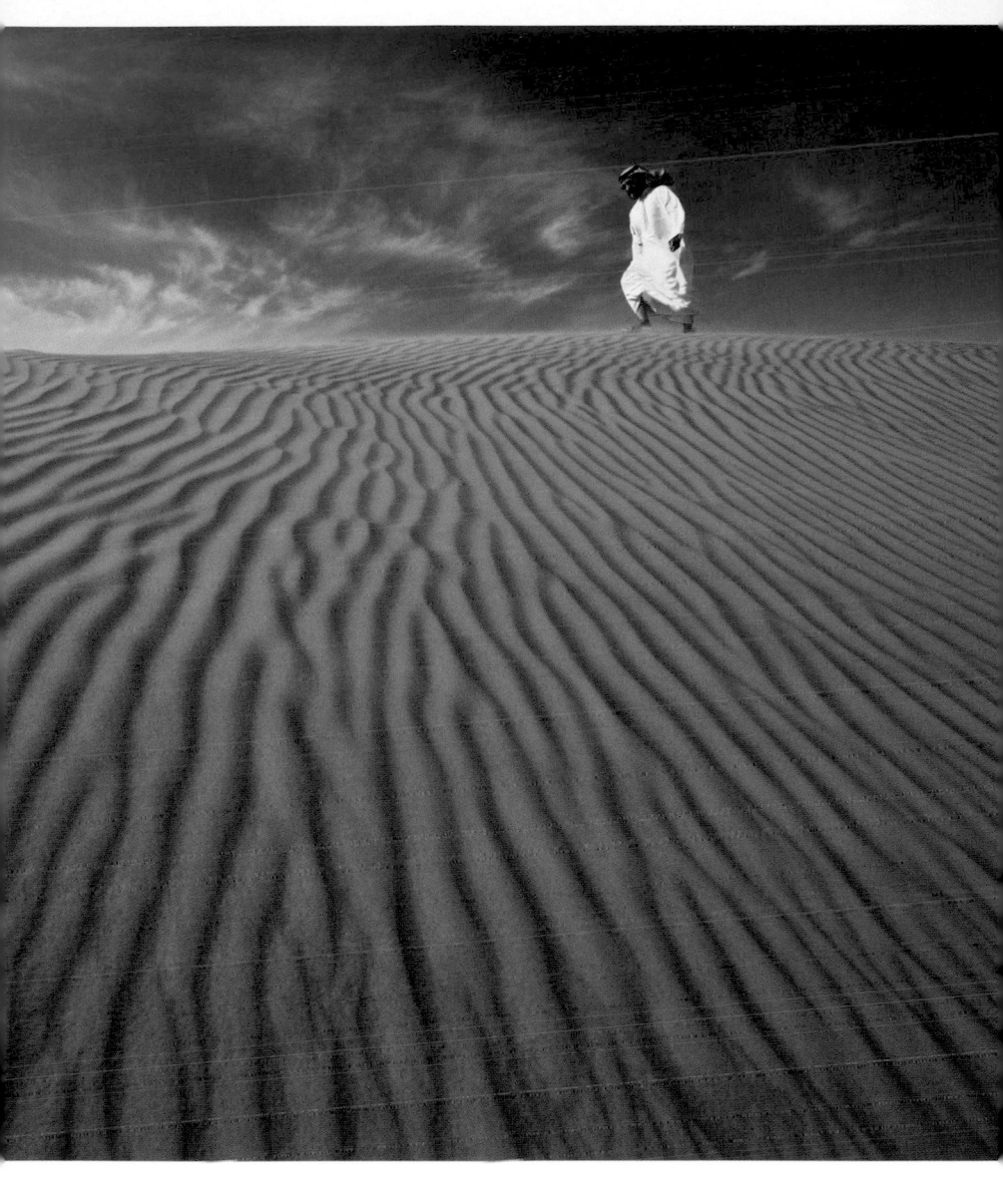

ADDING INTEREST
IN THE FOREGROUND

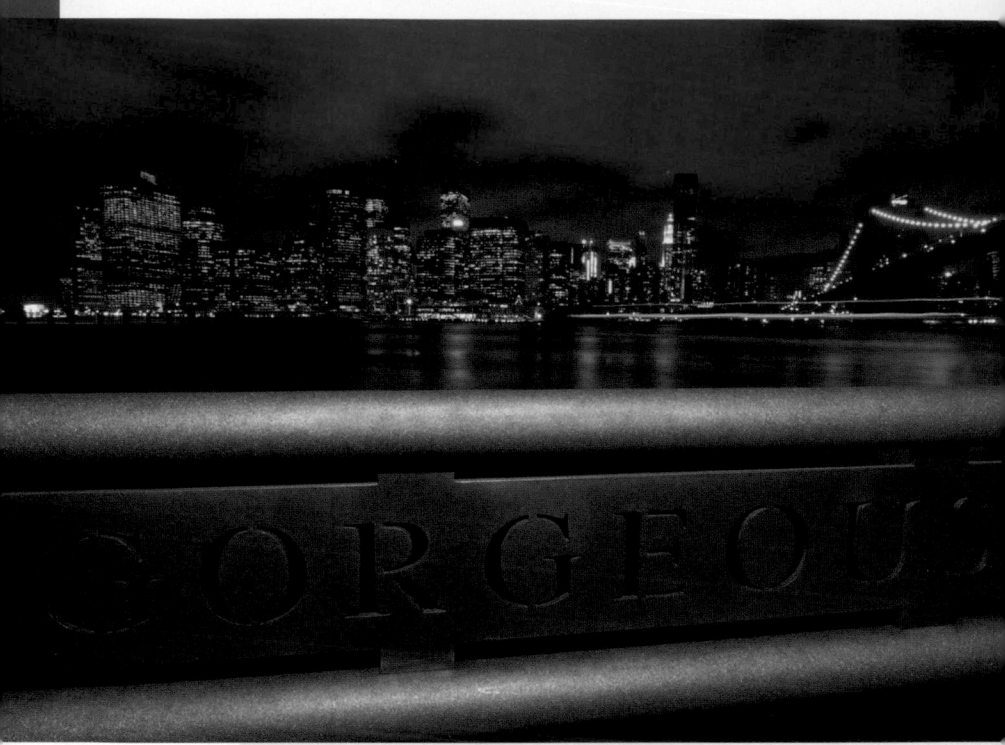

I have shot the New York City skyline for years, usually from Brooklyn, near the Brooklyn Bridge. But I had not shot the west side of the Brooklyn Bridge in more than nine years, so when I did finally visit it with some workshop students, I was quick to notice several new (to me, at least) phrases and words in the railings along the riverfront. Why not use a word or two in much the same way I use foreground flowers in landscapes? I soon caught sight of the word *GORGEOUS* and knew immediately that this was where I wanted to set up. With my Nikon D3X and 16–35mm lens at the 19mm focal length, I framed *GORGEOUS* in the foreground with the city beyond. This is classic "storytelling" aperture stuff, so f/22 was my obvious choice for a deep depth of field. I manually set the focus to 3 feet on the distance scale, and all that remained was to take a meter reading off the dusky sky. According to my meter, and with an ISO of 100, my shutter speed indicated 4 seconds as a correct exposure for the ambient light. (No filters here of any kind.)

Without benefit of my flash, however, no one would have been able to see *GORGEOUS*, so out came my Nikon SB-900 flash set in manual exposure mode (as always!). With the flash set at full power (1/1), and the aperture dial on the back of my flash set to f/22, I discovered that the flash-to-subject distance needed to be about 7 feet for a correct exposure. (I also placed an amber gel on the flash to warm up the blue-gray railing.) I fired the camera and, over the course of that 4-second exposure, the ambient light was recorded with the flash, set for rear curtain sync, firing at the end of the exposure. And voilà, here is the result!

Nikon D3X with 16–35mm lens at 19mm, f/22 for 4 seconds, ISO 100

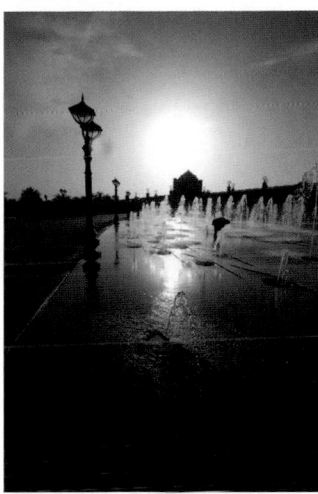

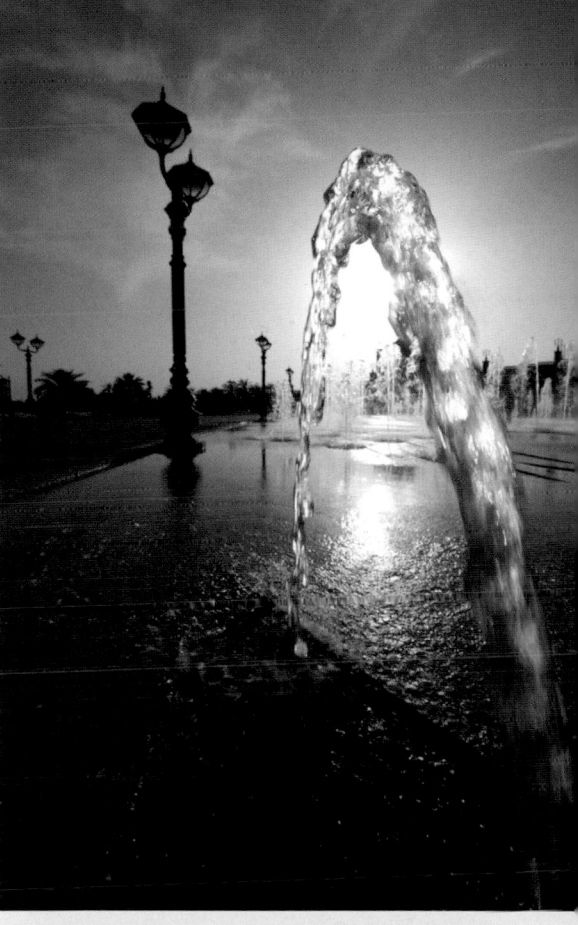

Leading lines play an important role in this image of the entrance to the Emirates Palace Hotel in Abu Dhabi. The line in the second shot leads your eye into the scene. When compared to the first image, it is even clearer that the line gives the picture greater depth, creating a much cooler and far more refreshing image.

By the way, with many of today's weather-sealed DSLRs, it should not be of any major concern if your DSLR gets damp or even a bit wet, *unless* the dampness or dousing comes from saltwater. If your camera should ever take a dip in saltwater, remove the batteries immediately and douse it with freshwater as soon as possible, then towel it dry. Let the camera dry out and reinstall the battery. Quite possibly, you will be up and running once again.

Both images: Nikon D3X with 16–35mm lens at 18mm, f/22 for 1/200 sec., ISO 100

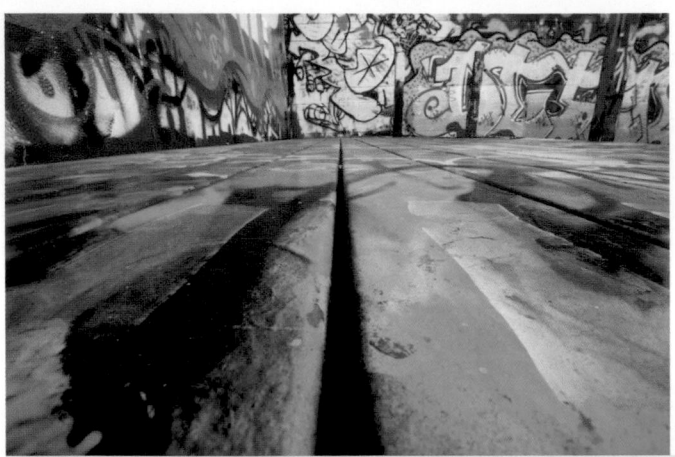

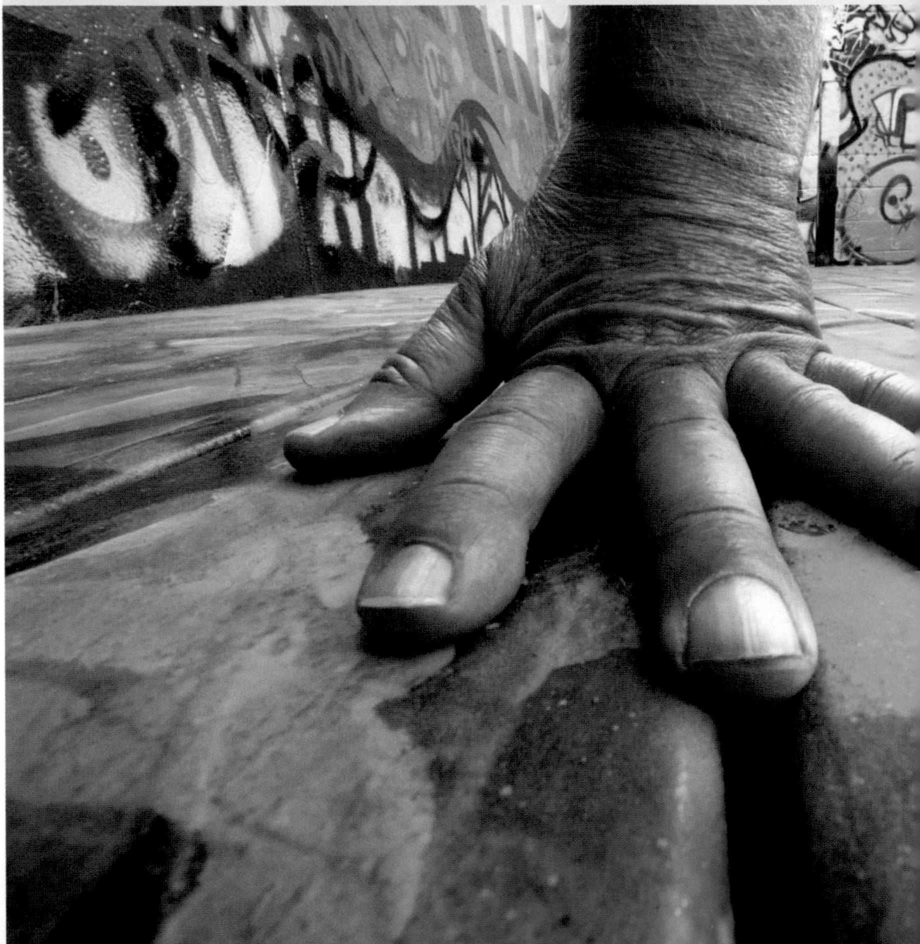

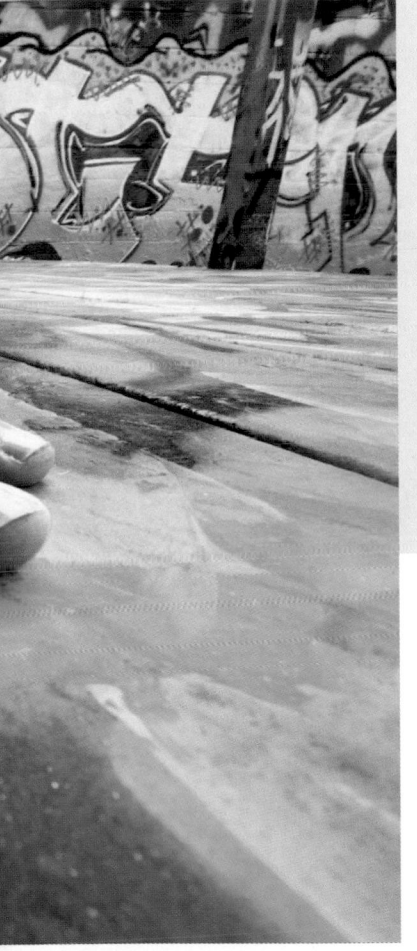

Here is another example of the power of foreground interest and its effect on the overall composition. One day I found myself in an area of Seattle where graffiti artists are given free rein to practice their art. With my camera set up at the end of a very colorful wooden deck, I captured the first image, which creates depth by emphasizing the lines of the wooden planks. But since lines lead the eye, it is best if they lead the eye *to* something, and in this case there was no "something." I thought it would be cool to include someone's foot in the foreground, but since there was no one whose foot I could use, I used my own hand instead. With the camera's self-timer engaged, I sat on the deck just out of camera range with only my hand and wrist in the frame. In a side-by-side comparison, it's fair to say that the use of an immediate foreground subject creates a far more compelling composition. And if we break it down further, my hand and wrist are nothing more than line and texture.

Nikon D3X with 16–35mm lens at 20mm f/16 for 1/125 sec., ISO 200

ADDING INTEREST
IN THE FOREGROUND

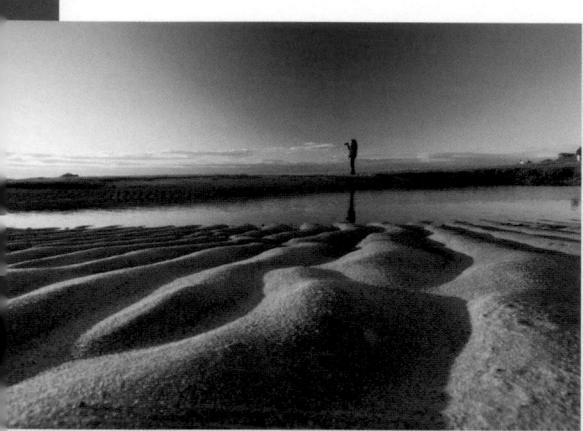

We have established that the use of line can effectively lead the viewer into a scene or, at the very least, extend an invitation to enter the scene. But line can also make it clearer what we wish our audience to look at; that is, what is of primary importance. In the first image shown above, notice how the lines come to a screeching halt at the small pool of water, even though the lines were intended to lead you to the intended subject, Kathleen Clemons, photographer extraordinaire and the director of student happiness at my online school, PPSOP.com. In the second image, shown at right, the lines *do* lead to Kathleen. Rather than stopping at the water's edge, they seem to frame Kathleen, or at least her reflection.

Both images: Tripod, Nikon D3X with 16–35mm lens at 16mm, f/22 for 1/30 sec., ISO 100

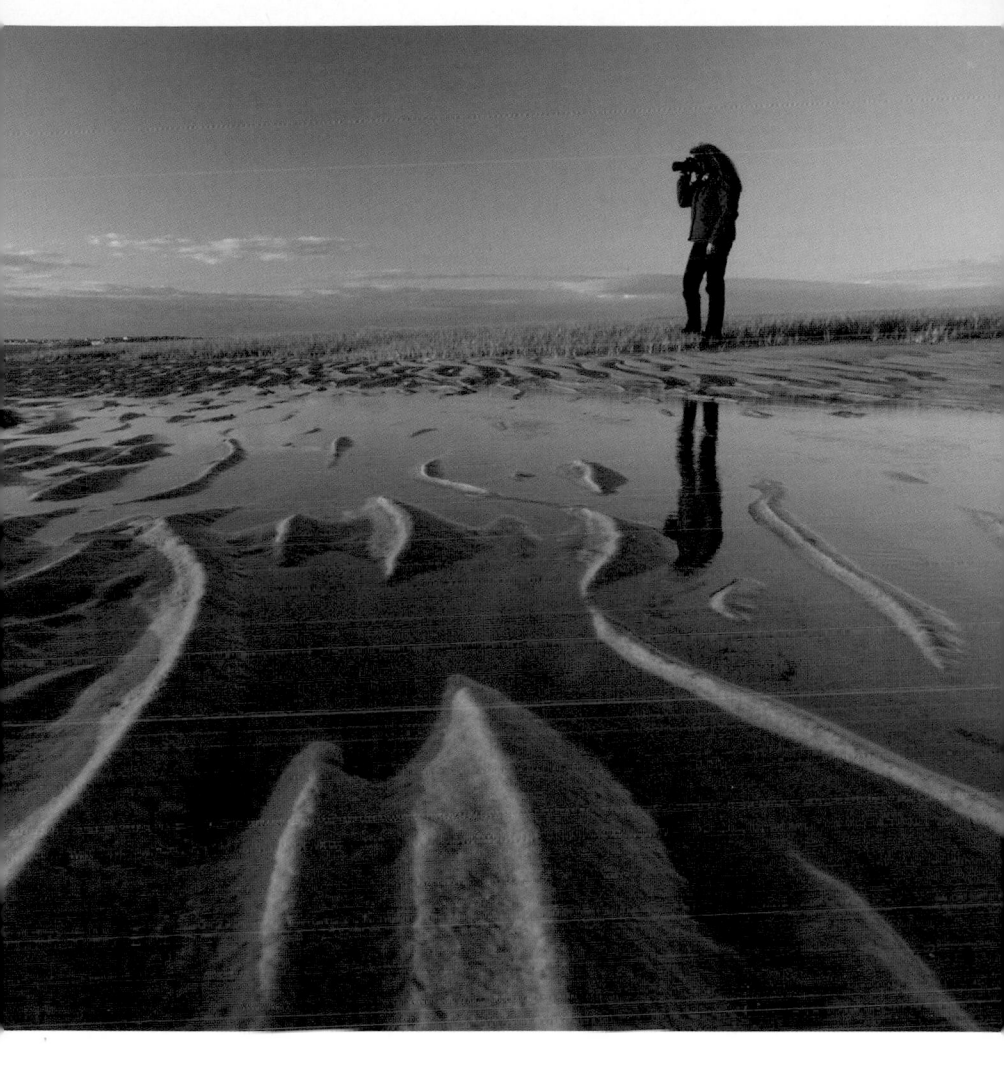

113

ADDING INTEREST
IN THE FOREGROUND

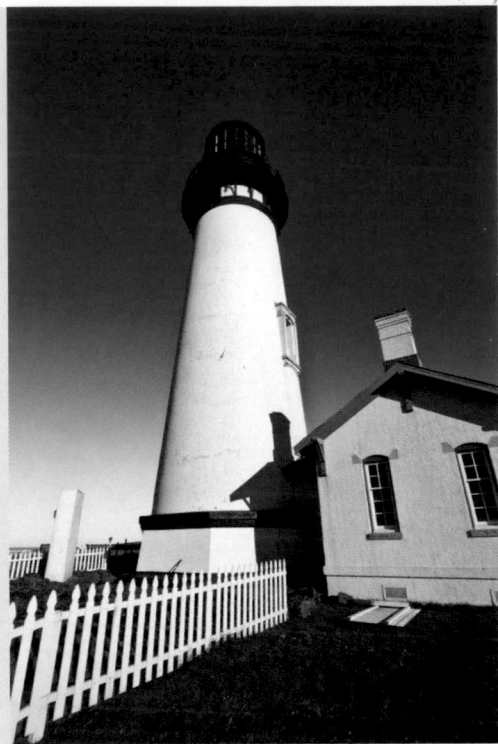
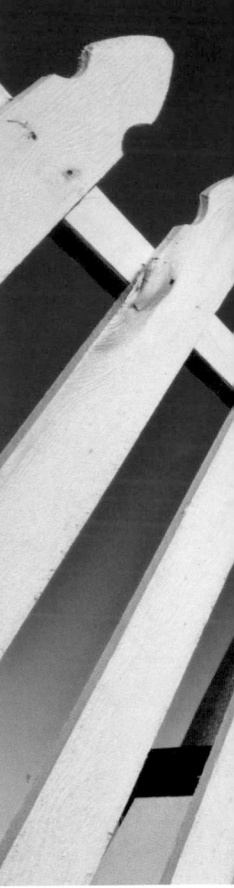

It should be clear by now that when shooting with a wide-angle lens, lying on the ground is the norm, not the exception. I am not opposed to shooting my wide-angle lens from my knees, at eye level, or from above on a ladder, either. But it has been my experience that shooting from down low offers the greatest assortment of lines and textures. When I see wide-angle compositions that do not incorporate line or texture in the foreground, I cringe—just as I do when I see someone eating chunks of wasabi with each bite of their sushi.

Yaquina Head Lighthouse, just north of Newport, Oregon, is one of the central Oregon coast's "hot spots," primarily for the sea life that thrives on the beaches below, the pelicans and seals, and the colorful display of orange and purple starfish, sea anemones, and sea urchins at low tide. Shooting the lighthouse up close at eye level requires a wide-angle lens *if* your intent is to "get it all" inside the frame. The trouble with this up-close, wide-angle view is that the lighthouse quickly becomes distorted, as if it's falling over, as in the first photo above. When faced with distortion like this, I find that sometimes the best solution is to exaggerate it even further. If you have ever stood next to a tall building and looked up with your wide-angle lens, you know how quickly you can send that building much higher and farther into the sky. The same was true for this lighthouse and the picket fence surrounding it. Lying at the base of the picket fence and handholding my camera, I could quickly see how the lines of the fence could be used not only to frame the lighthouse but also to thrust the viewer into the scene, which of course they do, as in the photo at right..

Both images: Canon 5D with Canon 17–40mm lens at 17mm, f/16 for 1/60 sec., ISO 100

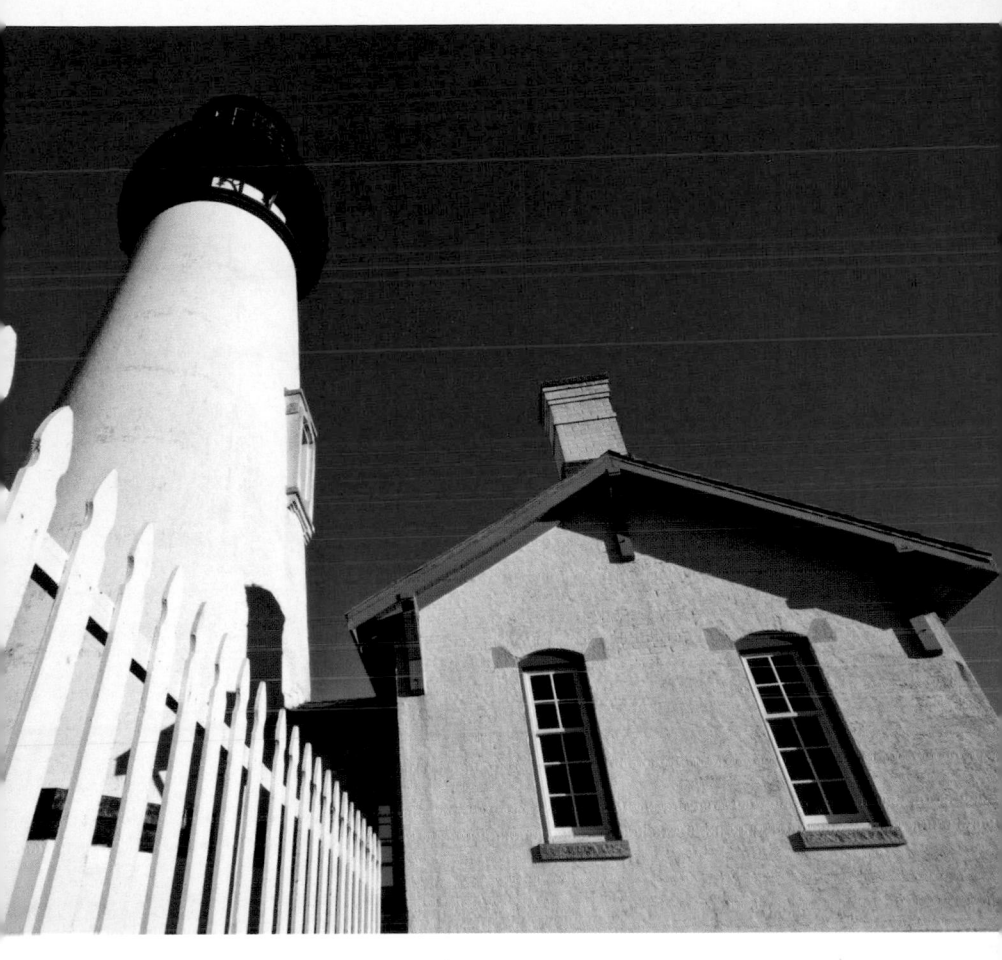

115

ADDING INTEREST
IN THE FOREGROUND

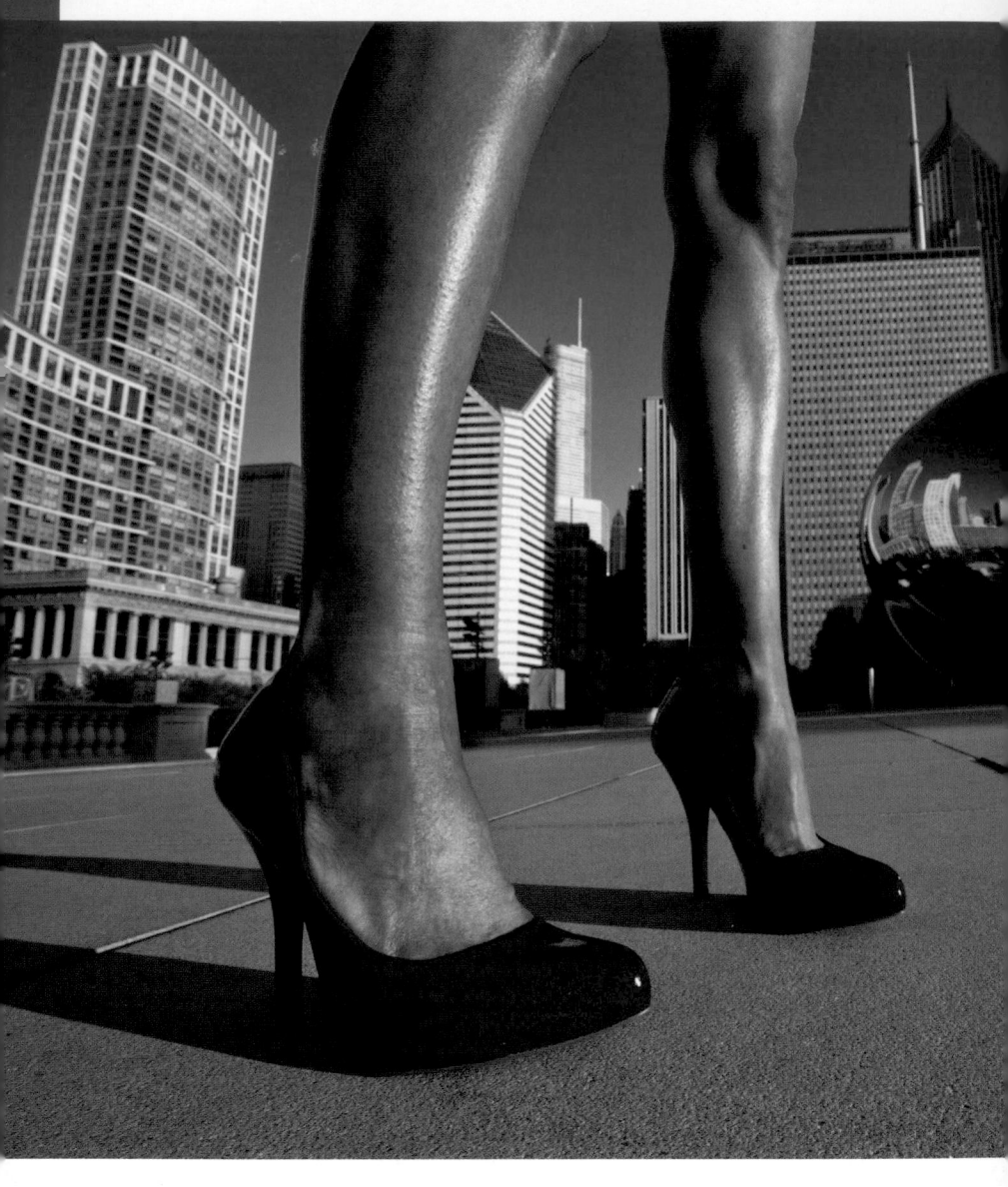

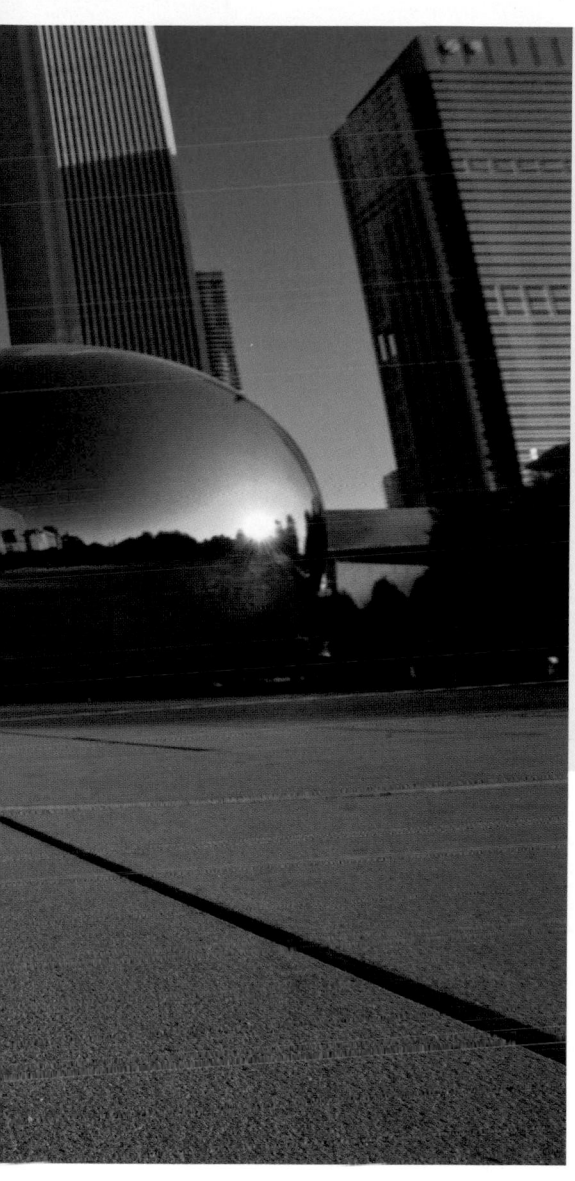

The "Bean" sculpture in Millennium Park has quickly become one of Chicago's most popular sculptures. I have photographed the Bean in all sorts of light, in different seasons, and at different times of day, and was quickly reaching the point where, short of seeing the perfect rainbow arching over the Bean, I would probably have little reason to photograph it again. That was until I hit on the idea of a woman in red high heels. A few quick phone calls and I had my model, complete with the requested red heels, for something a bit more memorable than the "standard" Bean shot. This image, taken with a handheld camera, is again about line, along with a dash of color, but more than either of those it is the point of view and use of foreground interest that make the image possible, thanks to a wide-angle lens and a small aperture.

Nikon D3X with Nikkor 16–35mm lens at 22mm, f/22 for 1/60 sec., ISO 100

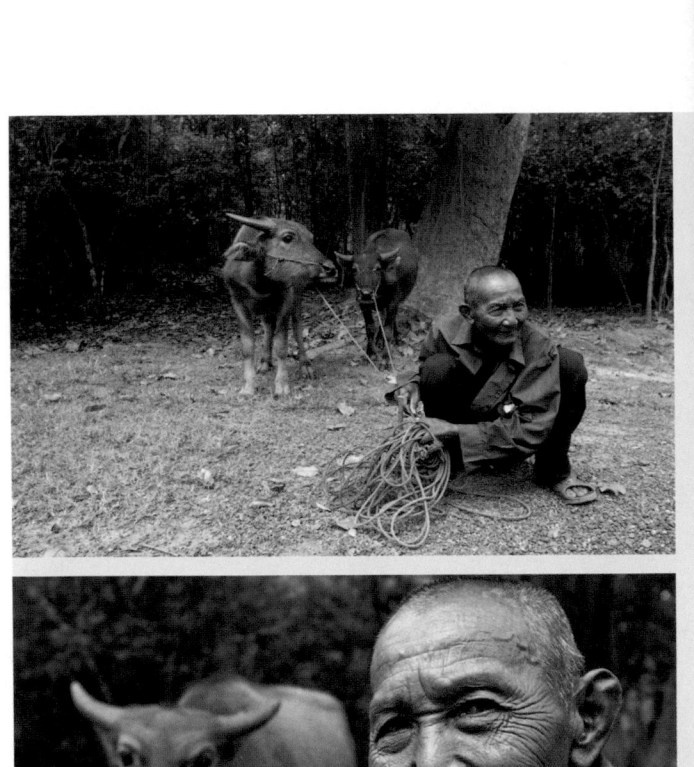

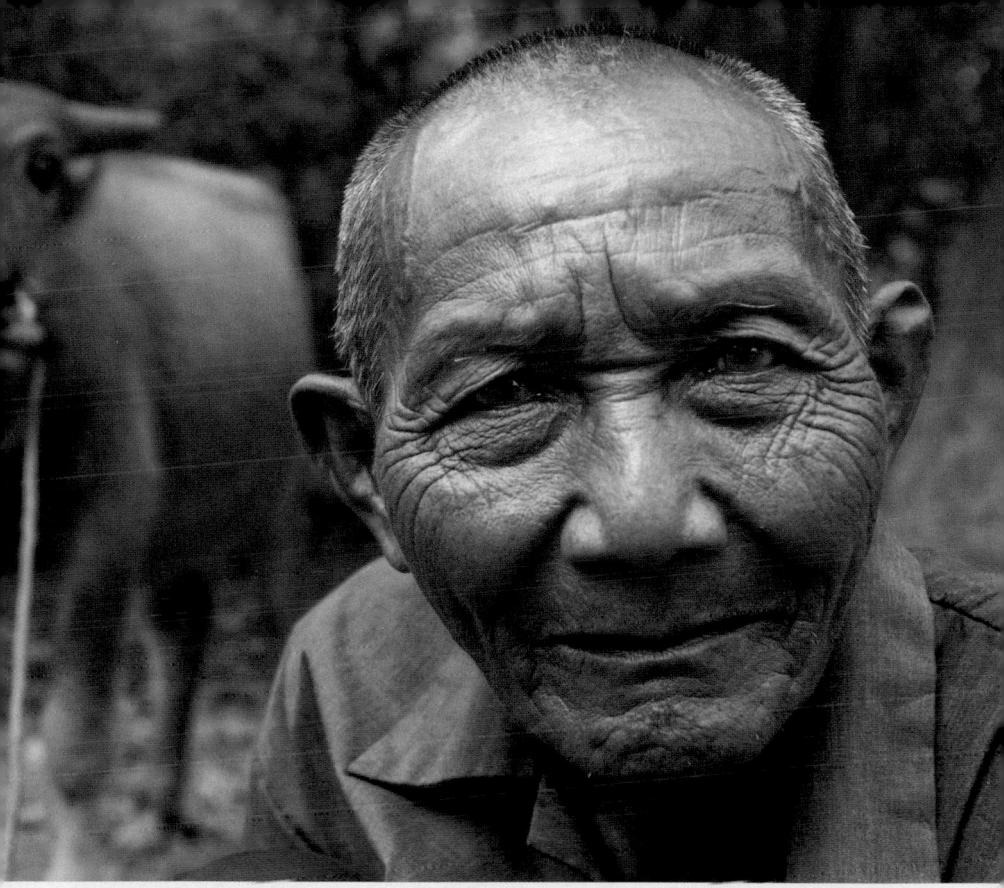

A few miles west of Angkor Wat, we passed a farmer on the side of the road who seemed to be having some trouble controlling his two young water buffalo. As we slowly drove past, I noticed a smile coming from the man's face. "Still smiling in the face of adversity," I remarked to myself. I saw this type of attitude time and time again among the people of Cambodia, who, as I am sure you know, are no strangers to adversity.

We pulled over and asked the farmer if he would mind posing for some pictures. In the first image (top left), you can see many tourists' approach to shooting candids: Stand far back, don't engage the subject in any way, then go home and do your best to crop it in Photoshop for something a bit more compelling. You already know my feelings about this approach, so let's simply look at what I did next. In the second photo (bottom left), I am obviously engaging with the subject. He is fully aware of my presence and I am fully aware that I have used his body to hide one of the buffalo behind him (a "crying baby," in this case). But I am still left with a rope rising up from the ground below and into his chin. In the third shot (above), you see how a slight shift in my point of view, as well as a slight shift in the man's point of view, delivers the cleanest and most compelling composition (as luck would have it, both he and the water buffalo seem to be making the same quizzical and lovable face!). Since the man was the real focus of my composition, I chose an aperture of f/5.6 to keep the focus limited to the man. I handheld my camera and kept my focal length at the 35mm range, a moderately wide-angle range, as I still needed a wide angle but did not want to distort the man's face.

All images: Nikon D3X with 24–85mm lens, f/5.6 for 1/160 sec, ISO 100

ADDING INTEREST
IN THE FOREGROUND

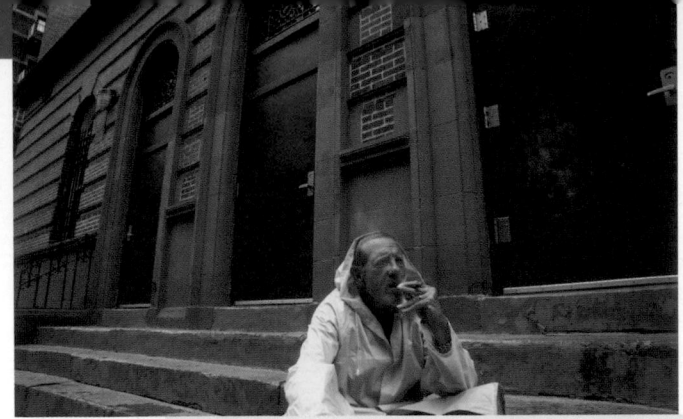

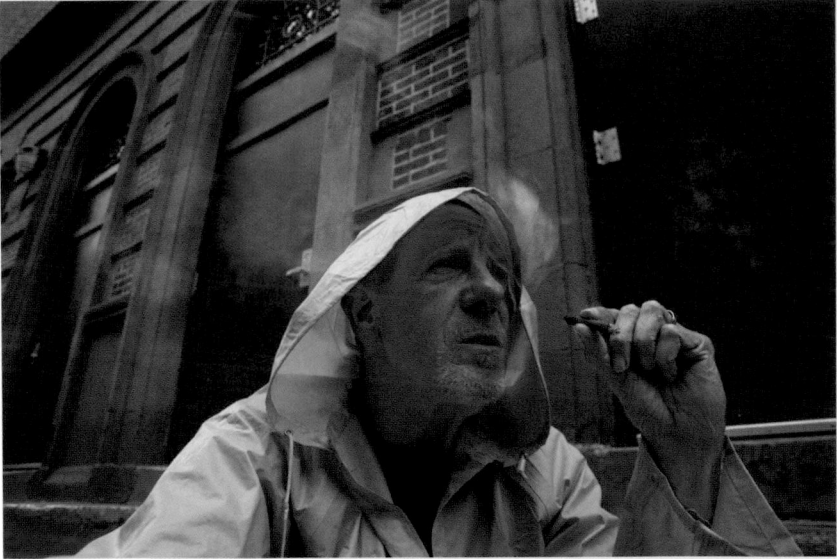

If there is one hurdle to overcome when using your wide-angle lens, it is the constant need to get closer, closer, closer—and when you think you are close enough, get closer still! Getting close enough is something we all struggle with, and with a wide-angle only more so, as we have to be ever mindful of the wide-angle lens's tendency to push subjects toward the "back of the stage." Once we recognize this, we can simply place one foot in front of the other and walk closer to the stage.

With great anticipation, my students and I awaited the "big one" to arrive in Manhattan last August—the Hurricane That Wasn't, as we soon were calling it. But, hey, we were not going to sit around and cry about what could have been! So out the door we went, into the deserted streets of Lower Manhattan. I asked one of my students, dressed in his yellow rain slicker, to sit against the backdrop of several red doors. I then asked each of the students to take a shot with their wide-angle lens. Not one got close enough—at least, not initially. Compare the two examples shown here. The first image is what most of the students shot, and the second is what I recommend. It's about getting closer. If you want to create an intimate encounter with your wide-angle lens, you need to be much closer than 5 feet!

Nikon D3X with 24–85mm lens at 28mm, f/16 for 1/60 sec., ISO 100

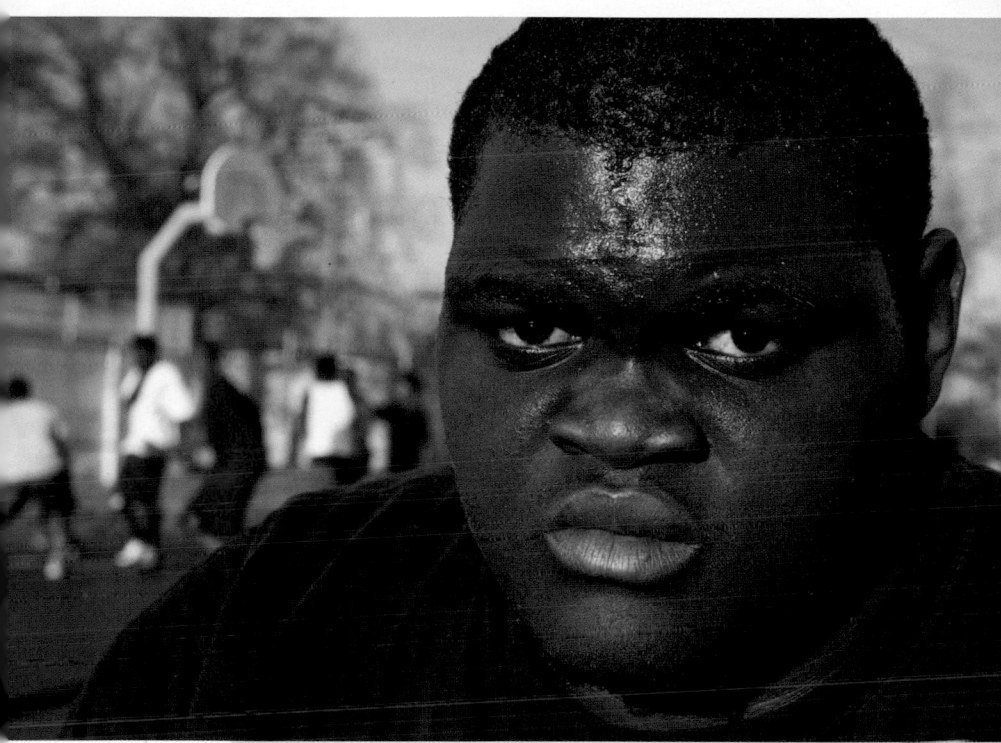

I shot this image with a moderate wide-angle lens, focused very close, while handholding the camera. Notice how the subject occupies a large part of the foreground, while subtle "clues" in the background tell us about the overall scene. Much like the composition of the flower image shown on page 122, this composition offers the viewer an intimate encounter. These are the kinds of encounters that await all of us once we get in the habit of looking for interesting foregrounds. What are you waiting for?

Nikon D300S with 24–85mm lens at 35mm, f/22 for 1/250 sec. for the ambient light in background and f/22 with Nikon SB-900 flash for light on model

ADDING INTEREST IN THE FOREGROUND

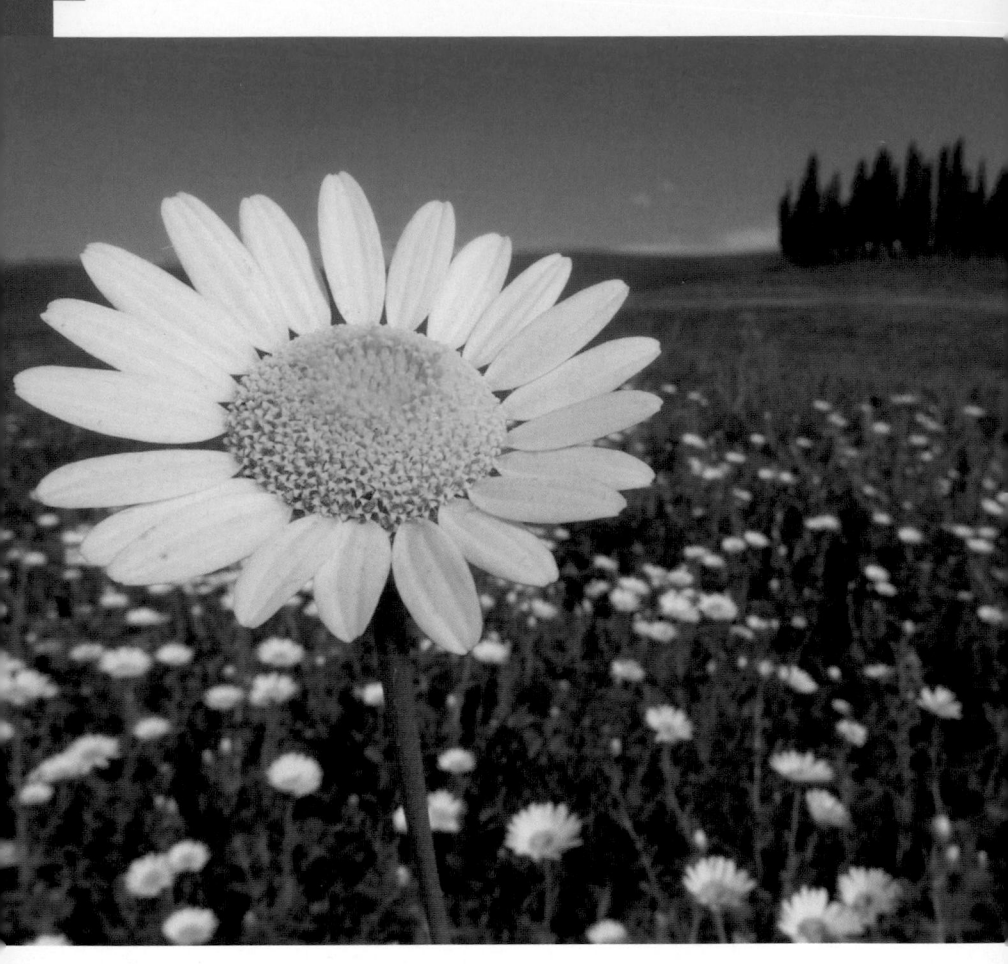

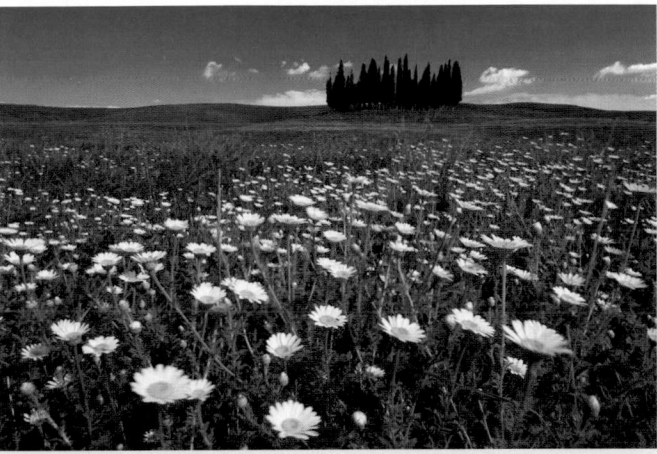
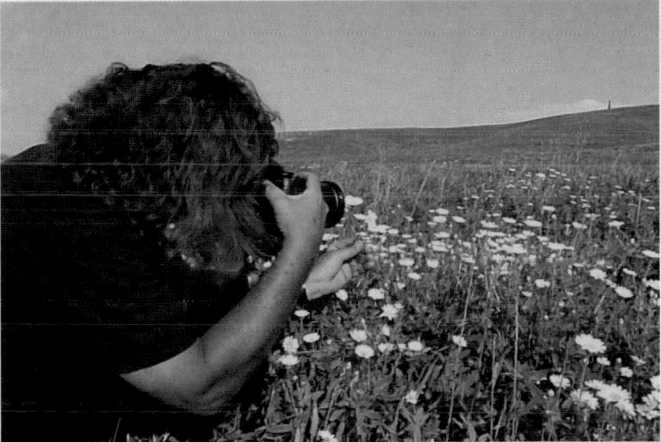

In the Tuscany region of Italy, near Siena, I came upon one of the most photographed fields in all of Tuscany. With its large group of cypress trees sitting among the rolling hills, it screams, "Take my picture!" No matter what the season, these rolling hills and cypress trees always make for a pleasant image—*if* composed well, of course.

I strode into the field with my camera and 16–35mm wide-angle lens, determined to shoot an up-close-and-personal "portrait" of a lone daisy against the familiar Tuscan hills and trees. As you can see in the photograph top right, taken with the camera and lens on a tripod, I did manage to capture another "flowers in the foreground, cypress trees in the background" composition. Now compare that result with the image at left. Which is more intimate? Which makes you reach for your Claritin? Which might make you recall the smell of a flower? There is no secret about how this photo was created. I picked a flower, and with the camera and lens on my tripod, I simply focused in manual, as close as I could, and brought the flower to that close focus point. Imagine the possibilities!

Top right: Nikon D3X with 16–35mm lens at 20mm, f/22 for 1/30 sec., ISO 100;
Left: Nikon D3X with 16–35mm lens at 20mm, f/11 for 1/125 sec., ISO 100

ADDING INTEREST
IN THE FOREGROUND

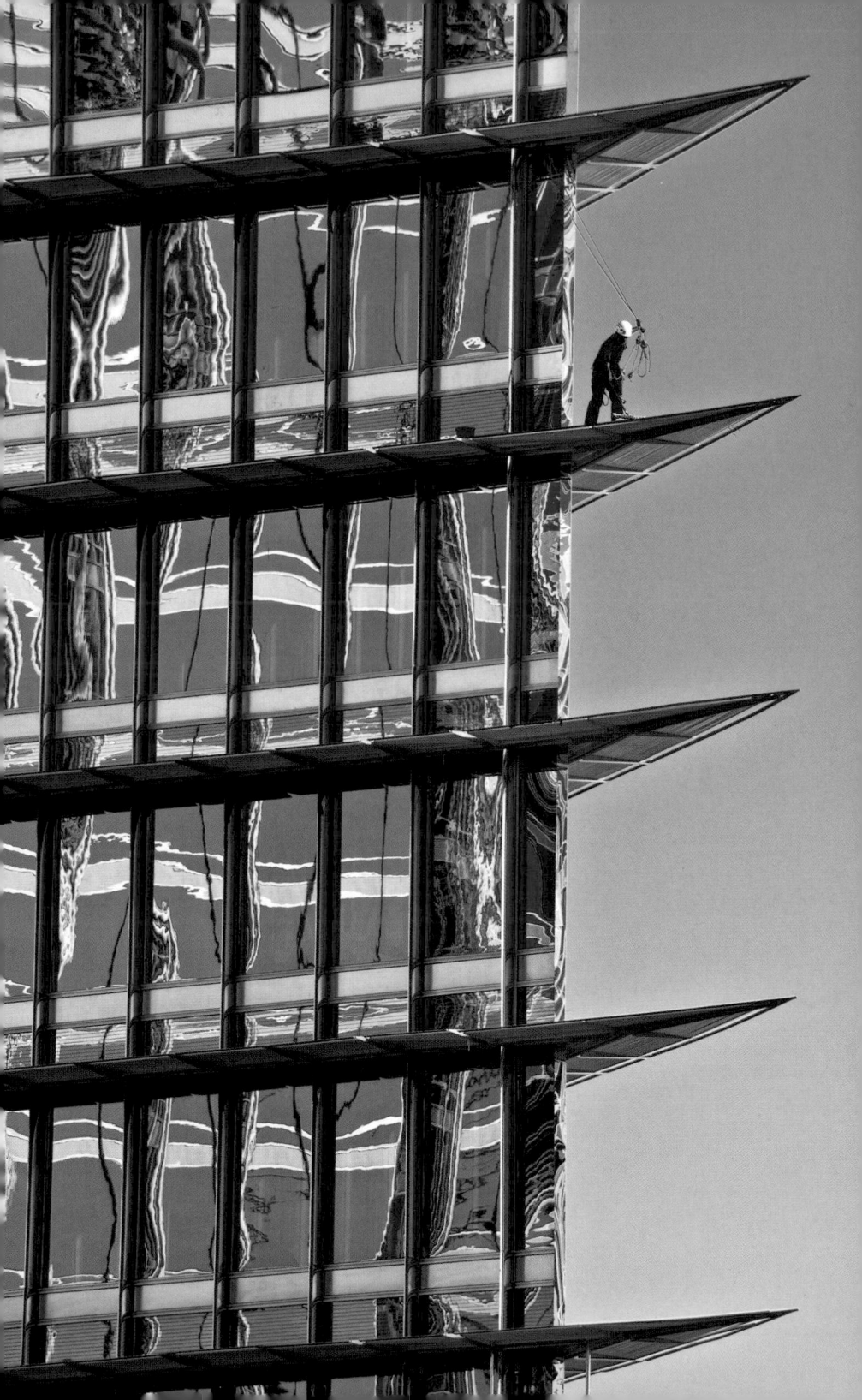

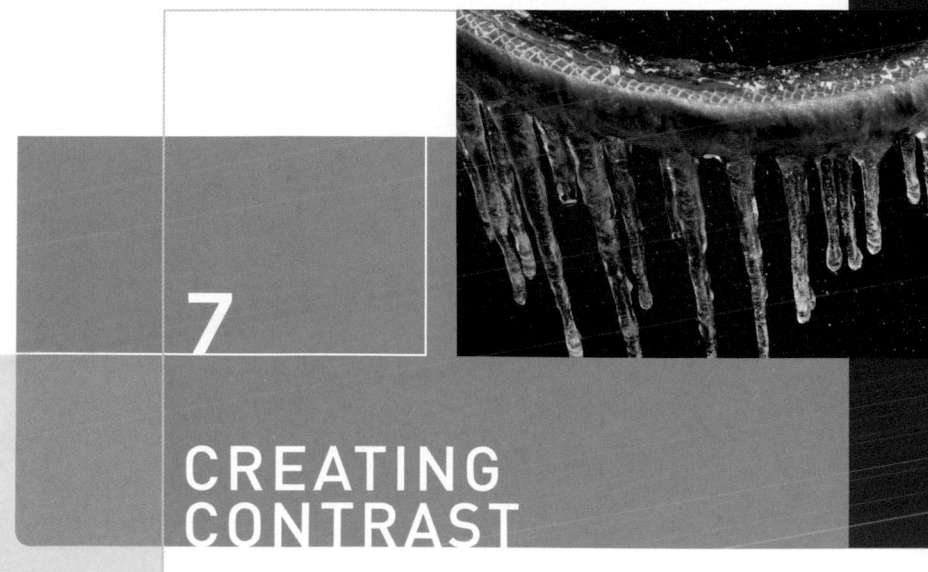

7

CREATING CONTRAST

We are quick to see a ketchup stain on an impecca-
bly dressed man's white shirt, just to the left of his
red tie and surrounded by the "frame" of his black
suit. We are just as quick to notice the small but lin-
gering piece of green leafy spinach stuck between
the two front teeth of the office secretary as she
greets you for your afternoon appointment. Why?
Because they create *contrast*, another vital element
of compelling photographic compositions.

How many of us would reach for a black piece of
paper when drawing with a black pen or for a white
piece of paper when drawing with a white pen? Obviously, none of us would, unless we were looking for
ways to make our drawings invisible. Surprisingly,
there are more of us out there than you might think
who, though not intentionally, reach for black paper
when "drawing" with a black pen or for white paper
with a white pen. Not surprisingly, your eight-year-
old son, dressed in his Count Dracula black cape,
would all but disappear if photographed outside

Nikon D3X with Nikkor 70–300mm lens, f/11 for 1/320 sec., ISO 100

against the dark of night, even with a flash. If not for the contrast between his face (or maybe just his eyes) among all that dark, we might at first see it as a blank, dark canvas of nothingness.

Contrast can be good and contrast can be bad. But either way, contrast is vital. It is the difference between good and bad, big and small, smart and stupid, ambitious and lazy, short and tall, and so on. Without its contrasting mate, each would cease to have meaning. But contrast alone is not enough. It is, once again, the *arrangement* of the contrast that is important.

As is true with most "first" outings, my first trip to the Bugaboos, a small yet concentrated mountain range in the Canadian Rockies west of Banff, will probably prove to be the most memorable. While I plan to go back, hopefully several times, I do not expect to experience the same wide-eyed wonder I had the first time. That is, unless I am treated to another day of remarkably clear air with blue sky and white puffy clouds! The subtle wind on one such afternoon produced the same rolling contrast mentioned earlier. In the image opposite, the long but narrow shadow falling across the rocky outcropping near the top third of the frame creates contrast between the dark and surrounding light, and thus a sense of depth. Again, my exposure here is for the light, so any resulting shadows appear as dark, underexposed areas. Because dark is perceived as a heavier, thicker mass than light, the rocky outcropping is given much stronger force than when seen in the light, as in the image at right.

Both images: Leica D-Lux 5 with 24mm lens, f/8 for 1/320 sec., ISO 80, Aperture Priority

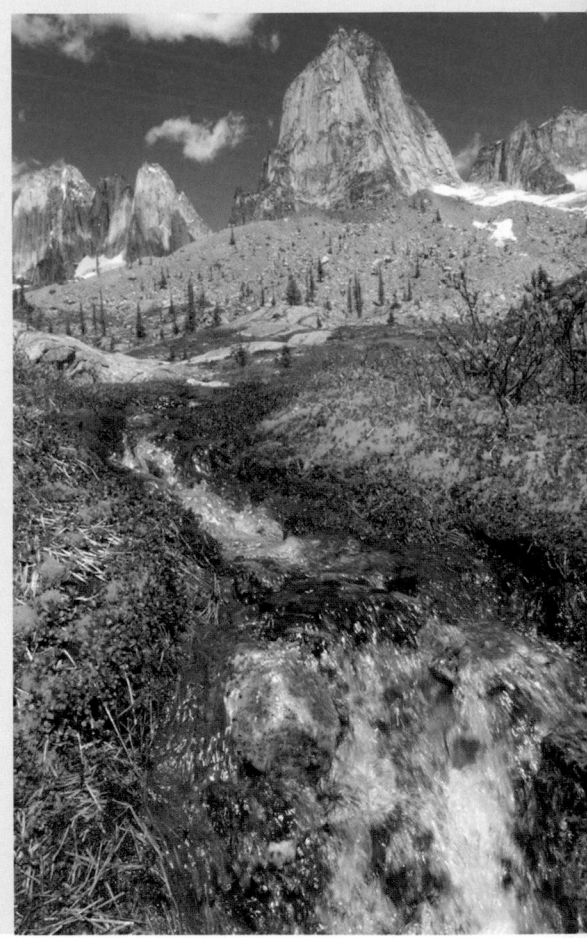

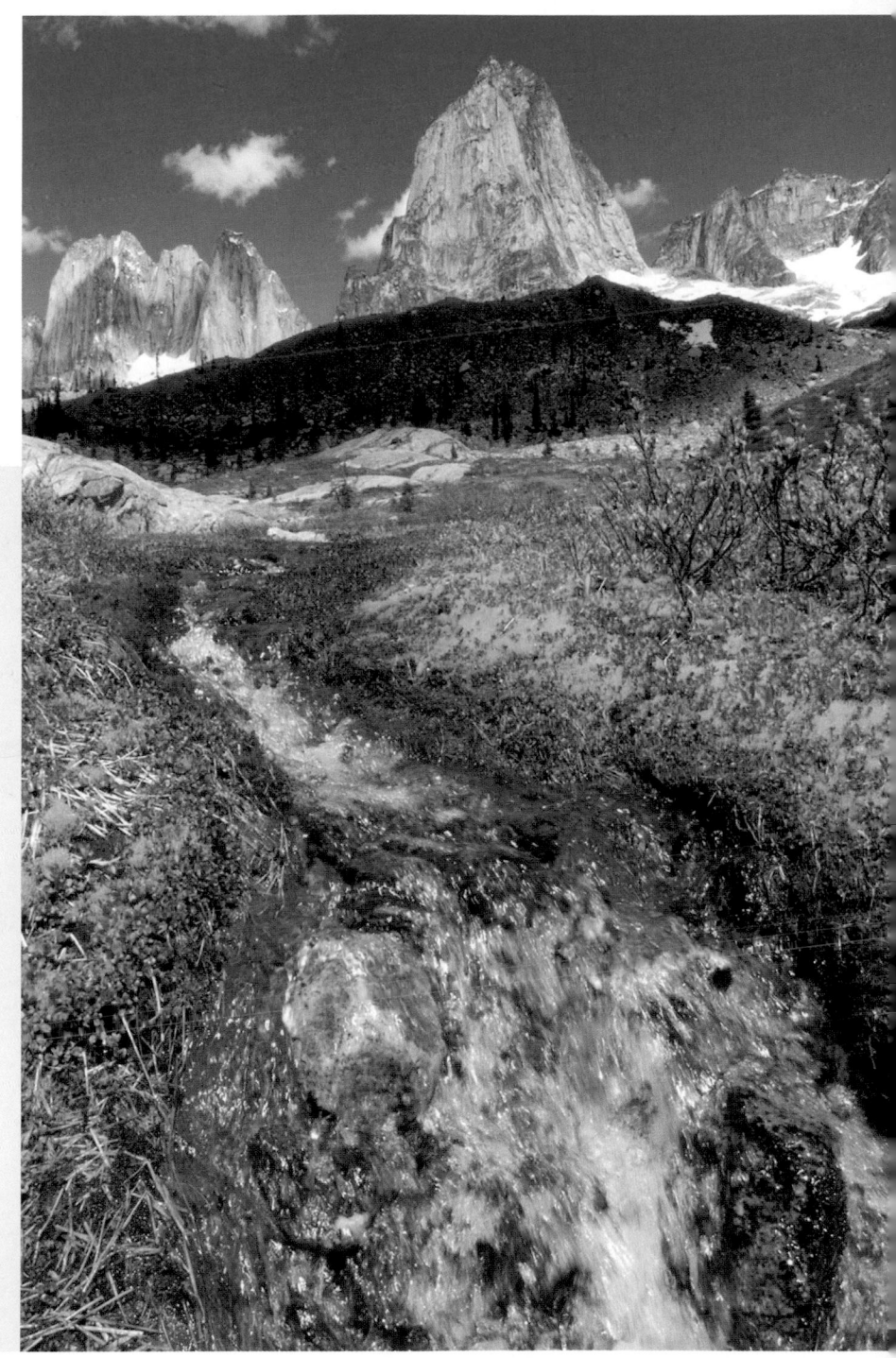

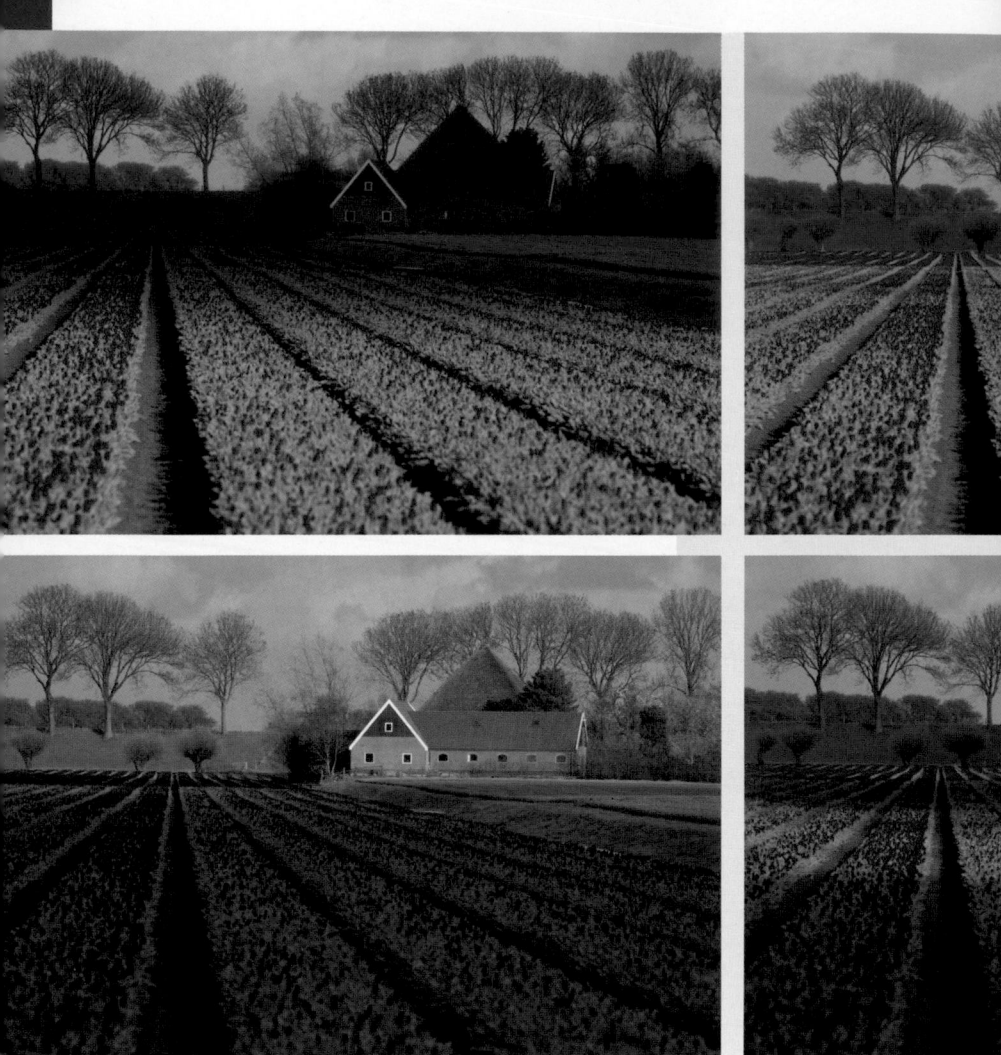

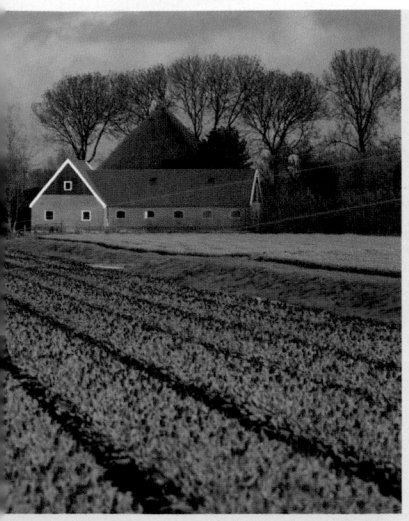

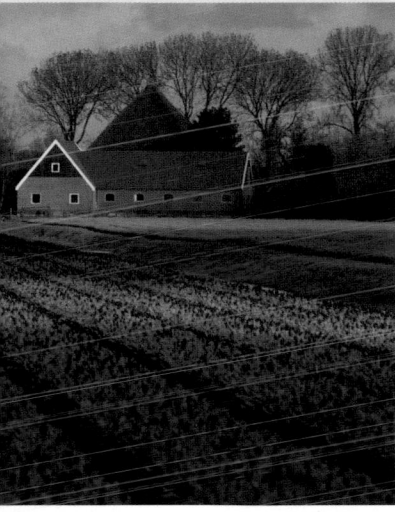

Spring has always been a wonderful time of year for landscape photographers in Holland. Throughout much of the area called West Friesland, the once-frozen dark soil is transformed into an explosion of color as thousands of tulips rise from the tulip fields. Throughout much of April, the clouds and sun jockey for position, each claiming victory for only a few seconds at a time, thanks to a constant sharp and biting wind.

As this battle rages overhead, large swaths of sunlight and shadow roll across the landscape, and not surprisingly, stunning landscapes await any photographer. It's one of those classic lighting situations where no experience is necessary! All you have to do is keep your finger on the shutter release and have a big enough memory card. By the end of the day, you can retire to the cozy confines of your room, fire up the laptop, and enjoy the certainty that on this day you got something really special. Such is the outcome when shooting what I call *rolling contrast*. Not every image will be a winner, of course. In some shots, the distribution of sunlight and shadow will be off—for example, all light except for one dark corner. But in others the distribution will be perfect: light in two-thirds of the frame, shadow in one-third, or shadow in two-thirds, light in one-third.

If there is any doubt about exposure in these kinds of situations, let there be no mistake: this is time for the Sunny 16 Rule! The Sunny 16 Rule says that any front-lit scene (with the exception of less than 90 minutes before sunset or after sunrise) should be exposed at f/16 with a shutter speed that equals your ISO. For example, if your ISO is 100, your exposure should be f/16 at 1/100 sec. With my 70–300mm lens set at f/16, and my shutter speed at 1/100 sec., I simply fired a number of frames as shadow and sun rolled across this particular landscape. Of the four images shown, my favorite is the last one. I wish every day of shooting were this easy!

All images: Nikon D3X with 70–300mm lens, f/16 for 1/100 sec., ISO 100

CONTRAST AND VISUAL WEIGHT

As I review my own photographic journey, I remember with great vividness how almost five years after I picked up a camera, contrast suddenly became vitally important. Although it had been apparent in much of my work prior to that, I had not had any real appreciation for it. I was merely responding to whatever contrast presented itself before me but was not actually "seeing" its role in the overall composition. It was only at this point that I realized how, with a bit of thought and planning, I could actually control contrast and its effectiveness in my compositions. With this realization, I turned a major corner in my photographic maturity and was soon exploiting contrast to my advantage.

There are many ways to describe contrast, as we have already seen, but this section will explore contrast in light (dark versus light), tone (soft versus hard), color (monochromatic color versus vivid color), and the disruption in a pattern.

Almost without fail, our eye first goes to whatever area of an image has the highest contrast (either dark or light). The viewer then assumes that this area *is* the main subject—and rightly so! Unlike the distraction of that crying baby I spoke about earlier, this area of highest contrast can be thought of as the warm and inviting smile of a happy baby.

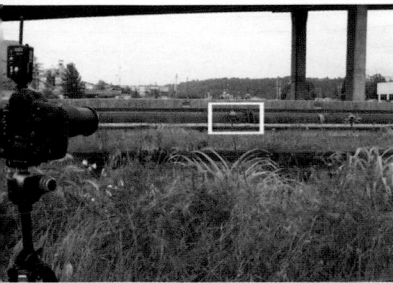

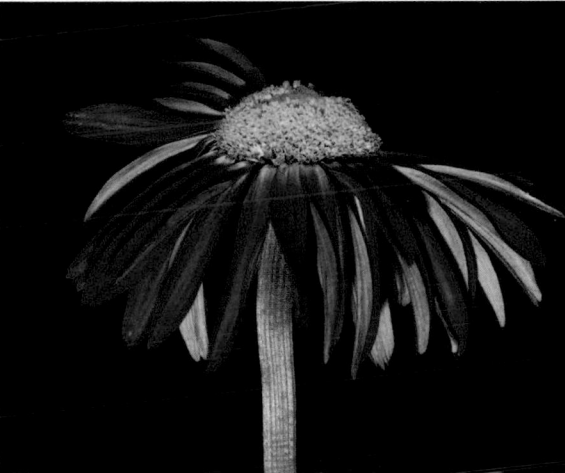

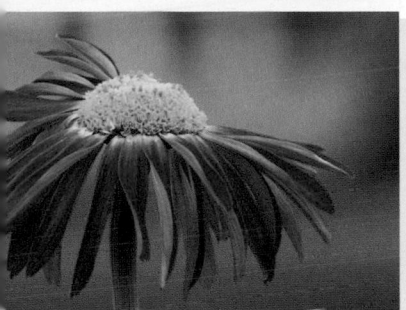

Another effective way to create contrast, especially when photographing flowers, is to use a portable electronic flash or a ring flash, which is almost guaranteed to record black behind the flower—*if* you use a fast-enough shutter speed. Let me explain.

A correct flash exposure is 100 percent dependent on the right aperture. As long as you are using the "right" aperture, in conjunction with the correct flash-to-subject distance for that aperture, you will get a correct flash exposure. But what about shutter speed? Its role is, for the most part, reduced to controlling the exposure of your ambient or available light, and therein lies the secret to recording black backgrounds.

In the example shown here, it was a cloudy day and the lone purple flower was in an industrial setting. In the bottom left photograph, you can see how, without benefit of any flash, I was able to record a correct exposure of the flower at f/8 for 1/30 sec. We can both agree that this is a far-from-compelling image. At this point, I got out my flash and set it to manual. I dialed in an aperture of f/8, and the flash-to-subject distance scale told me that for a correct flash exposure, my flash would need to be 18 feet from the flower. I was only about 6 feet away, so I simply dialed down the power of the flash until the distance scale indicated a flash-to-subject distance of 6 feet. Just before I took my next exposure, I adjusted my shutter speed to 1/250 sec., which meant that my ambient light would be 3 stops underexposed. (How did I get that? My original ambient exposure was f/8 for 1/30 sec. Compared to the new ambient exposure of f/8 for 1/250 sec., that equals a -3-stop difference.) When the flash fires, it will correctly expose the flower, but the faster shutter speed of 1/250 sec. will be too fast to record any of the background ambient light, resulting in a black, severely underexposed background and lots of contrast.

Bottom left: Nikon D300S with Nikkor 70–300mm lens, f/8 for 1/30 sec., no flash; Right: Nikon D300S with Nikkor 70–300mm lens, f/8 for 1/250 sec., with flash

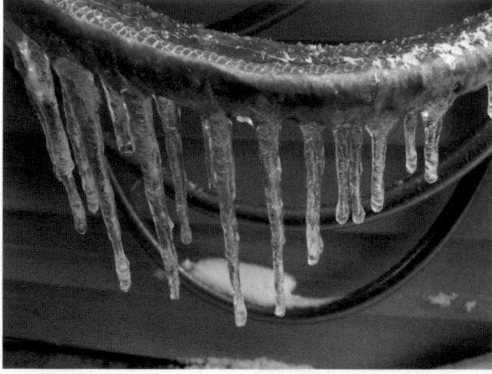

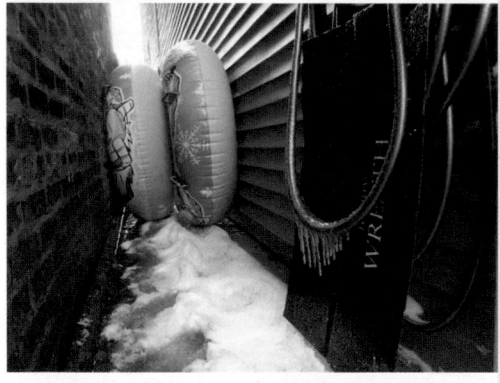

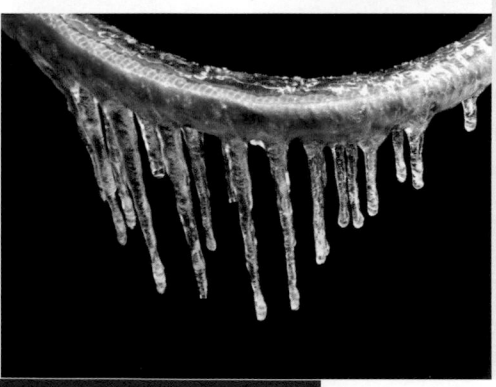

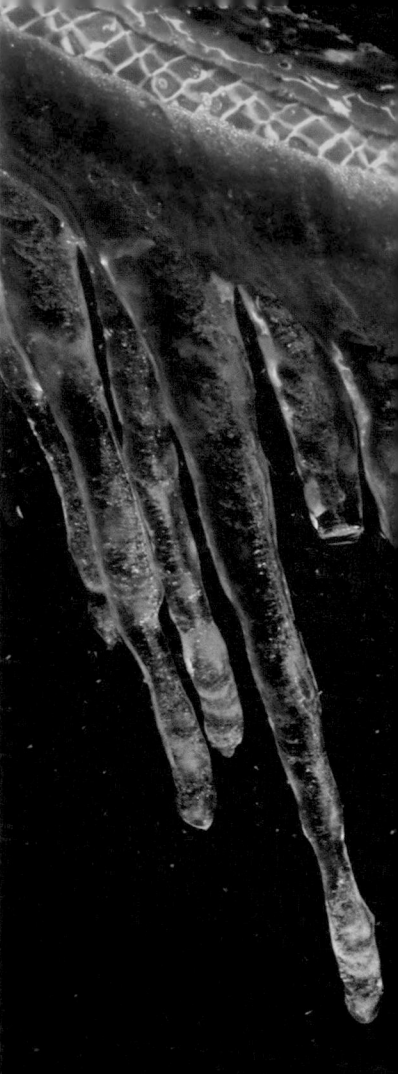

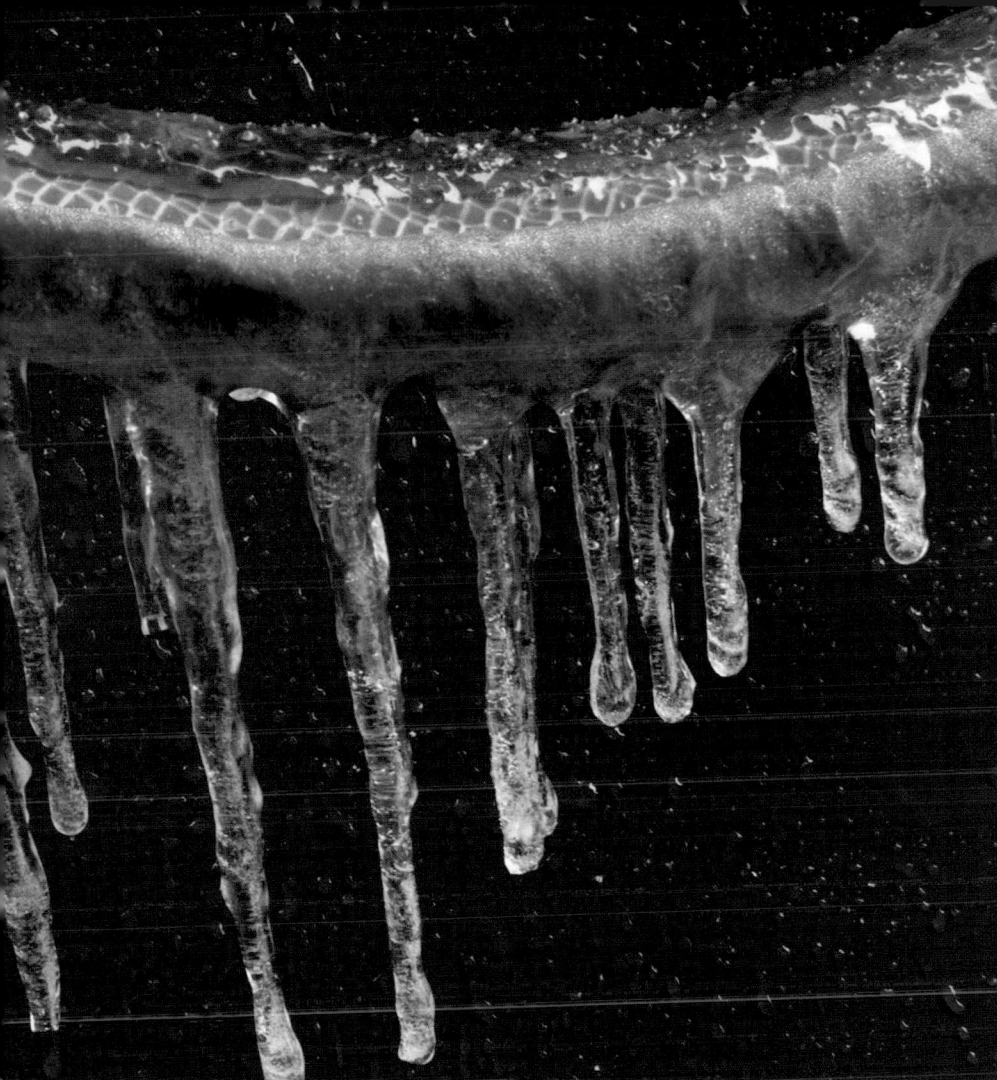

There are several ways to create contrast. Perhaps the simplest involves the use of your flash or seamless backgrounds, such as colored poster board, fabric, or even just a solid-colored piece of cardboard. That was surely the case when I went outside one cold winter's morning and discovered that a beautiful ice sculpture had formed around my garden hose. Apparently, it was just sunny and warm enough to melt the snow on the roof 20 feet above but cold enough to freeze the steady drips as they hit the garden hose in the open shade below.

In my first shot (opposite, top), the dull backdrop of the tan siding offers little contrast to the much more vivid hose. Dashing back inside the house, I grabbed a red cardboard box from the closet and leaned it up against the side of the house. Better! Handholding my Leica D-Lux 3 set to Aperture Priority mode, I set the aperture to f/4 and recorded this pleasingly festive winter scene of green and red (above).

Just for fun, I then went back in the house to grab a piece of black cardboard, and was soon shooting the garden hose against a dark, deep, and mysterious black background for a completely different look.

All images: Leica D-Lux 3 with 24mm lens, f/4 for 1/100 sec., ISO 100

TAKING CONTRAST
TO THE NEXT LEVEL

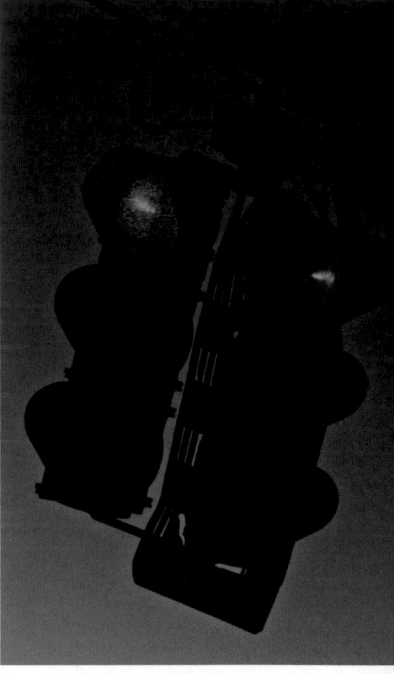

With a single shift in contrast, your arrangements can become more poignant, more meaningful, more important. I can't say with certainty when it happened, but at some point early in my career, when I started shooting with a macro lens, I began to notice how the slightest shift in my point of view could alter the overall contrast. This was particularly true when shooting sidelit flowers in the garden. When I moved to the right, for example, even just a fraction of an inch, the unsightly "black hole" to the left of my yellow gloriosa daisy would disappear. Now, when I look up through the branches of a tree at a lone red cardinal with my 70–300mm lens, I am quick to notice the bright white holes of distant, overcast sky showing through the leaves. With a subtle shift in my point of view, a bit to the left or right, forward or back, I am often able to reduce, if not eliminate, these jarring shifts in contrast, allowing the viewer to focus on the red cardinal, for example, without any visual interruption.

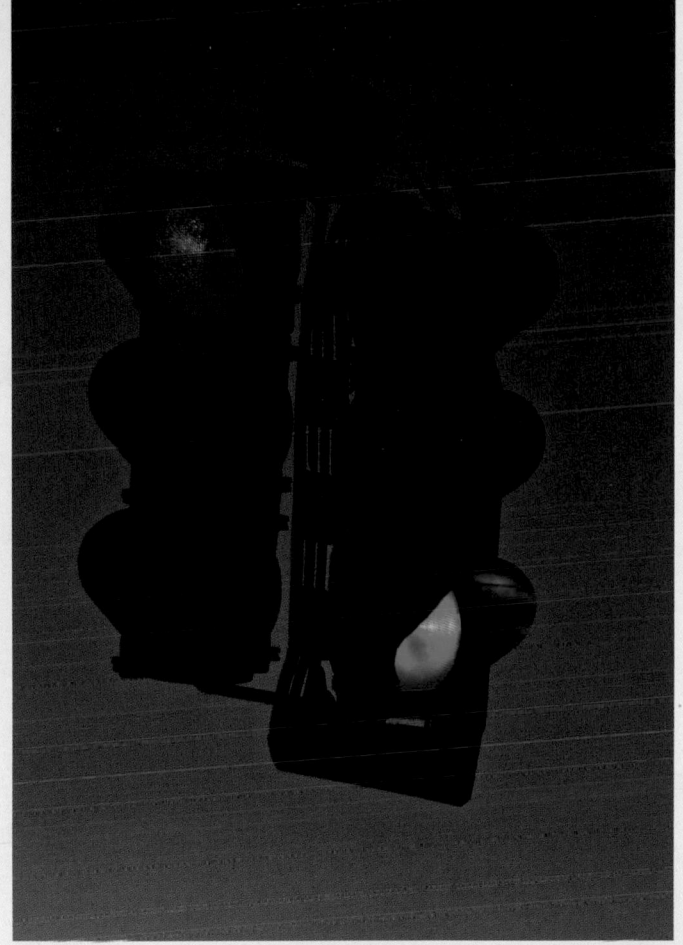

It was one of those early mornings where you find yourself in a new place, not really knowing the lay of the land and challenging yourself to come up with something interesting. On this particular morning, my goal was to find a suitable location from which to shoot the Tampa Bay skyline in the predawn light, but I got sidetracked by a traffic light, of all things. As I was about to cross the street, I was seduced by the contrast between a red light and a green light. I've often felt that much of what I shoot is a "self-portrait" of my inner psychology, and this image is no exception. Just the day before, my eldest daughter and I had a major disagreement and this image surely spoke to that: green says "yes" while red says "no"! A few minutes later, I felt compelled to shoot that same light with both traffic lights aligned. Perhaps this image reflected my wish that my daughter and I could be in total agreement?

Above: Nikon D300S with Nikkor 70–300mm lens, f/11 for 2 seconds, ISO 200; Opposite: Nikon D300S with Nikkor 70–300mm lens, f/11 for 1/2 sec., ISO 200

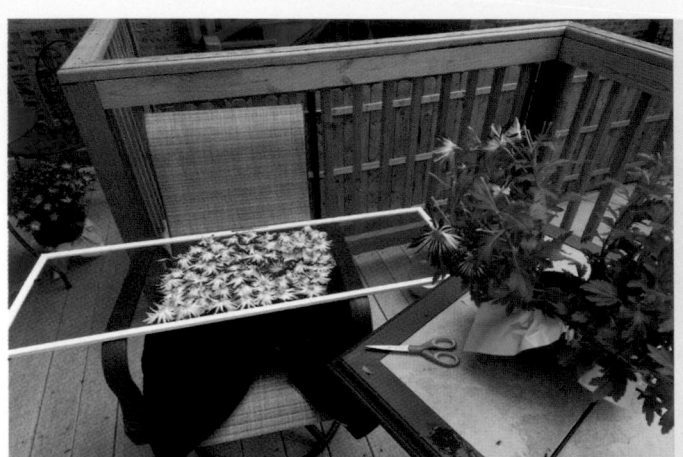

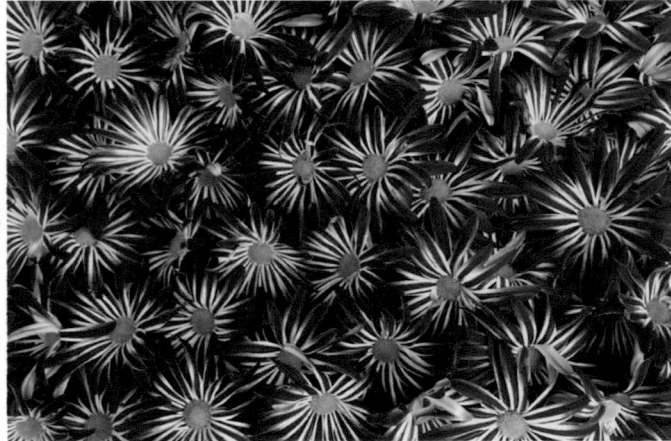

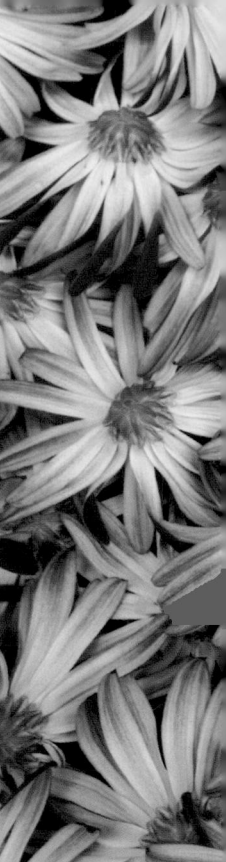

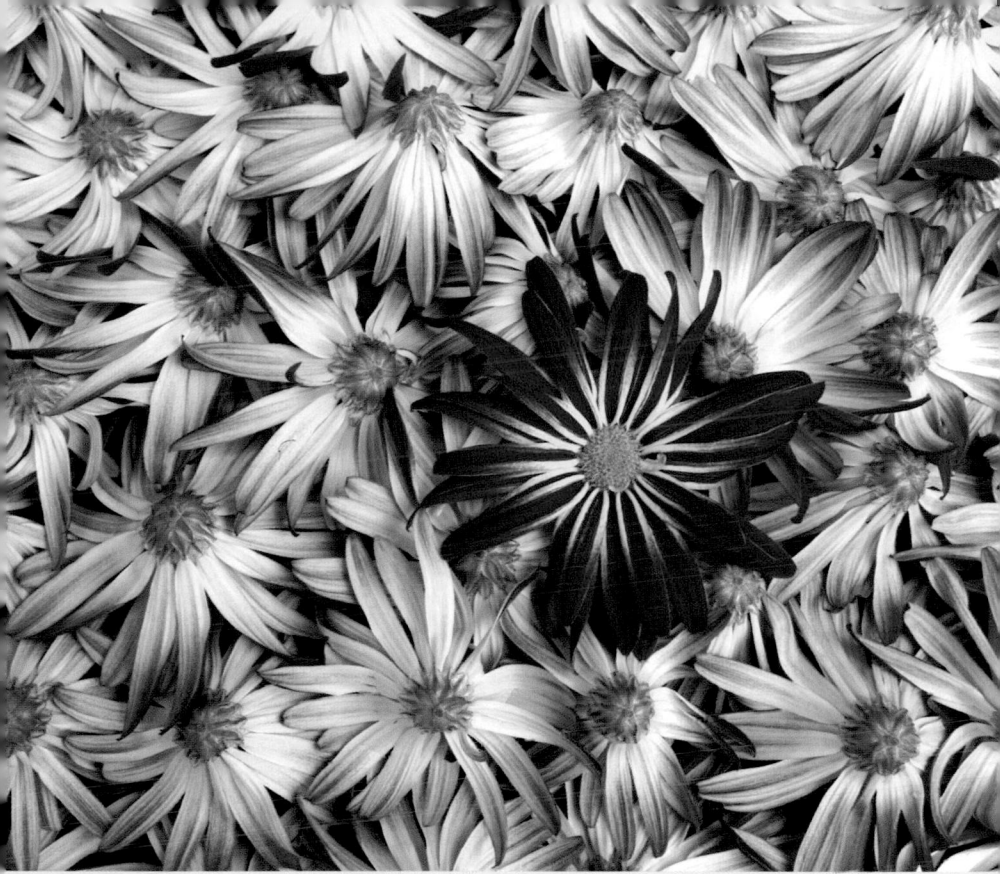

Over the years, February has always been a tough month for me. Perhaps for you, too? If you suffer from seasonal depression, the absence of actual sunshine over the course of three to four weeks can deeply affect your overall energy and mood. Only recently, did I get smart and start booking workshops in sunny locales during those dark winter days. But for years, I suffered through it and often found myself coming home from the grocery store laden with bouquets of flowers. I could pretend that spring was just around the corner, and if nothing else, the mere act of shooting flowers outside my house on many a cloudy day elevated my mood just enough to make the remaining winter tolerable.

Returning home from the grocery store one such day, I made quick work of these chrysanthemums, clipping their heads from the stems and laying them on a piece of window screen. I started by making what I consider one of the most compelling and, surprisingly, one of the easiest arrangements: the mere composing of a pattern, as shown bottom left. When done correctly, the volume of the subject is turned up, the once-single voice of the subject, here a flower, now joined by many others. The key to a successful arrangement of pattern is to fill the frame—edge to edge, top to bottom—so that viewers feel as if the pattern runs beyond the edges of your frame. This illusion of an infinite number is certainly not limited to flowers. Any subject will convey the same message—bottle caps, paper clips, hats, baseballs, shoes, leaves. The key is to fill the frame in its entirety.

Assuming you have done that, you are now ready to create an image of extreme contrast, as shown in the second example above. I simply turned all but one of the flowers over. Recalling our earlier discussion about layering and backgrounds, it should be clear here that we have, in effect, a background of one dominating tone, and a foreground with one lone contrasting shift in color and tone.

Both images: Nikon D300S with Nikon 24–85mm lens at 85mm, f/16 for 1/30 sec., ISO 200

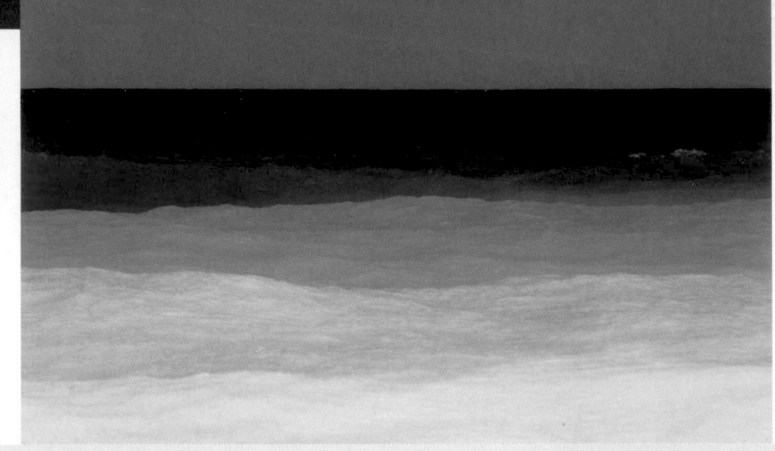

Just like the migratory birds that fly north or south depending on the time of year, I, too, have my annual migration that finds me flying south to Cancún every August. August is a great time to go, when both the crowds and the prices are low. Over the course of one August getaway, the Caribbean put on a particularly stunning show of color. As shown in the first image (above), the various tones and shades of blue were quite distinct from foreground to background. It wasn't until 30 minutes or so later, however, that I spotted a large sailboat coming in from the right, as shown in the second image (right). The contrast created by this white sailboat is another example of an extreme shift in contrast. And just as with the "lone" flower in the previous pair of images, this lone sailboat is key to creating a more compelling composition.

Both images: Nikon D300S with Nikkor 70–300mm lens at 300mm, f/22 for 1/100 sec., ISO 200

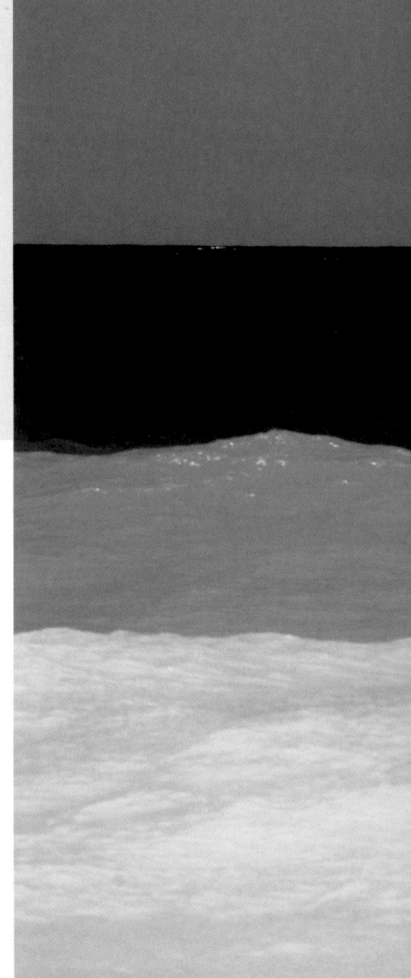

139   CREATING CONTRAST

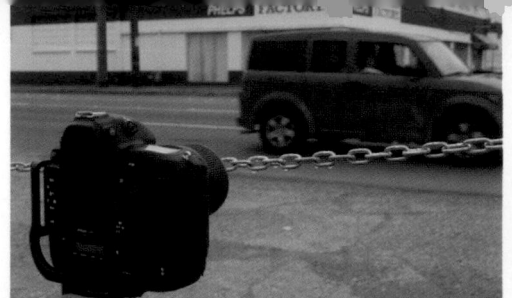

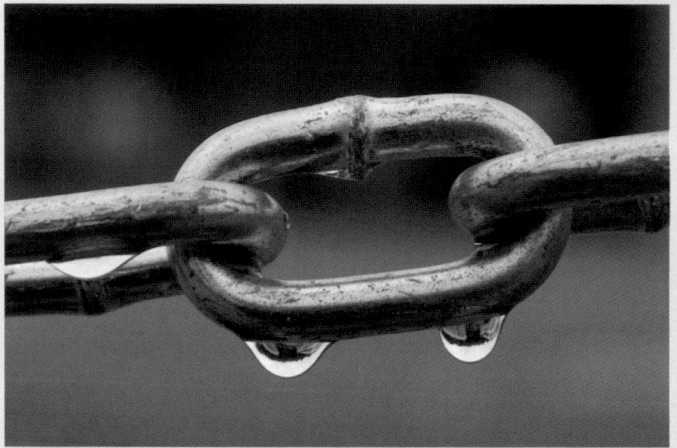

I am convinced that anyone who lives in the Pacific Northwest and chooses to make a career as a photographer will have an advantage over photographers from less "hostile" environments. When you live anywhere near the I-5 corridor, from the Canadian border to as far south as Eugene, Oregon, there is an almost daily grind of waiting for light. During that constant wait, one of three things will eventually happen: you will give in to the frustration and find another hobby, you will move to a sunnier climate, or you will learn to be inventive and creative and to work quickly with whatever light you have. As one who grew up in the Pacific Northwest, I have had many a frustrating day of "no light."

But, in large part, these days of "no light" also brought many an idea to the surface that may have otherwise gone unnoticed. As we all stood around an empty parking lot of an abandoned warehouse a bit south of Safeco Field, I suggested to the students that we shoot a "spiderweb with dewdrops" against a background of out-of-focus color. Soon we were all hanging out in front of a large length of chain, each claiming a few links. After spraying the links with water, we waited for the right car to pass in the background. We were all quick to notice that the abundance of white, gray, and black cars passing by offered little contrast, so when red, deep-blue, and lime-green cars passed, shouts of joy were heard from everyone!

In this first image (above), with the absence of any contrast, the links appear soft-spoken, passive, and quiet. But when photographed against a background of red (opposite), they come alive, thanks to the contrast in the background. Playing the role of background layer, the red contrast is vitally important to the success of this image.

Both images: Nikon D3X with Micro-Nikkor 105mm lens, f/11 for 1/125 sec., ISO 100

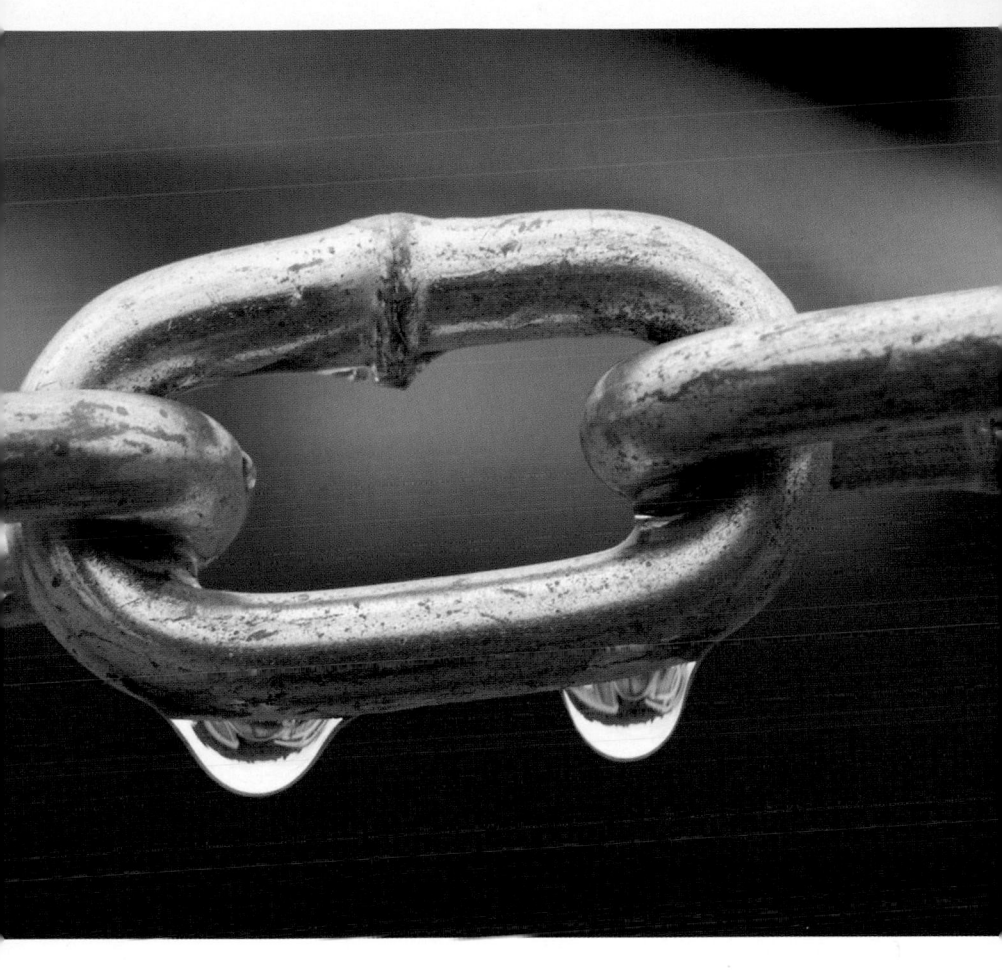

GOING TO EXTREMES

Perhaps you are familiar with the phrase *going to extremes*. It is often used to describe intense behavior that veers outside the norm. But going to extremes is also a way of creating compositions that are both surprising and dramatic by letting color or tone dominate. When that color or tone consists of mostly white, it is referred to as *high-key contrast*; when it is mostly black, it is referred to as *low-key contrast*. The use of a dominant color or tone is a great way to exaggerate the main subject, which is often quite small in the overall composition.

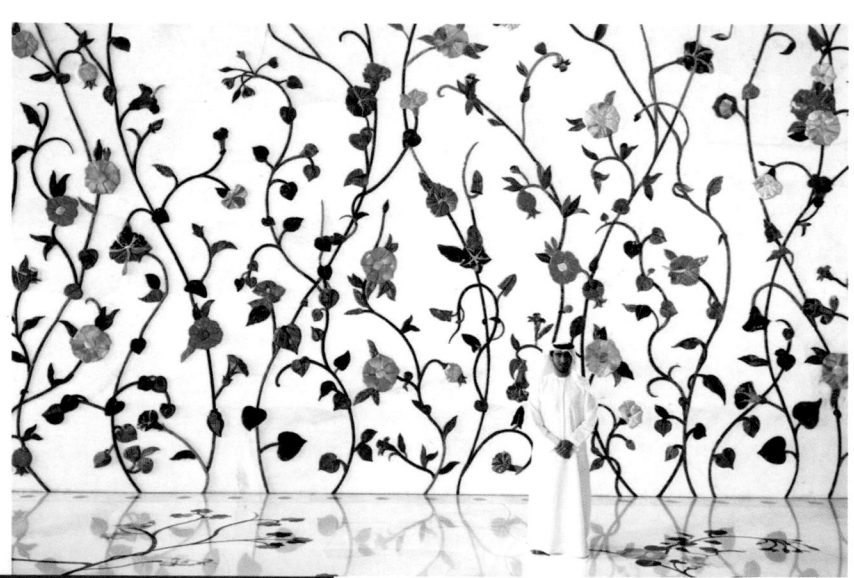

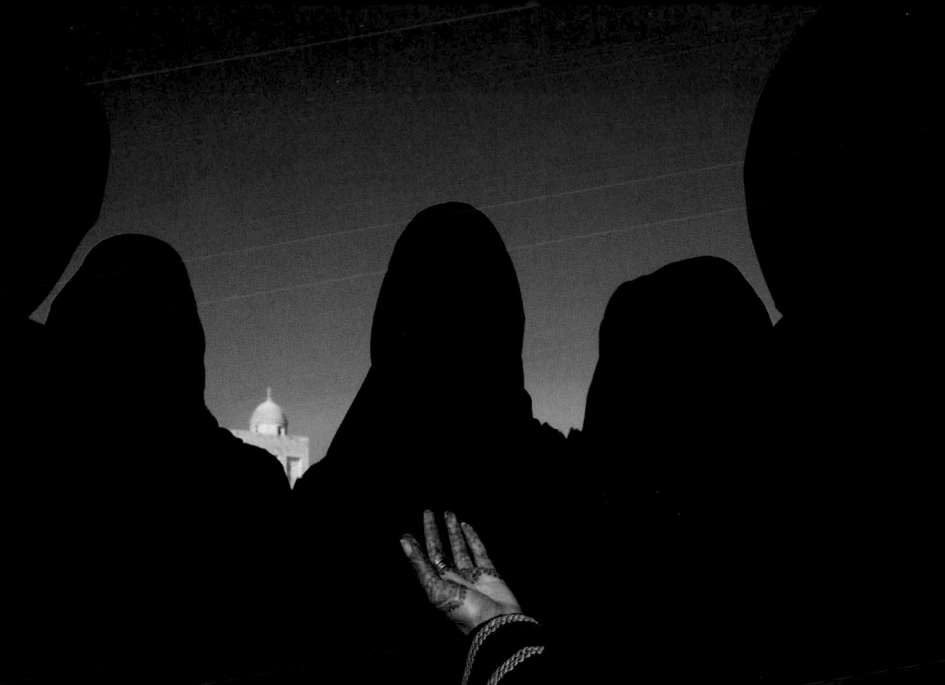

Above: The low contrast of a frame filled with mostly black has been shot many times in the past by studio and location photographers worldwide. In the black of night or a darkened room, and with flashlight in hand, you can create sudden surprise or shock by shining the lone beam of light on something that was once lost. On a recent trip to Doha, Qatar, I was following a group of female students as we walked toward a mosque. One of the women was being quite animated with her hands as she spoke, and it was then that I saw all the black surrounding her hand. I asked the women to simply stand facing the mosque and I asked the woman on the right to raise her left hand, palm up. After setting my exposure off the blue sky, I fired off about a dozen frames, changing my composition slightly each time. All the black from the women's burkas creates, of course, a "darkened room," allowing the lone henna-painted hand to look as though it were being lit by a flashlight, when in fact it is only being lit by the sun overhead. The small hand is the "surprise," and against all this extreme contrast, it gets the greatest attention.

Nikon D3X with Nikkor 16–35mm lens at 16mm, f/16 for 1/125 sec., ISO 100

Opposite: Like most things that leave a lasting impression, the Sheikh Zayed Mosque in Abu Dhabi, UAE, will be forever remembered not so much for its massive size and truly beautiful architecture but for the single image shown here. It is another image of low contrast with a small and important surprise. At first glance you may see only the wall of ceramic flowers, but soon you see the "surprise"—my friend Mohammed, one of several tour guides at the mosque. If not for the tone of his face, we might not see him at all. Are you by chance finding yourself now thinking about a host of ideas for low-contrast compositions? The possibilities are truly endless!

Nikon D3X with Nikkor 16–35mm lens at 16mm, f/8 for 1/80 sec., ISO 100

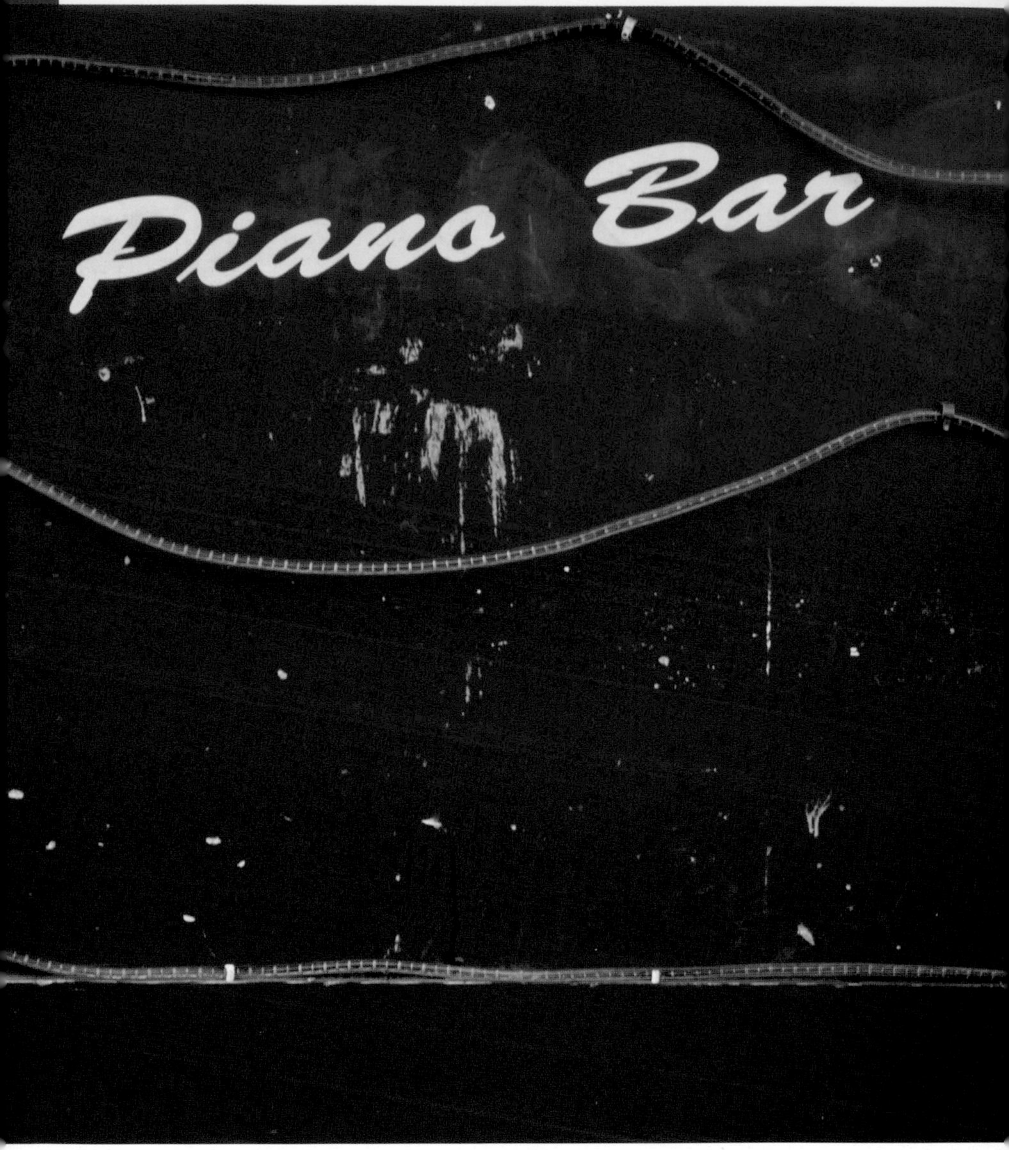
Piano Bar

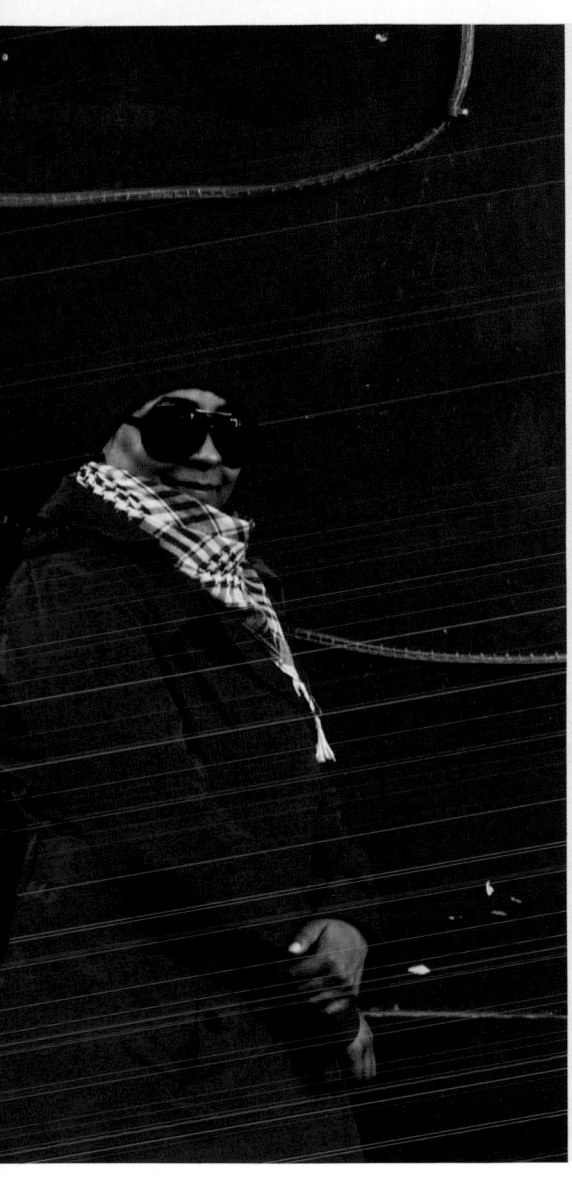

At the beginning of this chapter, I asked if it made sense to write with a black ink pen on a black piece of paper, and of course, most of us would agree that this made no sense unless we were trying to hide our words. Sometimes it can actually be fun to "hide" some of our words, and with this hiding of words, our images can take on new meaning. Images with little contrast are called *low key*, by the way, yet ironically, some low-key images are extremely surprising!

On a recent workshop in Paris, my students and I were shooting near the Basilique du Sacré Coeur de Montmartre when I asked one of them to pose against a nearby red wall. The result is a low-key composition that offers up the small surprises of a piano bar, a scarf, two hands, and a face covered in sunglasses.

Nikon D3X with Nikkor 24–85mm lens at 70mm, f/11 for 1/100 sec., ISO 100

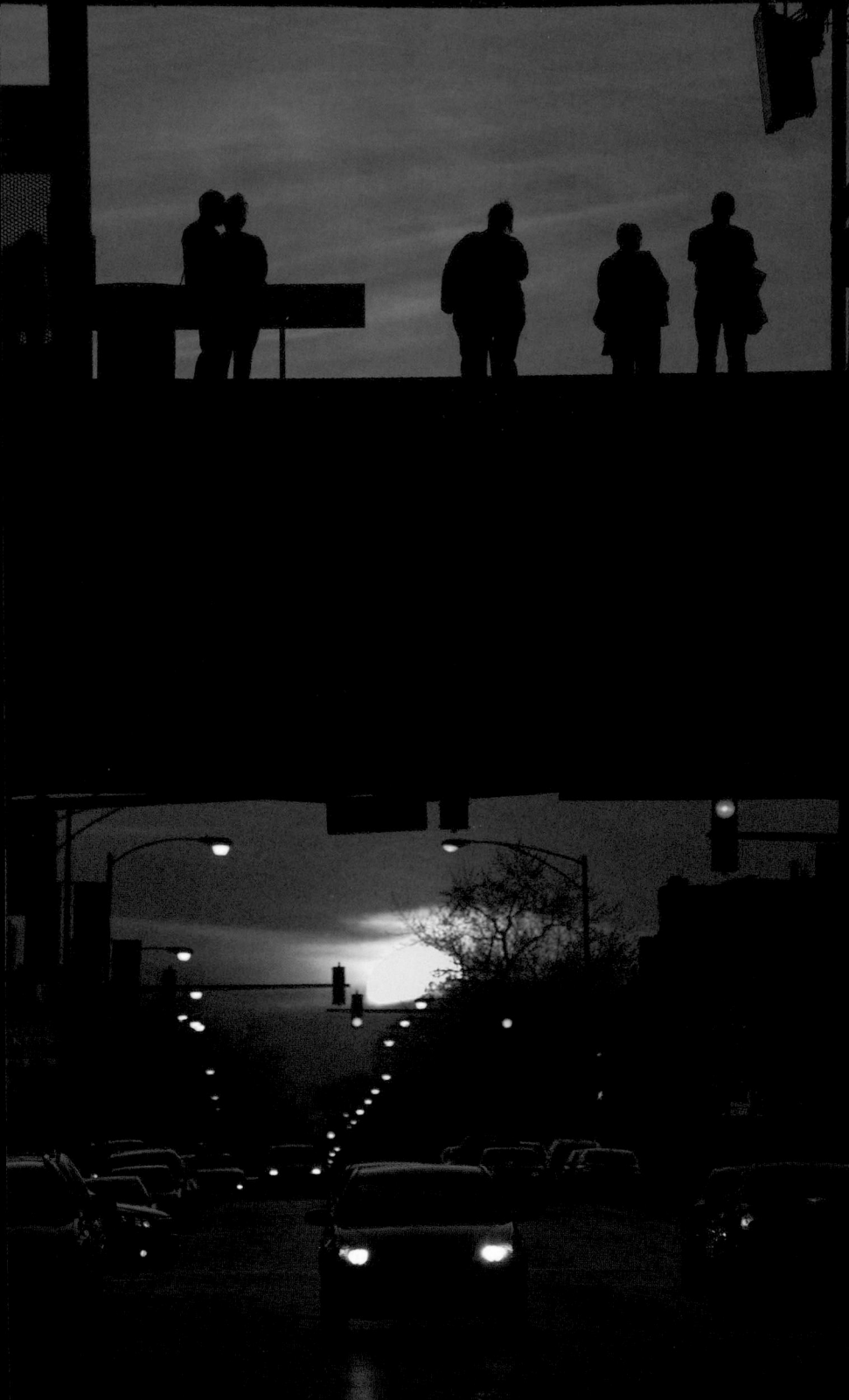

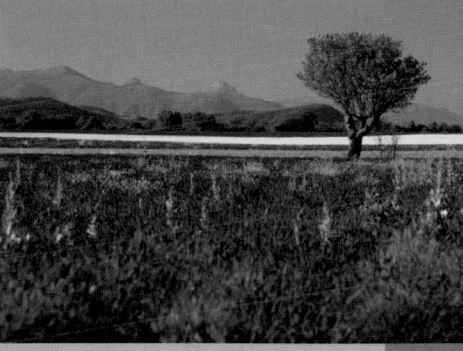

8

THE GOLDEN SECTION, THE RULE OF THIRDS, AND THE RULE OF VISUAL WEIGHT

Since a compelling photograph is usually about an effective arrangement rather than about the content, are there "rules," or guidelines, for creating the most effective and engaging composition? Interestingly enough, there are. I call them the *rules of engagement*, and we'll cover two of the biggest in this chapter: the first is what the Greeks called the *Golden Section*, which, as many photographers will suggest, was later identified in many photographic tutorials as the *Rule of Thirds*; the second is about using line to define *visual weight* in your image.

Nikon D3X with Nikkor 70-300mm lens, f/16 for 1/250 sec., ISO 100

THE GOLDEN SECTION

The *Golden Section* refers to an arrangement of two lines that was found to be the most pleasing to the eye. The ratio of these lines is approximately 8 to 5. This means, for example, that an 8-inch line next to a 5-inch line looks more pleasing than an 8-inch line next to a 4-inch line. Interestingly, the fraction $5/8 = .63$, and $8/5 = 1:63$. If we expand the Golden Section into a rectangle 8 inches long by 5 inches high, we end up with what is known as the Golden Rectangle.

Although there is ample evidence that the Golden Section was used by the Egyptians—for example, in the building of the pyramids—it wasn't identified until ancient Greek mathematicians began studying the paintings of their fellow artists and they recognized a pattern. Certain objects in a scene were often two-thirds as large as others: Landscapes often placed the horizon line with two-thirds of the landscape below and one-third sky above (or vice versa), and in still lifes, artists seemed to favor compositions in which two-thirds of the frame was filled with the round shapes of fruit and the remaining third with the round shape of the bowl. These artists and architects had a "natural eye,"

an innate sense about how to create compelling and effective compositions. Thanks to the Greek mathematicians, especially Pythagoras, this compositional arrangement became known as the Golden Section, a rule stating that when any object or shape had two distinct parts, the smaller part should be two-thirds the size of the larger part.

The Golden Section was soon applied with vigor to numerous buildings in Athens, most notably the Parthenon. And ever since, just about anything that has been successfully designed, engineered, and constructed has utilized the Golden Section. The CN Tower in Toronto, for example, which is the second-tallest tower in the world, is exactly 553.33 meters tall and the observation deck is located two-thirds of the way up, at 342 meters. Perhaps not surprisingly, Leonardo da Vinci applied the Golden Section to the *Mona Lisa* with precision! And I would be remiss if I didn't mention the Fibonacci numbers.

Fibonacci was an Italian mathematician famous for his calculations predicting how many rabbits would result—and how quickly—from two rabbits breeding under ideal circumstances. I will spare you the details, but a series of numbers arose from his calculations: 1, 2, 3, 5, 8, 13, 21, 34, 55, 89, 144, 233, 377, 610, and so on. Do you notice the pattern in this series of numbers? Beginning with 3, each number that follows is a combination of the two numbers before it. For example, 3 (1 + 2), 5 (2 + 3), 8 (3 + 5), and so on. Fibonacci's numbers have a direct correlation to the Golden Section. Look at what happens when you divide each of Fibonacci's numbers by the number before it: 1/1 = 1, 2/1 = 2, 3/2 = 1.5, 5/3 = 1.666, 8/5 = 1.6, 13/8 = 1.625, 21/13 = 1.61, and so on, most resulting in a variant of 1.6. Is this merely a coincidence? I hardly think so, and you might agree with me in light of what you are about to read next.

What is perhaps most interesting about the Golden Section is that nature abounds in it. Every living and breathing thing in Mother Nature's closet, from flowers and ferns to the smallest microbe, is evidence of the Golden Section. Lilies and irises each have three petals; buttercups, columbines, and pinks have five petals; delphiniums have eight, some daisies and corn marigolds have thirteen, asters and black-eyed Susans have twenty-one, and Michaelmas daisies have fifty-five petals—all Fibonacci numbers. Not surprisingly, a poppy seed head has thirteen ridges and the common sunflower has eighty-nine spirals—all Fibonacci numbers again! Pythagoras may have been the first to realize that even the human skeleton was based on the Golden Section; my upper arm bone is roughly two-thirds the length of my lower arm bone.

Entire books have been written about the Golden Section, and discussing it in more detail is beyond the scope of this book, but it is vitally important that I state *emphatically* that the use of the Golden Section in your compositions will more often than not lead to far more engaging and compelling photographs. The sooner you embrace it, the sooner you will start hearing compliments from complete strangers about your photographs.

Think of the Golden Section as a Golden Rectangle, with the two shorter sides roughly two-thirds as long as the two longer sides. Not surprisingly, 35mm cameras and the sensors of most DSLRs approximate the dimensions and shape of this Golden Rectangle (the "rectangle" of your camera's viewfinder and sensor is 3:2). The more common 3/2 figure is what has been used in 35mm photography, but both the 8/5 of the Golden Rectangle and the 3/2 of the 35mm frame are Fibonacci numbers; 8/5 expressed as 1:63 and 3/2 as 1:67.

THE RULE OF THIRDS

Now let's fast-forward to only a few hundred years ago and we discover perhaps the first evidence of the term *Rule of Thirds*. In his book *Remarks on Rural Scenery*, written in 1797, John Thomas Smith wrote,

Analagous to this "Rule of Thirds" (if I may be allowed so to call it) I have presumed to think that, in connecting or in breaking the various lines of a picture, it would likewise be a good rule to do it, in general, by a similar scheme of proportion; for example, in a design of landscape, to determine the sky at about two-thirds; or else at about one-third, so that the material objects might occupy the other two: Again, two thirds of one element (as of water) to one third of another element (as of land); and them both together to make but one third of the picture, of which the other two-thirds should go for the sky and aerial perspectives. . . . In short, in applying this invention, generally speaking, to any other case, whether of light, shade, form or color, I have found the ratio of about two-thirds to one third . . . a much better and more harmonizing proportion, than the precise formal half. . . .

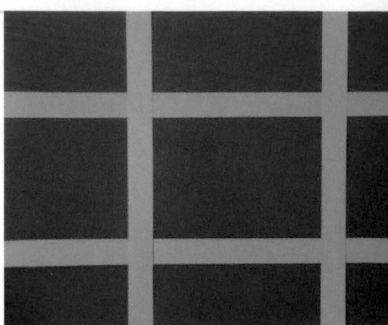

This diagram shows the Rule of Thirds as defined by John Thomas Smith in 1787. Note that there are four horizontal lines (including the top and bottom of the rectangle) and four vertical lines (again including the outer sides of the rectangle). Last I checked, 4 + 4 = 8, and 8 just so happens to be a Fibonacci number.

So there we have it; possibly the first use of the term *Rule of Thirds*, though it had in fact already been in use for thousands of years as the *Golden Section*.

Applying Mr. Smith's Rule of Thirds (see diagram) to the 35mm frame is becoming more and more common-place with camera design. Only recently are we finding DSLRs with grids built into the viewing screens, something many of us have been advocating for years. On some models the grid is an option that you turn on inside your menu; on others, it shows up on your monitor when you use Live View.

Although some may disagree, I believe we *must* be bound by the Rule of Thirds—though if the word *bound* makes you uncomfortable, feel free

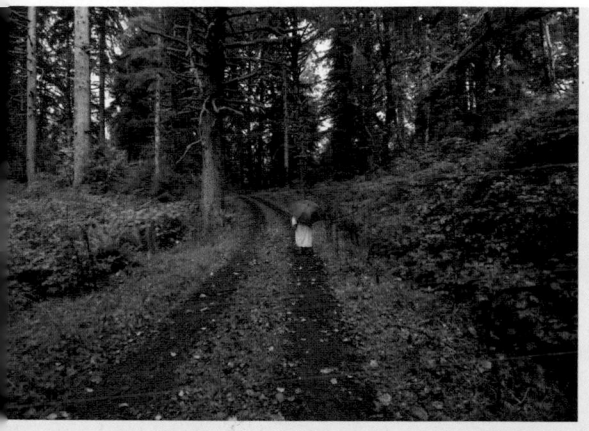

In the first photograph (left), the subject is too centered, and with the all-important horizon line in the middle, we are not sure whether the trees or road are the "winning" subject of the image. In the second image (below), the winner is clear: not the converging parallels of the road but rather the tall trees. By tilting the camera up, I was able to bring the horizon line down to the lower third and place the visual weight on the trees. The soaring trees now call even greater attention to the "smallness of man."

Both images: Nikon D3X with Nikkor 16-35mm lens, f/16 for 15 seconds, ISO 100

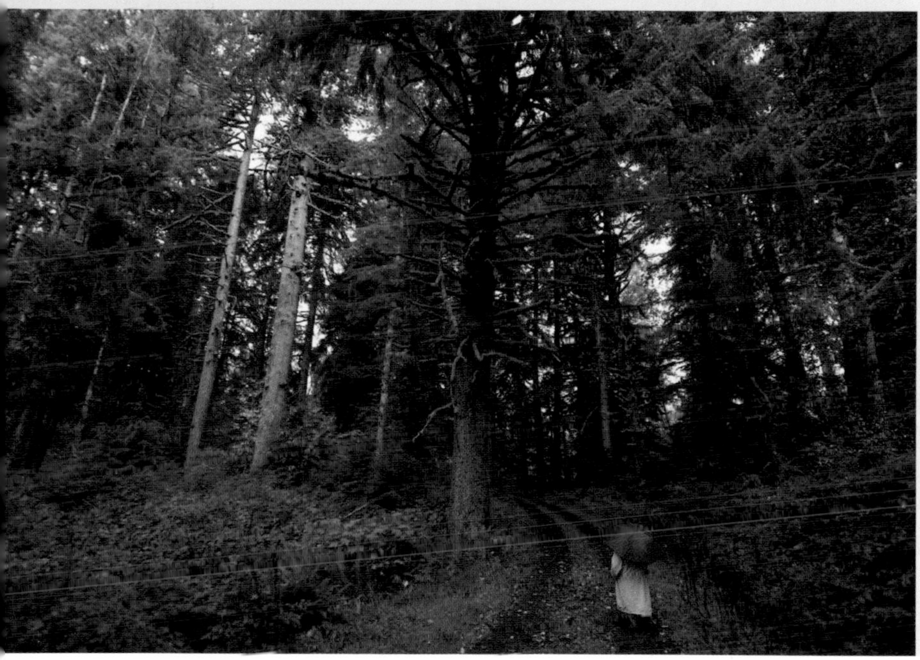

to refer to it as the "Suggestion" of Thirds. At its core, the Rule of Thirds can serve you well and should serve as the foundation of every image, much as a firm and solid foundation should be the basis of every house or skyscraper. That said, if you are not clear about what you wish to say in your photograph, then the Rule of Thirds won't make it any clearer. And unless you have a thorough understanding of the language of line, you will never fully understand why some arrangements fall short.

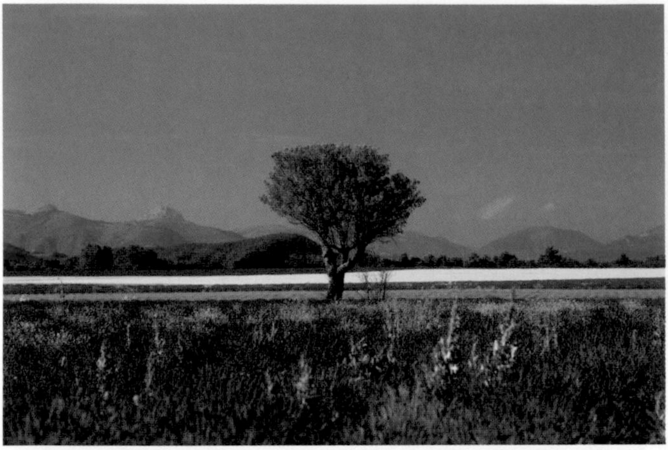

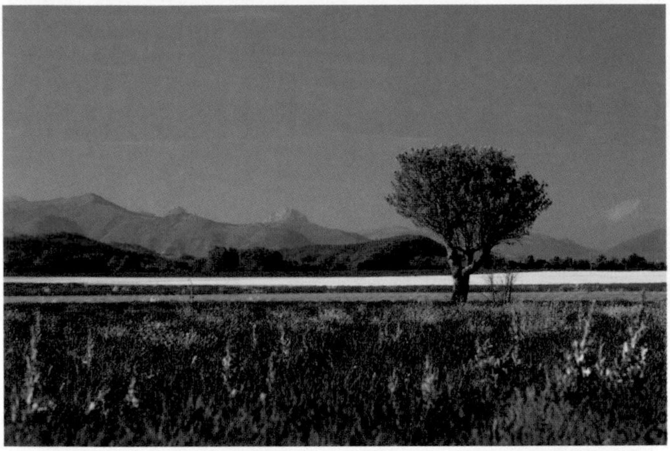

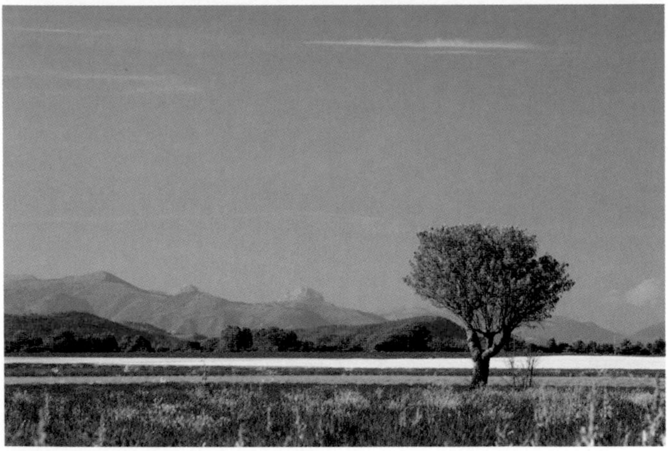

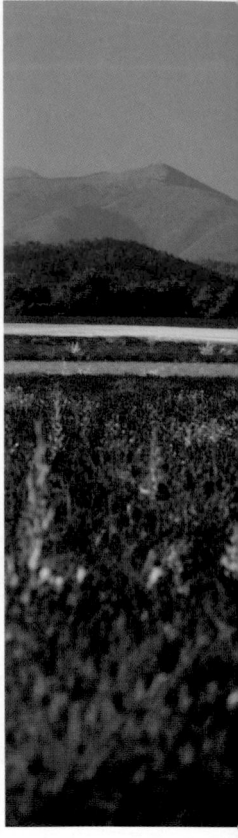

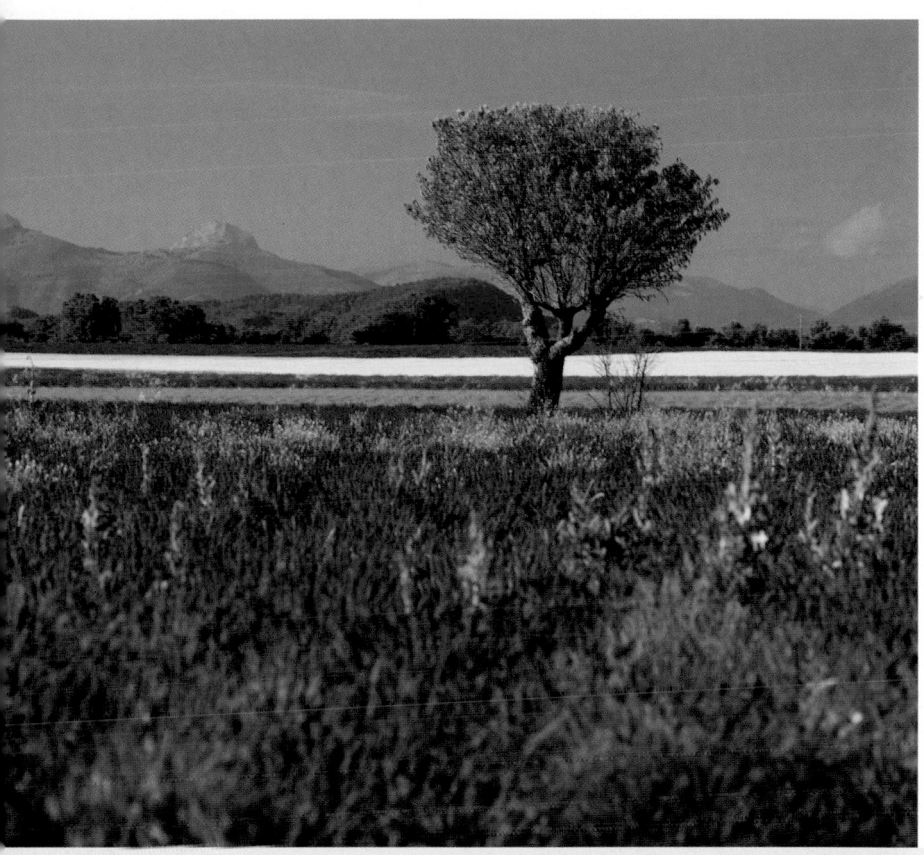

As I drove down one of the many back roads in the Valensole Plain of Provence, I caught sight of a lone tree in the distance. The first image I shot (opposite, top) may look familiar to some of you, as it depicts what I often see from students in our beginner classes. The horizon line runs through the middle of the frame, and the subject, the tree, is smack dab in the middle of the frame—and why not? This is where you focus, after all, right? (More about this focus issue in a minute!)

But as we can see in the next image (opposite center), it now "feels" better with the tree in the right third of the frame. And as we see in the next two images (opposite bottom and above), it feels even better still when we place the tree on the right and the horizon line in the upper or lower third of the frame. Why? Because you are now catering to your "inner eye," the eye that instinctively knows about the Golden Section and only needs to be awakened to it.

With regard to the focus issue, I have heard many times that the reason we place a subject in the middle of the frame is that it's where the focusing takes place. Not true! You can set autofocus points on your camera left, right, above, or below. You can also focus on your subject, engage the focus lock, and then recompose the image so the subject is no longer centered. Even better, you can turn off autofocus and focus manually!

All images: Nikon D3X with 70–300mm lens at 200mm, f/32 for 1/60 sec., ISO 200

THE GOLDEN SECTION,
THE RULE OF THIRDS, AND
THE RULE OF VISUAL WEIGHT

AWAKENING YOUR EYE TO THE RULE OF THIRDS

One of the easiest exercises I know, and one that will certainly wake up your eye to see the Rule of Thirds, involves the use of blue-, red-, green-, and yellow-colored construction paper. Start with a sheet of blue paper and fill up your frame with the blue. Feel free to crank up the ISO and shoot handheld near a window, or do this outside, weather permitting.

Now take the green paper and cut out four strips, each 1/2-inch wide and 11 inches long. Place just one of those strips so it runs through the middle of the red paper and take a shot. Now take a second strip and place one across the top third of the paper and the other across the bottom third. Take another shot. Finally, leaving those two strips in place, get two more strips and place them vertically along the right third and left third (as if you were creating a tic-tac-toe board). Take a fourth shot. You just photographed the Suggestion of Thirds grid.

Now get the yellow paper and cut out a circle roughly 2 inches in diameter. Place the circle on one of the points where your vertical and horizontal lines cross and take a picture. Repeat for each point where the lines cross. For your final image, remove the strips and place just one green strip so it runs through the middle of the frame. Then place the yellow circle right in the middle so it sits atop the strip and take that shot. Now show your family or a friend the eight shots you just took and ask which arrangements are the *least* appealing. The odds are good that they will not like the first and last images. This has much to do with our innate sense of order and tension. In the first and last shots, you have *only* order: an even 50/50 division of the paper.

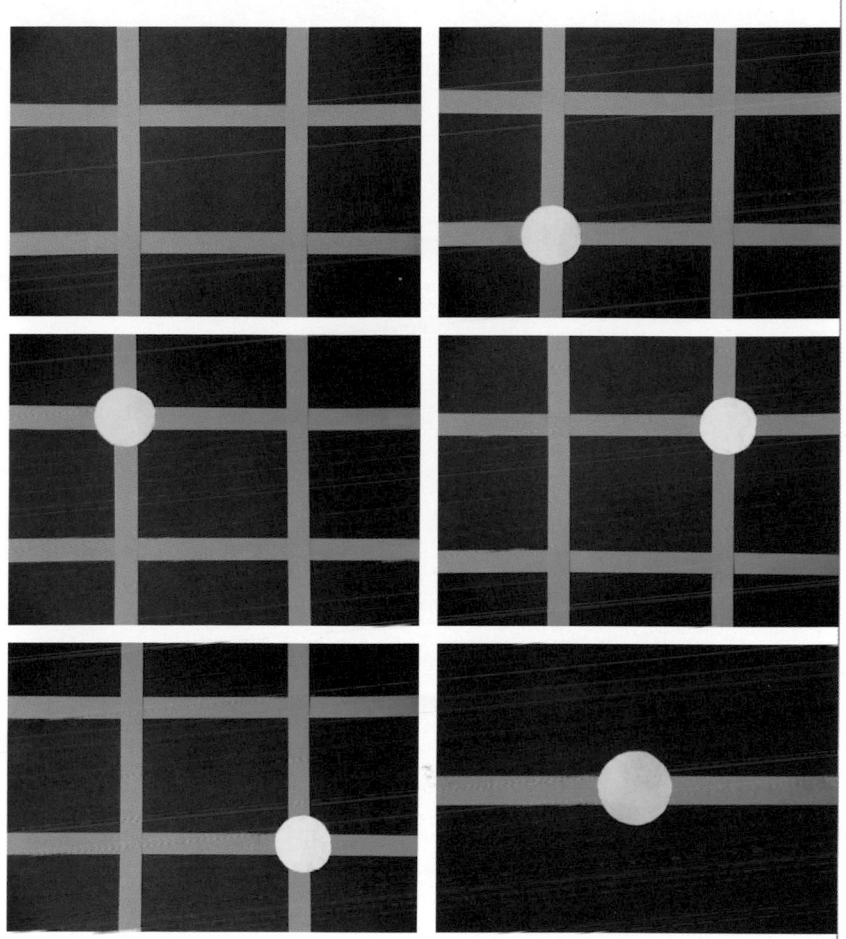

THE GOLDEN SECTION,
THE RULE OF THIRDS, AND
THE RULE OF VISUAL WEIGHT

155

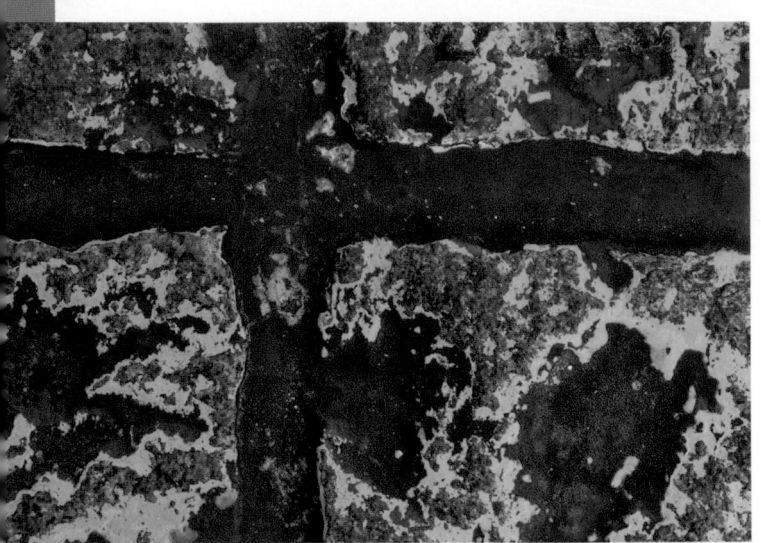

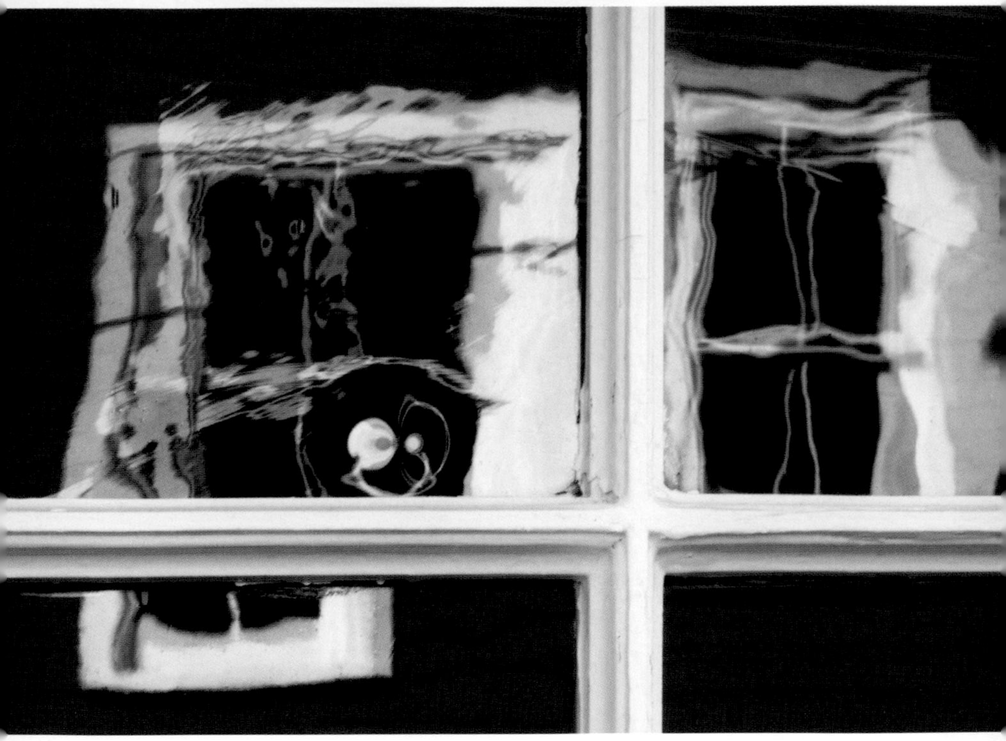

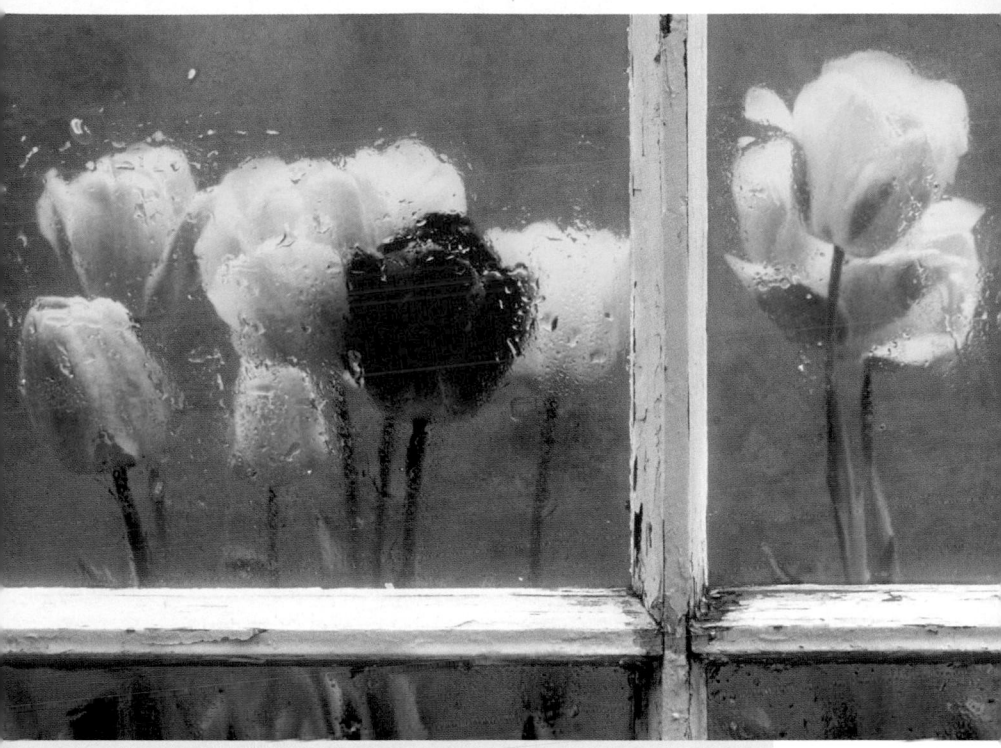

Did you enjoy the exercise with the colored construction paper? I hope so, because now it's time to head outside and spend a day looking for grids. You will find plenty of grids in brick walkways and walls, as well as in the windows of older homes and barns. You goal is to find interesting examples of the Suggestion of Thirds, even if the subject limits itself to textures and colors. Here are three examples to show you what I mean. The first (opposite top) was shot outside my hotel in Singapore. The second image (opposite bottom) shows a really old red building I came across in the town of Lunenburg, Nova Scotia. I was quick to spot the reflection in the old float glass but also made sure to incorporate the grid of the window frame. Lastly, I shot the third image (above) years ago on my farm in Oregon. It was my first grid image of a barn window, with several large pots of tulips I had placed in the background. After lightly spraying the glass with water, I got the textured look I wanted and shot a number of frames with my Nikkor 35–70mm lens.

Opposite top: Nikon D3X with Micro-Nikkor 105mm lens, f/11 for 1/200 sec., ISO 200; Opposite bottom: Nikon D3X with Nikkor 70–300mm lens at 180mm, f/11 for 1/60 sec., ISO 100; Above: Nikon F-3 with Nikkor 35–70mm lens at 70mm, f/8 for 1/60 sec., Kodachrome ISO 64 film

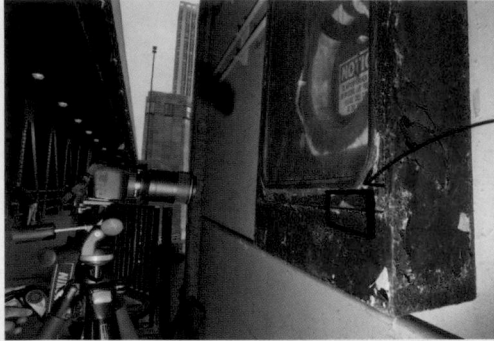

Late one afternoon in downtown Chicago, my students and I came upon a battered and bruised fire-hose box. With my camera and lens mounted on tripod, and with the aid of my SB-900 flash, I set up this "mountainous landscape" of red. Note the "horizon line" placement near the bottom third, as well as the fact that there are three distinct sections of red in this composition. Some might argue that the mountain is dead-centered, and I would agree. But this "mountain" is not a single, static line; rather, it comprises three lines that form a triangle whose very design suggests movement: "up" one side and "down" the other. This suggested movement avoids any static feeling normally associated with centering an object.

Micro-Nikkor 105mm lens, f/16 for 1/250 sec., SB-900 flash off camera, ISO 200

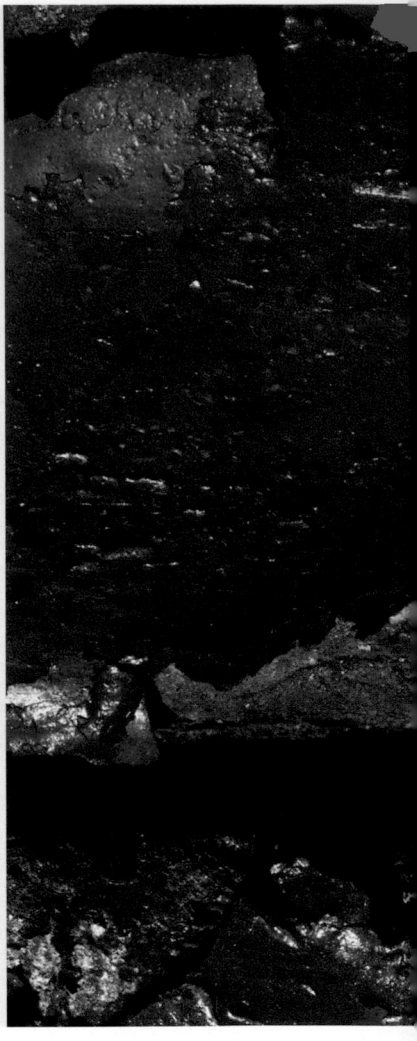

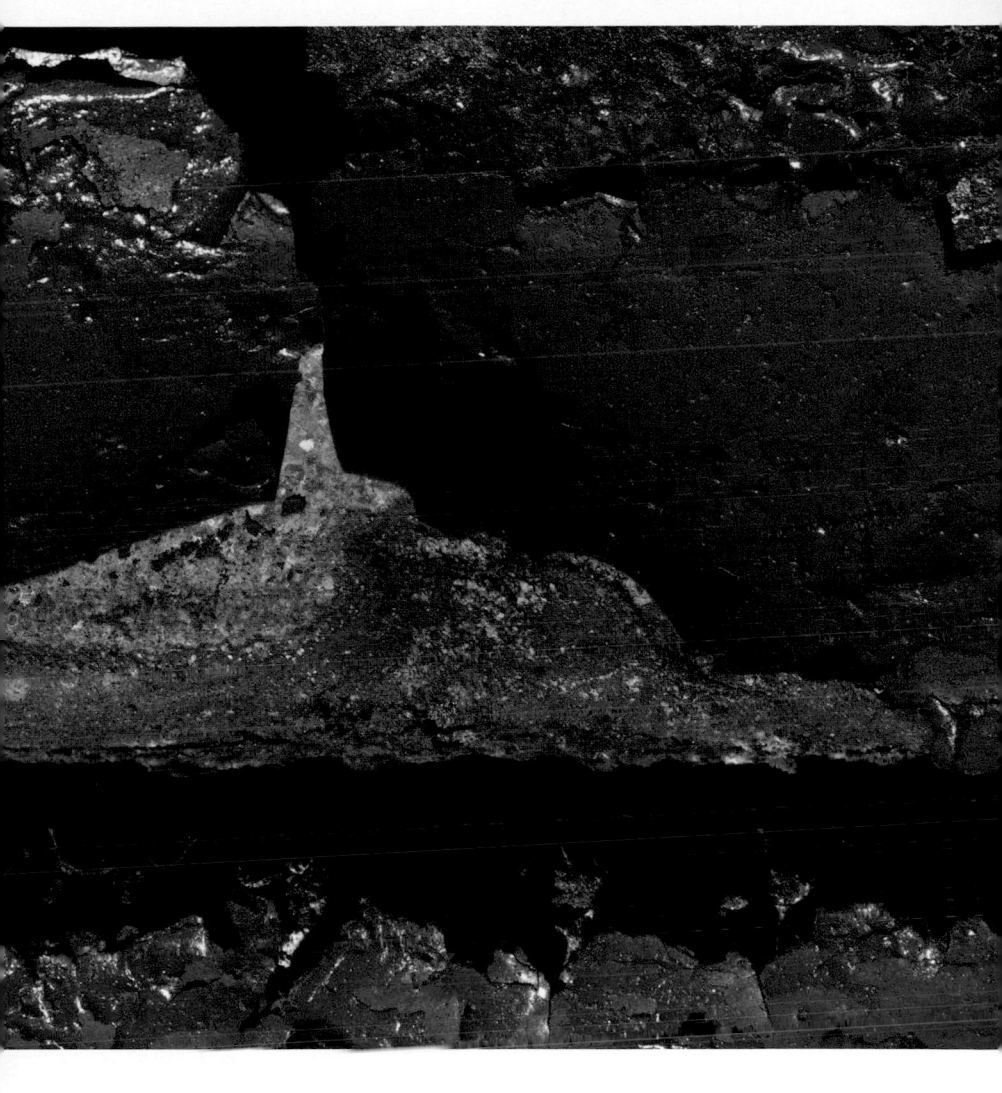

THE GOLDEN SECTION,
THE RULE OF THIRDS, AND
THE RULE OF VISUAL WEIGHT

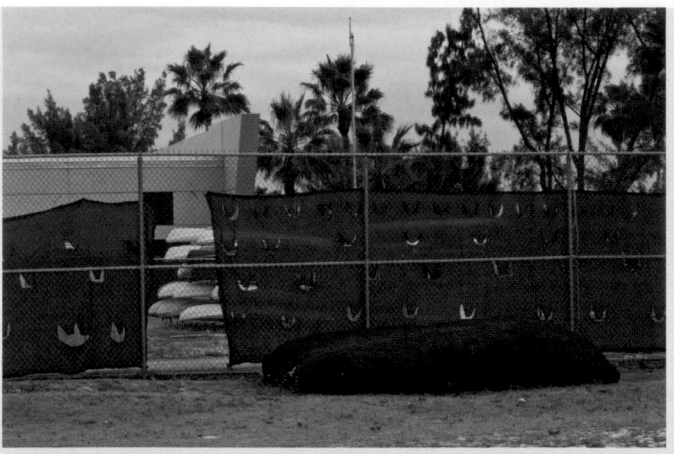

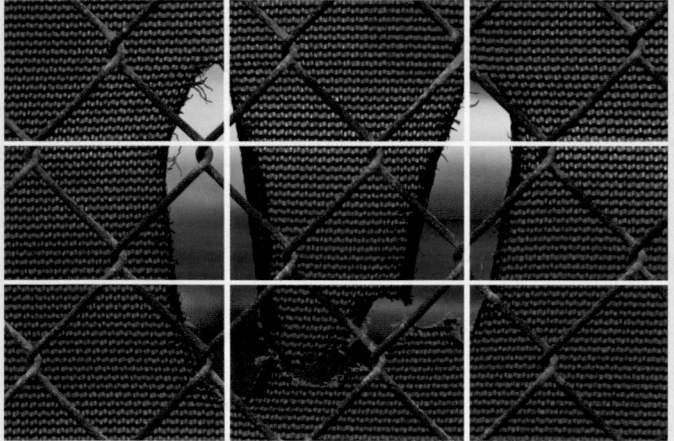

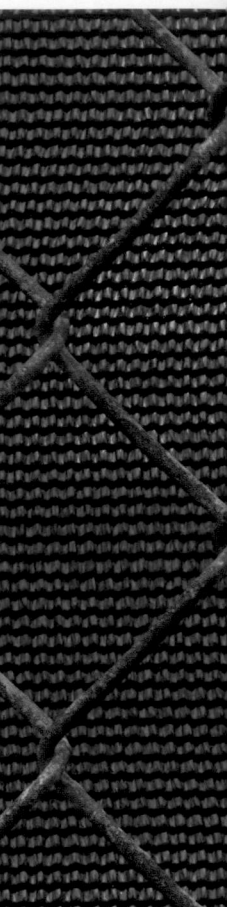

It's hard to imagine that a storage yard for kayaks would lead to compelling compositions, but there was much "gold" to be mined here. As you can see, behind this tall, cloth-covered fence was a plethora of line and color. Reduced to its simplest elements—line, texture, and color—this image is composed of three layers: the top layer is composed of rusty lines, the second layer of green textures and a torn shape brought to life by the third layer, an out-of-focus background of vivid color. As one who always likes to put an image to the test, look at this same image with a grid placed it over it. The Rule of Thirds, aka the Golden Section, is alive and well here, too!

Nikon D2X with Nikkor 70–200mm lens at 200mm, f/9 for 1/60 sec., ISO 200

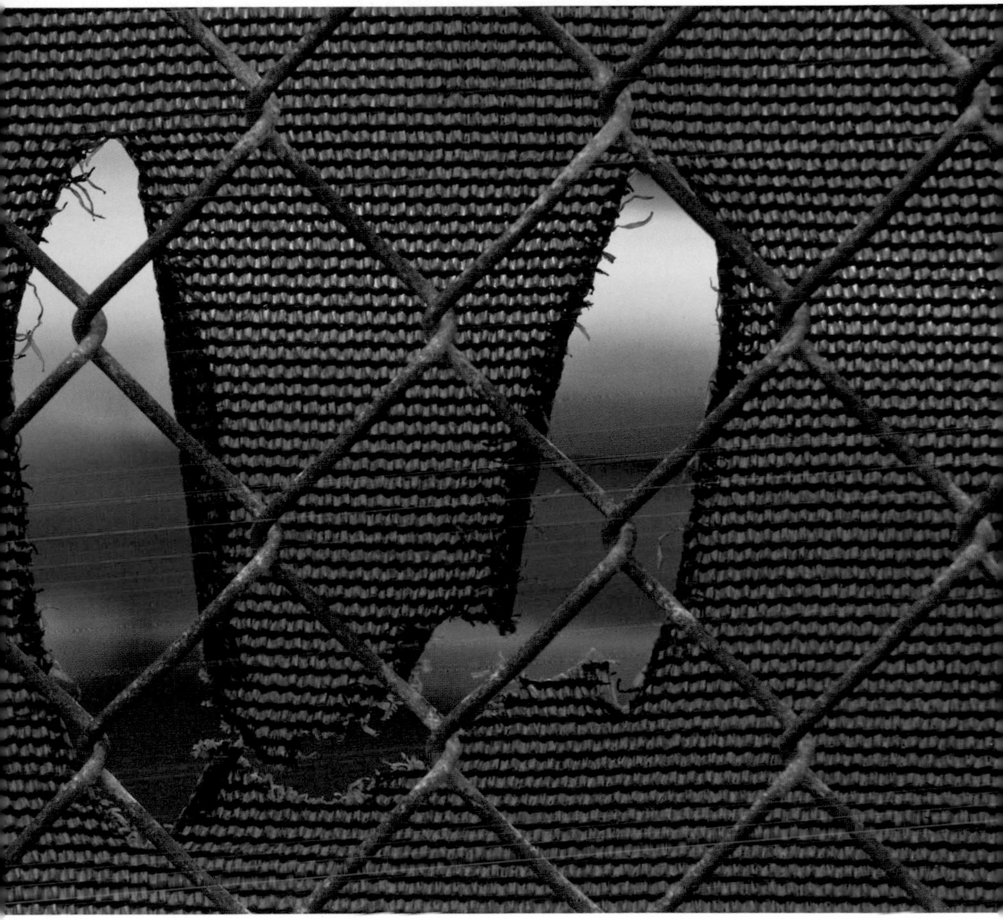

THE GOLDEN SECTION,
THE RULE OF THIRDS, AND
THE RULE OF VISUAL WEIGHT

THE RULE OF VISUAL WEIGHT

In general, the Rule of Thirds asks that you make a decision about visual weight. Every photograph is composed of *visual weight*, or the dominating theme in your overall composition. And it is up to you, the photographer, to control the placement of that visual weight. You do this by making decisions, including where to place the horizon line (near the top or the bottom of the frame), and by your use of selective focus (what is in focus and what is not), suggested motion (frozen action or implied motion), contrast (light tones are perceived as lighter in weight than their darker-toned counterparts), and color (reds, oranges, and yellows are advancing colors, while blues, greens, and purples recede).

If you like shooting landscapes or cityscapes, the rule of visual weight dictates that something in the landscape—either the sky or the land—needs be declared the "winner." If interest is greatest *below* the horizon line, then you should "push" the line near the top third of the frame. If interest is greatest *above* the horizon line, then it's best to push the horizon line down near the bottom third.

What drives this high or low decision? Your message, what you wish to say, and the subject itself. Generally speaking, if you have an incredible sky, a rainbow, or a dark and foreboding sky, then chances are good that you would be better off placing the horizon line low and emphasizing the sky. (As a sidenote, most sky-filled compositions call on the wide-angle lens for its far-reaching angle and ability to diminish the size of subjects in the landscape below.)

It may sound odd, but if you listen closely, you can hear the language of the landscape right in front of you. The reason you are standing there, awestruck by what lies before you, is that you have already heard its voice. Maybe it was a simple shout from the sky: "Hey, look at me! I am offering up rainbows for you." Or maybe it was the red barn, boasting about its fresh coat of red paint and how it contrasts with the rolling green hills around it. Now that you hear its voice, you just have to make the decision about the final arrangement. Where will the visual weight, the visual emphasis, be placed? What lens choice, combined with what point of view, can best convey your message of hope or courage or lust or fear or victory? These decisions are all part of the process—decisions that will result in the most compelling image possible at that moment.

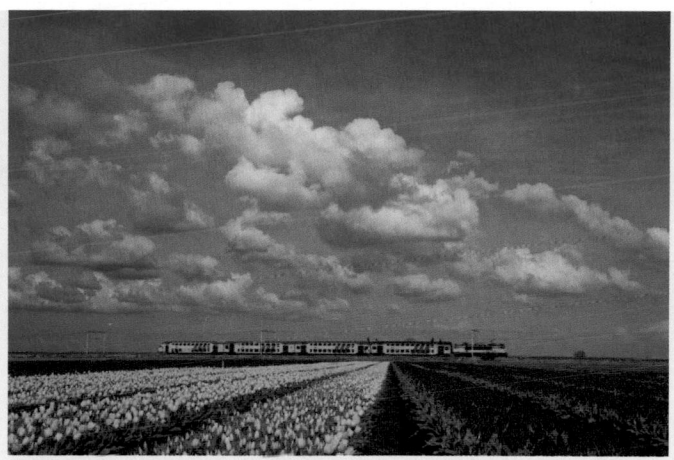

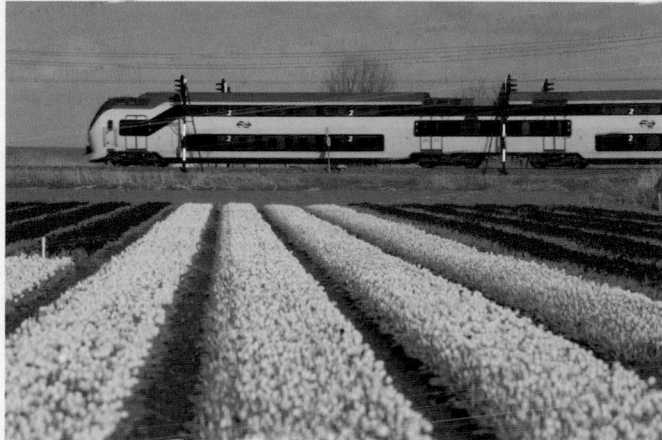

In the first image shown above, I chose to give the "Rembrandt sky" the visual weight, placing the horizon line near the bottom of the frame. With such a massive amount of visual weight on the sky, the landscape below was humbled. A few minutes later, when the next train passed, it was time to give the landscape the visual weight by placing the horizon line near the top third of the frame. Note how the train itself is being used as the top-third "line," and due to the converging parallel lines formed by the rows of tulips, all eyes are directed to the train. By the way, would this still be a visually strong image if the outer rows of tulips were not red but all the same color yellow? Probably not. The red tulips offer some welcome color contrast and even do so in classic thirds—two-thirds yellow, one-third red. Will wonders never cease!

Top: Nikon D3X with Nikkor 16–35mm lens at 18mm, f/11 for 1/400 sec., ISO 200;
Bottom: Nikon D3X with Nikkor 70–300mm lens at 220mm, f/8 for 1/800 sec.

THE GOLDEN SECTION,
THE RULE OF THIRDS, AND
THE RULE OF VISUAL WEIGHT

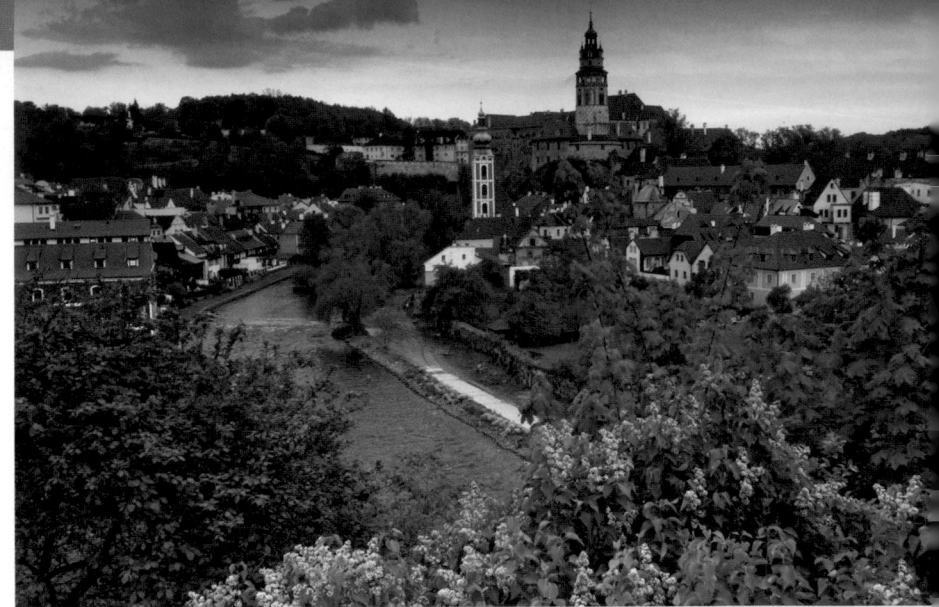

The decision over where to place the horizon line is often an easy one, especially when the sky is an ordinary cloudless dull blue color or gray and overcast. By the way, when the sky is gray, overcast, or simply a dull blue, I might use a tobacco-, gray-, or blue-colored graduated-color filter, as I did here. This image was taken in the lovely Bohemian town of Český Krumlov, in the Czech Republic. Setting up my camera with a graduated-blue filter, I photographed the scene you see here. Note my placement of the curving line of the small river and how it is used as the "dividing line" to separate the landscape below into a one-third/two-thirds division. Clearly, it was my choice to declare the right side of the frame as the winner. Note also the language of the curvilinear line: curvilinear lines are passive, restful, and gentle, and thanks to this meandering line of the river, the scene does indeed look passive, restful, and gentle.

Nikon D300S with Nikkor 18–55mm lens, f/16 for 1/60 sec., ISO 200

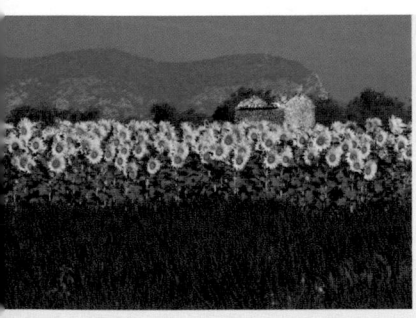

In this image of lavender and sunflower fields and an old stone well house in Provence, France, I decided to keep the focus on the landscape and place the horizon line in the top third of the frame. The first image (left) shows a standard eye-level view, which captures four shifts in tone. As we know that even numbers seldom work as well as odd ones, I decided to shift my point of view for the second shot. By standing on the front seat of my car and shooting out the open sunroof, I elevated my perspective to garner seven distinct tonal shifts, creating a more compelling composition (right). Additionally, note that I shifted from a horizontal to a vertical frame.

Both images: Nikon D300S with 70–300mm lens, f/32 for 1/60 sec., ISO 200

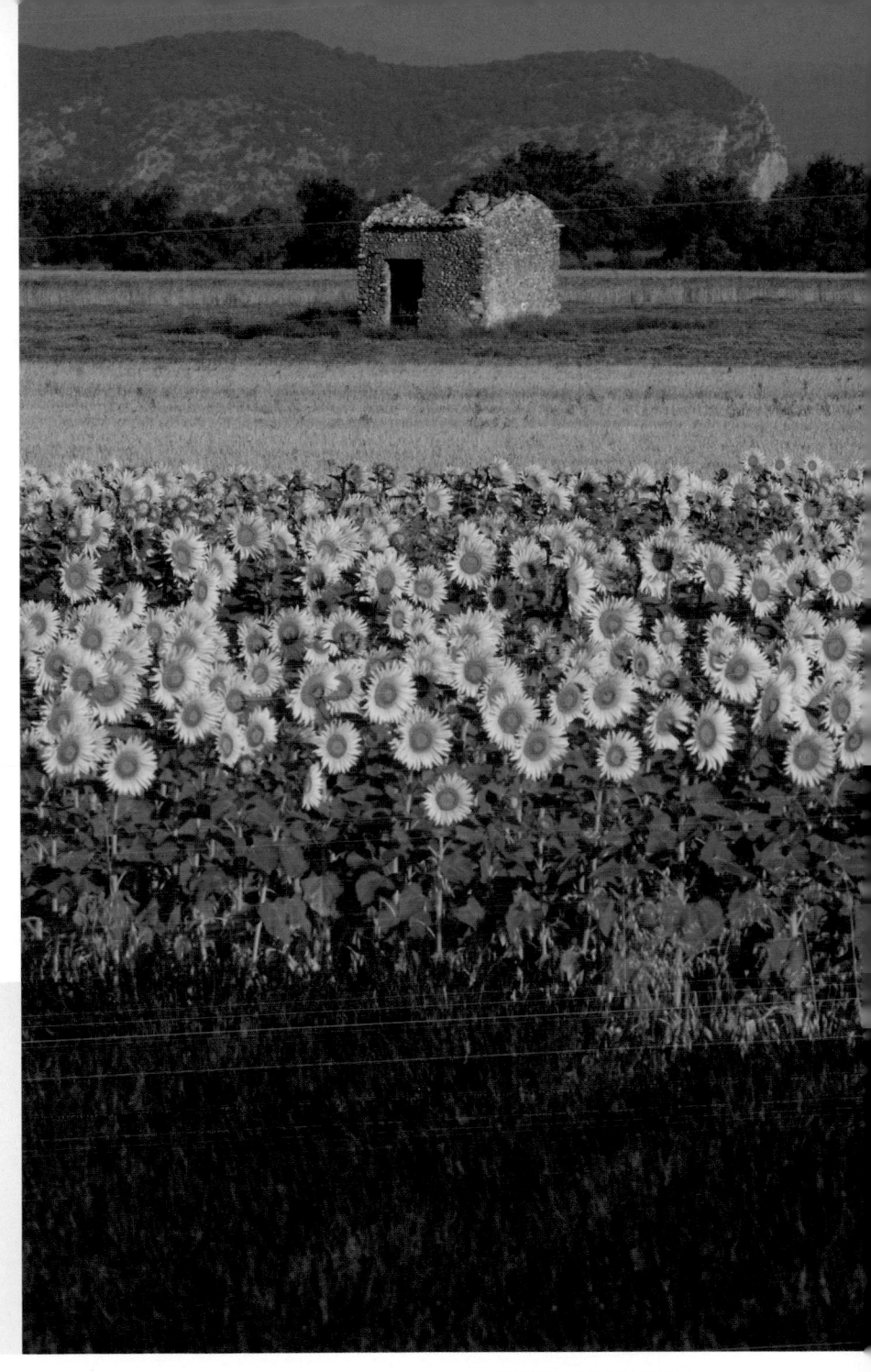

THE GOLDEN SECTION,
THE RULE OF THIRDS, AND
THE RULE OF VISUAL WEIGHT

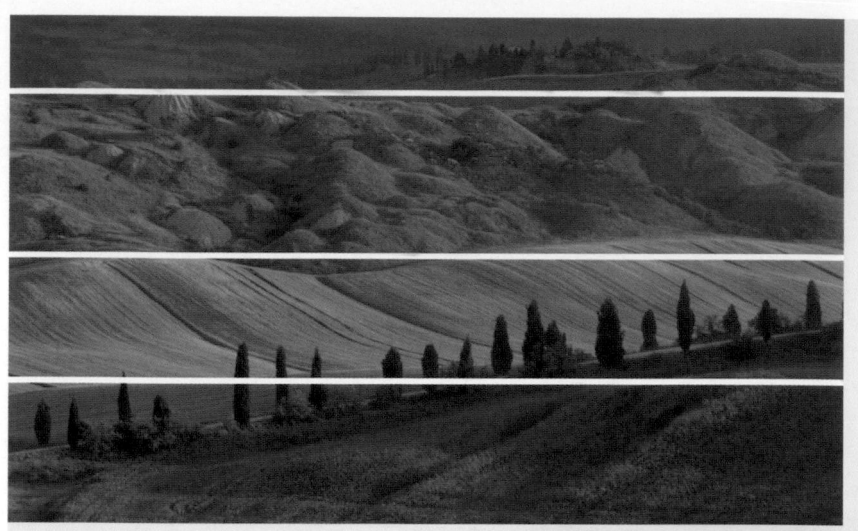

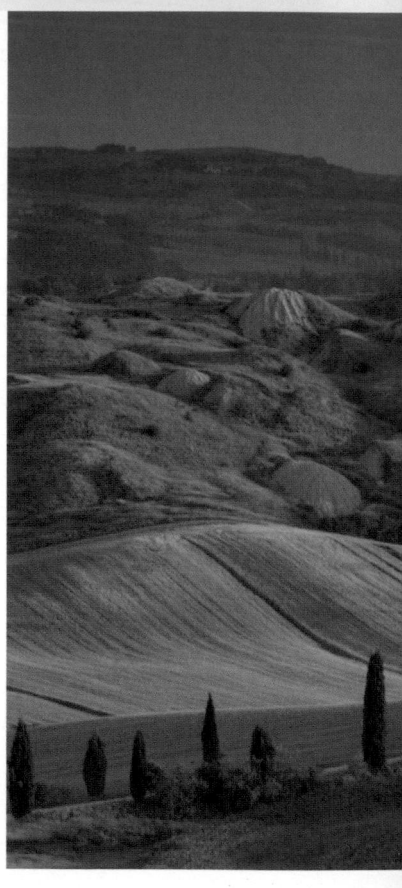

This idyllic Tuscany landscape awaits anyone willing to get up at dawn and venture east on state road SP438 toward the town of Fiorentine, a bit south of Siena. If you do so, you will have no trouble spotting a somewhat surreal landscape of rolling hills of wheat interspersed with large mounds of what look like boulders. As the narrow road unfolds, one compelling landscape after another beckons. This day proved to be one of those hot and humid early summer mornings, resulting in a hazy dull-blue sky, but I would not be deterred and once again called on a graduated-blue, neutral-density (ND) filter. With my camera and 70–300mm lens mounted on a tripod, and my graduated-blue filter in place, I was quick to make the decision to push the horizon line near the top of the frame. Note the varied textures and tones of the landscape below. There are five distinct "lines" here—tones, actually—beginning with a green tone, followed by the golden tone of the wheat, the yellow/orange tone of the hillside and rocks, the blue tone of the distant hills, and finally the lighter blue tone of the sky. And while this pleasing landscape does not follow the normal Rule of Thirds, there are five distinct lines found here, a Fibonacci number. Compare this to the composition at left, with only four distinct tones, and I'm sure you'll agree that the shot below is much stronger.

Nikon D3X with Nikkor 70–300mm lens at 300mm, f/22 for 1/60 sec., ISO 100, graduated-blue filter for the sky

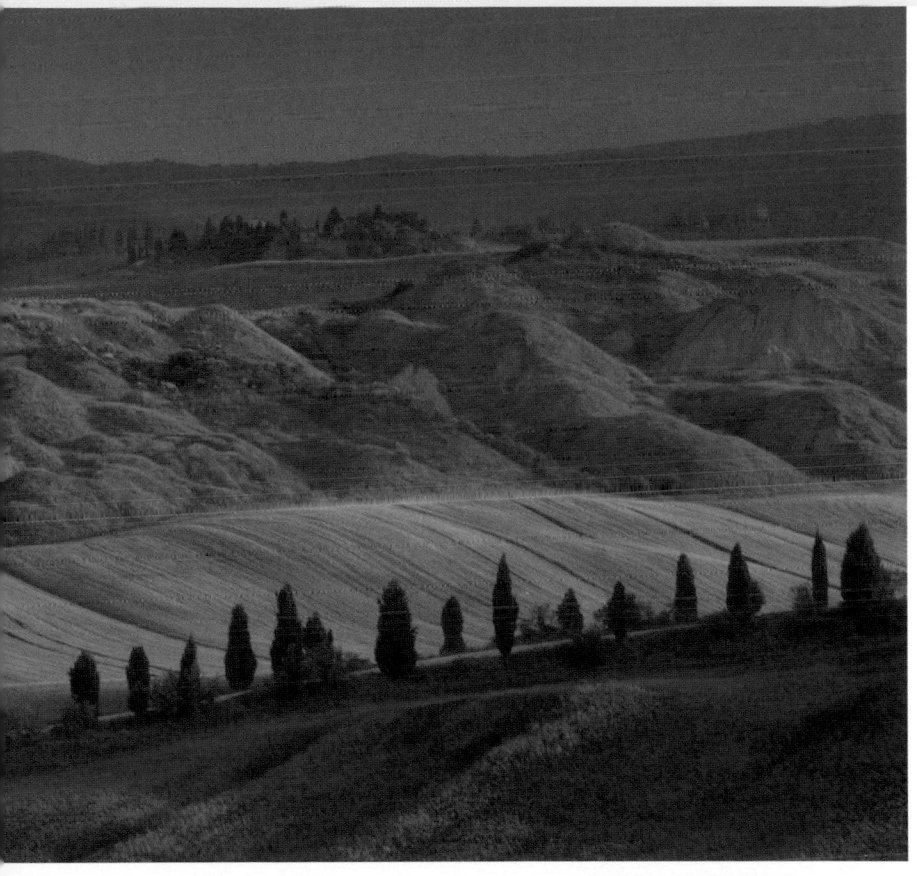

THE GOLDEN SECTION, THE RULE OF THIRDS, AND THE RULE OF VISUAL WEIGHT

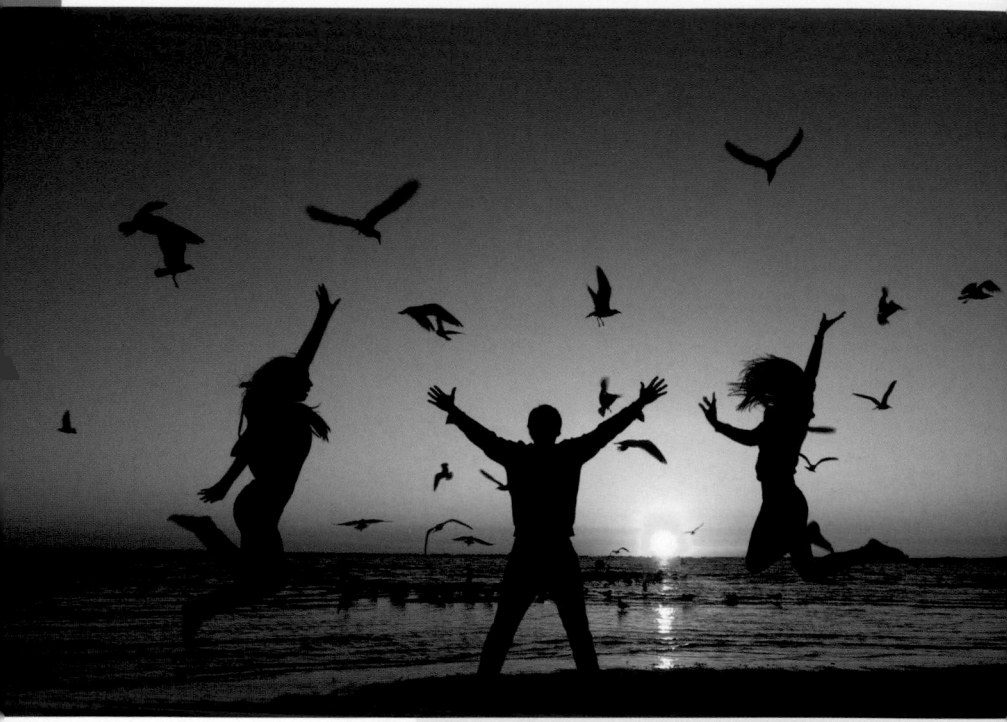

A bag of Doritos almost always guarantees a flock of seagulls, so all that remained was to have the two girls on either side of the central figure jump, arms outstretched, on the count of three—and jump they did. Handholding my camera and 24–85mm lens, I chose to tilt the camera up a bit while seated in a baseball catcher's stance and fired off a number of frames. The moderate wide-angle, coupled with a low horizon line, assured me of getting a large canvas above the horizon filled with flying gulls and "flying" youth, all silhouetted against the sunset sky.

Nikon D300S with Nikkor 24–85mm lens, f/11 for 1/500 sec., ISO 200

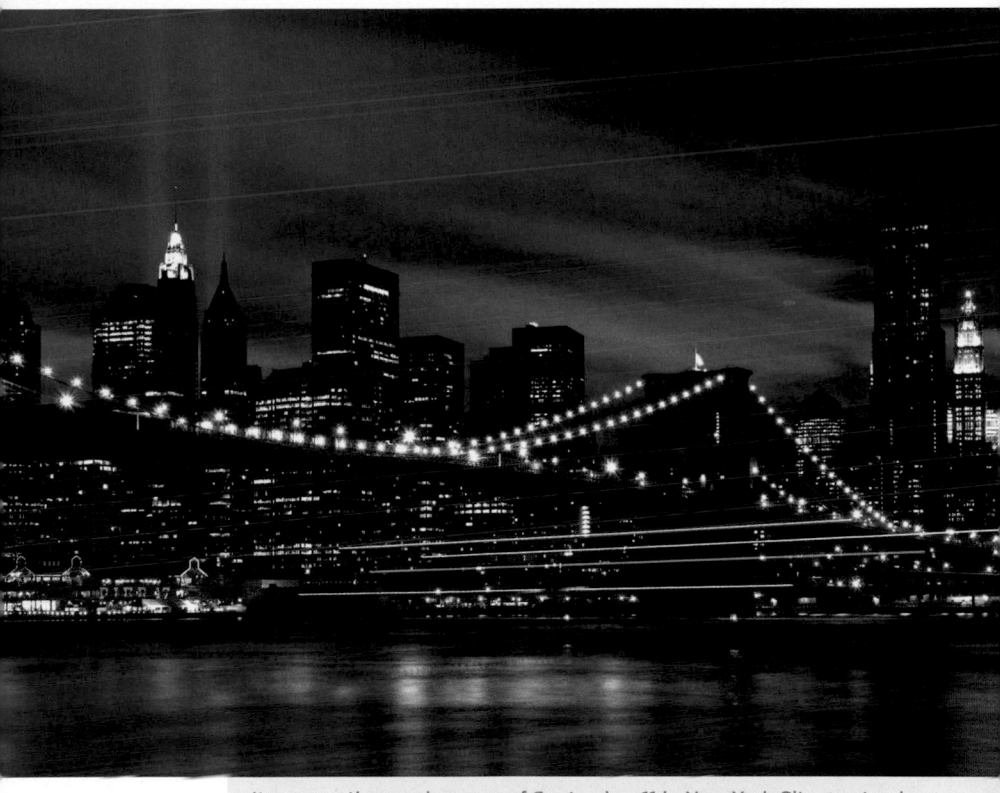

It was another anniversary of September 11 in New York City, so standing shoulder to shoulder with fifty-plus other photographers at Brooklyn Bridge Park to shoot the Manhattan skyline was to be expected. The decision to place the horizon line near the bottom third was an easy one. I wanted to fill the upper two-thirds of the frame with the New York City skyline and the all-important spotlight tribute to the World Trade Center's Twin Towers.

With my camera and 24–85mm lens mounted on a tripod, I determined that this would be a classic "who cares" composition and chose an aperture of f/11. With the camera in manual exposure mode, I pointed it toward the dusky-blue sky and adjusted my shutter speed until 2 seconds indicated a correct exposure. I then recomposed the scene you see here and, with the camera's self-timer engaged, tripped the shutter.

Nikon D3X with Nikkor 70–300mm lens at 300mm, f/11 for 2 seconds, ISO 200

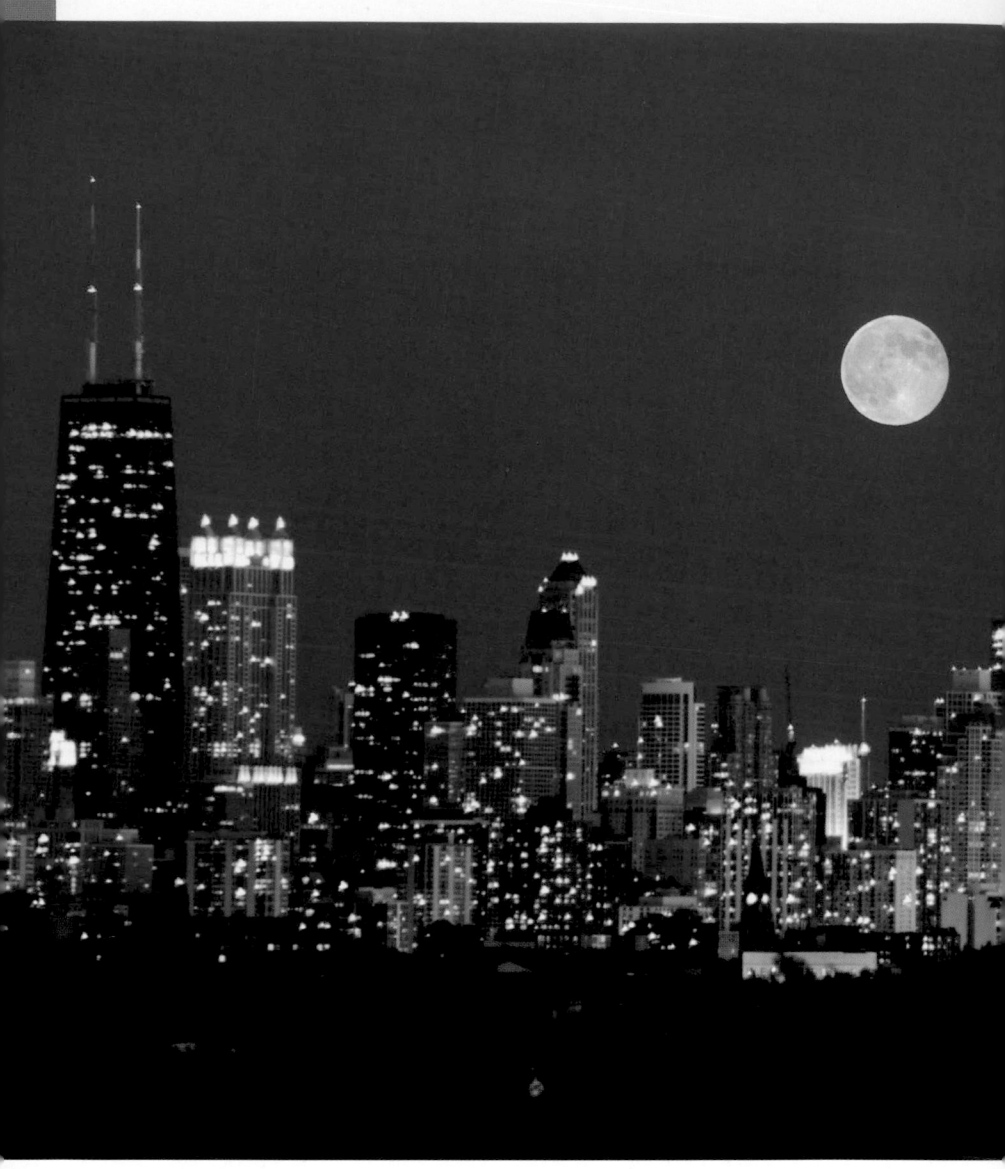

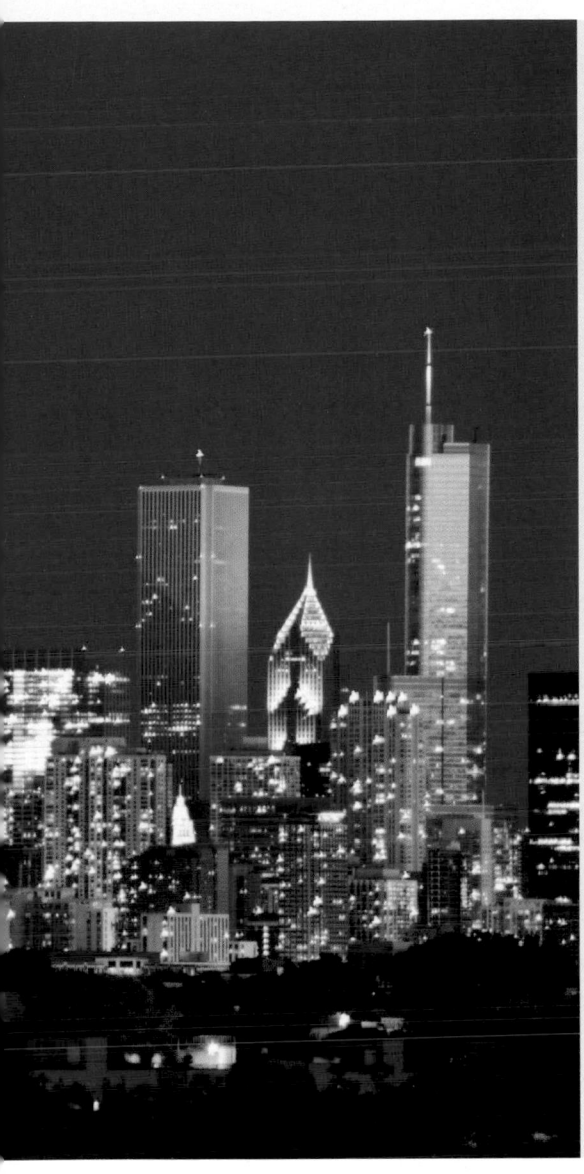

The second most impressive sky-line—after New York City's—is, in my view, Chicago's. I am fortunate that my studio has a large rooftop deck with great views of the Chicago skyline, and a few times each year, the full moonrise comes up right over my city view. But like all full moonrises, shots like these are 100 percent weather dependent; a cloudy sky in the forecast spells doom for a shot like this. The night I took this image, we were blessed with a clear night, so my decision over where to put the horizon line was easy. This image was all about the vast universe and the full moon, and as such, the city would be "pushed down" toward the bottom third of the frame, allowing the dusky blue sky and moon to dominate the composition. Note, by the way, how an upside down "triangle" emerges, formed by the lines of the city's buildings, as if to cradle the full moon.

Nikon D3X with Nikkor 70–300mm lens at 300mm, f/11 for 2 seconds, ISO 200

THE GOLDEN SECTION,
THE RULE OF THIRDS, AND
THE RULE OF VISUAL WEIGHT

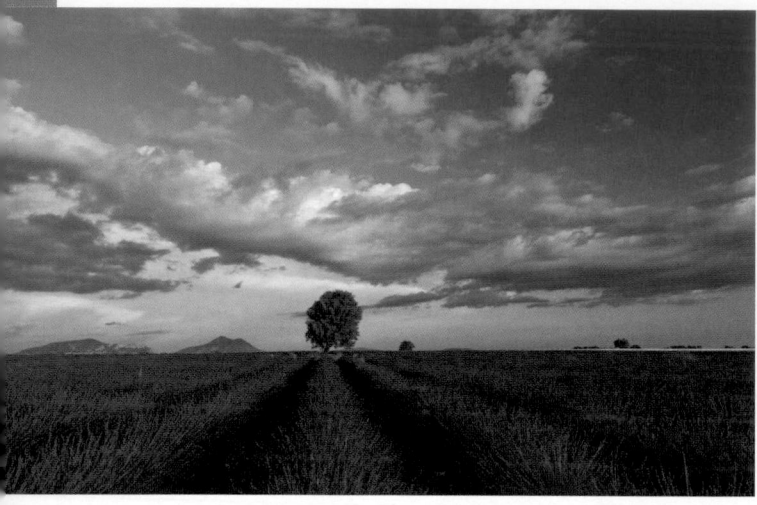
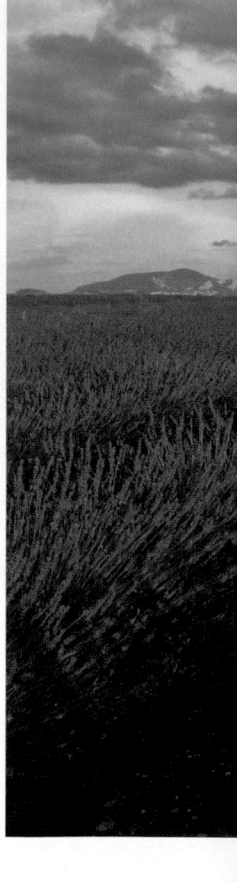

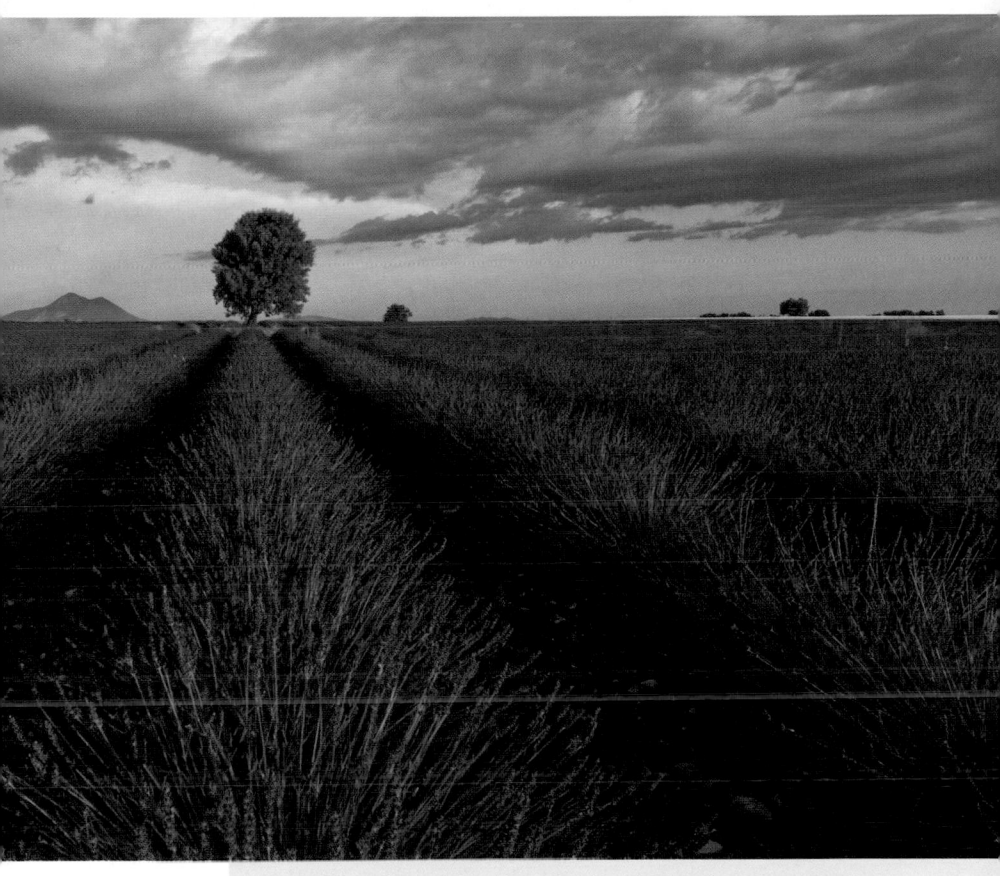

Whether to place the horizon line high or low is an important question, and as you may have surmised by now, sometimes you may choose to do both. But what is important to note is that there is a real visual difference. When the horizon line is placed near the bottom third, you create the illusion that objects are smaller and the foreground is farther away. For example, compare these two images. The tree in the first image (opposite), where the horizon line sits near the bottom third, appears farther away than the tree in the second photo (above), where the horizon line is near the top. In truth, I am the same distance from the tree in both shots. As often happens when placing the horizon line near the bottom third, a large and expansive sky fills the upper two-thirds of the frame, and as such, the "universe" trumps everything on the ground below.

Both images: Nikon D300S with Nikkor 12–24mm lens at 18mm, f/22 for 1/40 sec., ISO 200

THE GOLDEN SECTION,
THE RULE OF THIRDS, AND
THE RULE OF VISUAL WEIGHT

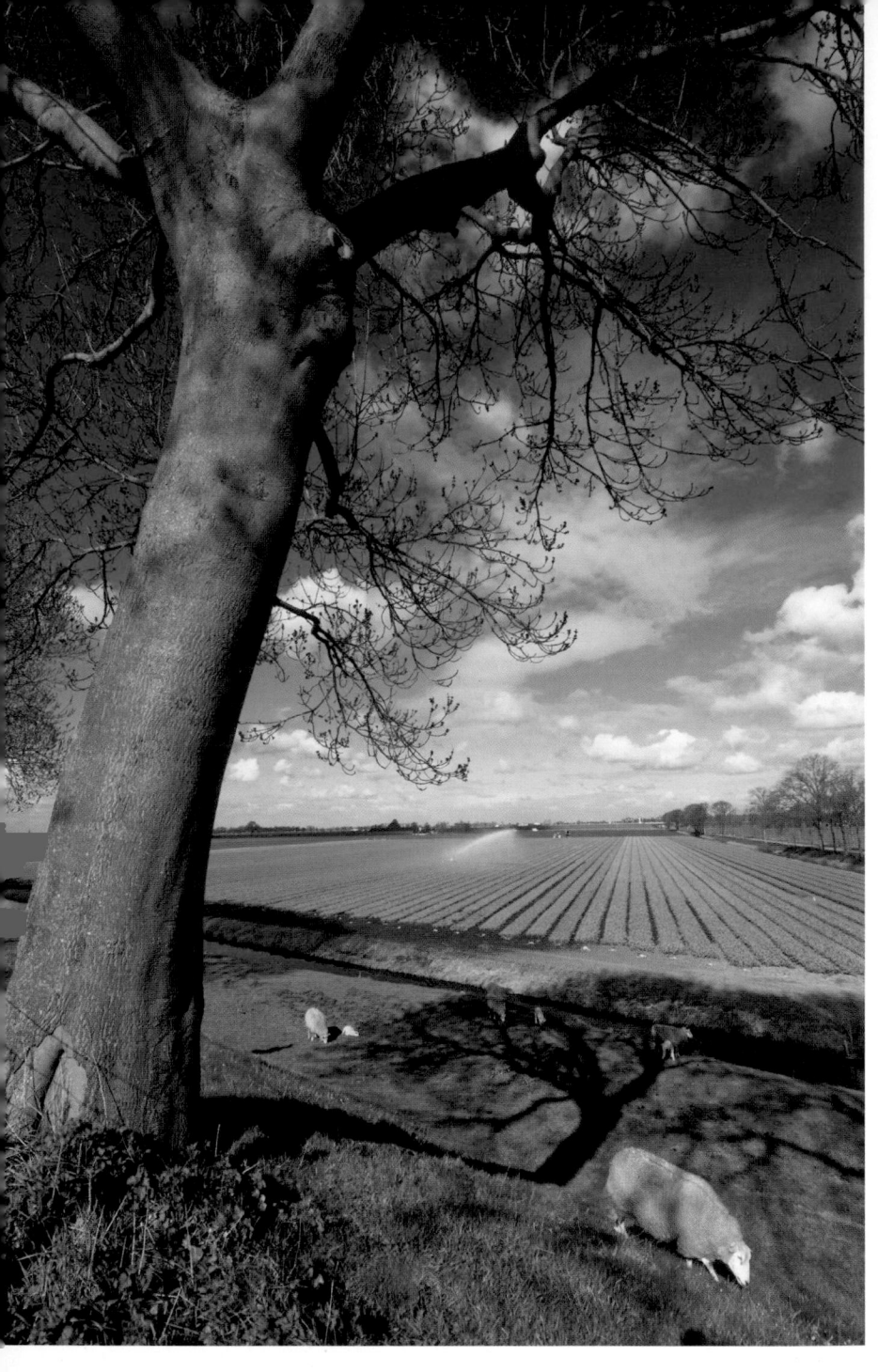

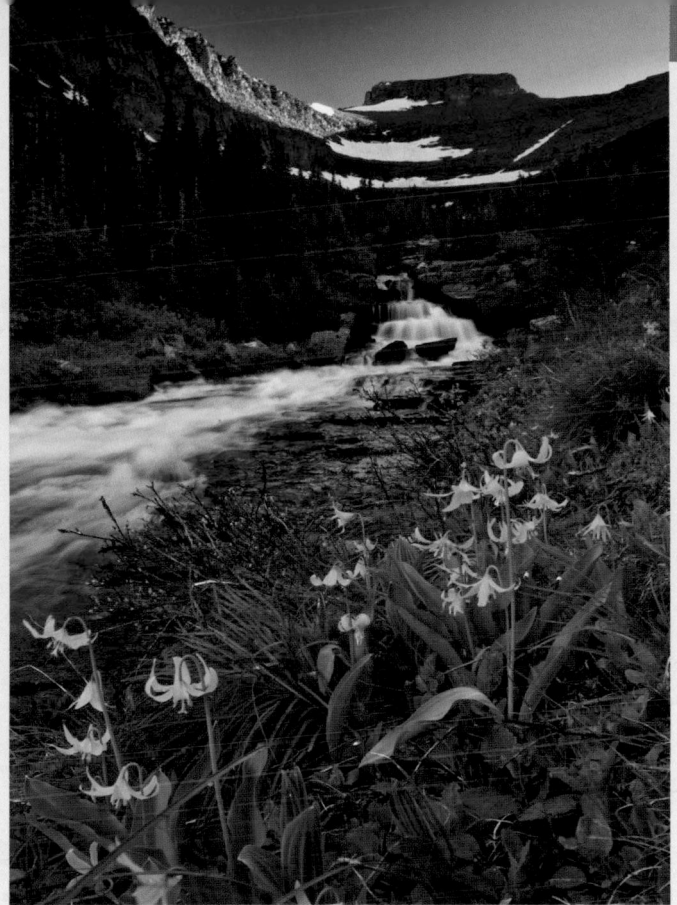

Here are two more examples where the placement of the horizon line is obvious—low in the first, high in the second. But what may not be as obvious are the dominant lines found in both images.

In the first image (opposite), notice how the tree rises up, carrying the eye into the infinite sky. Then, just as quickly, we slide down the tree to investigate the landscape below.

In the second image (above), the river's meandering line finds us slowly wandering upstream to investigate the landscape before us. Slowly we slide down the stream and stop to "smell the roses" along the way. This second image clearly offers an immediate foreground, and subsequently we sense the depth and distance that follow. In the first image, we do not have immediate foreground interest, yet depth and distance are obvious here, too, again attributed to line. The foreground line of shadow leads our eye to the distant and converging parallel lines of the rows of tulips, which then take our eye deeper into the scene.

Opposite: Nikon D300S with Nikkor 12–24mm lens at 14mm, f/22 for 1/125 sec., ISO 200; Above: Nikon D3X with Nikkor 16–35mm lens at 16mm, f/22 for 1/15 sec. with 2-stop graduated ND filter, ISO 100

WHERE HAVE THE HORIZON LINES GONE?

Once you've learned to take two steps closer to fill the frame and use the Rule of Thirds, the next big hurdle is defining a compelling composition when no horizon line is present. Many students struggle with this; it seems that an image without a horizon line is like a map without any roads. We know the roads are there, but the map only shows the terrain.

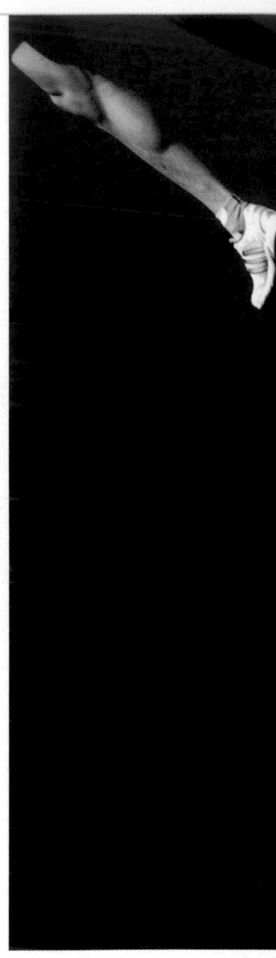

Perhaps by now you are starting to get that every composition, with or without obvious horizon lines, is made up of lines. First and foremost there are the Suggestion of Thirds lines, but on top of this we see perhaps a single layer of lines, or multiple layers of lines: lines that are thick and wide or thin and narrow; lines that are short; lines that are long; lines that run diagonally, vertically, and/or horizontally. And, as you may know, when a line closes on itself, it becomes a shape. Just like lines, shapes come in varying sizes and tones and thus have their own visual weight. All of us perceive lighter-toned lines and shapes as more delicate, fragile, and quieter than heavier-toned lines and shapes, which we perceive as stronger, more decisive, and forceful. With practice, you will begin seeing and speaking the language of effective composition with or without horizon lines. By the way, if you have yet to engage the built-in grid on your camera, or if you have yet to make your own, now is the time to do that as we move toward compositions where no defined horizon lines are present within the photograph.

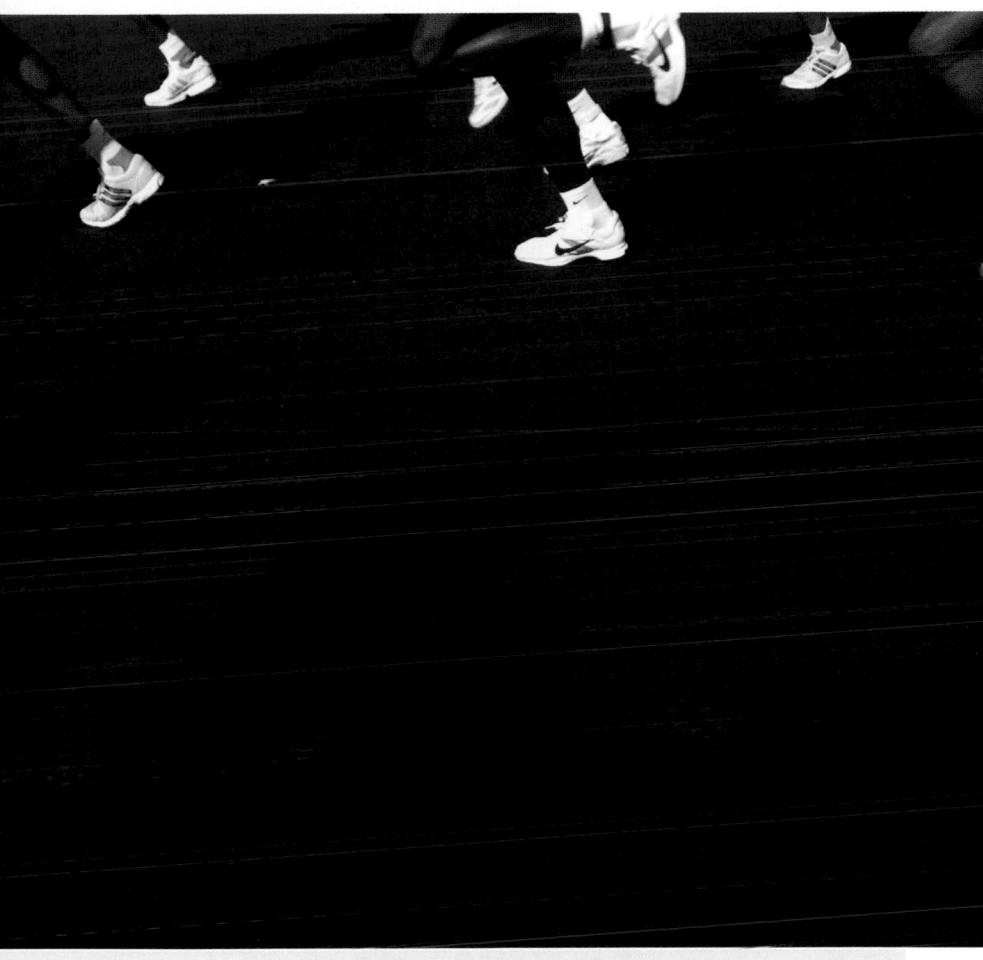

Do you see the suggested horizon in this image? It is the feet of marathon runners moving across a blue carpet in Prague, very near the top of the frame. The feet and simple silhouetted shapes jutting out are just enough to compete this simple arrangement, which is nothing more than the use of the Suggestion of Thirds. This is an example of how simplicity can lead to a graphically strong composition.

Nikon D300S with Nikkor 12–24mm lens at 16mm, f/8 for 1/1000 sec., ISO 200

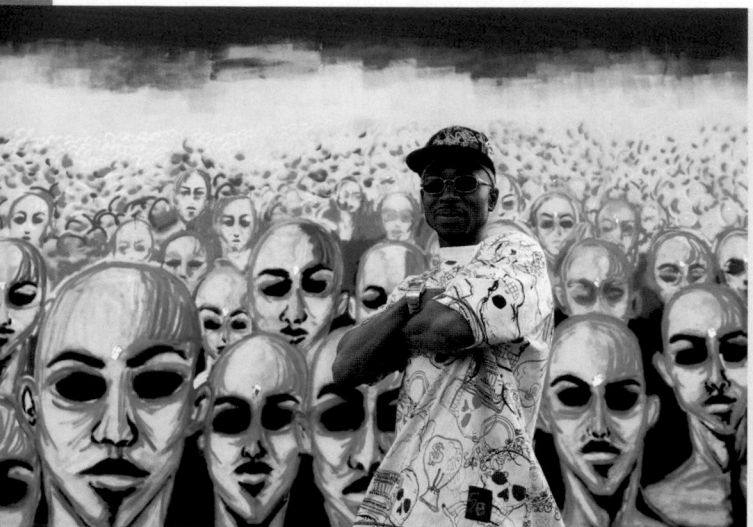
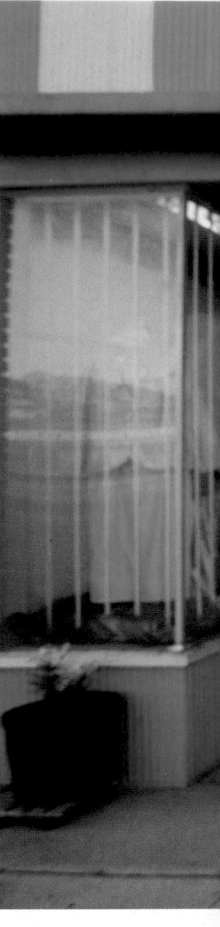

Again, note the suggested horizon line here: the red section in the mural. This young man in Miami just happened to stop by to chat while I was shooting the mural. Within minutes, he had become my new subject. The red skulls on his shirt were a stroke of luck and played an important role in tying the background to the subject. Note the obvious use of the Suggestion of Thirds here, as well.

Nikon D3X with Nikkor 24–85mm lens at 35mm, f/8 for 1/500 sec., ISO 100

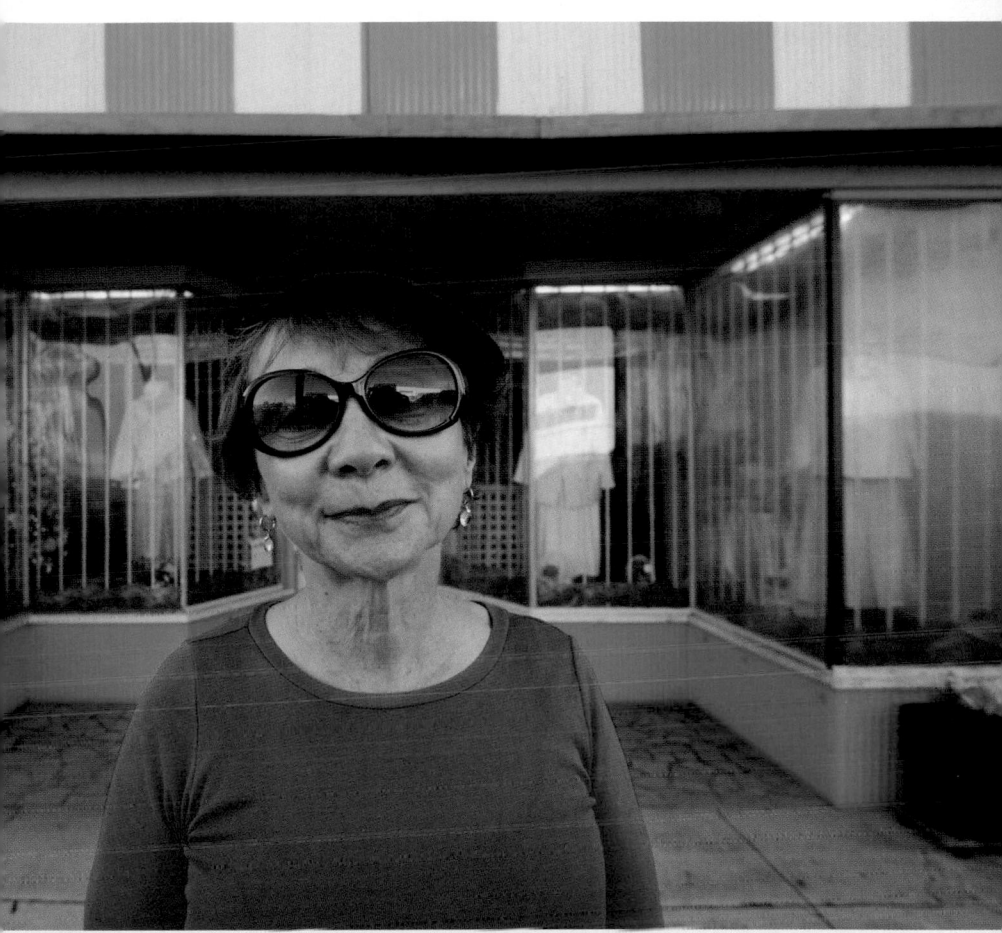

This photo and the one on pages 180–181 also share a common thread. Yes, they are both "people shots," one a posed portrait and the other a candid. But what I really want you to notice is that both rely on the Rule of Thirds despite the absence of any defined horizon lines. It is challenging to arrange a compelling composition in the absence of a defined "line" to get you started, which is, at least initially, all the more reason to either activate the grid that came with your DSLR or make your own from a piece of plastic and a Sharpie, cutting it to the same size as your digital monitor and taping it on top of it.

Here, it's true that my subject is posing right in the middle of the frame, but she is also supported by a background of lines that converge at her neckline. These converging lines act as two arrows, leading the eye to the subject and emphasizing her importance as the key element in this composition. The inclusion of the sidewalk (a lower-third horizon) and the store's awning (an upper-third horizon) serve to hold the viewer's attention—to keep the viewer from leaving the subject. It was pure luck that my subject was wearing a pink top and the building behind her had pink trim.

Nikon D3X with 24–85mm lens at 35mm, f/6.3 for 1/200 sec., ISO 100

THE GOLDEN SECTION,
THE RULE OF THIRDS, AND
THE RULE OF VISUAL WEIGHT

In this photo, there are two large blocks of color: a golden one covering the right two-thirds and a bright-pink one comprising the left third. As luck would have it, I happened to be set up and ready to shoot when two women entered the scene from the left while the lone woman on the right continued to hang her laundry. I love how the lone woman plays off the smaller pink wall opposite her, just as the other two women play off the larger wall opposite them. With regard to exposure, because the two women are walking in an area of deep shade and my exposure is set for the much brighter sunshine, they were recorded as silhouettes.

Nikon D2X with Nikkor 70–200mm lens at 200mm, f/16 for 1/125 sec., ISO 200

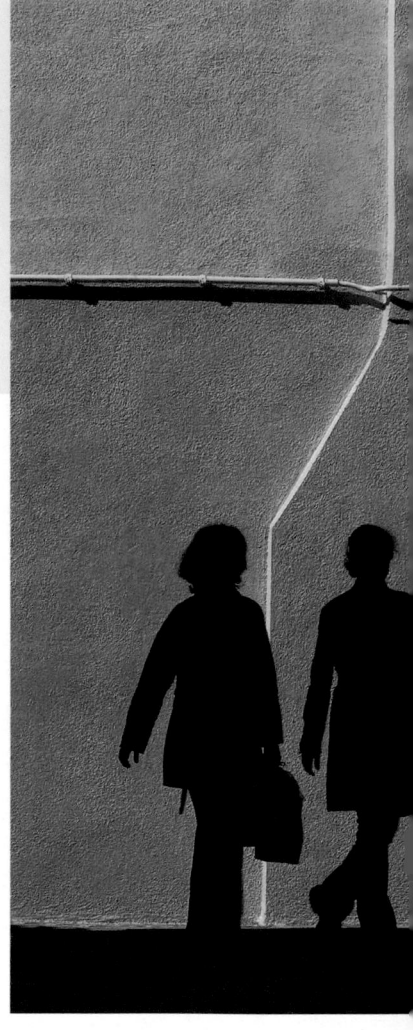

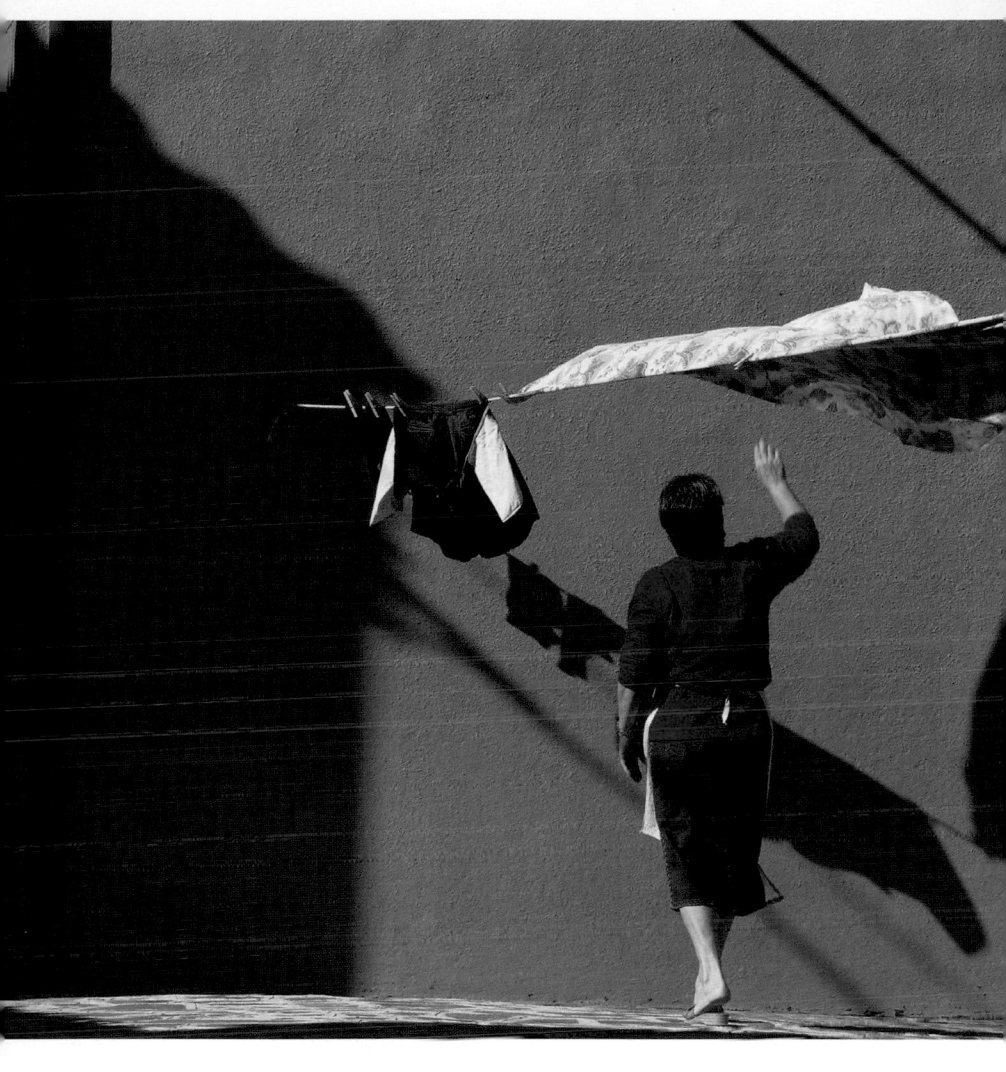

THE GOLDEN SECTION,
THE RULE OF THIRDS, AND
THE RULE OF VISUAL WEIGHT

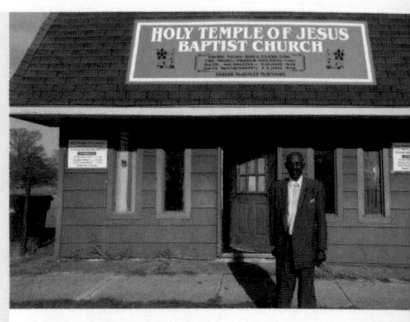

As the sun sank low in the western sky of Clarksdale, Mississippi, I caught sight of this hot pink church. As I pulled over to the side of the road, I spotted a preacher heading for the church's side door. Within a few minutes of exchanging pleasantries, Pastor Mckinley McKnight agreed to stand out front with an open Bible in hand, quoting scripture while I photographed him with my 16–35mm lens. Although he is surely centered in this composition, it works because the background offers some welcome two-thirds/one-third divisions: namely, the blue line of the window trim and how the area inside it encompasses roughly two-thirds of the background.

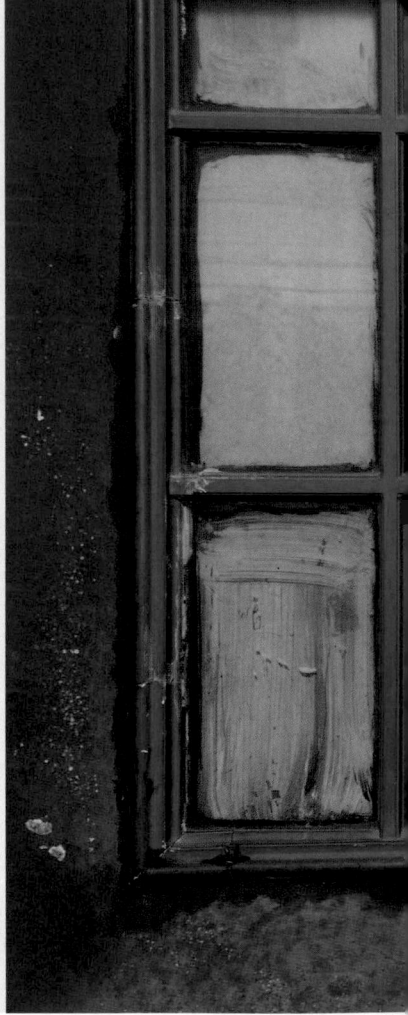

More often than not, most compositions fall short because they have too much going on inside the frame. And, let's face it, this is an easy trap to fall into. No matter where we turn, with the exception of a clear sky or a blank wall, we see nothing but busy canvases, some more cluttered than others. When I looked at this scene, the empty canvas that emerged was the colorful entryway. I simply moved in close enough so the blue window trim and the contents inside the trim filled two-thirds of the frame. The bottom blue trim of the window put me in mind of a low horizon, so I placed it near the bottom. Also note how I used the right side, the "line" of the window, in the right third. Again, there is no real horizon line present, yet there are always lines that can fit the bill.

Now I was ready to bring in layer number two: Preacher McKnight. The intimate, up-close-and-personal portrait of him holding his Bible, with a painted cross in the glass just over his shoulder, provides just enough information to convey what he stands for.

Remember, your goal should always be to get your message across in a clear, concise, and articulate manner. You have about a tenth of a second to capture the viewer's attention with your image. If you make it a habit to focus on what to *exclude* in your composition, you will find the path toward what to *include* far less cluttered.

Nikon D3X with Nikkor 24–85mm lens at 26mm, f/8 for 1/500 sec., ISO 100

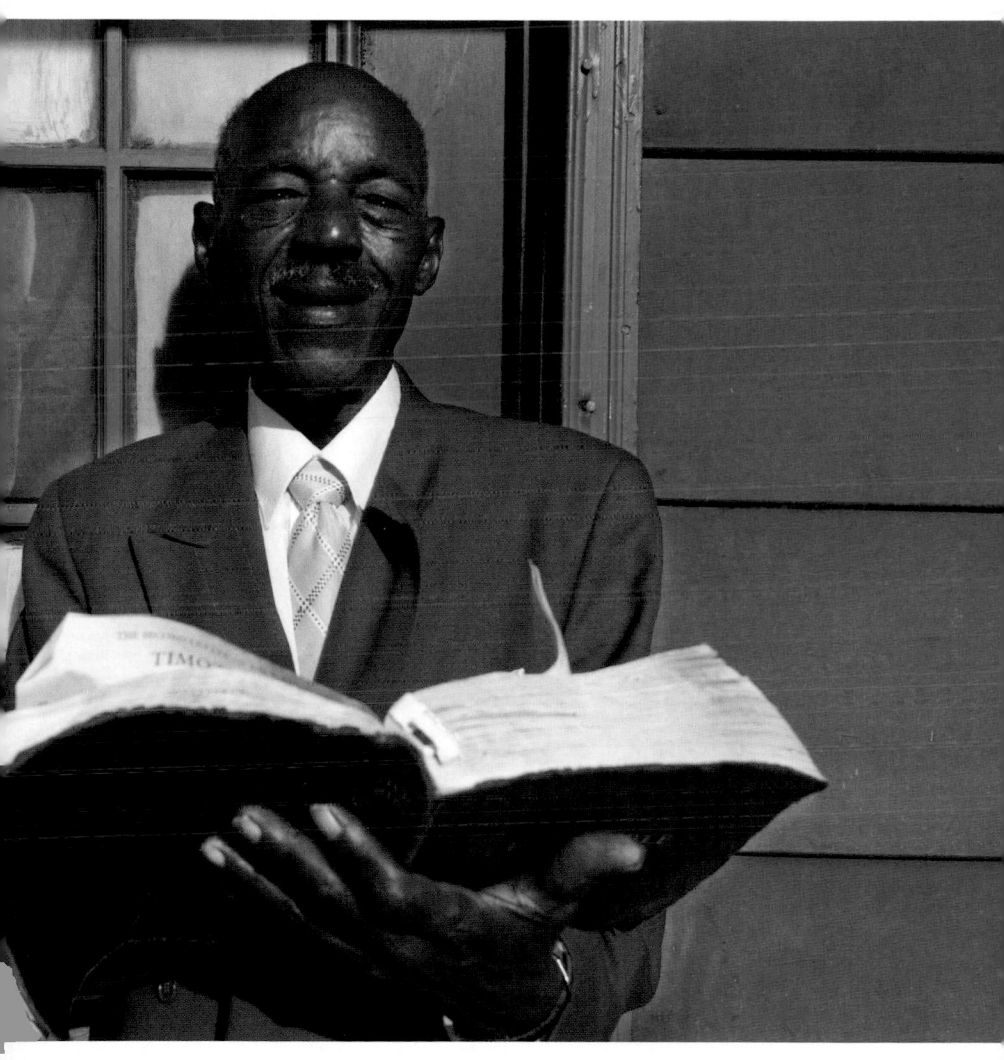

THE GOLDEN SECTION,
THE RULE OF THIRDS, AND
THE RULE OF VISUAL WEIGHT

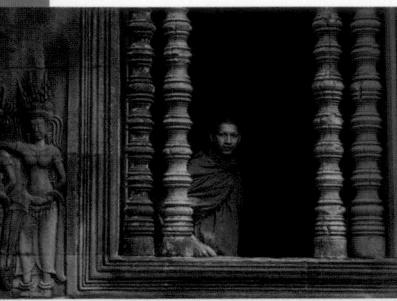

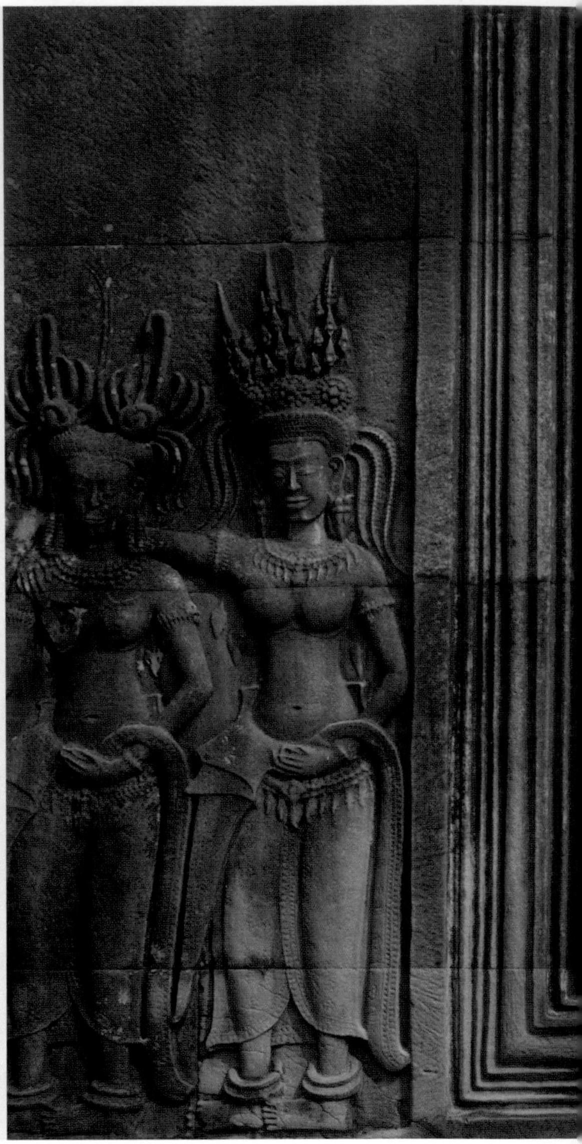

The first image (above) shows a monk posing in the open window of an inner courtyard at the Angkor Wat temple in Cambodia. As much as I liked that photo, I couldn't help but notice the two "dancers" etched in the stone wall just to the left of the open window. Knowing we had two monks, it made sense to pose them both, echoing the two dancers. Despite the somewhat evenly split frame in both images, the saving grace is once again *line*—in particular, the line of the window frame that runs with authority across the bottom of the frame where it meets its vertical counterpart along the left vertical third of the composition. This lower line of "authority" mimics the horizon line of a landscape and, like most horizon lines found in landscape photography, brings a greater feeling of stability to the composition.

Both images: Nikon D3X with Nikkor 24–85mm lens at 70mm, f/11 for 1/250 sec., ISO 100

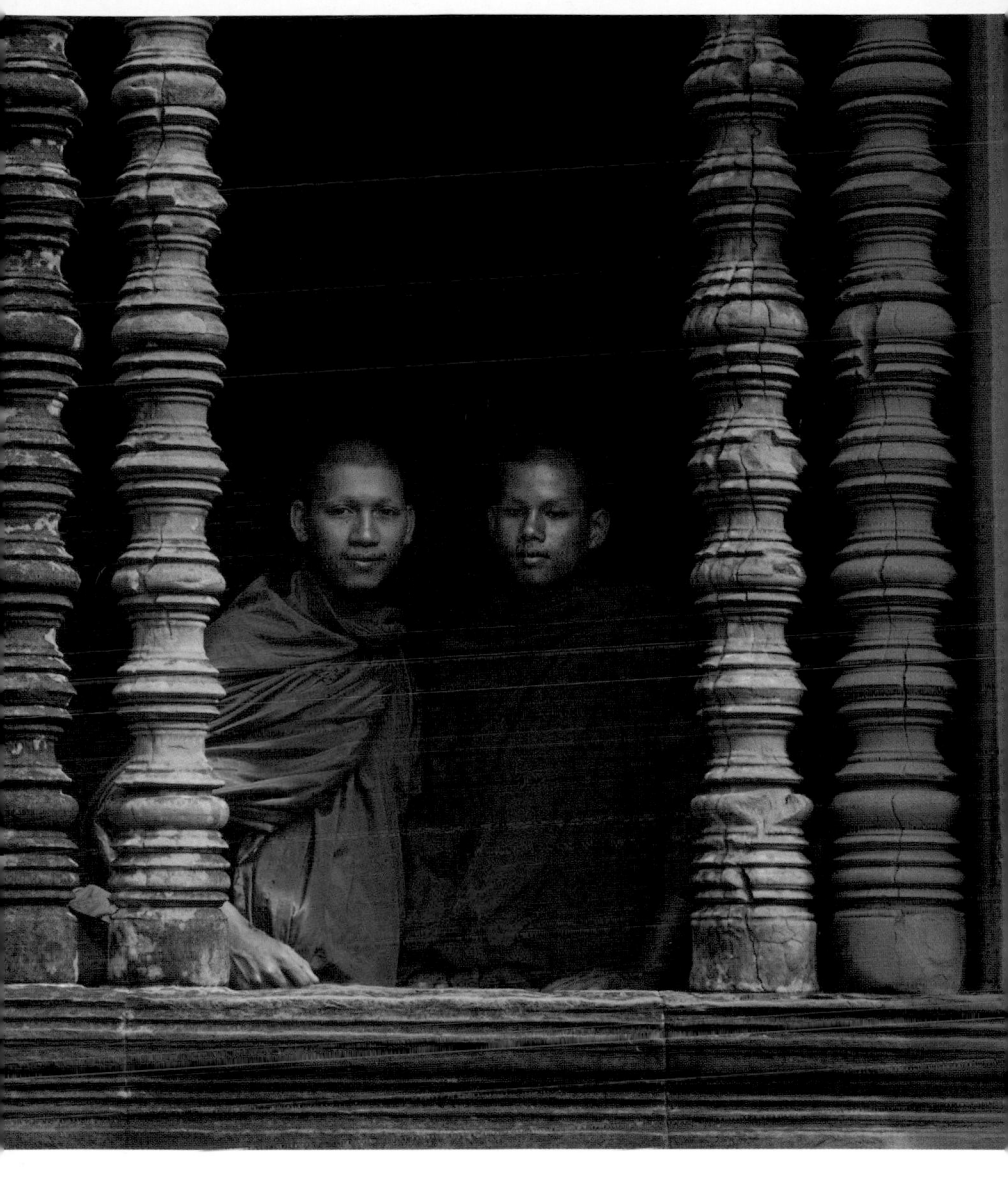

THE GOLDEN SECTION,
THE RULE OF THIRDS, AND
THE RULE OF VISUAL WEIGHT

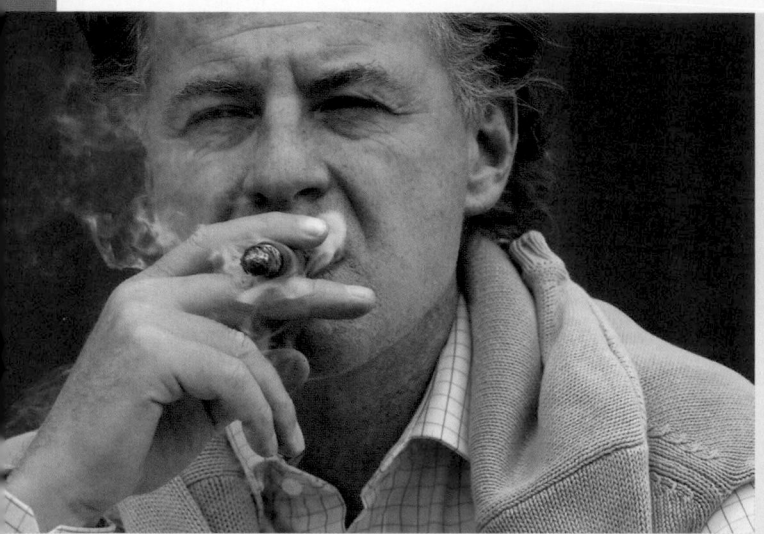

Sitting at a café with my neighbor in Old Lyon, in France, I was quick to notice that the red wall behind him would make a great background for his light blue sweater and shirt. It wasn't until he lit up his cigar, however, that I realized the need for such a "prop." As he drew on the cigar, his expression intense, the smoke created a wonderful sense of life and action in an otherwise pedestrian portrait. Note the use of the Rule of Thirds here, too. Just about two-thirds of the frame is in red, the other third in light blue. His eyes are in the top third and his chin in the bottom third, and his smoking hand takes up no more than one-third of the foreground.

Nikon D300S with Nikkor 24–85mm lens at 24mm, f/8 for 1/250 sec., ISO 200

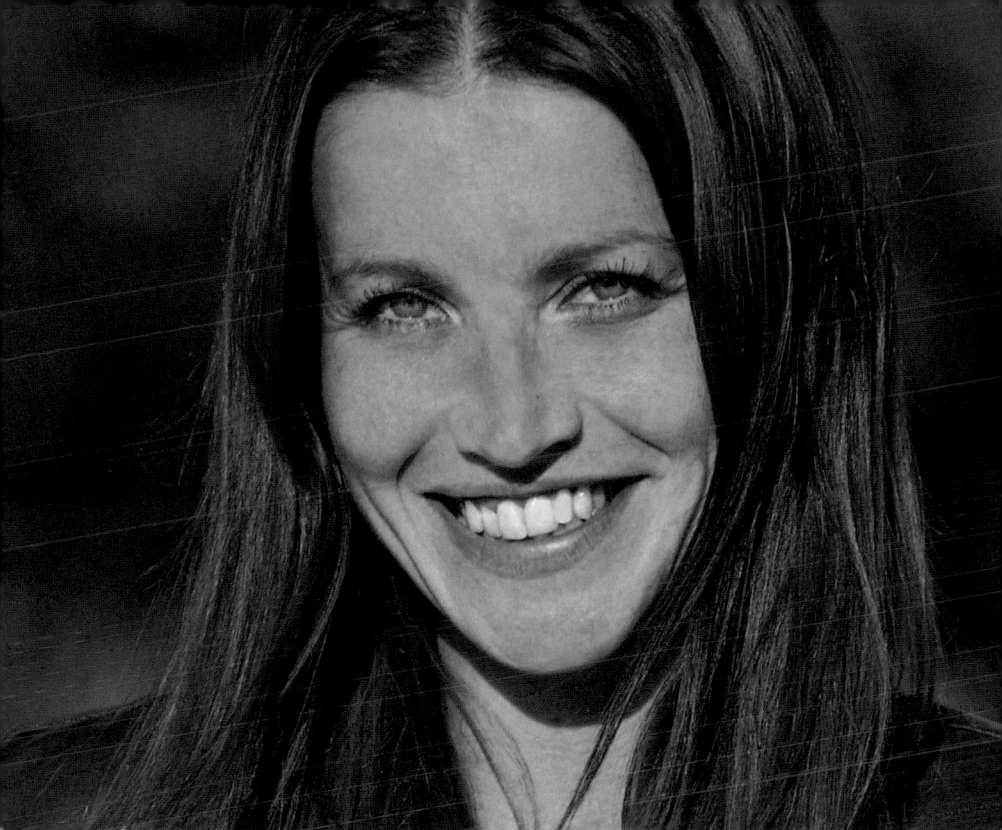

If there was ever a "foolproof" portrait composition, this would be it. Find a colorful background (in this case, flower beds at a local park) and make certain that there is a distance of about 20 feet between your colorful background and your subject. Then reach for your telephoto zoom. At no less than 200mm, and with the camera in the horizontal position, step back until you have just begun to cut off the top of your subject's head. Set your aperture to f/5.6 and adjust your shutter speed until a correct exposure is indicated, then press the shutter release. As I do when shooting most portraits in this fashion, I framed the subject off-center, yet composing within the framework of thirds. Sometimes the portrait takes up two-thirds of the frame, other times it only takes up one-third, but rarely, if ever, does it take up only half the frame.

Why cut off the top of the subject's head? I am not a big fan of the high school yearbook portraits of yesteryear, with all that empty space surrounding the portrait. It does nothing more than cast even greater attention to the static pose most of us are striking. By excluding a small portion of the forehead, the portrait becomes more intimate, creating the feeling of an in-your-face encounter, much like a kiss. This arrangement also tends to be in harmony with the Rule of Thirds, since it eliminates the additional horizon line that normally exists between the top of the head and the distant background. The hair and forehead can be thought of as the top third of the image, the mouth and chin as the bottom third, and, of course, the eyes and nose as the middle third.

Nikon D3X with Nikkor 70–300mm lens at 280mm, f/5.6 for 1/640 sec., ISO 100

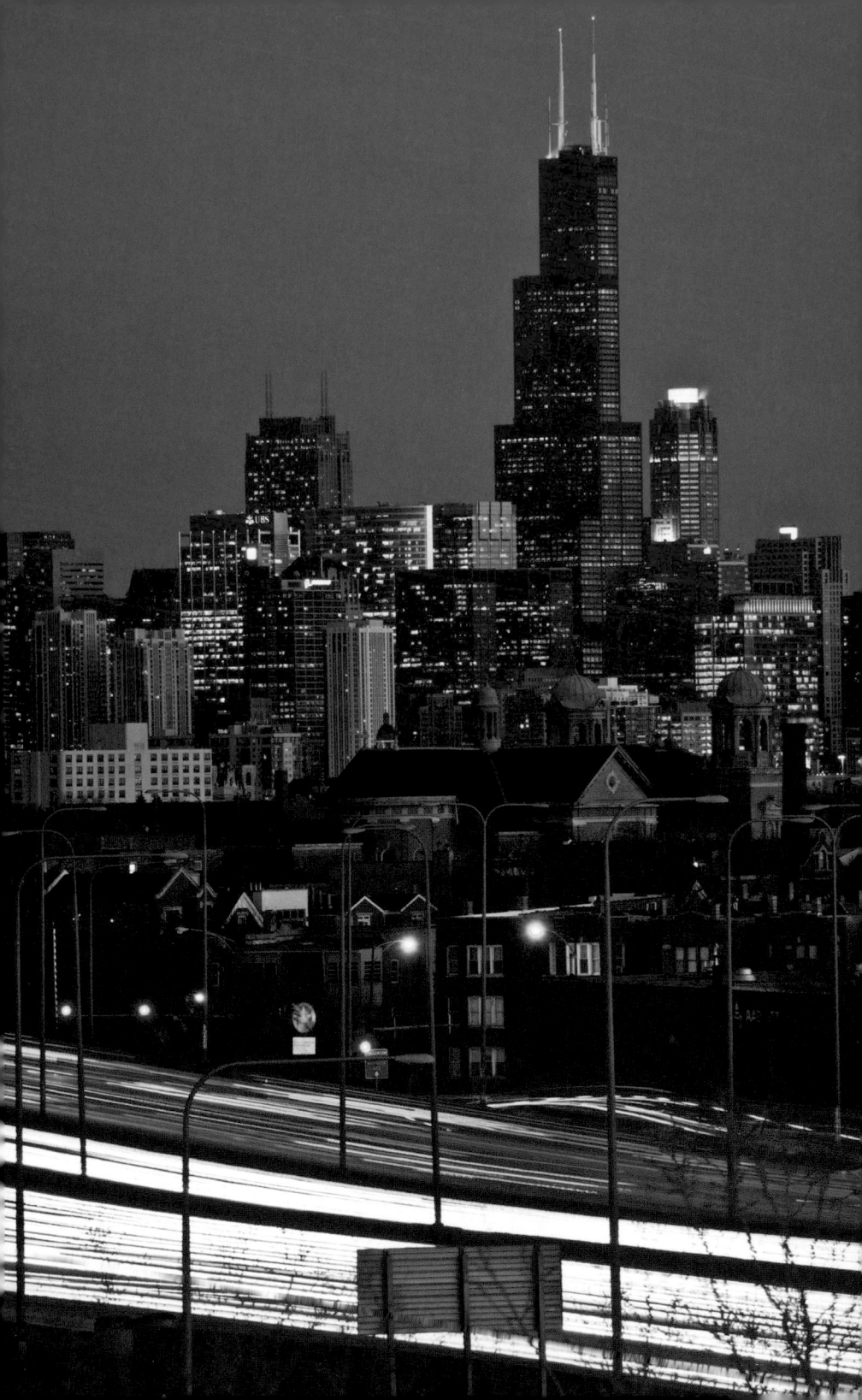

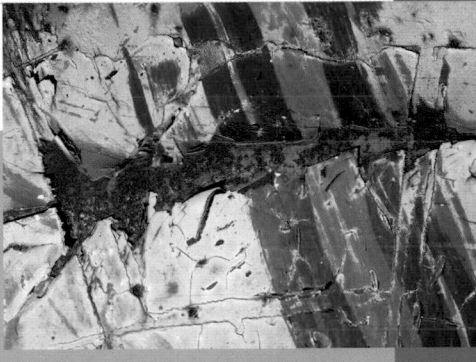

9

HORIZONTAL VERSUS VERTICAL

I had a student who once asked me if I thought it was wise to also buy a "vertical camera." When I heard the question, I was initially perplexed and asked where he had heard of such a camera. As it turned out, the student simply assumed that it took a "vertical camera" to make a vertical composition. Of course, I was quick to point out that vertical compositions were achieved by simply turning the camera to its vertical position. The student quickly replied, "And you can do that without damaging the camera?"

Yes, that is a true story, and even though most shooters probably don't believe they need a vertical camera to take vertical compositions, the evidence sure leans in that direction. If I were a betting man, I would wager that at least 80 percent of your compositions are shot in a horizontal format. I would also hazard a guess that no fewer than 20 percent of those horizontal compositions would have been *more* compelling had you simply turned the camera to its vertical position.

Nikon D3X with Nikkor 70–300mm lens, f/16 for 8 seconds, ISO 100

WHEN TO SHOOT VERTICALLY

When is the best time to shoot a vertical composition? As I've always said, the best time to shoot a vertical composition is right after you shoot the horizontal composition. Unfortunately, many shooters don't *see* the vertical composition until after they have returned home from shooting. It is only then that they make the bold attempt to crop any number of vertical compositions out of the plethora of horizontals that fill the computer screen.

Why do so many of us fail to see the vertical possibilities until it's too late? I am convinced that, at least in part, it has much to do with how cameras are designed to hang around our necks or on our shoulders, even how they are displayed on camera store shelves—always in the familiar horizontal position. Camera design also suggests that it simply "feels better" to hold your camera in the horizontal position. The trouble, of course, is that the world is filled with vertical subjects, and to place an otherwise vertical subject inside the much shorter horizontal frame, you need to move back, back, back, until the vertical has been "shrunk" to fit inside the horizontal frame. Natural verticals include compositions of the face (which is why the vertical frame is called *portrait*) as well as of trees, flowers, buildings, sports, fashion, and many abstract subjects. As a general rule, simply ask yourself if the subject you are photographing is taller than it is wide. If the answer is yes, then it is surely worth at least a look through the "vertical camera."

Shooting verticals in the vertical format and horizontals in the horizontal format is by no means a rule, but simply one more option to consider as you work toward developing your eye, your compositional voice, your style. Much of my portrait and people work is composed in *landscape* format, and I also have a number of horizontal subjects that work better or equally well as verticals. And if any of you have aspirations of one day "turning pro," you will discover the value of making it a habit to shoot both horizontals and verticals as much as possible—*if* seeing your work on the cover of magazines, annual reports, and brochures is important to you, that is.

Finally, it should come as no surprise that the *message* of a horizontal frame is different from that of the vertical frame. Landscape mode suggests calm and tranquility; think of it as lying in bed. Portrait mode, on the other hand, implies strength, pride, and dignity; think of it as being awake. Then again, there are any number of horizontal images that are lively and awake, and just as many verticals that feel calm and tranquil.

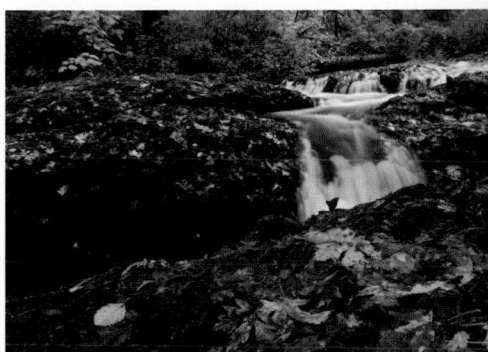

If there is one common refrain with my students, it is the overuse of the horizontal frame. As we just discussed, the world is full of vertical compositions, but they are not always as obvious as the horizontals found at every turn. As you head out the door for a day of shooting, make it a point to dedicate at least 25 percent of your image search to vertical compositions. It's a great habit to get into and before you know it, seeing the obvious verticals will become second nature.

Along the North Falls Trail in Oregon's Silver Falls State Park, several students and I settled in at this small waterfall, where one of my students got busy shooting a horizontal composition similar to the one shown above. I pointed out that he had, in effect, split the frame vertically 50/50, with the right half of the frame waterfall and the left half just leaves. This is a classic example of a vertical composition "hidden" inside a horizontal. A quick twist of the tripod head or flip of the camera, and you have a much more dynamic vertical composition of the same waterfall.

Both images: Nikon D300S with Nikkor 12–24mm lens at 12mm, f/22 for 1/4 sec. with a polarizing filter, ISO 200

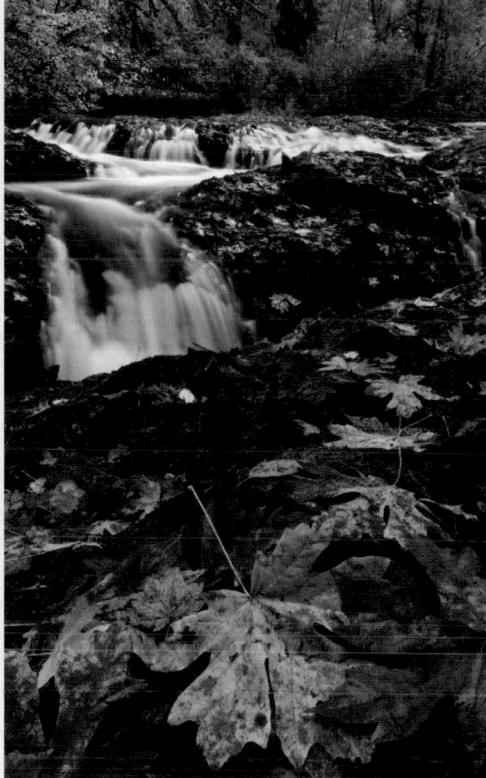

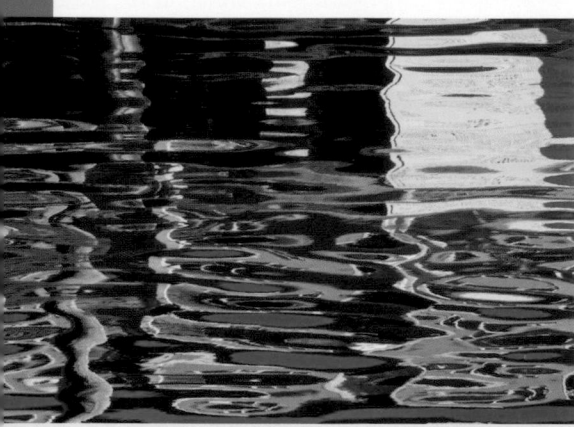

Sometimes hidden verticals are not that easy to spot, especially when they are "hidden" in the abstract. For example, notice how in the horizontal composition of colorful boats reflecting on the water (above), there is a large white "block" in the upper right of the frame. Note how your eye is drawn to that block, which gets the visual weight of the image, yet you are ultimately disappointed, since there is nothing interesting about it. As I mentioned earlier, the point of highest contrast gets the most attention, at least initially, and when the point of highest contrast is *not* the main point of interest, the eye/brain is quick to feel disappointment. What is the solution? Turn the camera vertically and, as if by magic, make the "eyesore" disappear! The vertical composition is cleaner and better balanced throughout, with a composition of classic thirds. The top third is mostly dark with a splash of red, and the remaining two-thirds is composed of contrasting shades of blue and brown.

Both images: Nikon D3X with Nikkor 70–300mm lens, f/32 for 1/30 sec., ISO 200

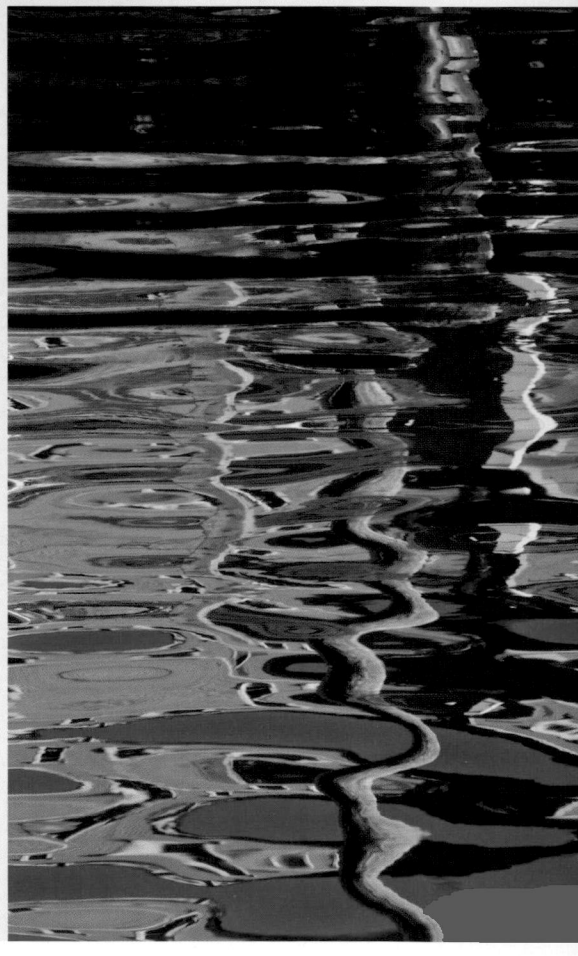

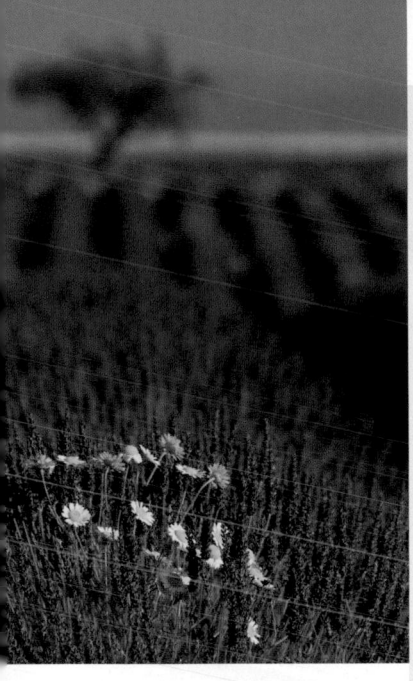

Caution! Sometimes the subject before you can work in either the horizontal frame or the vertical frame, so do not fret if you cannot decide which way to compose your shot. In fact, embrace this as a moment of discovery and shoot the subject both ways, then move on. I had a student a few years back who became paralyzed with indecision over which format he liked best. He must have stood there for no less than 15 minutes, inviting each of us to look through his camera and offering advice (while the most magical light slowly disappeared). Despite my telling him to shoot it both ways and then decide later on his laptop, he just couldn't do it!

Let there be no doubt that I, too, know the feeling of compositional uncertainty. The answer, as I am sure you'll agree, is to just shoot it both ways and move on! That is exactly what I did when shooting these lavender fields atop France's Valensole Plain. Both compositions are obvious examples of "selective focus," with the visual weight placed entirely on the yellow wildflowers in the foreground. Even today, a year later, I am still not sure which one is "best"!

Both images: Nikon D3X with Nikkor 70–300mm lens at 200mm, f/7.1 for 1/320 sec., ISO 100

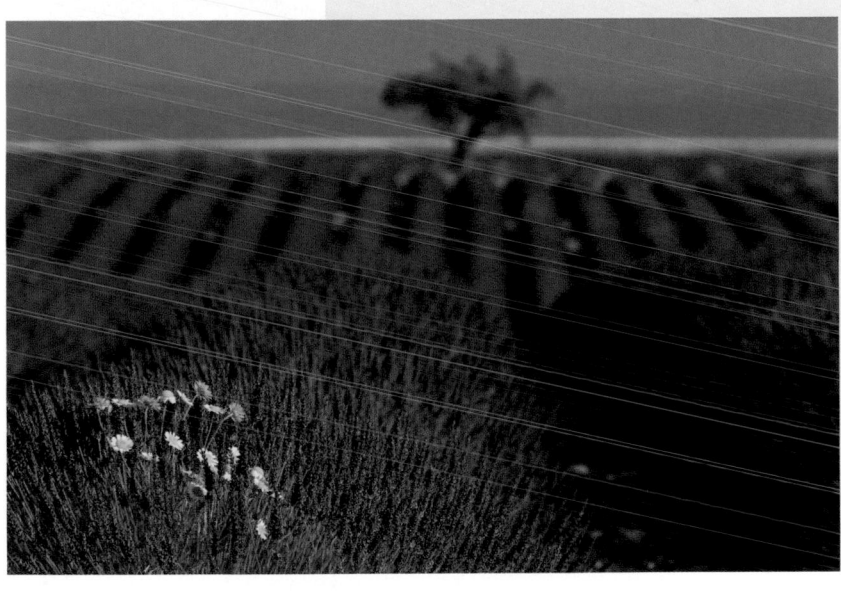

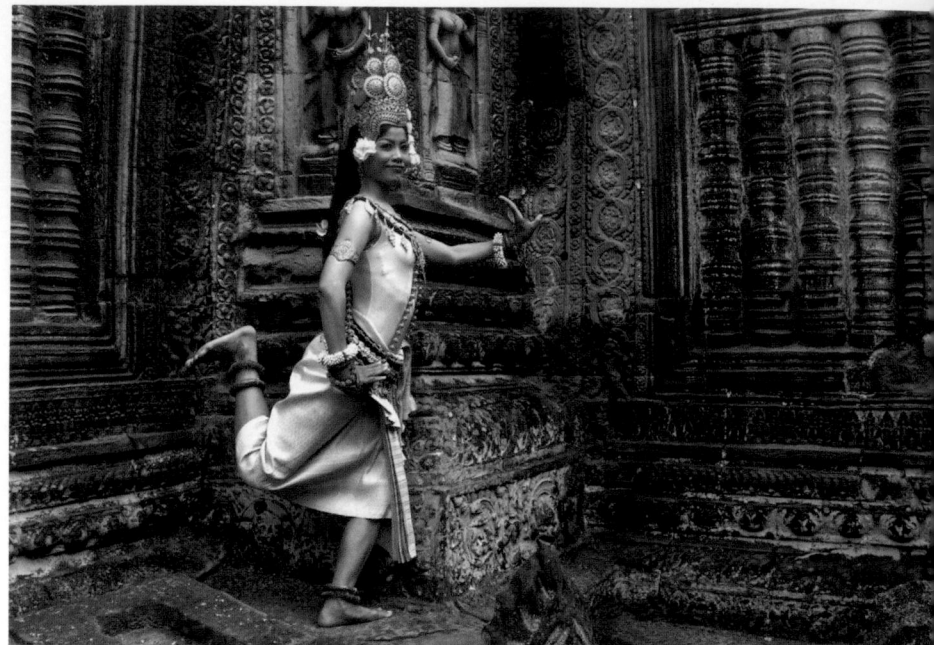

Make it a point to be on the lookout for the verticals everywhere; they really are as plentiful as the more obvious horizontals. This image reminds me of a student I had some years ago. She had a plethora of compositions that, almost without fail, would find the main subject on the left or right with "empty" space on the opposite side. I told her that she needed to shoot these same subjects inside the vertical frame, not only to fill up the frame with the natural vertical subject but also to have a shot at magazine and book covers. She quickly fired back that she had done this deliberately because her client, Argus Publishing, required a horizontal format *with empty space* on one side, since they used that space to place Bible passages and inspirational quotes. Did I ever get an earful that day! Now, whenever I review a large body of a student's work, I start by asking if the student is shooting for Argus Publishing. If the answer is no, only then do I give them a piece of my mind!

In all seriousness, I do call attention to the obvious verticals in my students' horizontal compositions, much as in these images of a young woman in "costume" in Angkor Wat. Note the stronger and more dignified vertical composition. Since it provides more room to fill the frame with my vertical subject, she also looks taller and more pronounced.

Both images: Nikon D3X with Nikkor 24–85mm lens at 35mm, f/11 for 1/60 sec., ISO 100

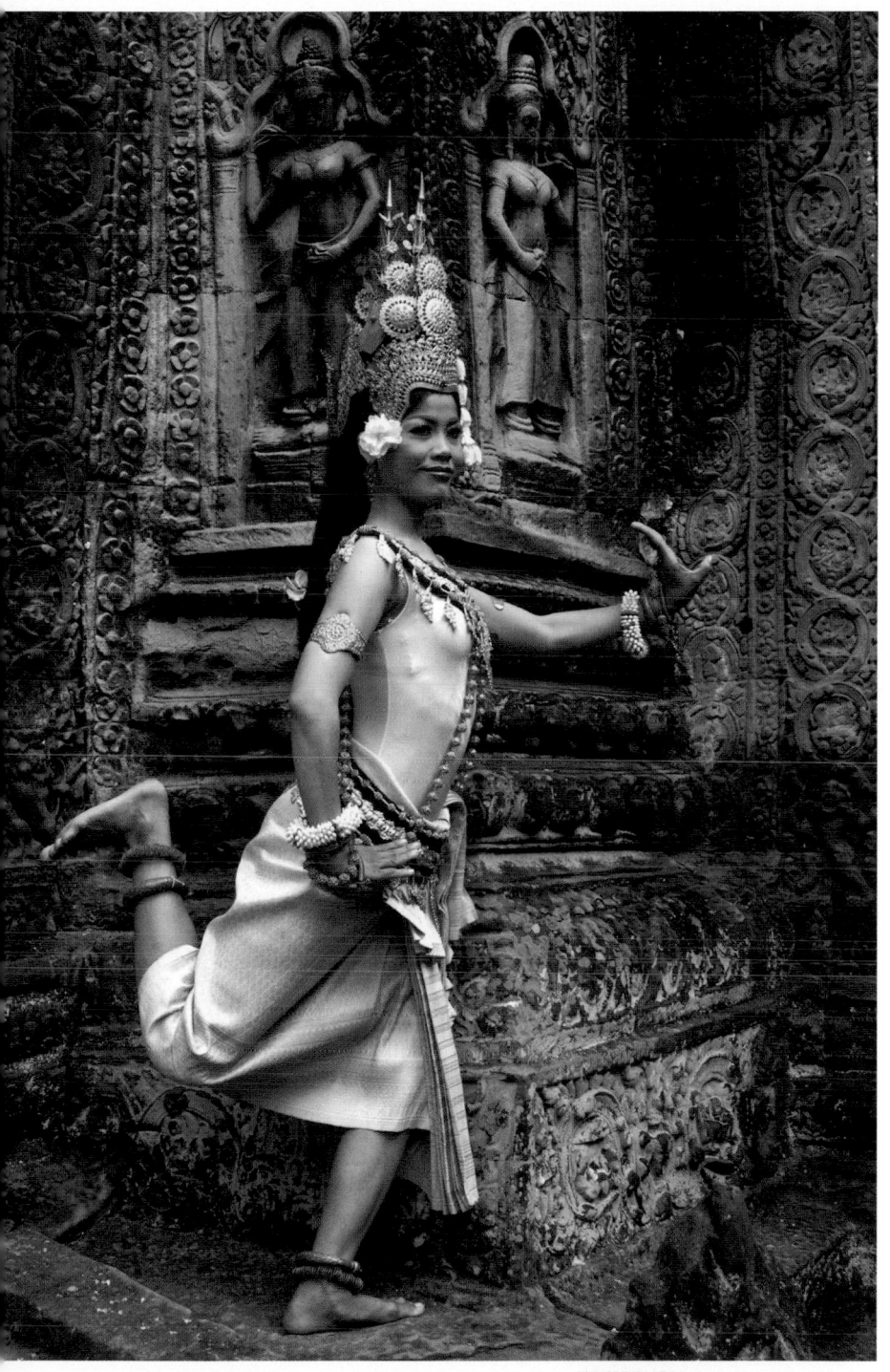

195 HORIZONTAL
VERSUS VERTICAL

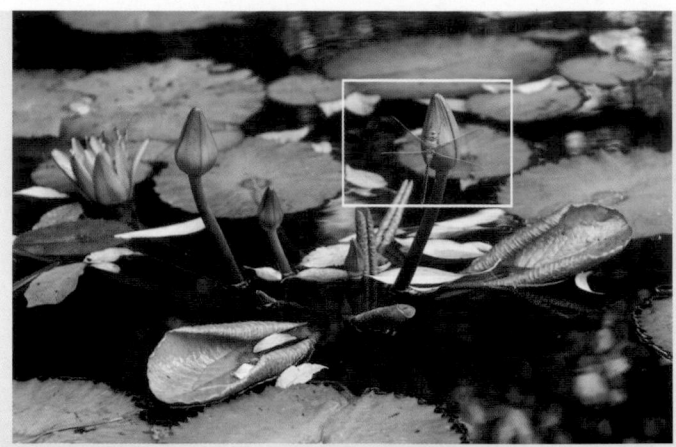

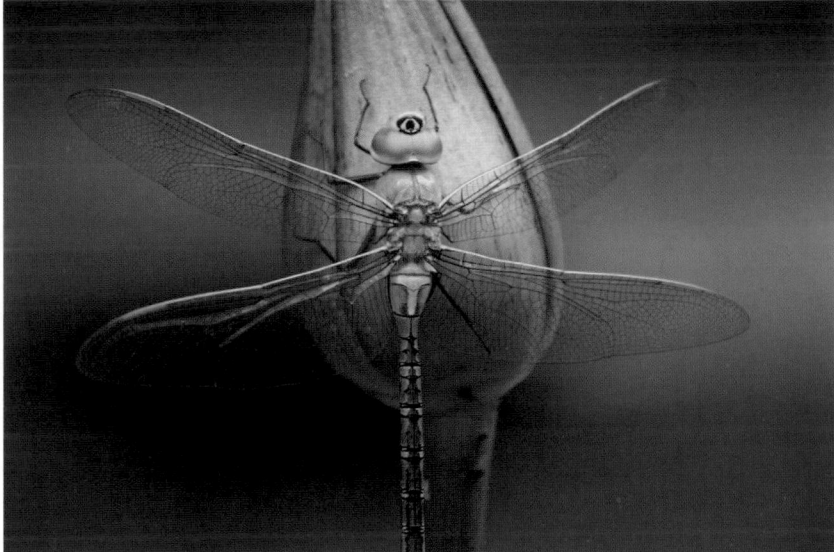

When one of my students spotted this dragonfly, a fantastic photo opportunity awaited those of us who had the "right" equipment to ensure a frame-filling and compelling composition. Sadly, only three of us had it. But whenever there is a shortage of the right equipment, I allow my students to take their SD or CF cards and place them inside my Nikon D300S (which uses both SD and CF cards). I am a firm believer in karma and that old adage "What goes around comes around." I can't tell you how many times, over the past thirty-five-plus years of shooting, I have been in need of a given filter, lens, flash, or reflector, and right next to me was a student holding out the requested piece of gear for the taking. And lest we forget: When is the best time to shoot a vertical? Right after you shoot the horizontal!

Both images: Nikon D300S with Nikkor 70–300mm lens and Canon 500D close-up filter, f/6.3 for 1/125 sec., ISO 200

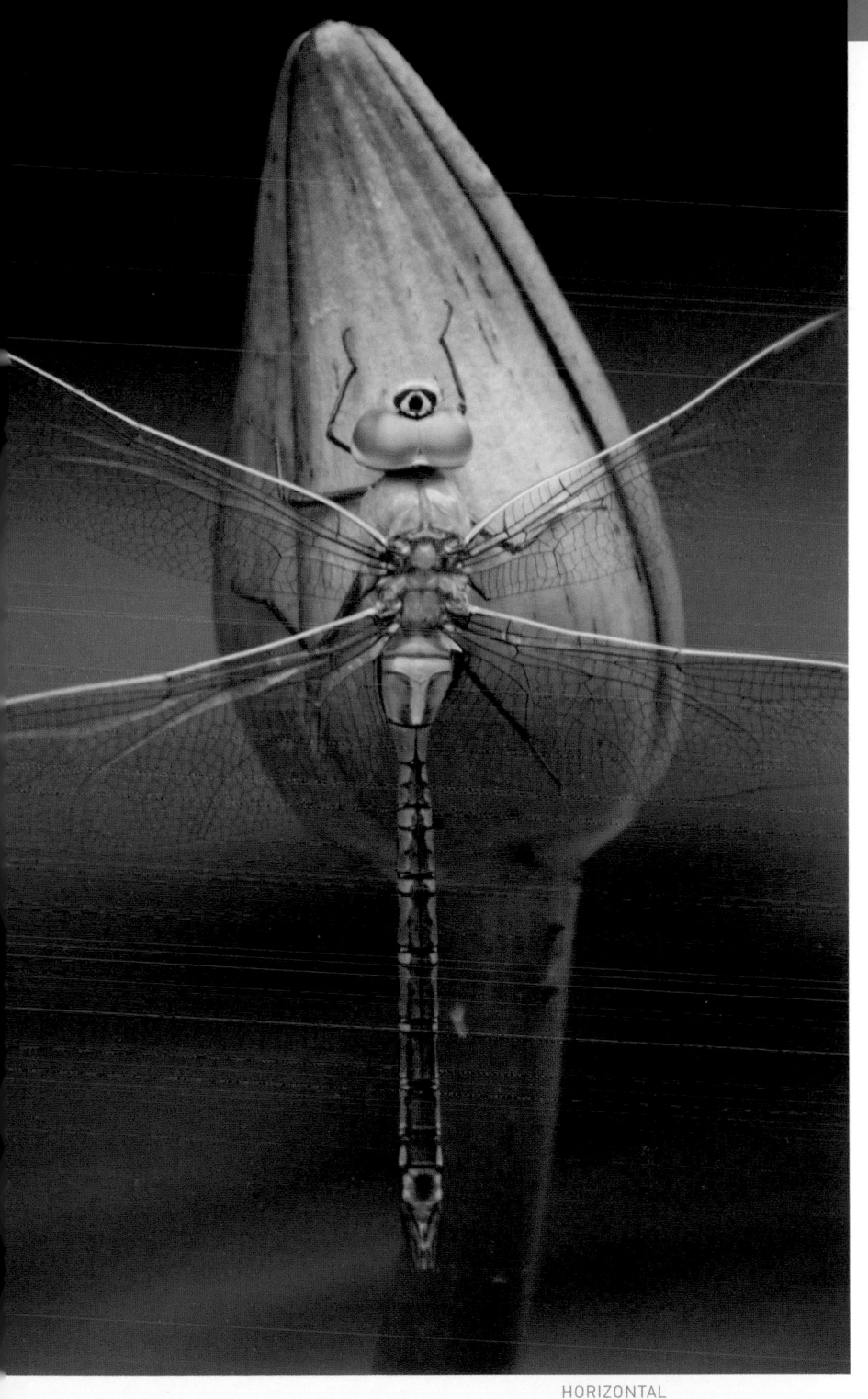

HORIZONTAL
VERSUS VERTICAL

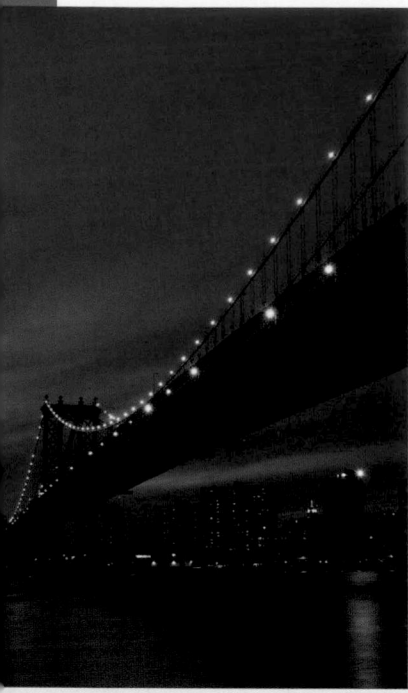

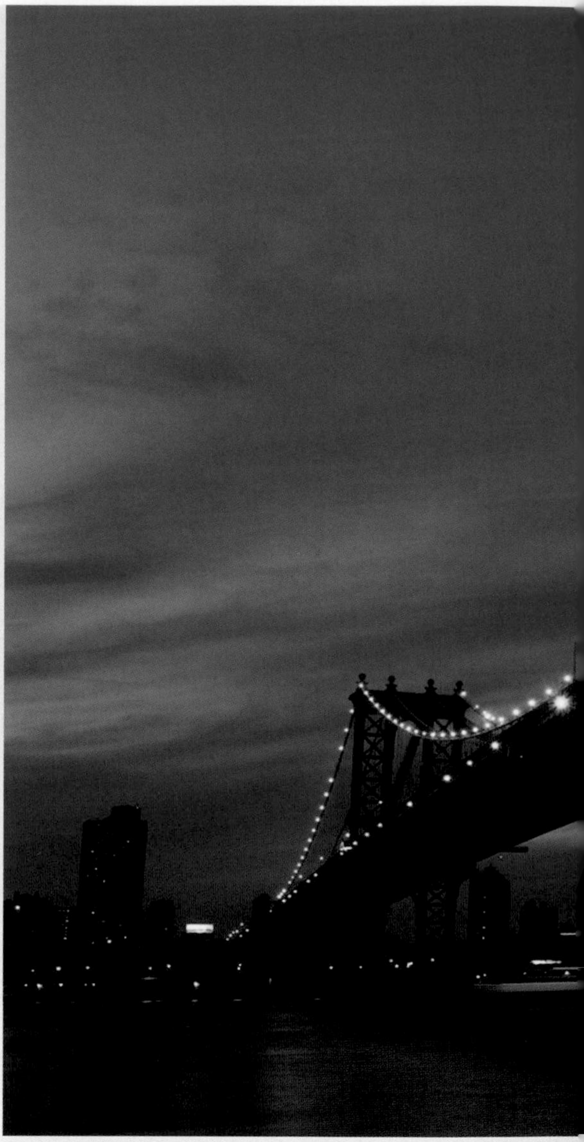

New York City's Manhattan Bridge is another subject that seems like more of a natural horizontal than vertical. In the first shot, a wide-angle lens was used in the much longer horizontal format to ensure that I would, in fact, record a very long bridge. Compare this to the much shorter Manhattan Bridge that has been "forced" inside a vertical frame. Sure, the bridge fits in either frame, but the message is clearly not as long when the bridge is composed inside the vertical frame.

Both images: Nikon D3X with Nikkor 16–35mm lens at 18mm, f/11 for 2 seconds, ISO 100

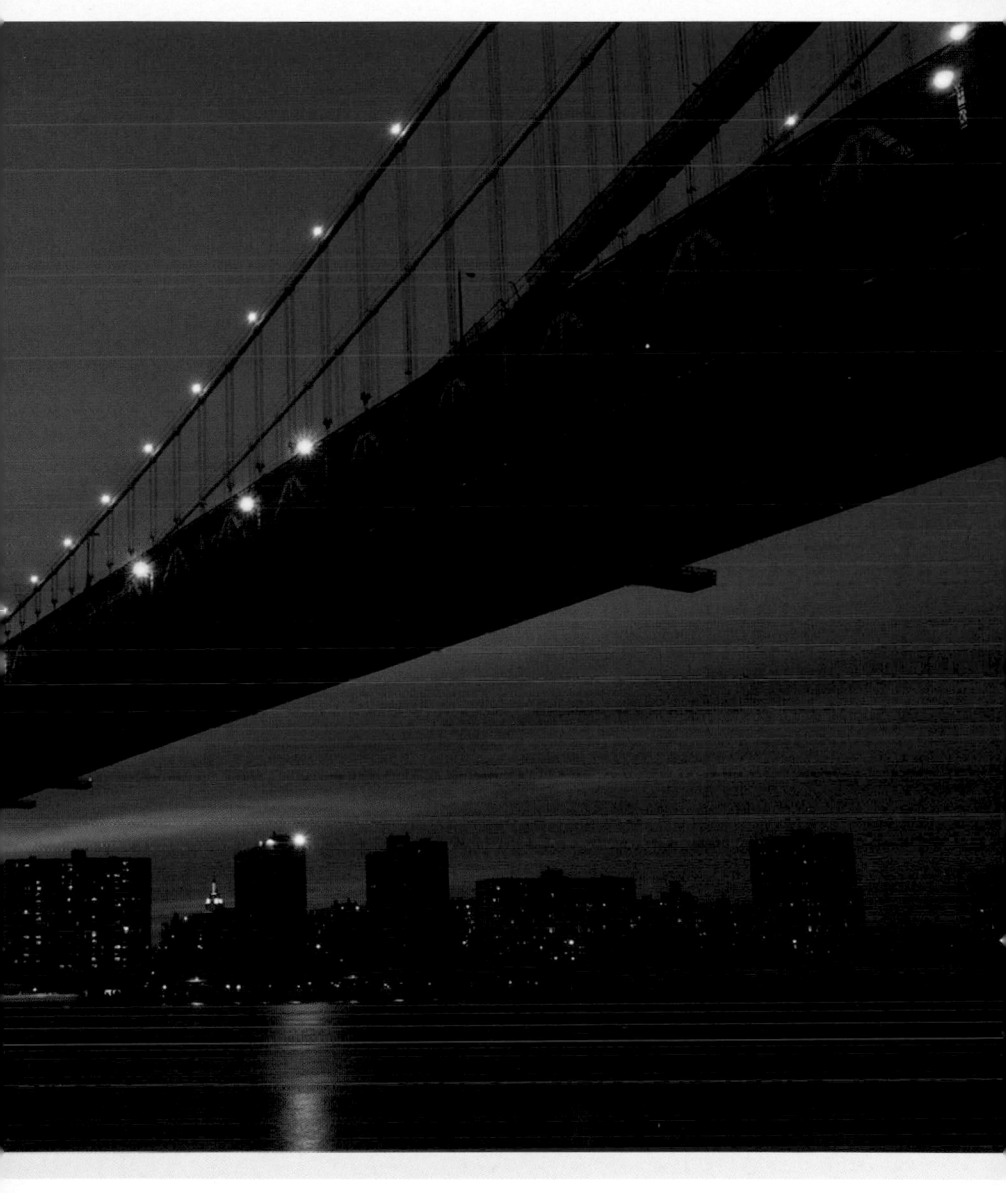

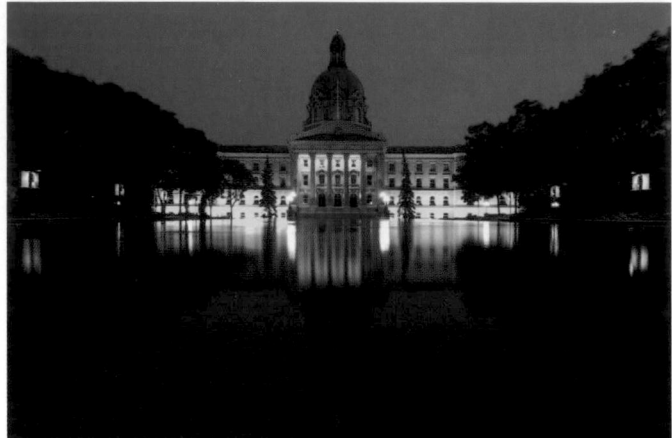

At first glance, the Capitol Building of Edmonton, Alberta, doesn't look like a "natural" vertical composition. It is surely longer and wider than it is tall and narrow—but look again. Sometimes a "normal" horizontal can be transformed into the vertical composition it deserves, thanks to the right lens choice. In the first image shown above, the Capitol Building is allowed to "flow" left to right in a horizontal composition by shooting with my 16–35mm lens at the moderate wide-angle choice of 35mm. Before moving on, I repositioned the camera to a vertical position and then zoomed to 85mm. The composition, the frame, is now narrowed, and as such, the focus can be placed on the "natural" vertical of the Capitol's dome, supported on the sides by the still-horizontal building. In effect, we have centered the building's pride and dignity while also maintaining the maturity, stability, and wisdom conveyed by the horizontal shape of the building on both the left and right sides.

Both images: Nikon D3X with Nikkor 16–35mm lens at 18mm, f/11 for 2 seconds, ISO 100

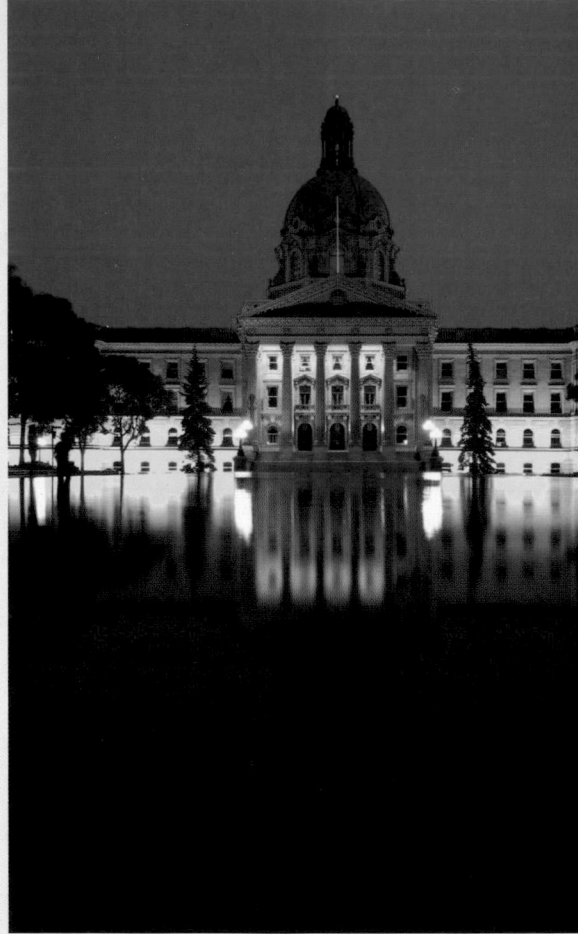

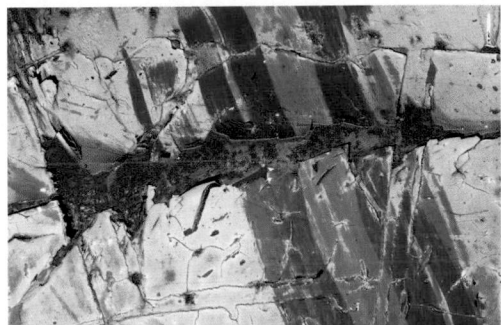

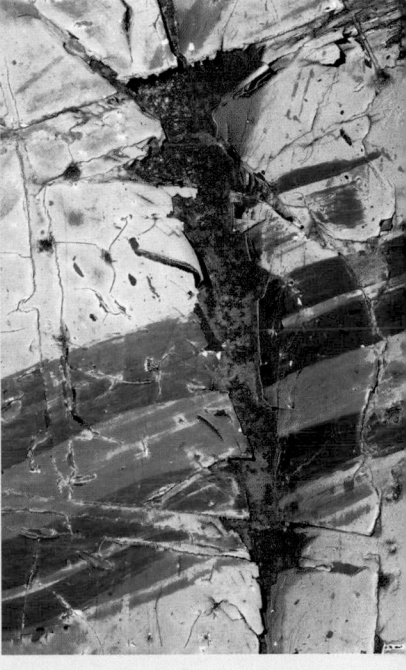

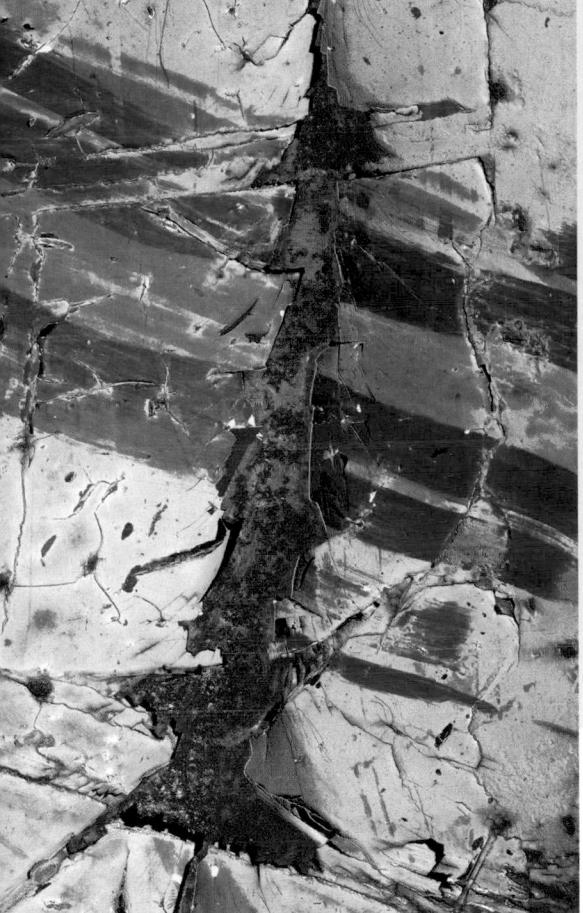

When lit by my SB-900 flash, this detail of chipped and peeling paint on the side of a Dumpster reveals wonderful color and texture. Nice as it is in the horizontal format, it takes on a whole new energy when flipped to a vertical in Photoshop. Depending on how it is flipped, the "lightning bolt" can also be seen as a syringe—either way, both verticals are much more active than the horizontal.

All images: Nikon D3X with Micro-Nikkor 105mm lens, f/16 for 1/125 sec., sidelit with SB-900 electronic flash

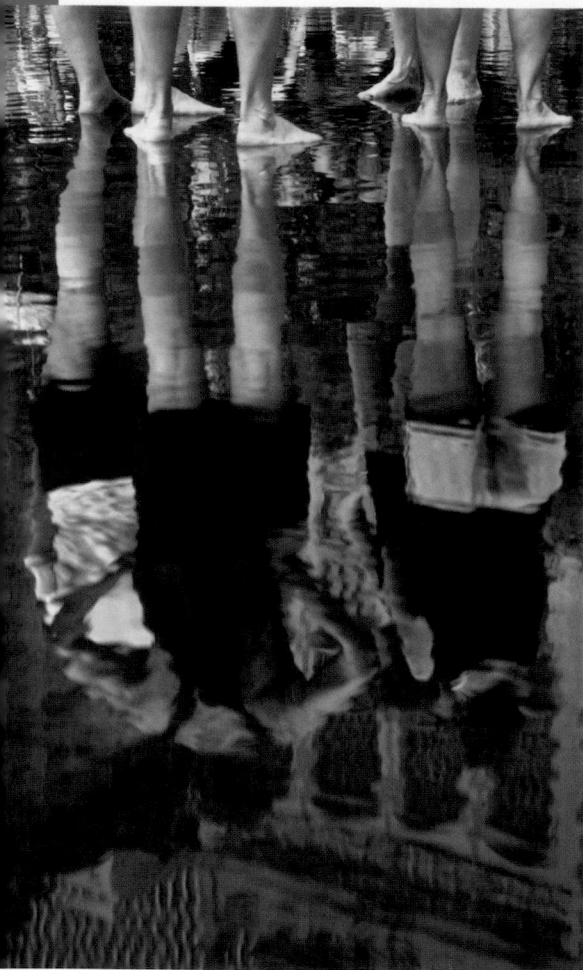

Are you fond of abstracts, such as reflections, rust, or peeling paint? If so, then try gathering a half-dozen or so of your abstract images. If my hunch is correct, you have never considered flipping your images, yet chances are good that if you were to simply "flip" them with your photo-editing software, you might discover an even more dynamic image.

Here is one example, taken in the early morning summer hours at Millennium Park in downtown Chicago. As you can see, we were shooting abstracts of the reflections of buildings and of locals and tourists strolling across the shallow reflecting pond. I framed up the composition at left, composing tightly around their reflection. When flipped for the second image (opposite), we are thrown off a bit, due to the abstract nature of this "new" composition. An effective abstract, in my view, is one that causes the viewer to stop and wonder, "What is that?" or "How was that done?"

Both images: Nikon D3X with Nikkor 70–300mm lens at 120mm, f/32 for 1/20 sec., ISO 100

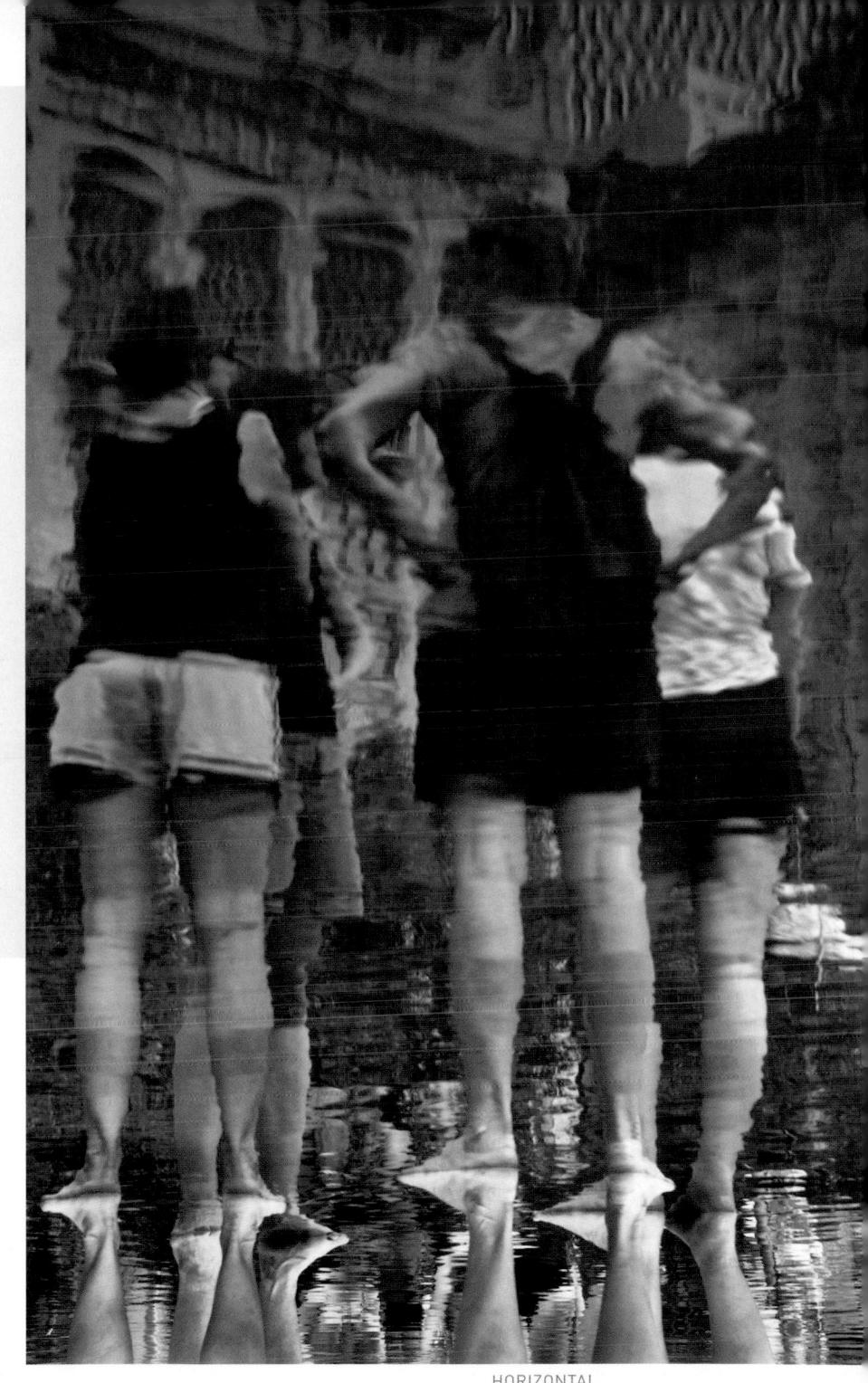

HORIZONTAL
VERSUS VERTICAL

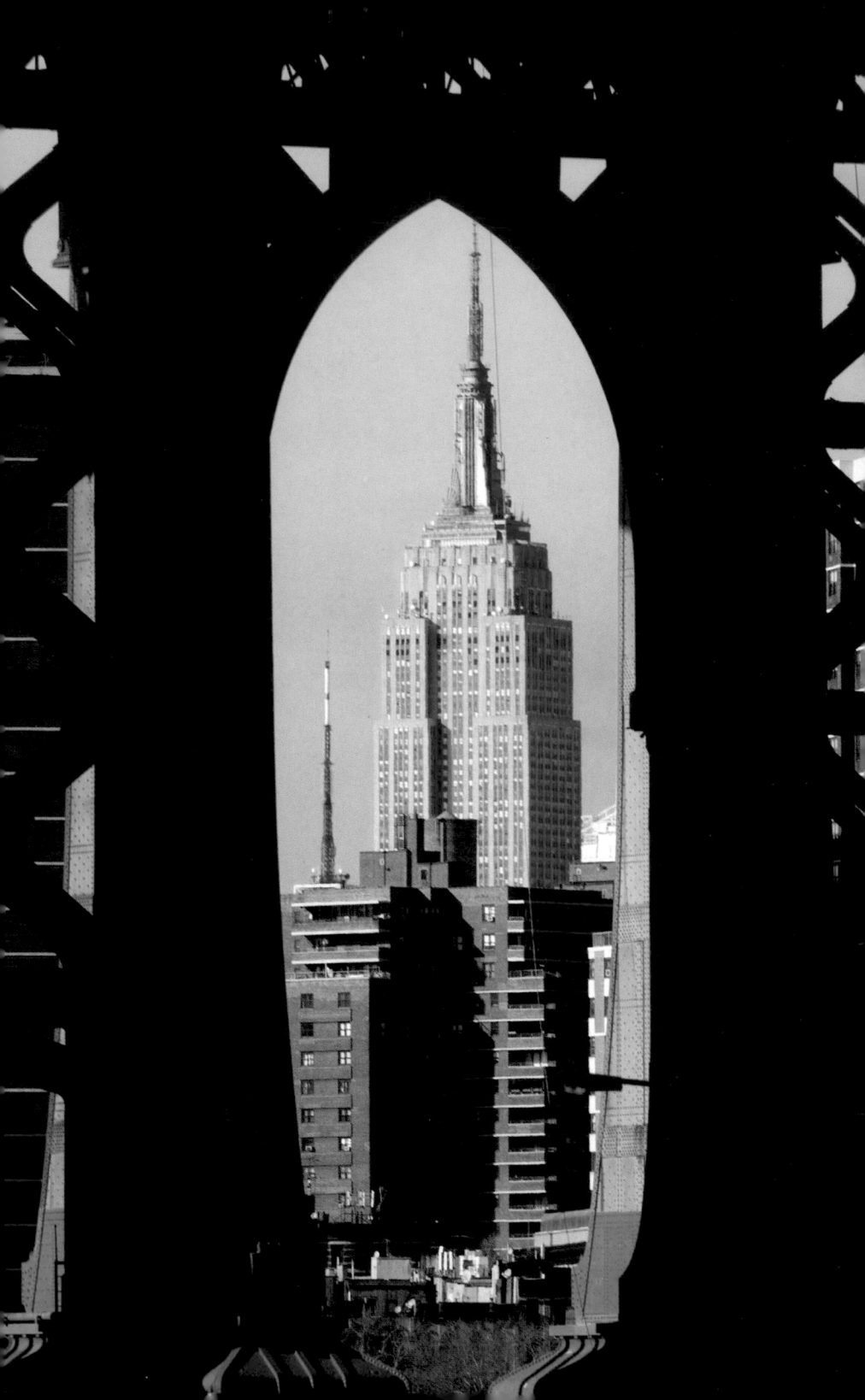

10
FRAMING WITH A FRAME

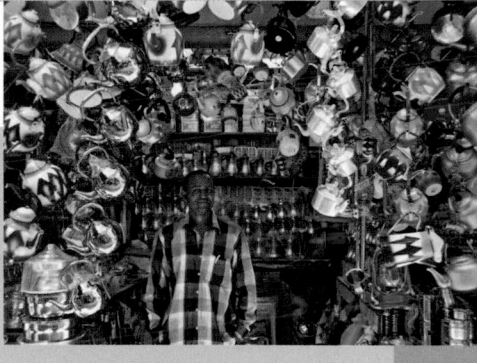

One surefire way to make an image more appealing is to introduce foreground subject matter that calls attention to, and frames, the main subject in the background. This technique is often referred to as *framing with a frame*. It is one of the simplest ways to create both depth and perspective in a composition. Opportunities to use framing with a frame abound: tree branches, fences, large boulders, framing through someone's feet or hands, tall grasses, and blooming flowers, just to name a few.

There are two ways to create the framing-with-a-frame effect, both highly dependent on the right aperture choice. If you want your foreground frame to be sharp, then, more often than not, you'll need a wide-angle lens combined with a small aperture of f/16 or f/22. If, on the other hand, you want your foreground frame to comprise out-of-focus tones or colors, use a telephoto lens combined with a large aperture.

Nikon D3X with Nikkor 70–300mm lens, f/16 for 8 seconds, ISO 100

To use this technique successfully, it's important to avoid using a foreground subject/frame that distracts the eye. For example, if your foreground frame consists of out-of-focus pink flowers that clash with sharply focused orange flowers and lines of textured tree bark, it might be more of a distraction than a frame that leads the eye to your subject in the background.

Think about whether your frame adds something necessary to the composition or is just an "extra" element that detracts from your main subject. Ask yourself the following: If I removed the foreground frame, would I miss it? If the answer is a resounding yes, then the frame is a good choice. If, on the other hand, it only serves to distract, then it's obviously not a good idea. As a general rule of thumb, a foreground frame should not dominate the composition. Its role should be limited to calling attention to the main subject.

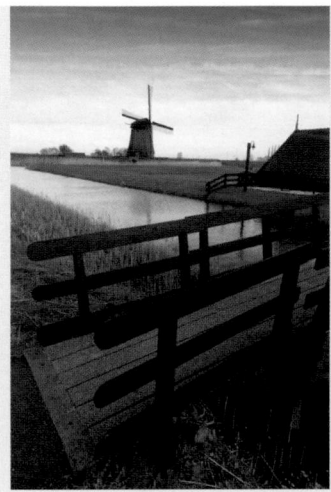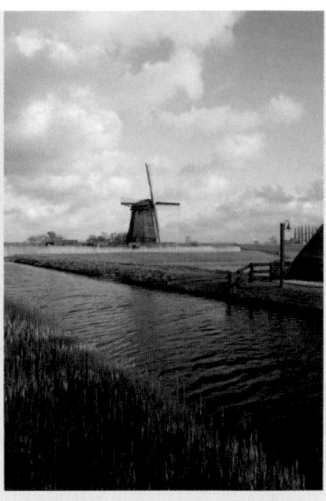

Over the course of several years, I have photographed the windmills of Schemeerhorn, in Holland, countless times. However, it had never occurred to me until this very afternoon that an opportunity to frame with a frame had been here all along. By getting down low with my 16–35mm and shooting at or near 16mm, I was able to frame the distant windmill with the dark textured wood of the little bridge.

Compare the windmill with and without the frame. Personally, I feel that the mere framing of the windmill makes it "feel" that much more important, and the foreground opening on the little bridge lends obvious depth and distance. It does not hurt that the wood is dark, adding some welcome contrast to the softer background of greens and blues.

All images: Nikon D3X with Nikkor 16–35mm lens, f/22 for 1/45 sec., ISO 200

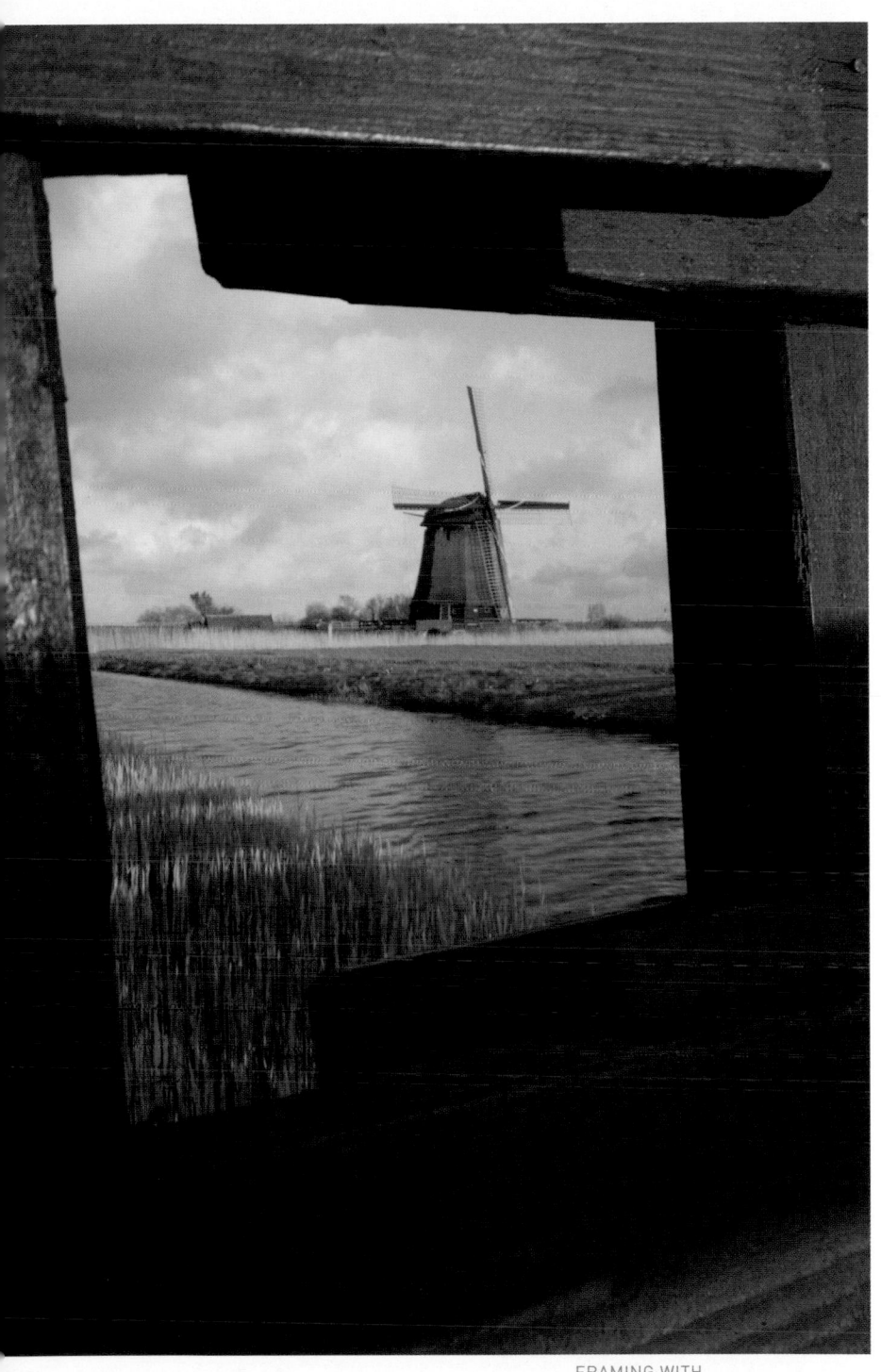

FRAMING WITH
A FRAME

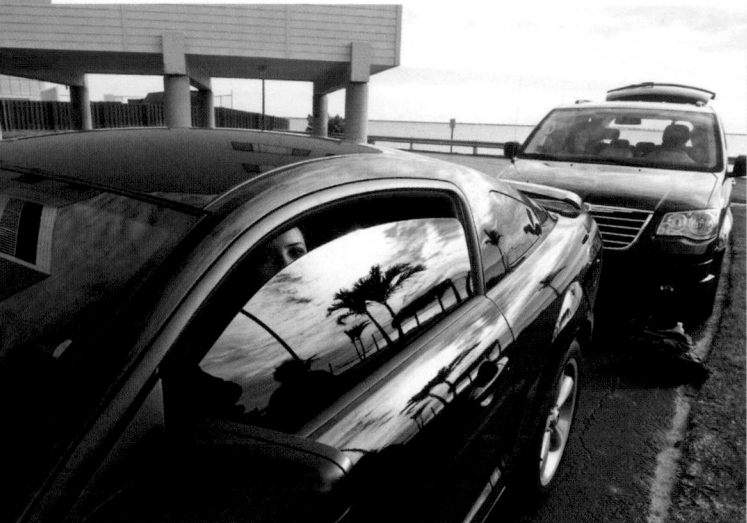

During a workshop in Tampa, Florida, one of the models, named Diana, got cold and asked to sit in my assistant's black Mustang. As she cracked the window open to let in some fresh air, I spotted the shot you see opposite and shouted, "Stop!" After a few tweaks with the opening of the window, I felt it was opened right where it should be and moved in closer to fill the frame with black shapes and one curvilinear line, revealing a pair of eyes. Fortunately, the Mustang had dark-tinted windows, which combined with the roof of the car to make a nice, dark frame around Diana.

How did I expose this shot? Before taking the exposure you see here, I had Diana roll down the window most of the way and filled the frame with her face. With my "who cares" aperture of f/11 in place, I adjusted the shutter speed until 1/125 sec. indicated a correct exposure, and then I had her roll the window back up to where you see it here. Not surprisingly, once the window was rolled back up, my light meter was influenced by all the black and told me the image was way underexposed. But as you can see here, my exposure was correct.

Nikon D3X with Nikkor 70–300mm lens at 70mm, f/11 for 1/125 sec., ISO 100

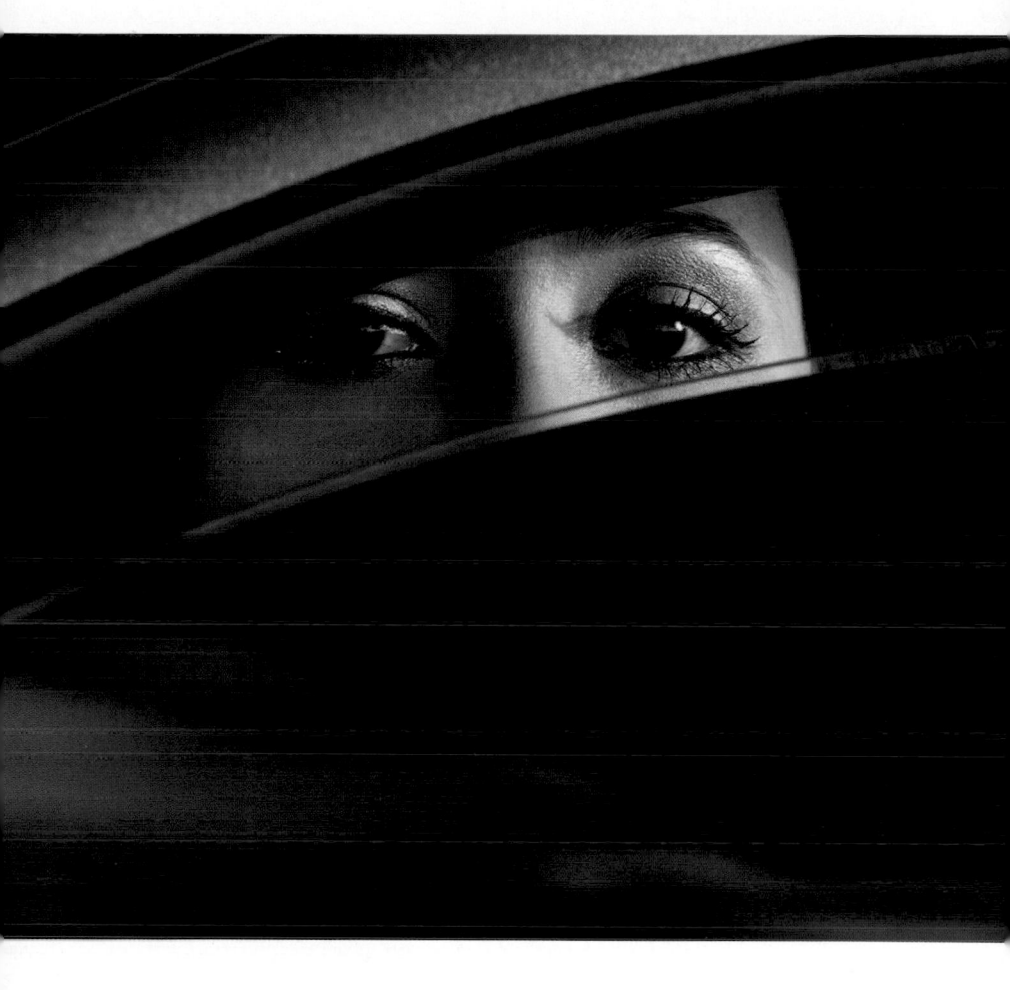

FRAMING WITH
A FRAME

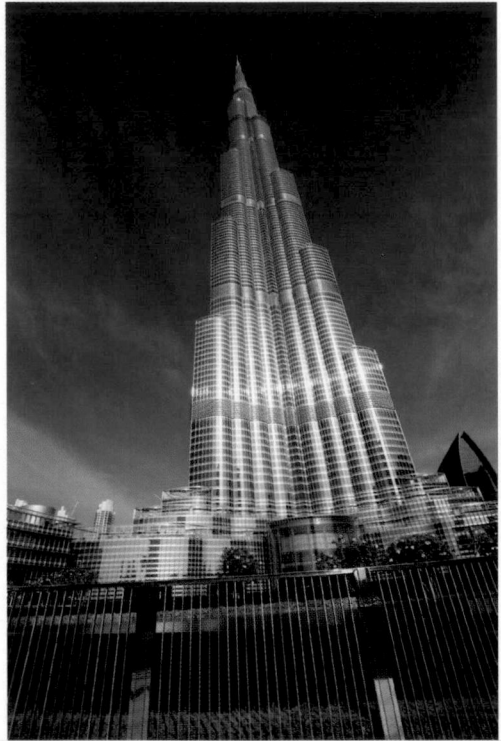

I don't know which of us was more excited—me or my daughter Sophie—but on this particular morning we were going to see the world's tallest skyscraper, the Burj Dubai (now Burj Khalifa) in Dubai. We got there early and within minutes were told by the security guard that we could not take pictures from "here" or "there." Despite my attempts at diplomacy, it was obvious this was one battle I would lose. Luckily, there is no shortage of views of the Burj Dubai, and even from 5 miles away, you can find a vantage point to make a nice picture. As shown here, Sophie and I did find our view and, with a bit of inventiveness, took advantage of a nearby fence and a super-wide-angle lens to frame the Burj Dubai.

Nikon D3X with 16–35mm lens at 16mm, f/22 for 1/60 sec., ISO 100

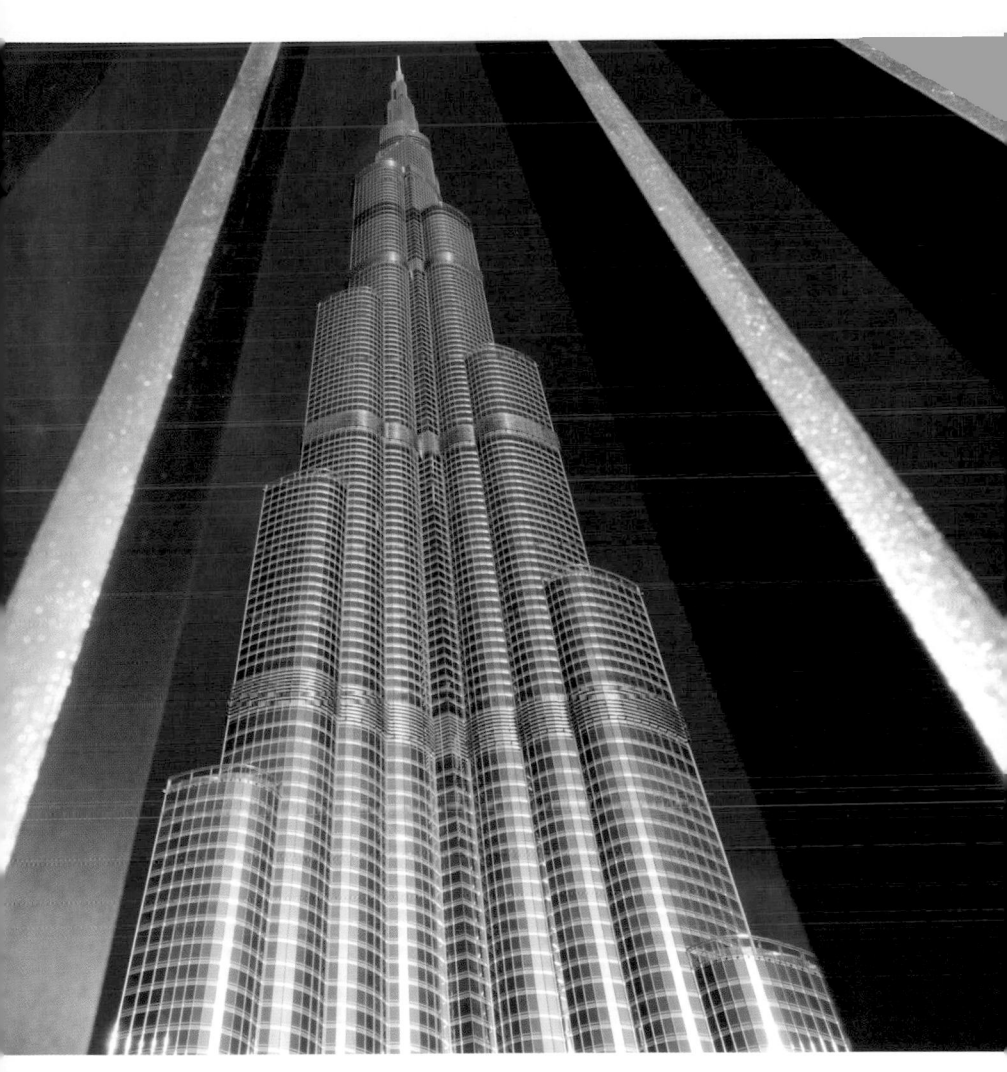

FRAMING WITH
A FRAME

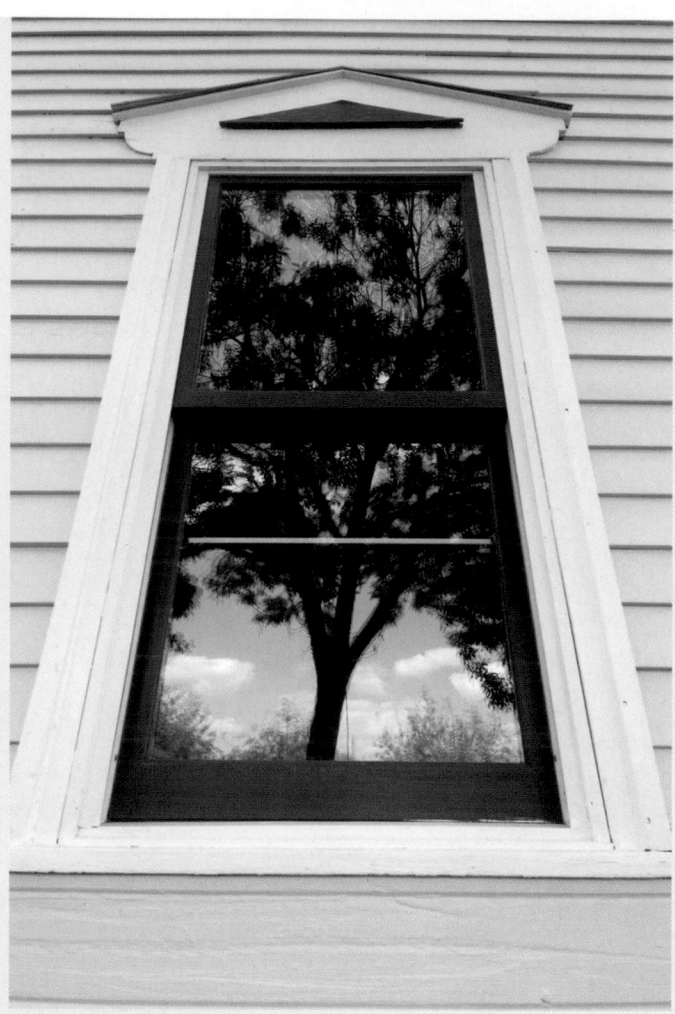

While shooting in a cemetery in Cape Cod, I happened to look up while moving past this small yellow church in the cemetery yard, and I caught sight of this lone window and its framed reflection. It was a tall window—about 6 feet off the ground—so when I framed it with my 24-85mm lens at the 24mm focal length, it came as no surprise that the distortion was quite magnified. Distortion like this is the norm when shooting up with a wide-angle lens, and it is further magnified when lines are present, such as the lines that make up the window as well as the lines found in the reflected tree. We are all familiar with the converging parallels of train tracks and how the two tracks create both depth and distance. Although these two converging lines of the window do not actually meet at a distant point, they still suggest depth and distance.

Nikon D300S with Nikkor 12–24mm lens, f/11 for 1/100 sec, ISO 200

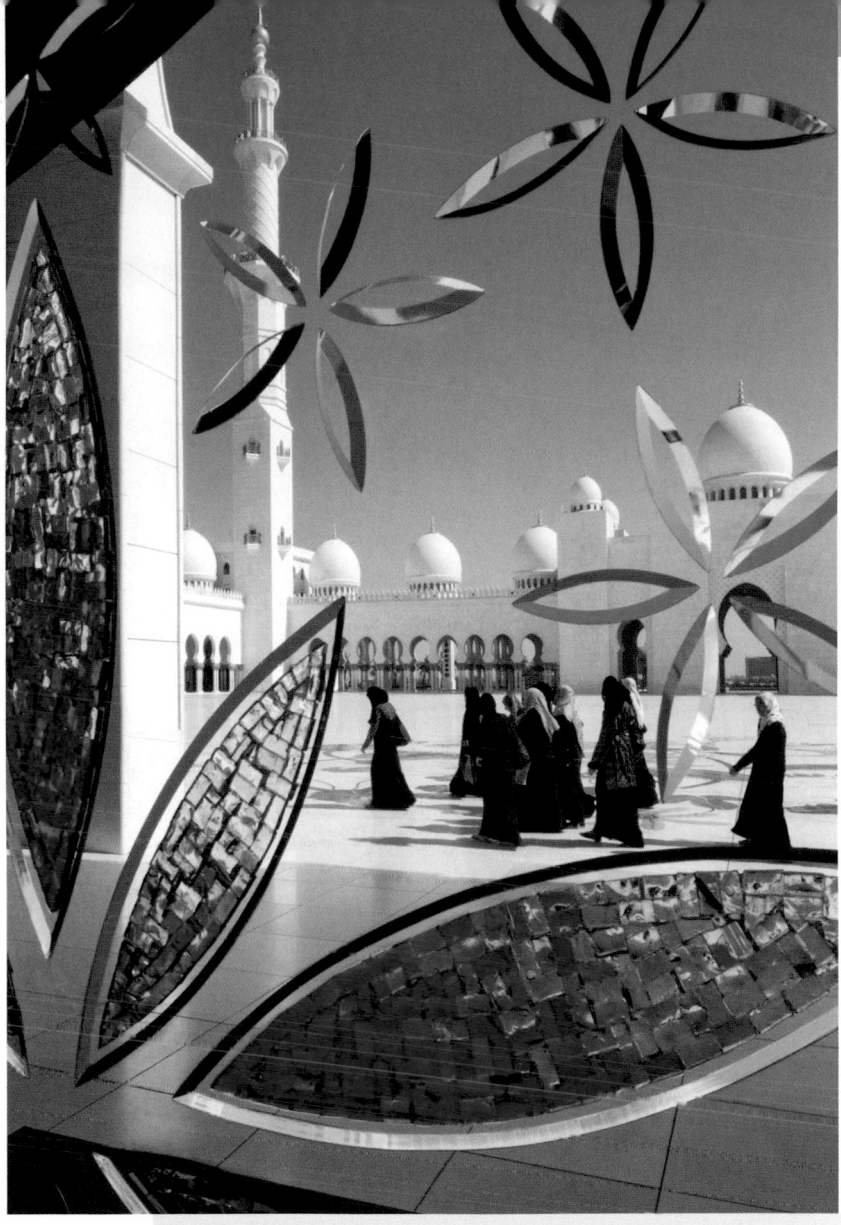

From inside the Sheikh Zayed Mosque in Abu Dhabi, you have marvelous views of the inner courtyard. Several large windows inside the mosque have truly intricate designs of leaded glass, and while framing one such design, a small group of burka-clad women strode past the window. Fortunately, I was ready and managed to get three shots, this being the best of the three. It is another example of framing with a frame and, not surprisingly, since I was using an aperture of f/22, I was able to render sharpness from the immediate foreground to infinity.

Nikon D3X with Nikkor 16–35mm lens at 24mm, f/22 for 1/100 sec, ISO 200

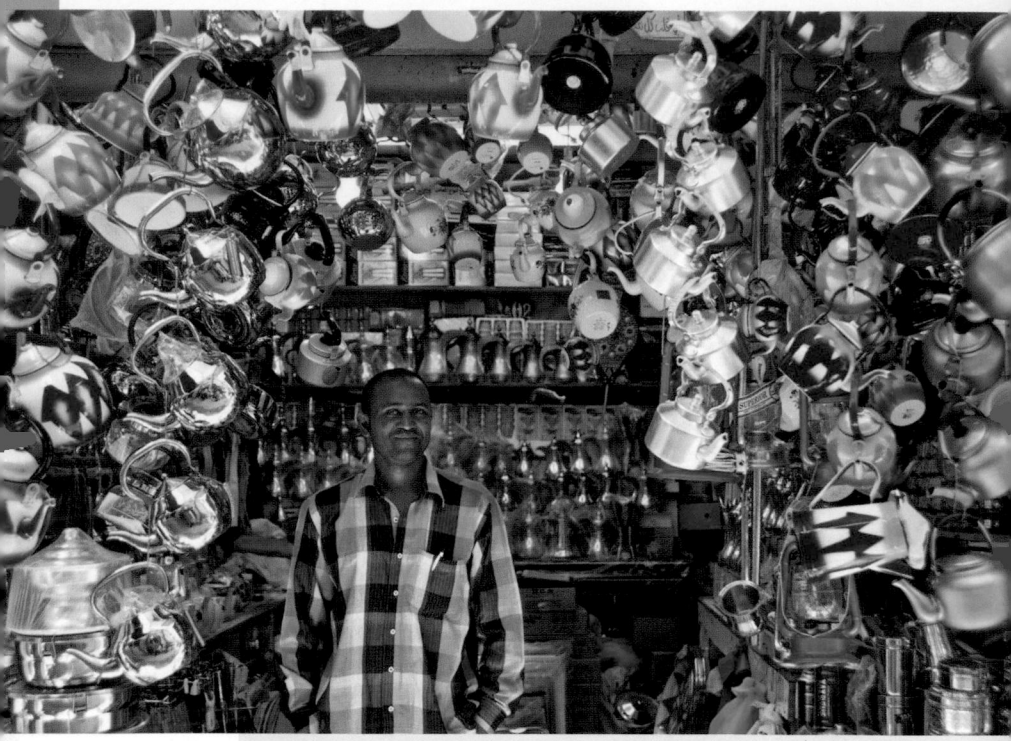

In downtown "old Kuwait," I came upon this vendor selling teakettles in all different styles, colors, and sizes. As you can see, he had no trouble posing and smiling for me, and when I was done, he presented me with a beautiful teapot for free, thanking "me" for coming to the aid of the Kuwaiti people following the invasion by Iraq.

Look closely and you see that once again, I drew on framing with a frame. The arching, rainbowlike shape of the teakettles spotlight the man, and since he is the only part of the composition that doesn't fit the pattern, his visual weight becomes the strongest. This is a good example of how a major shift in contrast calls attention to a much smaller subject. In doing so, the smaller subject is made "larger" and more important by comparison.

Nikon D3X with Nikkor 16–35mm lens at 20mm, f/11 for 1/60 sec., ISO 200

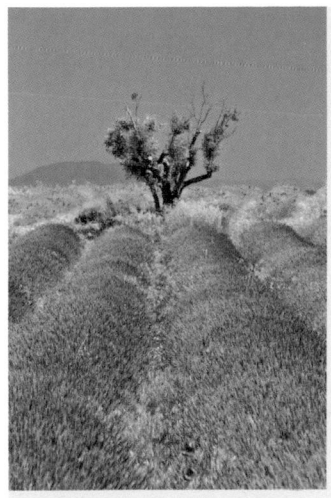

Atop the Valensole Plain in Provence, France, finding a lone tree among the plentiful rows of lavender is like finding the surprise in a box of Cracker Jacks. As we can see in the first example (left), taken with a wide-angle lens, the rows of lavender converge toward the tree, creating a sense of depth and distance, but the eye-level point of view still makes this a rather pedestrian image.

I then spotted some red poppies and a few yellow daisies amid the lavender and got an idea: What if I picked a few of each and held them close to my 70–300mm lens while focusing on the distant tree? With my aperture at f/5.6, I held the flowers about 18 inches from my lens, creating an out-of-focus red-and-yellow frame around the tree. With this frame in the foreground, a surprising landscape unfolds. The frame of color not only makes the tree seem more important but also implies a kind of secret, as if we are peeking in at the life of the tree.

Top: Nikon D2X with Nikkor 24–85mm lens at 60mm, f/22 for 1/60 sec., ISO 100; Bottom: Nikon D2X with Nikkor 70–300mm lens at 70mm, f/5.6 for 1/1000 sec., ISO 100

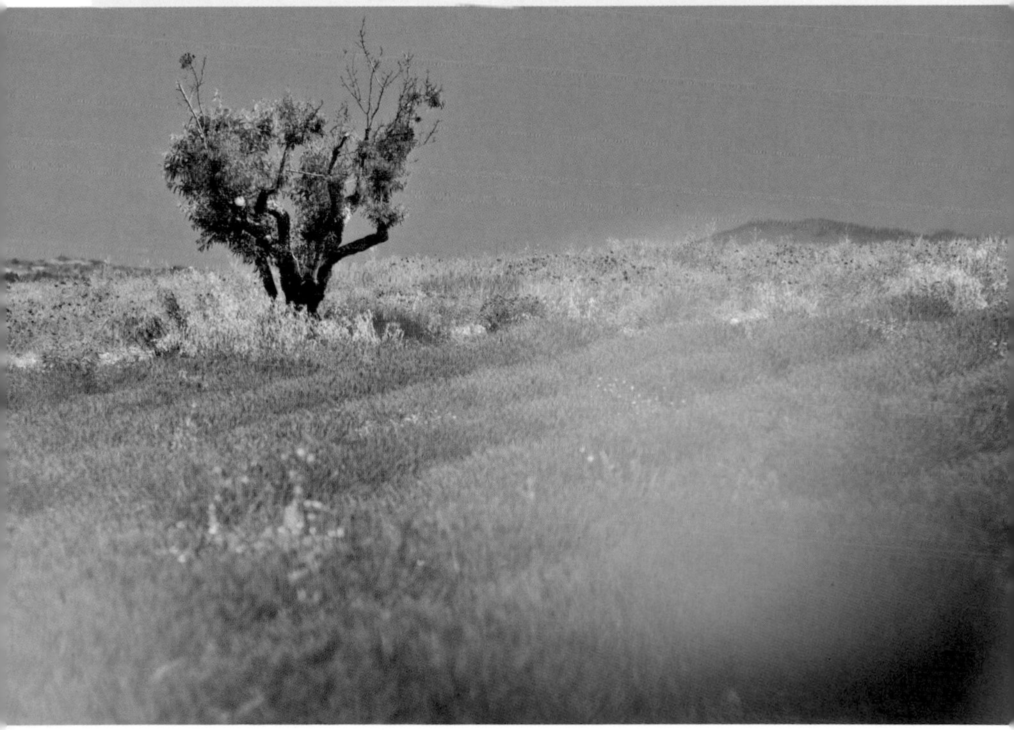

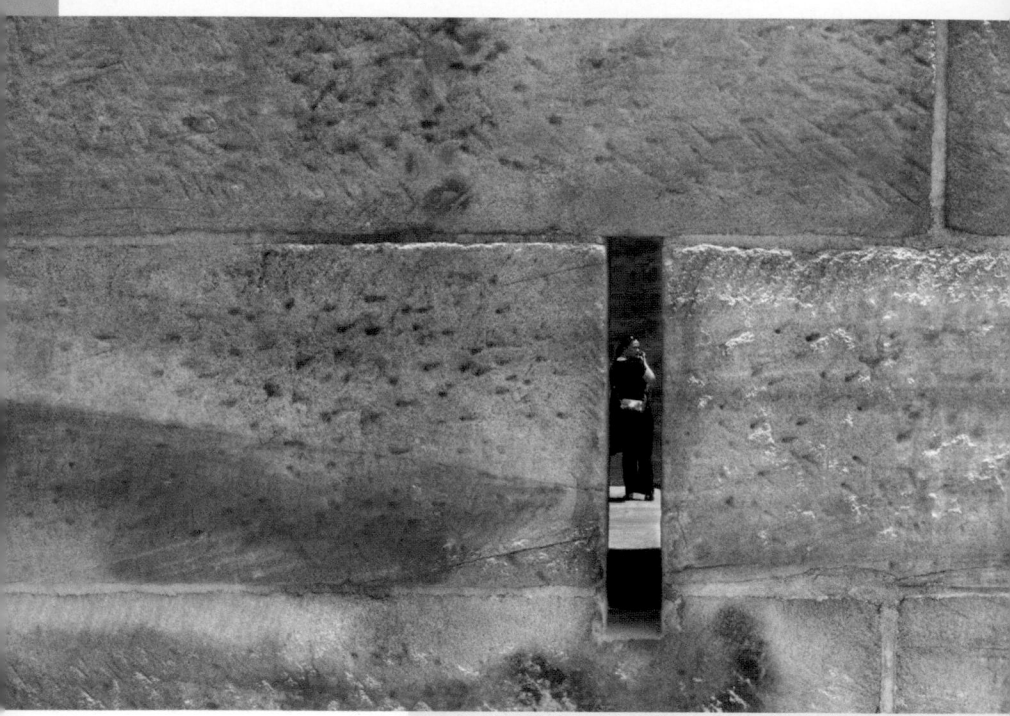

While shooting an old fort in Sydney, Australia, I spotted one of my students through a small opening in the fort's stone wall. I quickly placed the camera to my eye, and once I had what I felt was a nice composition, I hollered out her name. Just as she turned around, I fired the camera. Surrounded by the massive rock, this lone student is in marked contrast to the surrounding shapes and textures. Even though she is so small in the overall frame, she looms largest of all in terms of importance. This is in part because of the contrast between her and the surroundings but also because of the way she is framed.

Nikon D300S with 12–24mm lens at 12mm, f/22 for 1/100 sec., ISO 200

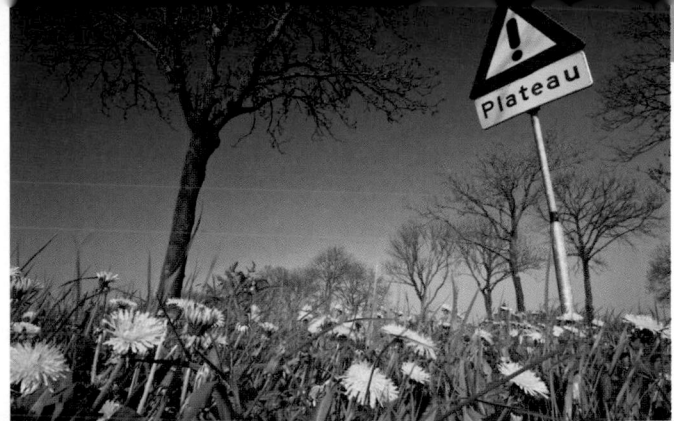

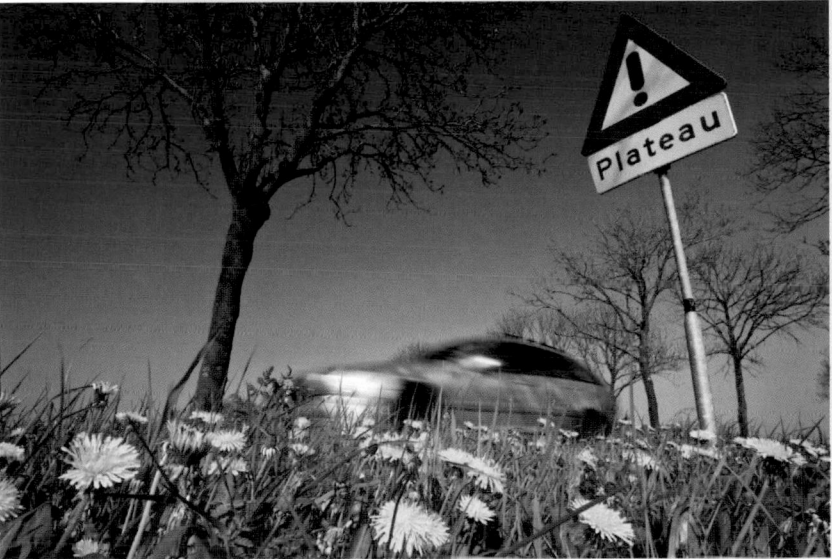

It's important to note that when framing with a frame, you are doing so because you want to elevate your subject's importance. As we have seen, the frame can be as simple as an actual window frame itself or lines that converge, point to, or wrap around the subject. Sometimes I have seen my students unknowingly create a framing with a frame yet have nothing inside the frame. This empty frame leaves the viewer feeling that something is missing. An effective arrangement is one that prompts the viewer to stick around and continue to look, to feel touched and affected by the work.

In the first example (top), we realize that something is missing because of the way the foreground tree on the left and the red road sign to the right seem to be framing "something." Was it a jogger who just passed by, or a person on a bicycle, or . . . ? Although I was hoping for a jogger or a bicyclist to pass, it wasn't to be. But I was nonetheless ready and in position when a lone car came by. As we compare the two images, I'll bet most of us would agree that the arrangement with the car makes more visual sense.

Both images: Nikon D3X with Nikkor 16–35mm lens, f/22 for 1/25 sec., ISO 100

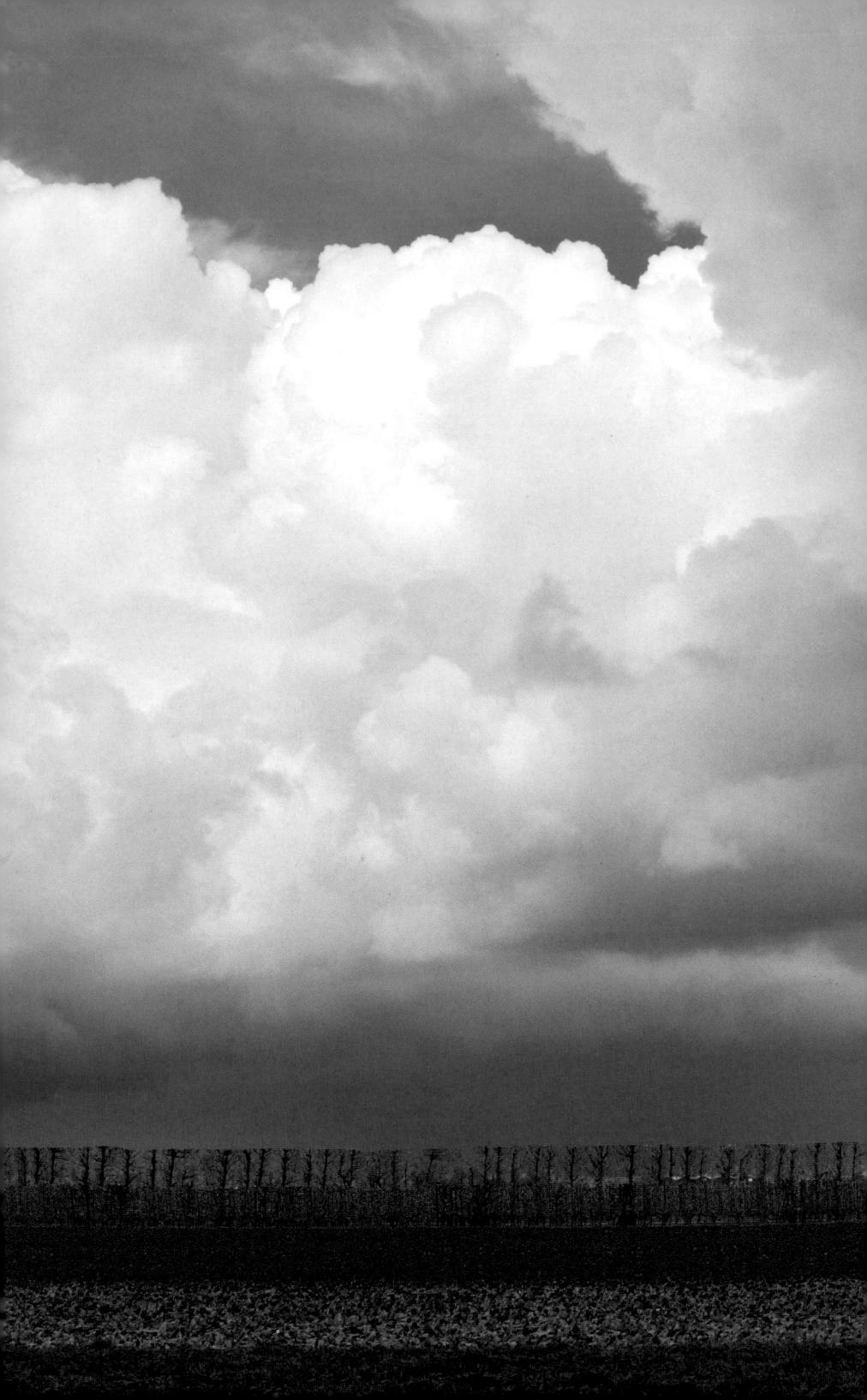

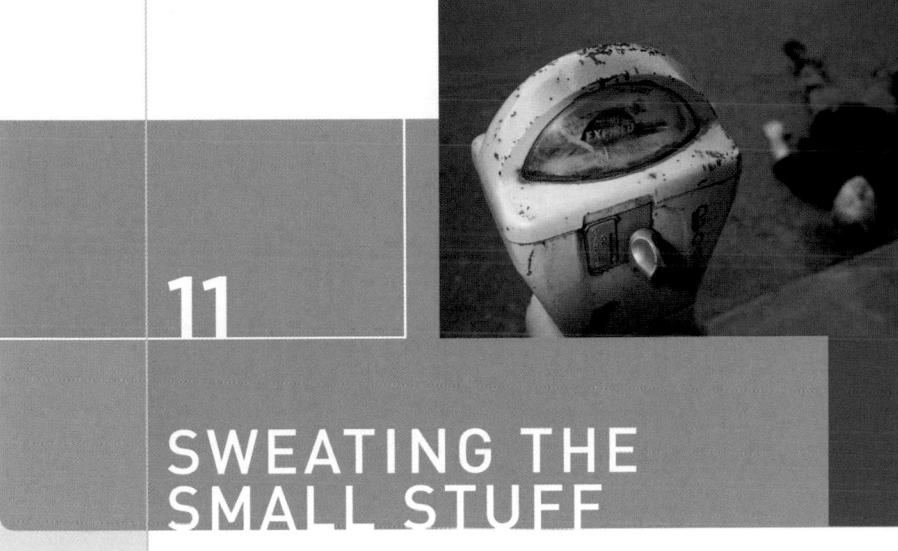

11

SWEATING THE SMALL STUFF

Have you ever been seduced by an advertisement that seemed to promise a really great deal for a particular product only to realize that it was not such a great deal once you read the fine print? I ask because many of my students' compositions remind me of these types of "great deals" that soon wither under careful scrutiny.

Beyond the obvious—split horizons, large and glaring contrasts and tonal shifts, excessive distance from the subject—these are the errors made at an even deeper level, a level that may be invisible to all but the most discerning eye, honed by countless image-making and/or image-editing experiences.

A discerning eye should be every photographer's goal. A discerning eye catches the smallest of details—details that would otherwise have a negative effect on the overall composition. A discerning eye also picks up places where just a minor shift may lead to a major and positive change in the photograph's overall appeal. If there is a barometer of

Nikon D3X with Nikkor 70–300mm lens, f/11 for 1/200 sec., ISO 100

photographic maturity, reaching the level of "weeding out the fine print" would be it. Fine print is often hidden—that is why it's called *fine print*. But it is there—those small and subtle shifts in contrast, color, and tone that the discerning eye refuses to tolerate. Repeat after me: "I am an artist. And just like a painter, I always have the option of starting with a blank canvas. I also can decide *what* I place on my canvas, *where* I place it, and in how many layers!"

Most of us would have no trouble spotting white flour spilled on a dark apron, the contrast clear enough for even the least discerning eye to notice. The trick is spotting the white flour spilled on a white or cream-colored apron. Honing your eye to see such "fine print" is an advanced step toward making your compositions more mature.

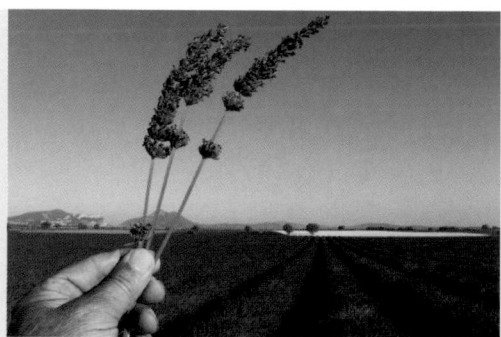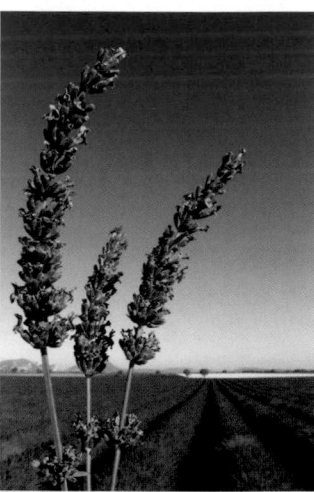

If you have read my other books, you know I am a huge fan of the Leica D-Lux camera. My first one was the D-Lux 3, then I moved to the D-Lux 4, and now I am embracing, with the greatest zeal of all, the Leica D-Lux 5. This might not be the camera for you if you are not a fan of doing extreme close-up work, but this is the biggest reason why I have loved the Leica D-Lux since its inception: it has the uncanny ability to focus really close—1/3-inch close—when at the wide-angle setting (24mm equivalent in 35mm terms). It is also an extremely small and lightweight point-and-shoot, so any time I wish to shoot a "quick" macro shot, I just whip out the D-Lux 5.

Last summer, while on the Valensole Plain in France, inspiration struck. What if I were to pick three stalks of lavender and hold them close to the wide-angle lens, incorporating them into a background composition of the plain? As you can see, a great sense of depth was created by layering this extreme foreground over the background of converging, parallel rows of lavender. However, look closely at the second image above; notice how the distant mountain is obscured by the middle flower. It's an easy fix, so I simply push the flowers up a bit higher into the frame and now the distant mountain is no longer hidden from view.

Both images: Leica D-Lux 5 with 24–105mm lens at 24mm, f/8 for 1/500 sec., ISO 100

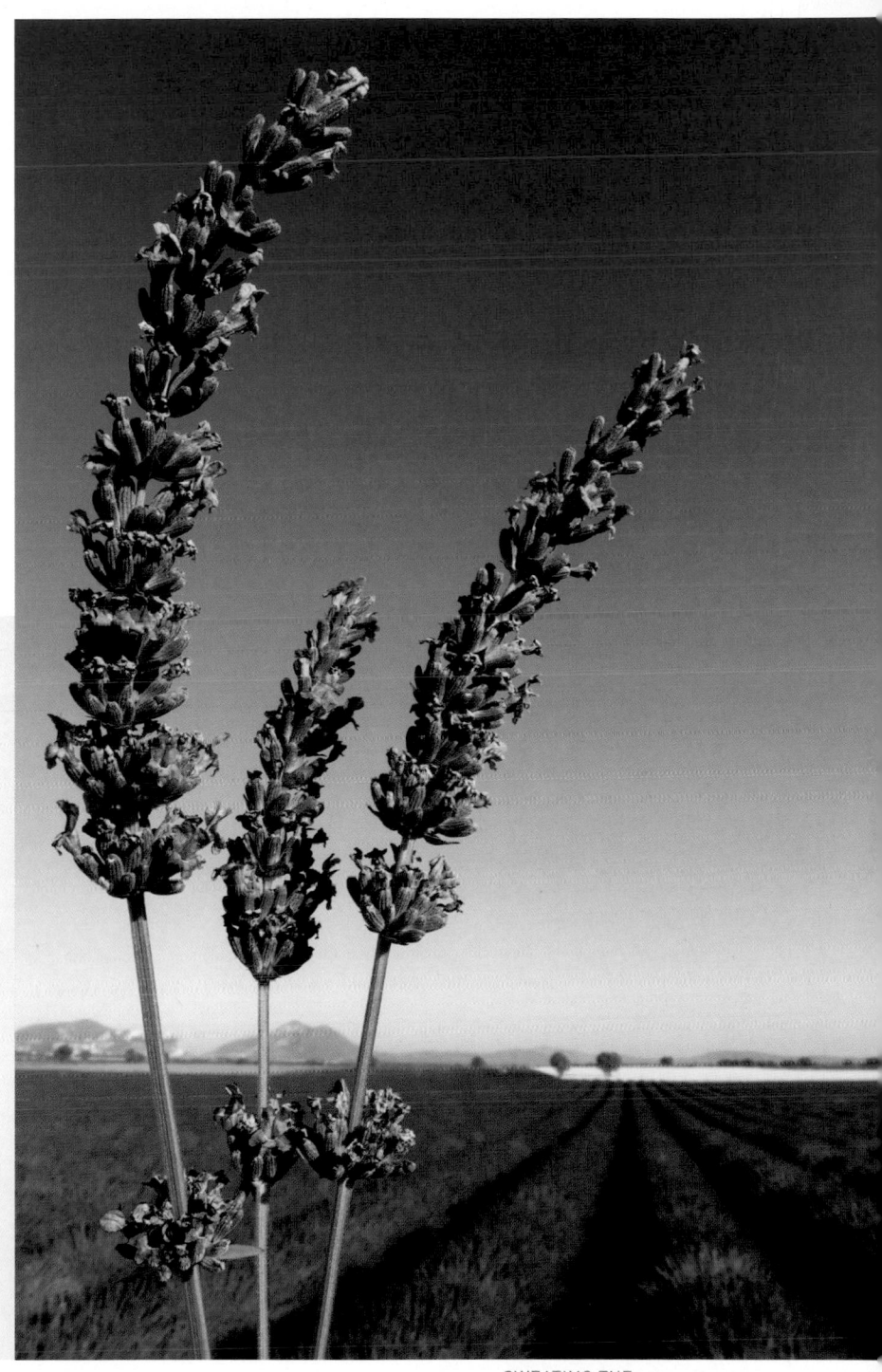

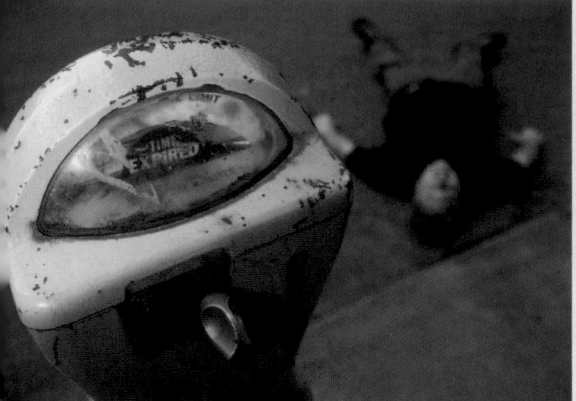

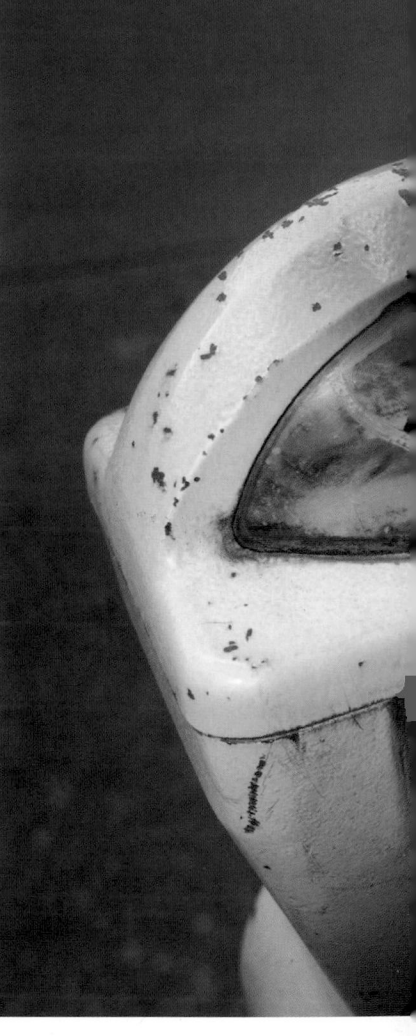

This humorous play on the word *expired* finds one of my friends, Joe, playing the "expired" man lying in the street. Notice how in the first example (above), Joe's arm merges with the yellow parking meter: this is an example of fine print. After moving slightly to my right for the second image (opposite), the merger has been eliminated. The merger was jarring because there aren't many elements in the image: only a piece of roadway, a yellow parking meter, and a "body." It is as if you were standing in an otherwise empty elevator with one other person, and that person stood right next to you instead of a normal distance away. If this image were more crowded, any potential merger would go unnoticed or, at the very least, be excused, since the eye/brain would allow for the crowded and carnival-like atmosphere—just as you wouldn't notice the stranger standing right next to you if the elevator were full of people. Those of you with a discerning eye may have noticed that my flash exposure is a wee bit better in the first image, but given the choice between the two, I still prefer the nonmerging image.

Nikon D3X with Nikkor 24–85mm lens at 35mm, f/11 for 1/125 sec., ISO 100, Nikon SB-900 flash

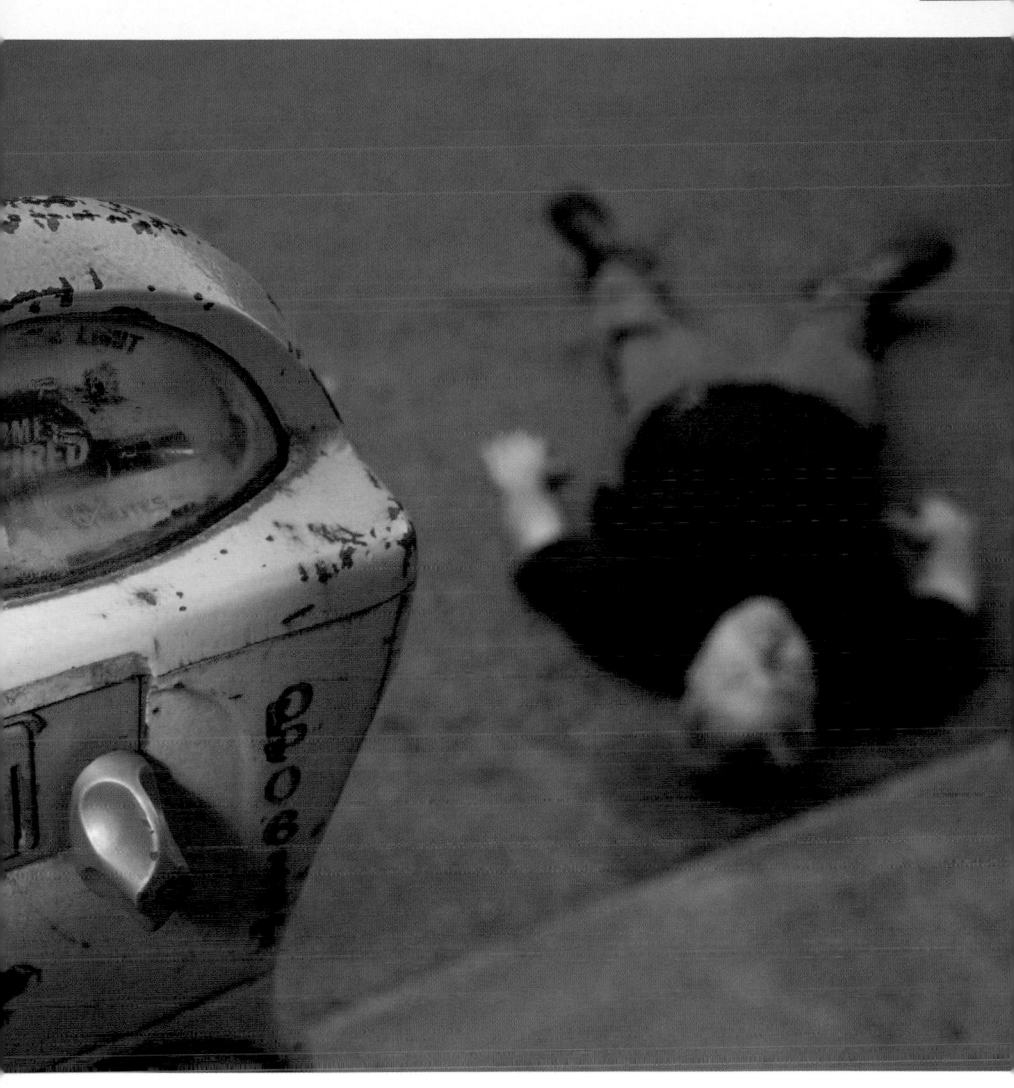

SWEATING THE
SMALL STUFF

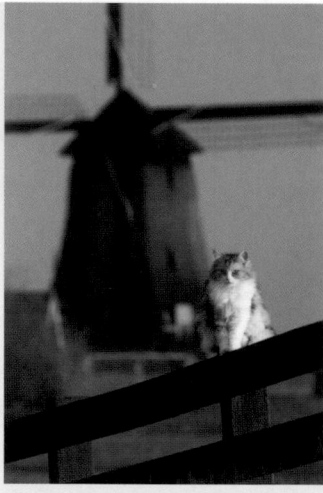

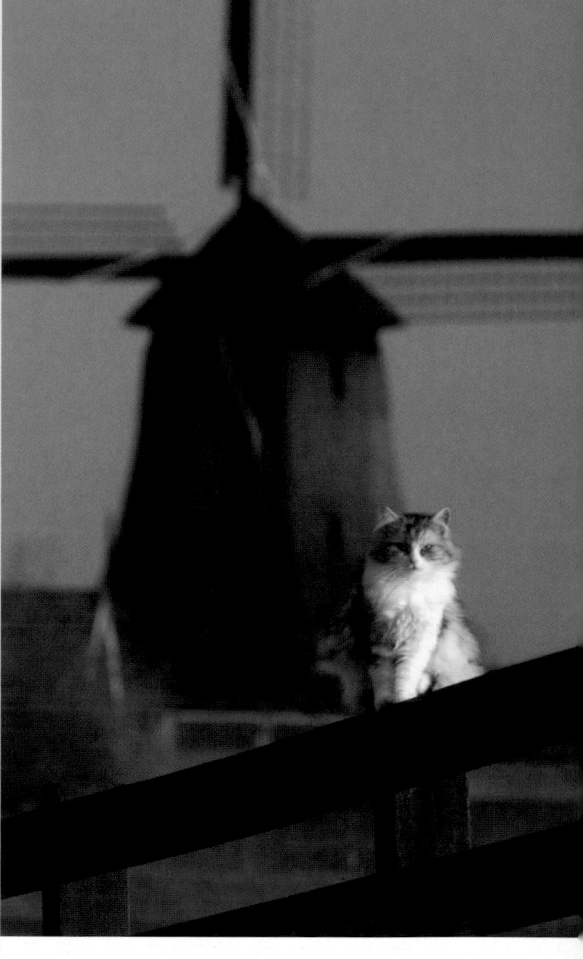

These images were taken in West Friesland, Holland, during what would prove to be one of the most wonderful afternoons and evenings of light that I have ever experienced in that area.

In the first example above, taken with my camera and 70–300mm lens on a tripod, note the fine print. What—you don't see it? It's there, just to the left of the cat. I am speaking about the "white" doorway of the distant windmill. Do you notice how it merges with the tone of the white cat? I find that distracting, much as you might find it distracting to have a conversation when, just a few feet away, someone is talking over you. For the second image (right), I moved up and to the right a wee bit, and just like that, the fine print was gone.

Nikon D3X with Nikkor 70–300mm lens at 300mm, f/8 for 1/400 sec., ISO 100

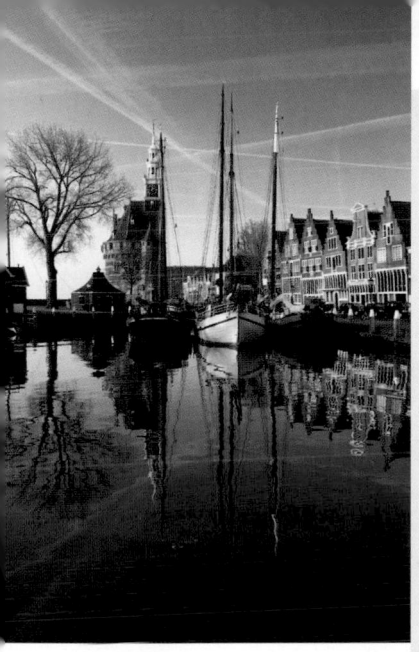

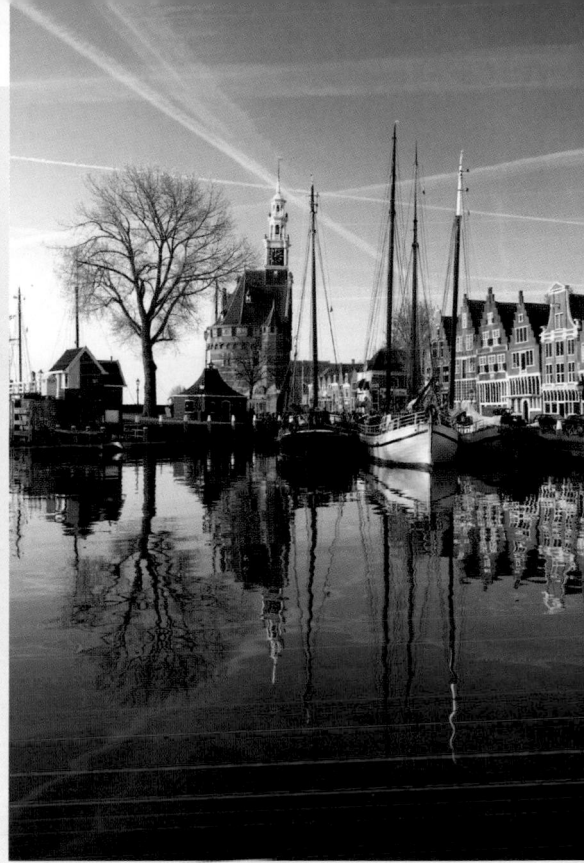

In the town of Hoorn, Holland, lies this truly quaint and photogenic harbor. Sitting at the edge of the seawall, and with my camera and 16–35mm lens on a tripod, I fired off several exposures of this calm and tranquil scene. Do you see the fine print in the first photograph (top left)? In the middle of the image, one of the boat's main sails merges with the very old brick lighthouse. By making a very subtle shift to the left, I erased the merger for the second image (top right). Then, in the tradition of practicing what I preach ("When is the best time to shoot a horizontal?"), right after shooting the vertical I rotated the camera for the third image (pages 226–227).

By the way, I am fully aware of the contrails in the sky in all three images. Why didn't I take out the healing brush and "fix" the sky in Photoshop so it was clear blue? Maybe I like contrails! Honestly, they don't bother me. In my opinion, the only way to eliminate them would have been to come back to this same scene on a cloudy day and use a 3-stop graduated ND filter, tweaking the in-camera exposure by shooting at about -1 stop. That way, you would end up with a truly dramatic, dark sky and no contrails.

Above and pages 226–227: Nikon D3X with 16–35mm lens, f/11 for 1/250 sec., ISO 100

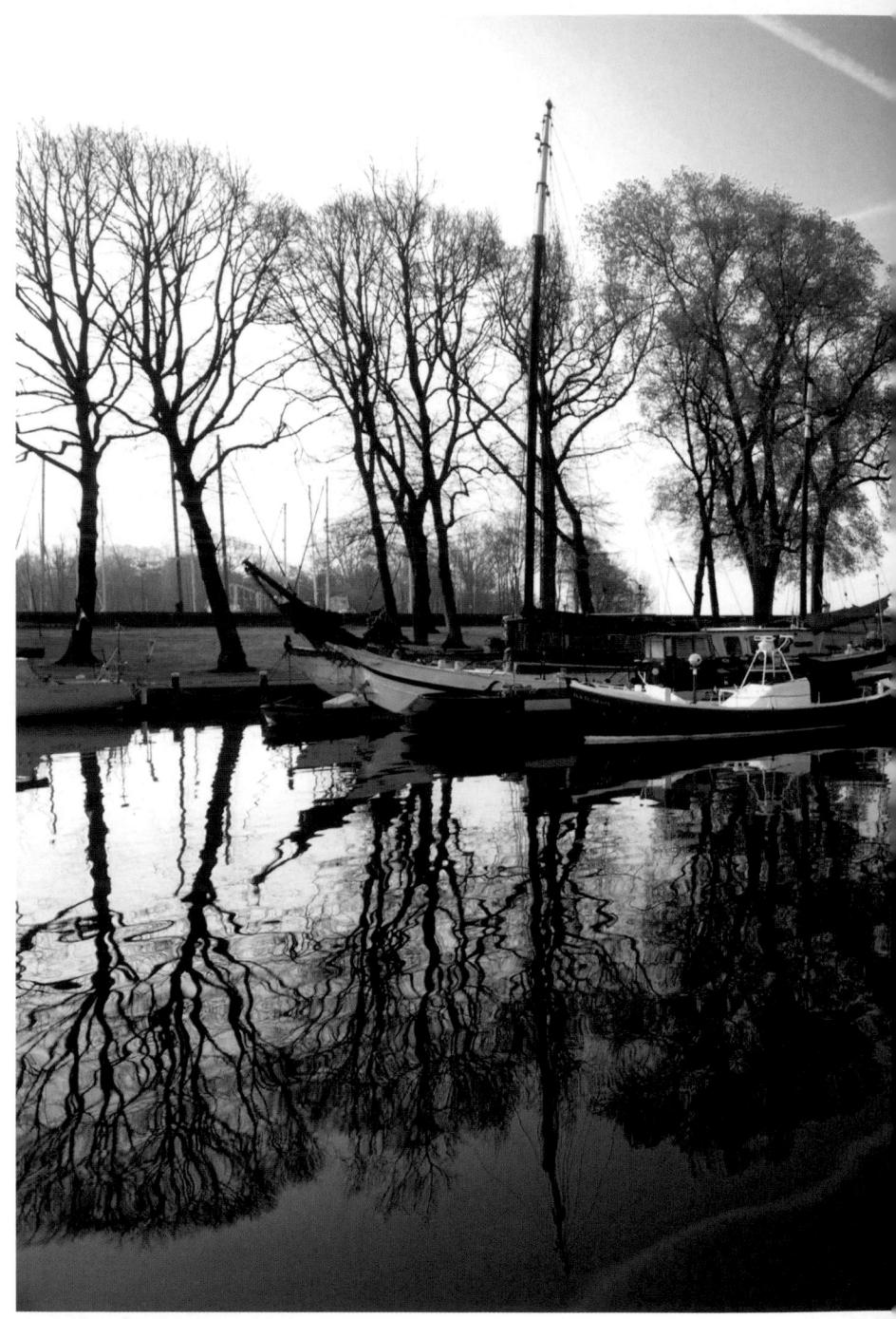

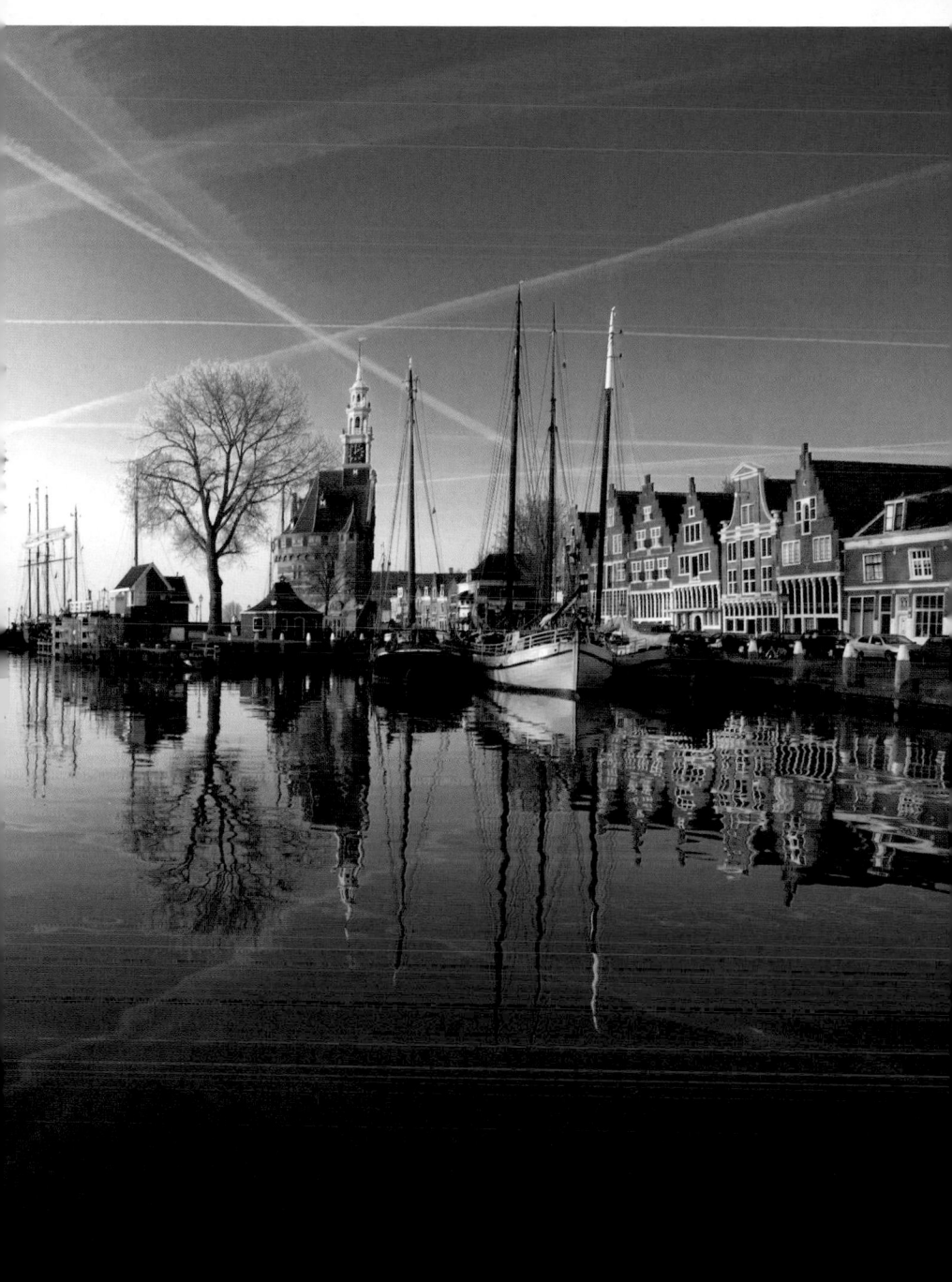

SWEATING THE
SMALL STUFF

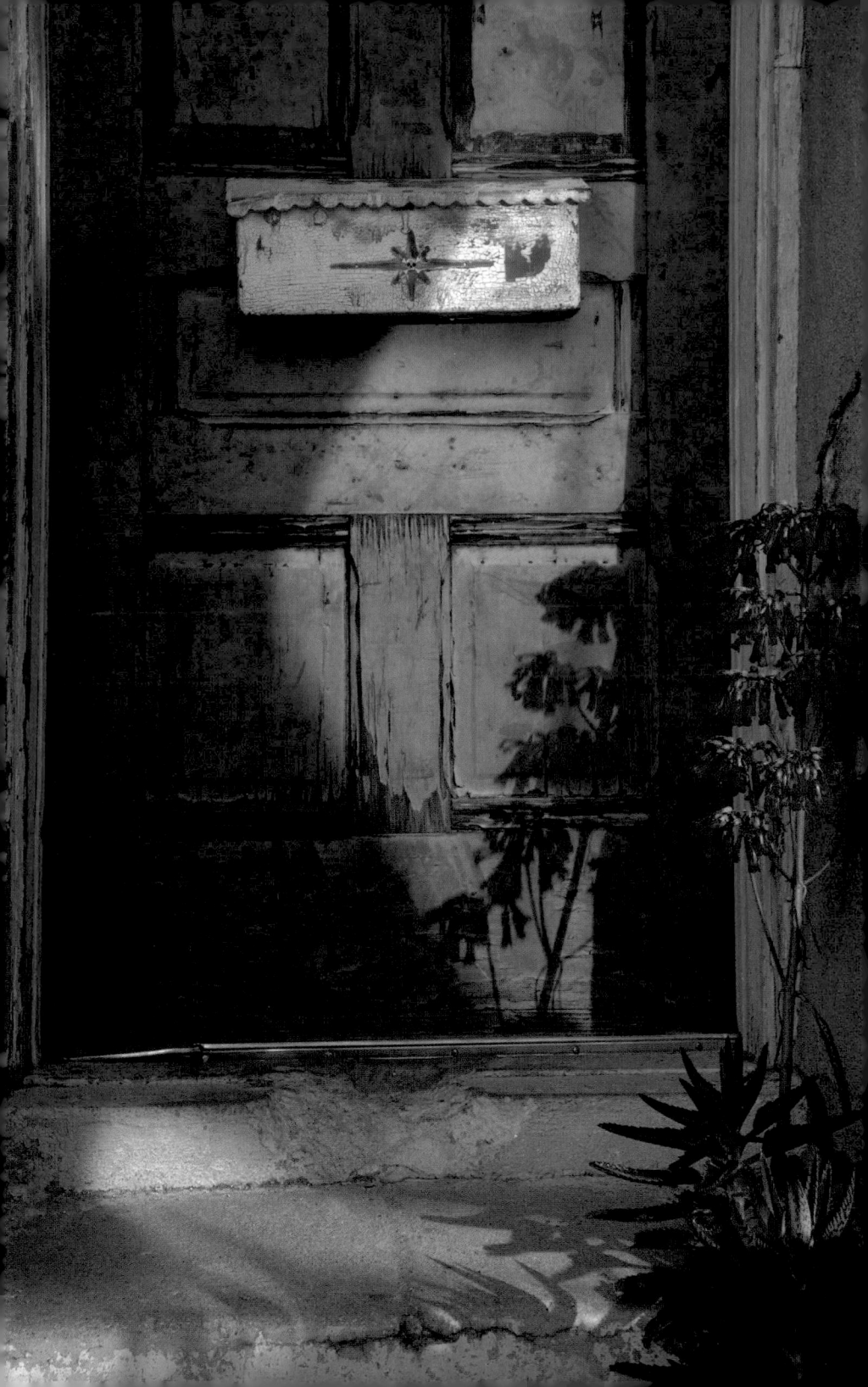

12

MINING IMAGES TO FIND THE MOTHER LODE

I have often felt that my approach to image making is akin to that of a miner who, along with a simple pick and his pack mule, goes into the wilderness looking for gold. Whether he spends his time panning at the edge of a stream or tunnels his way into the side of a mountain, he maintains the constant hope that with the next swing of the pick or dipping of the pan, he will discover an even larger nugget or, better still, the Mother Lode.

That hoped-for Mother Lode—or what others might call an "OMG image"—is the driving force for most of us. It is why we get up at 3 a.m. and chase up to Mt. Haleakala to shoot a sunrise. It is why we stay up all night shooting the northern lights. It is why we put ourselves in the path of danger, setting up a blind near a pride of lions or crossing into hostile lands under the cover of darkness. There are various reasons why each of us heads out the door with great anticipation, but more often than not, it is because we hope to come back with the Mother Lode!

Nikon D3X with Nikkor 24–85mm lens, f/11 for 1/60 sec., ISO 200

CHIPPING AWAY AT THE SCENE

It has been my experience that the Mother Lode—those larger-than-normal-sized golden nuggets—are often closer than most shooters realize. As I have been writing and showing throughout the pages of this book, the Mother Lode is often right inside the viewfinder. All you need to do to bring it completely to the surface is move a bit to the right or left or down or up or closer. Rarely do you simply step out the door and find the Mother Lode delivered to your doorstep. My search for the "big one" has almost always begun with the discovery of much smaller nuggets—nuggets that led me to believe that a much larger nugget *must* be nearby. This "chipping away" at the rock of image making is a constant; no matter where I go in this world, whether halfway around it or in my own backyard, there is almost always the process of "chipping away" at the scene, at the once "dirty" or "busy" canvas until that canvas is clean of all distraction.

This process of chipping away, as we have already discussed, may include a shift in point of view, a different lens choice, a very specific aperture and/or shutter speed, a de-liberate choice and use of a background color or texture. Call upon the Golden Section, or use a slower shutter speed or a larger aperture, or come back in warmer light or during a different season, or use a different model or a different wardrobe. And do not be afraid to move something out of the way or to add something to the mix!

Maybe it took only seconds, or maybe it required hours of planning, but before you, inside your camera's viewfinder, the Mother Lode is there to be discovered. When you do find those smaller golden nuggets, by all means trip the shutter release and embrace each magical moment. But watch out for the large wave of complacency that often follows such moments. Complacency can cause temporary blindness, and it is not until it's too late—later that night or the next day when you are at the computer—that you finally see the Mother Lode.

Practice the simple act of "looking deeper," looking further, looking past what you think is the "finished canvas" and ask yourself if there is at least one more image, possibly the Mother Lode, lying within. In many cases, the answer is an emphatic *yes*. If there is one constant refrain heard in my workshops, it is this: "Keep working it!"

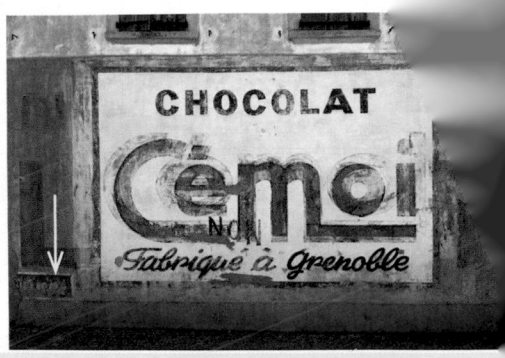

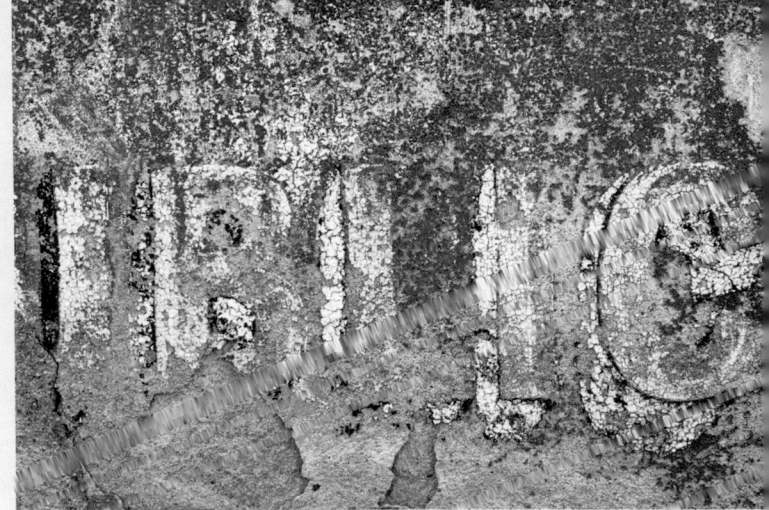

During one workshop, my students were seduced by this wall's appeal, commenting that it reminded them of an old-time poster from the 1950s. After a few minutes of shooting, they were all ready to get back in the rental van, each feeling they had gotten the shot. I stopped them, asking if anyone had noticed the lower left corner of the wall indicated with an arrow, with its peeling paint and what appeared to be another "poster" opportunity? No one had.

Over the years, I have often been hypnotized by the "Song of the Sirens" of Homer's *Iliad* and *Odyssey*. The Sirens have done their best many times to keep me from seeing other golden nuggets—and have at times been very successful. When I am really excited about stumbling across a fantastic image, I've learned that there is often an image of equal or even greater importance nearby, and needless to say, there is no better time to "mine" that other image than while you're there!

With my camera and Nikkor 24–85mm lens on a tripod, I moved closer to the wall, filling my frame with the remnants of what looked like "IBLIC." As you can see, this, too, is likely to be a "wow" if poster-sized!

Both images: Nikon D3X with 24–85mm lens, f/11 for 1/30 sec., ISO 100

MINING IMAGES TO FIND
THE MOTHER LODE

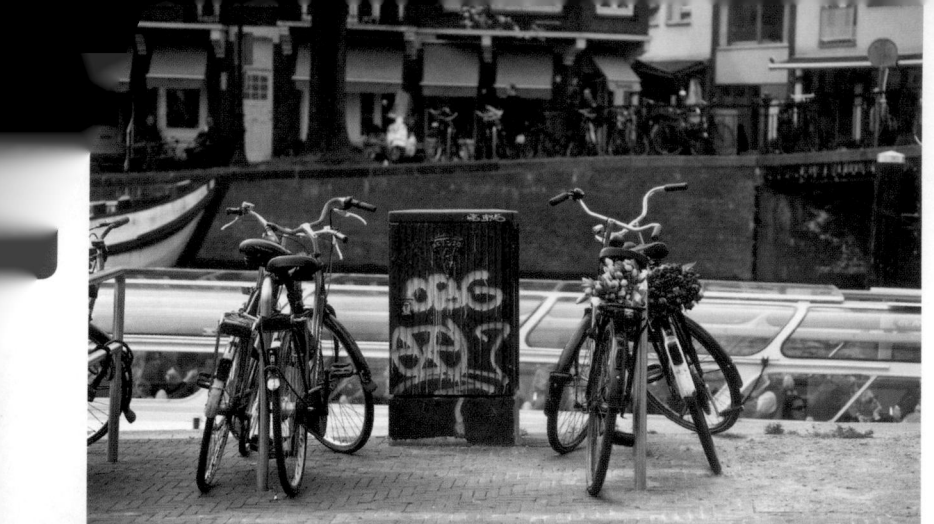

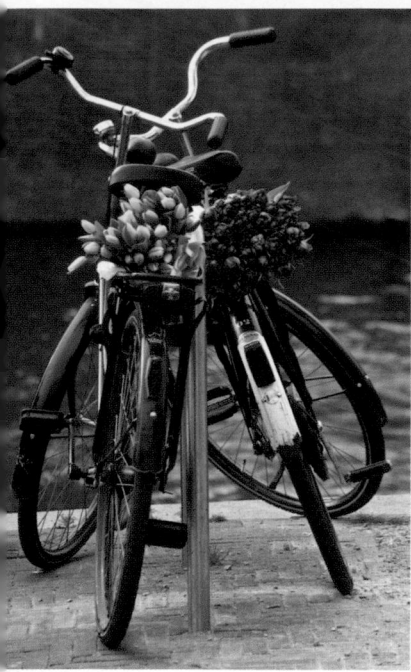

During my Holland workshop, each of the students must buy a bouquet of tulips at the flower market on Singelstraat in Amsterdam and create as many images as they can within a 60-minute period. There are no restrictions on how they use the tulips in the shot, whether as a still life, placed somewhere in the overall composition of a given scene, as a "prop" in a portrait, and so on. Following one such 60-minute period, the students and I met up on a street corner near Dam Square, where each of the students gave away their bouquet to a passerby. I was the only one who still had my bouquets because I wanted to share an idea with the group now that the contest was over. "Did anyone think of placing the tulips on the back of a bike?" Not surprisingly, no one had. So off we went in search of a bike-and-tulip shot and we didn't have to travel far, since Amsterdam is overrun with bikes (see top image). In the second image (left), taken with my 70–300mm telephoto lens at 240mm, the lens's narrow angle of view allowed me to isolate the two bikes. It was a typically overcast day in Amsterdam, and the exposure was easily shot in Aperture Priority mode at the "who cares" aperture of f/11.

For the final image (opposite), I waited a few minutes for a tourist boat to pass behind, adding some welcome tension to the overall composition. I stopped the lens down to f/22 and recorded a correct exposure of 1/15 sec. You can decide for yourself, but my opinion is that this final image, with the blurred background of tourists, is far more appealing. The added tension makes all the difference. Remember: work it, work it, work it!

Above and left: Nikon D3X with Nikkor 70–300mm lens, f/11 for 1/60 sec., ISO 200; Opposite: Nikon D3X with Nikkor 70–300mm lens, f/22 for 1/15 sec., ISO 200

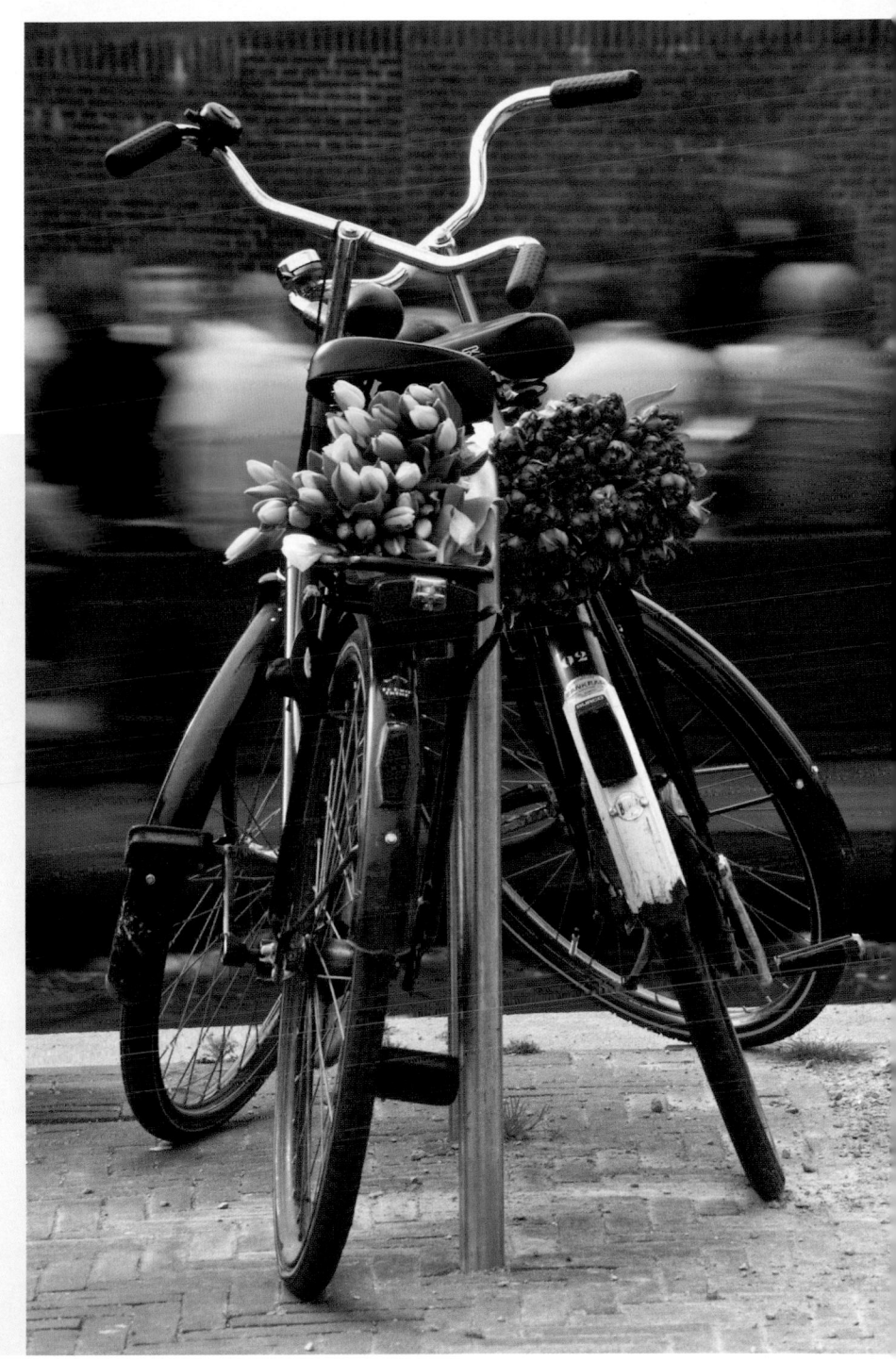

MINING IMAGES TO FIND
THE MOTHER LODE

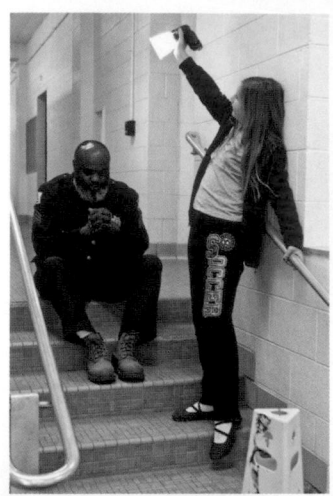

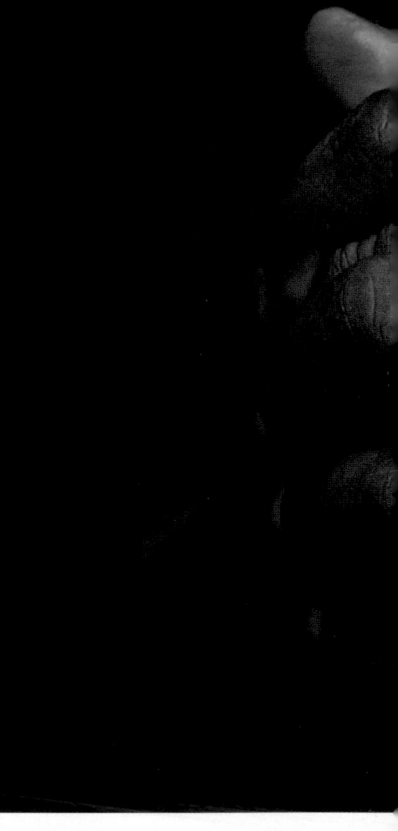

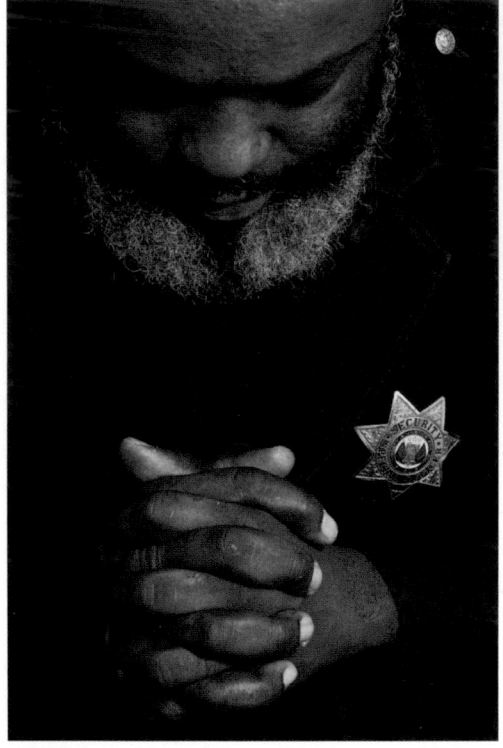

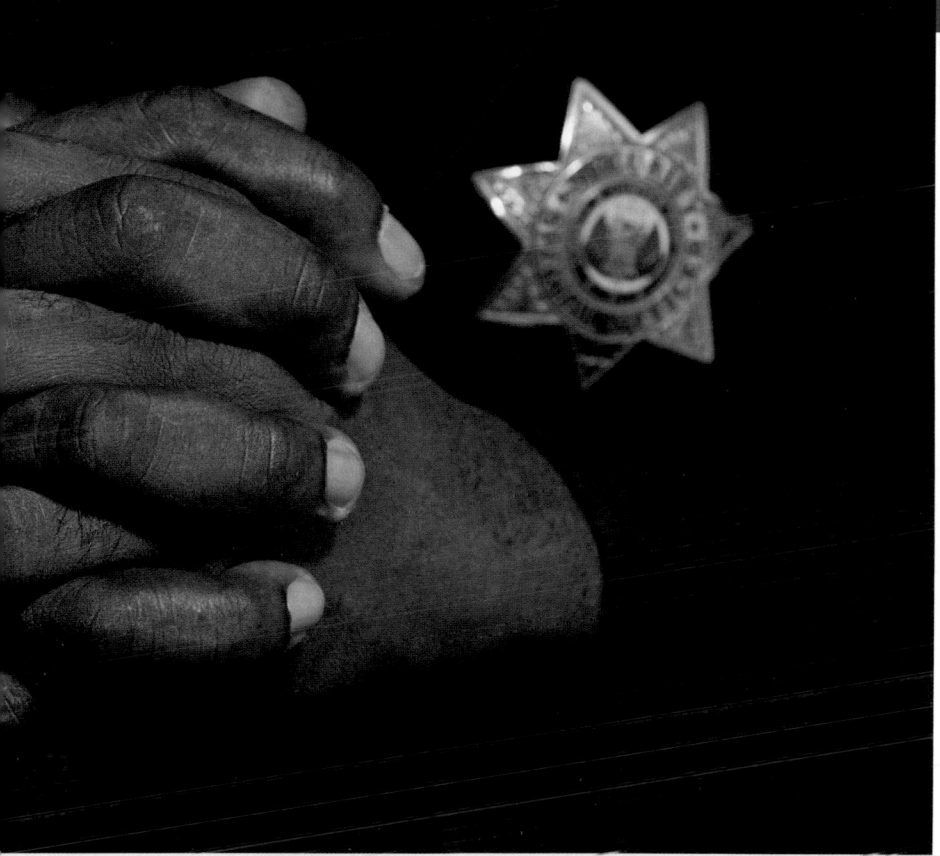

If they ever gave out an award for being the friendliest person in the world, Dennis would be first on my list. Dennis is the daytime security guard at the school my daughters attend here in Chicago. I "threatened" Dennis that one day I would come around with my camera and take his picture, and that day finally arrived about six months ago. With the help of my daughter Sophie and the ever-willing model Dennis, I made a simple on-location portrait using one flash. Sophie held my Nikon SB-900 flash (housed in a Gary Fong light dome) directly over Dennis. With my camera and flash in manual mode, I started by setting a "who cares" aperture of f/8 on the camera and then on the flash. I powered the flash down to 1/4 power; the flash-to-subject distance of 6 feet was now correct for my aperture of f/8. And since I did not want any ambient light to record, I set my shutter speed to 1/200 sec., more than 6 stops under what a correct exposure would be for the ambient light, assuring me that I had "killed" the ambient light.

The first image (left) shows a pleasing top-lit flash exposure of Dennis in a "prayer pose." It was a few shots later that the lightbulb went off and I saw the second image (above). I simply focused much more closely and composed much more tightly until only the hands and badge filled the frame. In my opinion, both images convey "faith" and "prayer," but it is the second composition that conveys "prayer" with an exclamation point. The same lighting was used in this second example, too, by the way, and I stayed with the aperture of f/8, knowing full well that at this close focal distance, it would not render enough depth of field to make the badge sharp. With the badge blurred, no reference can be made to any specific police or security agency, and as such, the image's market potential increases substantially.

Both images: Nikon D300S with Nikkor 24–85mm lens, f/11 for 1/200 sec., ISO 200, Nikon SB-900 flash

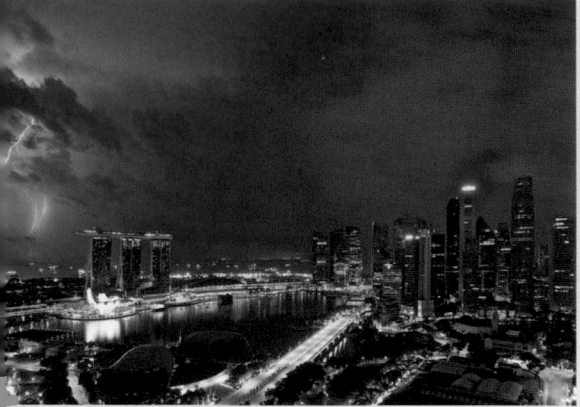

From my fourty-first-floor hotel room in Singapore, I was awakened at 3 a.m. by the loud crack of thunder, and a lightning strike that I estimated must have hit the hotel's sixty-ninth-floor rooftop. If I had not left the sliding-glass door to my outside deck halfway open, I might have simply stirred a bit and fallen back to sleep. But as it was, I was clearly awakened and soon on my balcony, shooting a number of 15-second exposures over the next 3 hours. I witnessed more than 100 lightning strikes in the area around me, and within the first hour had more than a dozen shots similar to the first image you see above. I was quite happy with these images, even though the bulk of the lightning strikes were taking place to the far left. Compositionally speaking, it was not ideal, but hey, I only have so much control over where lightning strikes! I knew that I had some great shots and should go back to bed, but. . . . And sure enough, sometime around 5 a.m., my persistence paid off, and I captured the lightning strike you see at right. It may have taken me more than thirty-five years, but I can finally say that I have an "awesome" lightning strike!

Both images: Nikon D3X with Nikkor 16–35mm lens at 18mm, f/11 for 15 seconds, ISO 100 and WB is set to Tungsten/Incandescent

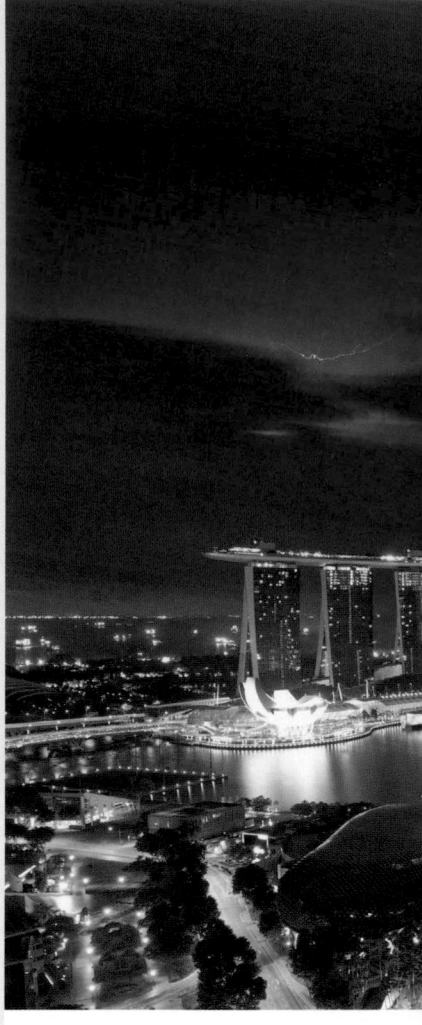

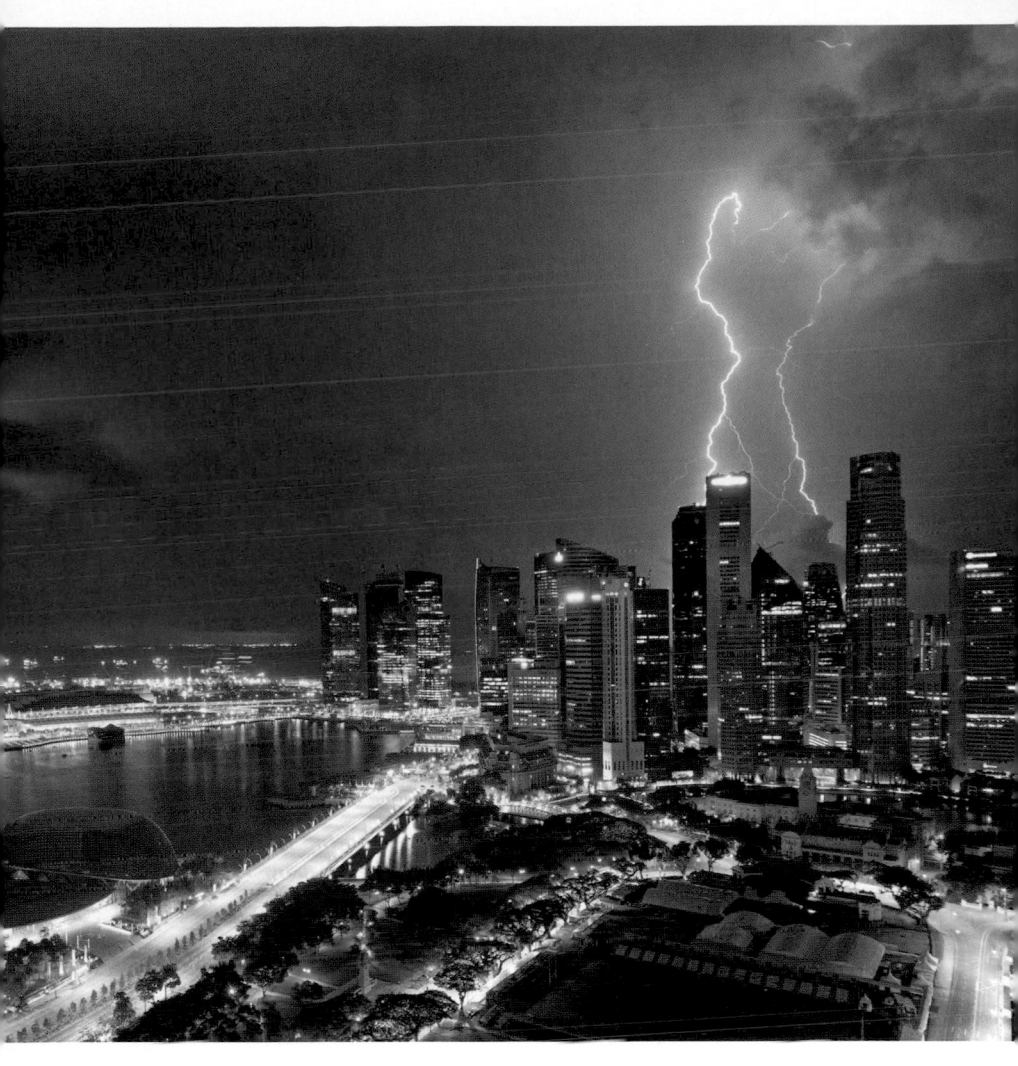

MINING IMAGES TO FIND
THE MOTHER LODE

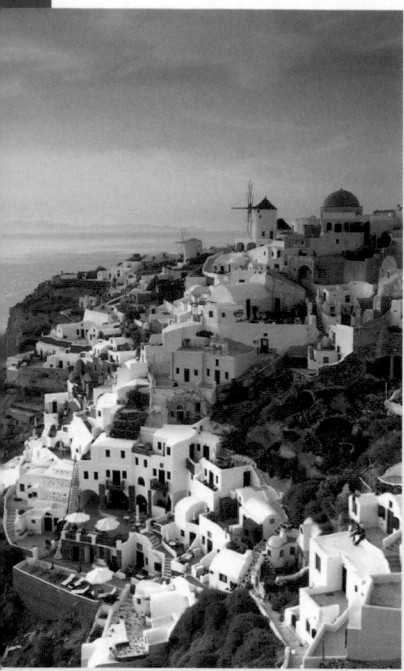

Particularly for those of you trying to market your work, do not forget to shoot the "magazine cover"! The best time to shoot a vertical is, of course, right after the horizontal, but for those choosing to market your work, the words *magazine cover* need to be in the forefront of your mind. Santorini, Greece, continues to be a popular tourist destination, so all the more reason to shoot the horizontal that may get used as a two-page spread inside a magazine and follow it up, 2 seconds later, with your vertical magazine cover.

Both images: Nikon D300S with Nikkor 12–24mm lens, f/11 for 1/125 sec., ISO 200

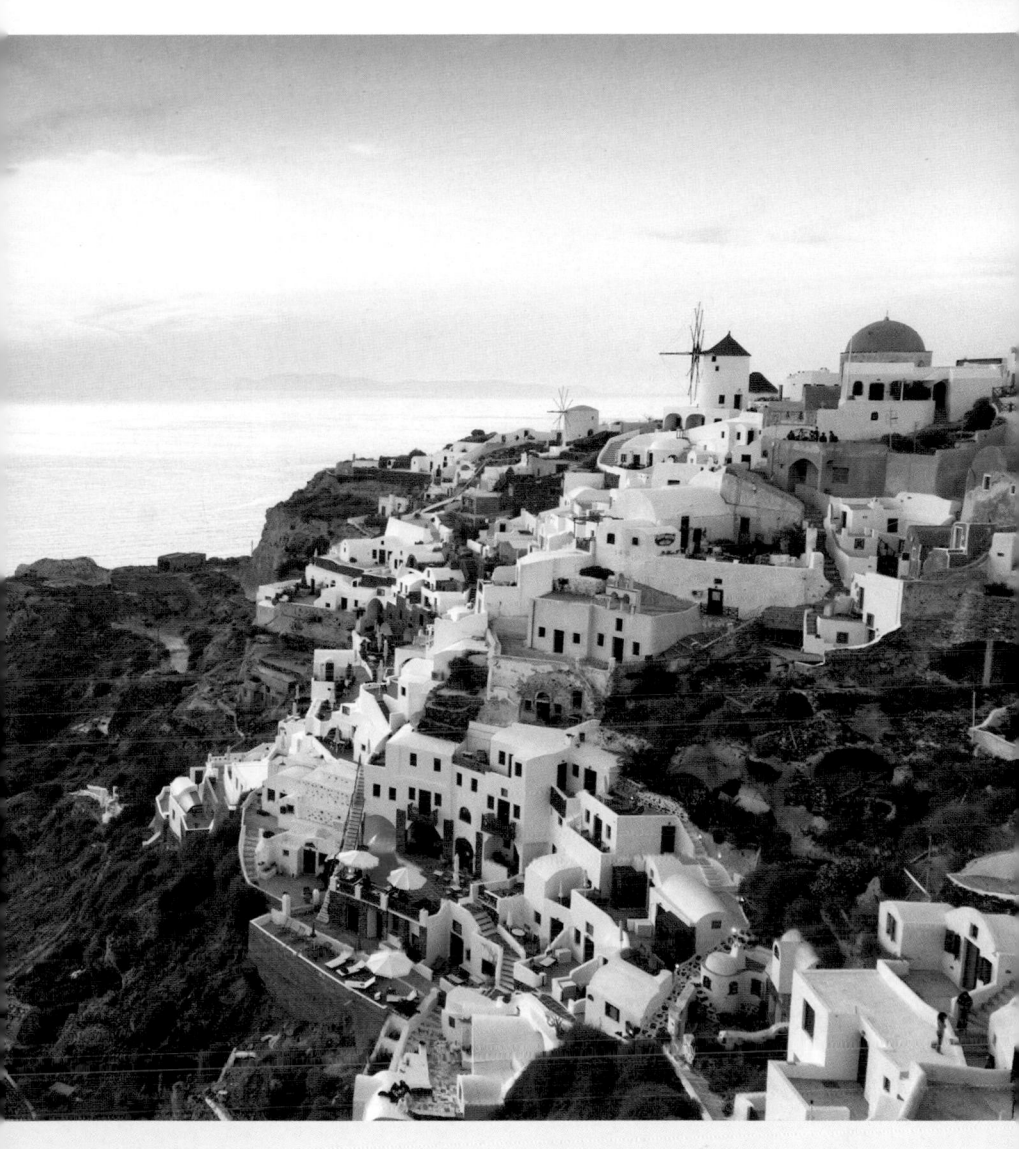

MINING IMAGES TO FIND
THE MOTHER LODE

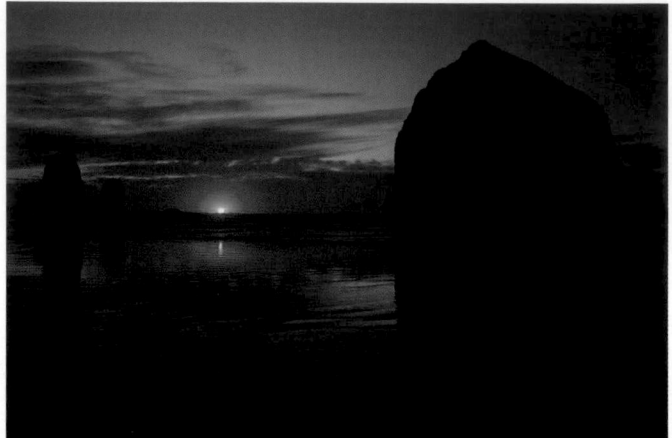

I remember shouting to Dennis James, "Work it, work it, work it!" He was one of the students in my Oregon workshop and the only one using a 28–300mm lens. If ever there was a good time to have such a lens, it was here, with one of the more magical sunsets taking place before us at Oregon's Cannon Beach. The ability to "mine" a number of images from a scene like this is limited by how quickly you can change from one lens to the next. In my case, I can change lenses quite quickly, but if you're just starting out, you may get a case of the "fumbles" *unless* you're like Dennis and have an almost "all-purpose lens" at the ready.

Clearly there is a wide-angle shot here, as the image above attests, but within this "bigger picture" there is an equally impressive telephoto composition, shown at right. At the end of the day, we all want to see a quality image, but with a bit of experience, a bit of lens know-how, and some persistence, your day can end with both quality and quantity.

Above: Nikon D3X with Nikkor 16–35mm lens at 16mm, f/22 for 1/30 sec., ISO 100; Right: Nikon D3X with Nikkor 70–300mm lens at 70mm, f/22 for 1/30 sec., ISO 100

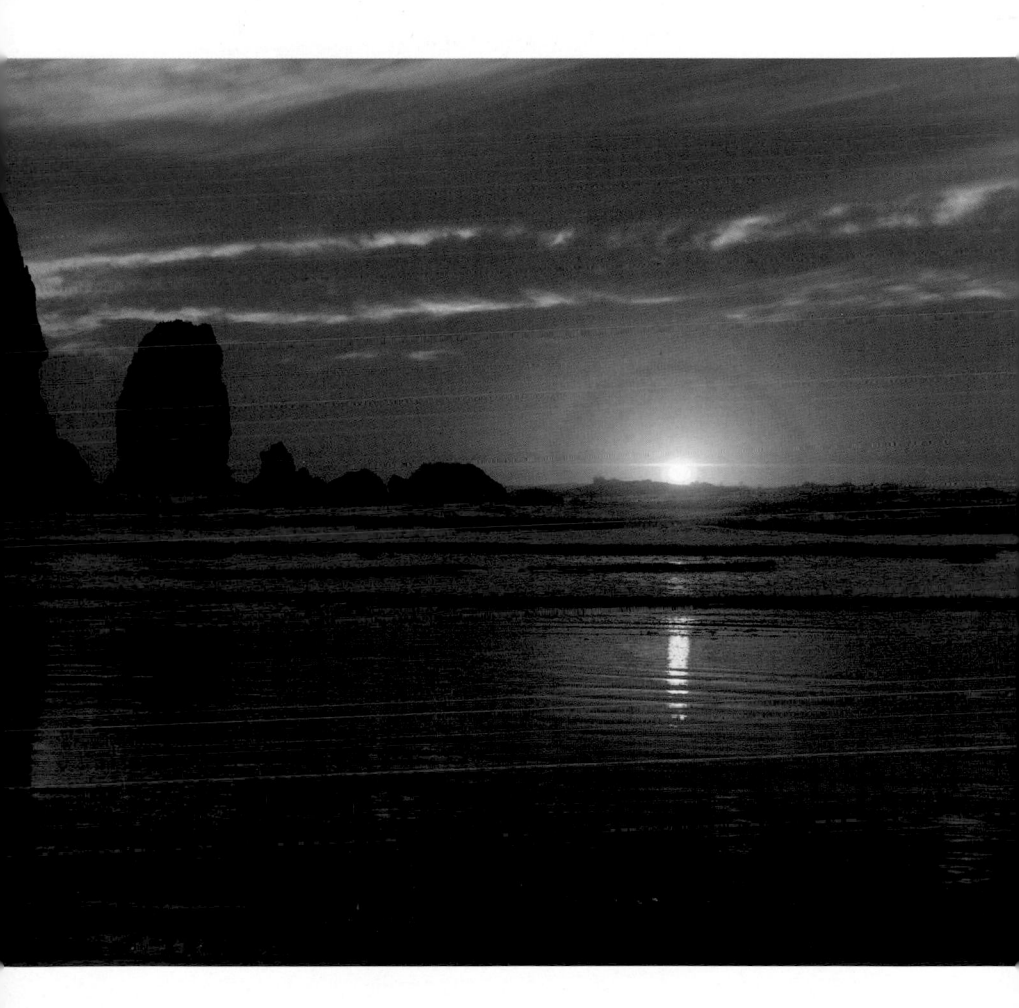

MINING IMAGES TO FIND
THE MOTHER LODE

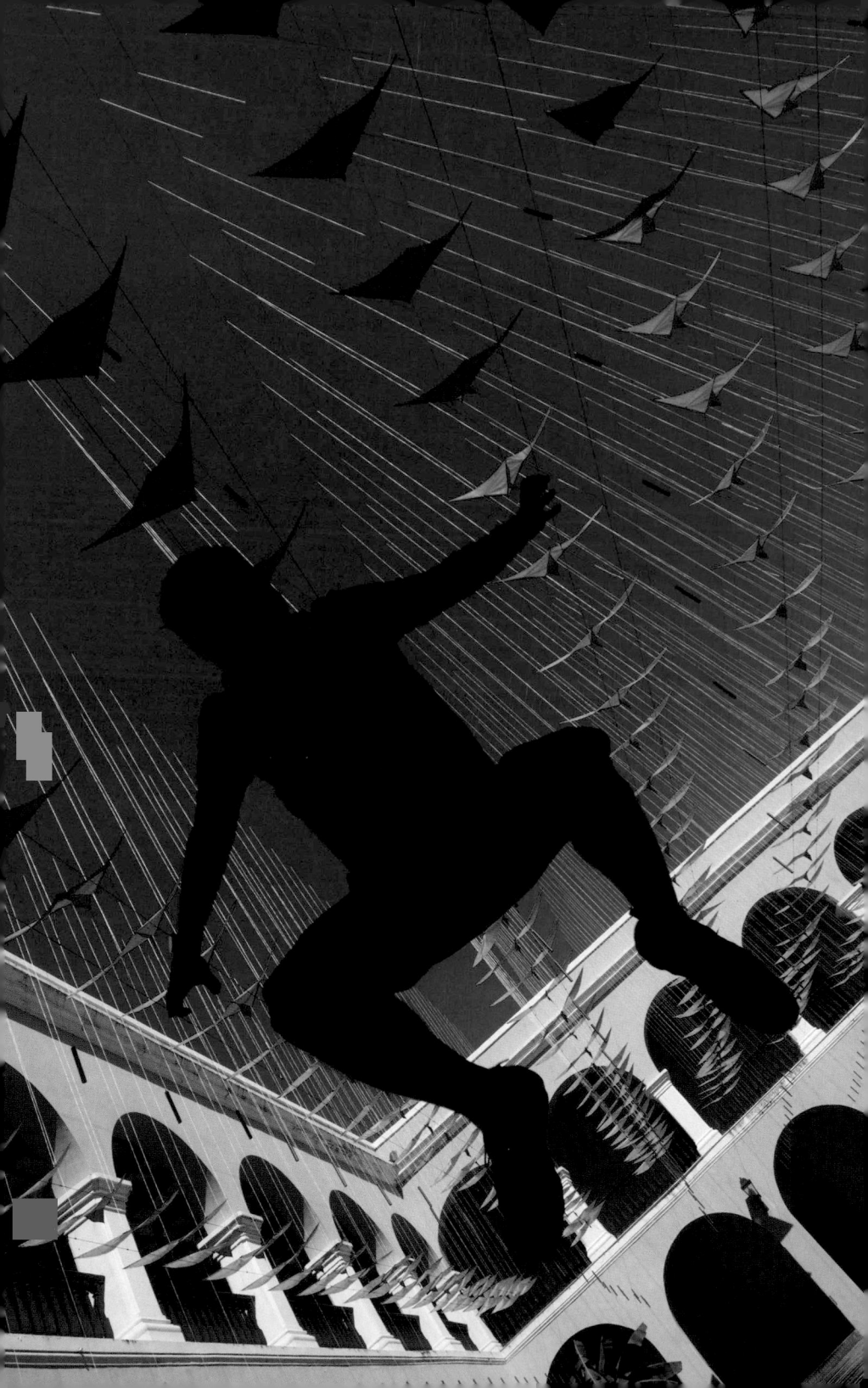

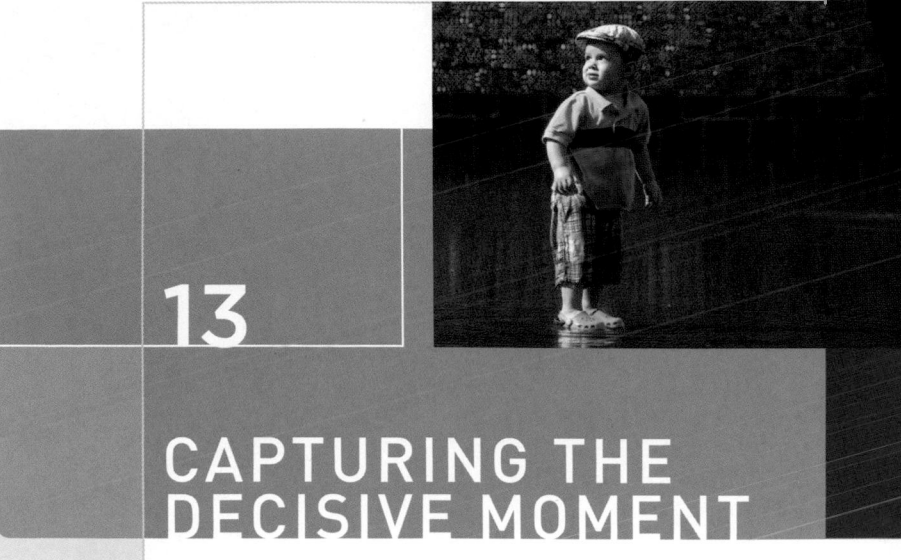

13

CAPTURING THE DECISIVE MOMENT

There are some compositions that owe their success to nothing more than capturing the "decisive moment," a phrase coined years ago by the famed French photographer Henri Cartier-Bresson. Still active in his nineties and spending his time doing oil painting, Bresson seemed perplexed by his fame, implying that perhaps photography was not art but simply the documentation of the world around us. I believe that if a picture I take is not possible to capture with any other medium, then it is at least uniquely achieved. But the art, as far as I am concerned, is in how we arrange the elements in the frame. I do not know of any other medium that allows for the creation of "art" so quickly. It is in many of these decisive moments where the photograph goes from a record to a piece of art.

Nikon D3X with Nikkor 16–35mm lens, f/11 for 1/400 sec., ISO 200

How is the *decisive moment* defined? For me and many others, it is that very brief fraction of time—a millisecond—when everything comes together in perfect synchronicity: the light, the lens choice, the point of view, the subject, the aperture, the shutter speed and, as is often the case, a healthy dose of luck. Decisive moments are not limited to an overt action, such as the now-famous image taken by Cartier-Bresson of the figure with an umbrella jumping over a mud puddle. In fact, you could be shooting a portrait when your subject makes a look you recognize as *that* look and at exactly that moment you trip the shutter, forever preserving that decisive moment. Whether it be the hurried action of a man jumping over a mud puddle with his umbrella, the subtle pursing of a model's lips, or a slight shift in the photographer's point of view, these actions are fleeting, yet when captured, each is what I see as a Kodak moment—a picture worth a thousand words.

I have seen, and have *missed* seeing, my share of decisive moments. Like the big fish that got away, those images remain in my mind as some of the best work I can never show. Am I just unlucky? Of course not! I have been lucky enough to photograph a number of decisive moments, too. I know of no successful artist who has put his or her camera or brush down and said, "I now have enough." Speaking for myself, it is the search for, the potential for, and the surprise of the decisive moment that drives me still.

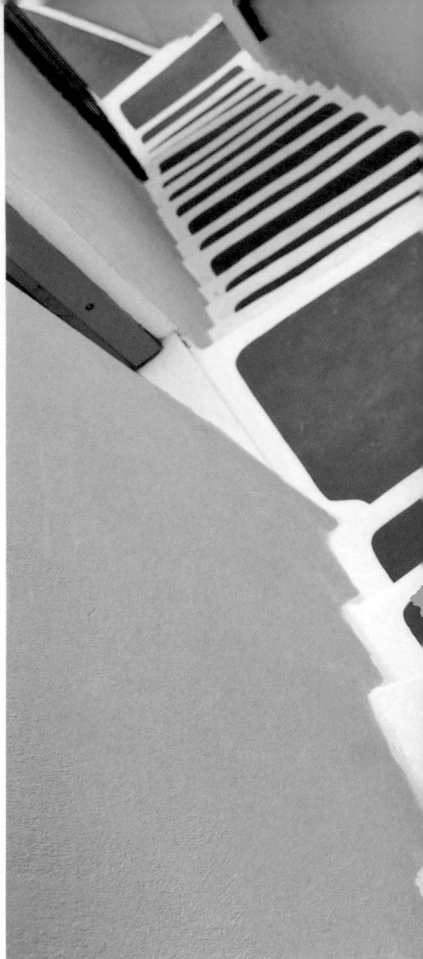

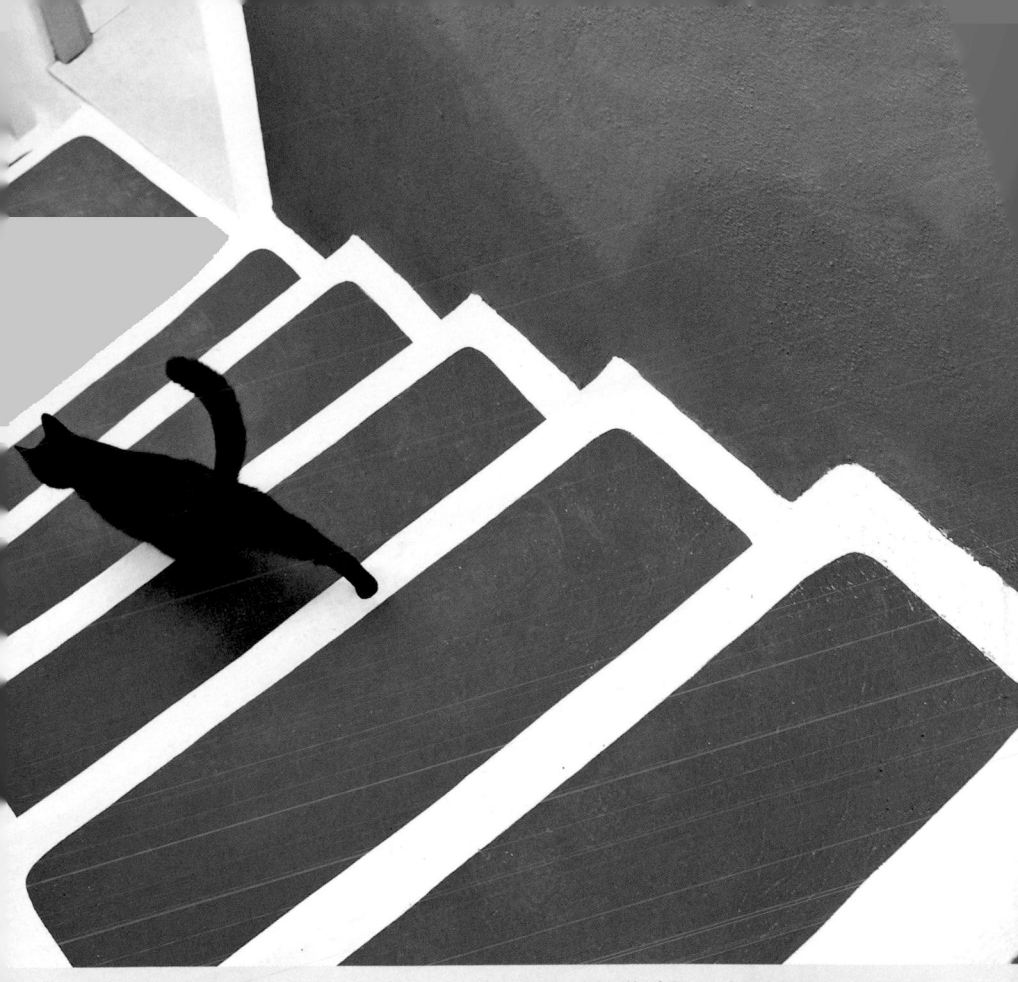

I had heard nothing but glowing reviews about the island of Santorini, Greece, so I finally put the spot on my workshop schedule in 2006. Within minutes of arriving, I began to question what all the glowing reviews could have possibly been about, since I didn't see all that much. But at my hotel, 30 minutes later, it all became clear. You've got to love these cliffside towns with their narrow alleyways and the locals using donkeys to carry goods up and down the steep cliffs. And, of course, where would these islands be without their cats? One of my favorite books, *Cats in the Sun*, showcases beautiful photography from the Greek islands, including Santorini. I had hoped to come away from Santorini with several outstanding cat shots, but by the last day of the workshop, it didn't seem as if it would happen—until, that is, this black cat crossed my path.

I realize that, for some, a black cat crossing your path is a sign of misfortune to come, but for me it proved most fortunate. I followed this cat for 5 minutes until he finally found a resting place at the top of some colorful steps. I moved into a position that allowed me to shoot down on the stairs from a diagonal point of view. All that remained was to see the cat take off, running down the steps, but he seemed rather content and was soon lying down, ready for a nap. Luckily for me, a large barking dog started coming our way and that was all it took to get this cat moving. Handholding my camera and 17–55mm lens, and with the ISO set to 200 and my shutter speed at 1/500 sec., I was ready, since I had already adjusted the aperture in anticipation of the shot. Needless to say I got the shot, complete with the cat in midstride.

Nikon D300S with 17–55mm lens at 17mm, f/8 for 1/500 sec., ISO 200

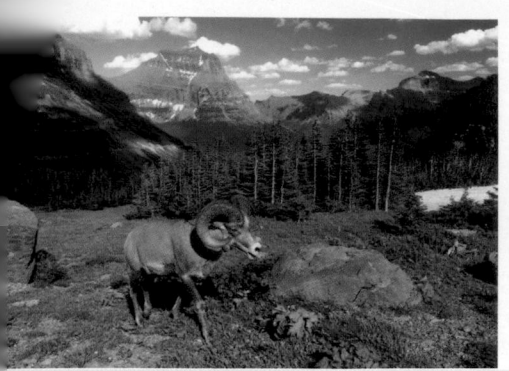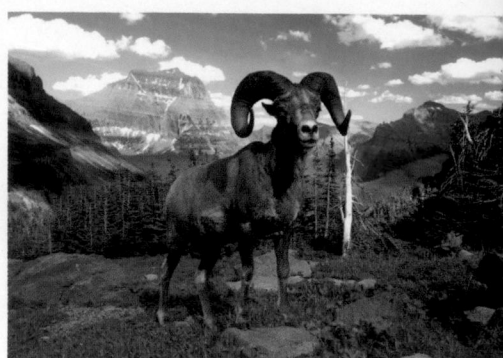

It has often been said that luck is about being prepared when opportunity knocks. This may be true, but on this particular day, something beyond preparation and opportunity were at work. It was July 16, 2010, and my students and I had spent the better part of the day in Glacier National Park. As we returned to Logan Pass, we pulled into a parking lot for a restroom break and a few minutes later spotted three bighorn sheep in the parking lot. Photographing bighorn sheep in a busy parking lot rarely qualifies as "compelling wildlife imagery," since the images you usually end up with are bighorn sheep walking through a busy parking lot. But within 10 minutes, the sheep began strolling to the edge of the parking lot, near a small rock wall beyond which lay a large meadow and pine trees, and Glacier's massive mountains could be seen rising from the forest floor. Not more than 10 seconds later, all three sheep jumped over the short wall and walked into the meadow.

At this moment, I had only my Leica D-Lux 4 around my neck. I raced back to the van and grabbed my Nikon D300S and 12–24mm lens. Returning to the wall, my heart sank—the three sheep had descended down the sloping meadow into the trees. If I were to have any "luck" at all, I would now need my 70–300mm zoom lens, hoping to capture the rams as they grazed below. Should I return to the van to get my telephoto zoom or stay put in case one or several of them returned up the hill? My students were using their telephoto lenses with glee, so why not join them? A little voice inside my head, however, seemed to shout, "Stay put!" So stay put I did.

Soon one of the rams began a slow trek back up the sloping meadow. Within seconds, he was right in front of me, only 4 feet away. He even placed both of his front feet on a small rock outcropping, as if to strike a pose! So there I was, seated on the small rock wall, the only one of us with a wide-angle zoom on the camera, framing a ram in the foreground and the all-encompassing mountains of Glacier Park in the background.

It was all wonderful, but I had one more request. I spoke to the ram in a muffled voice, "You look so regal and proud, but I need you to turn your head a bit toward me. This will allow me to get a small catchlight in your eyes and eliminate the subtle merger of one of your horns with the white pine tree in the background." No sooner had the words left my mouth than the ram turned his head until it was right where I wanted it. At that same moment, the sun, which had been dodging clouds, poked around a cloud and lit up his eye. I quickly fired off several more frames, with his head now clear of the merger and the subtle catchlight in his eyes. Several seconds later, he turned and disappeared behind a stand of pine trees in the meadow below.

All images: Nikon D300S with Nikkor 12–24mm lens at 16mm, f/22 for 1/30 sec.

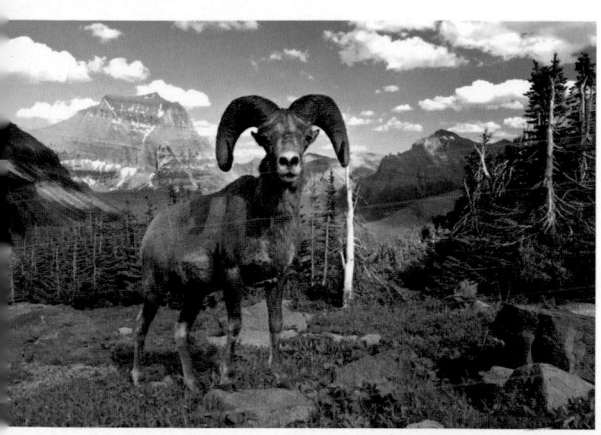

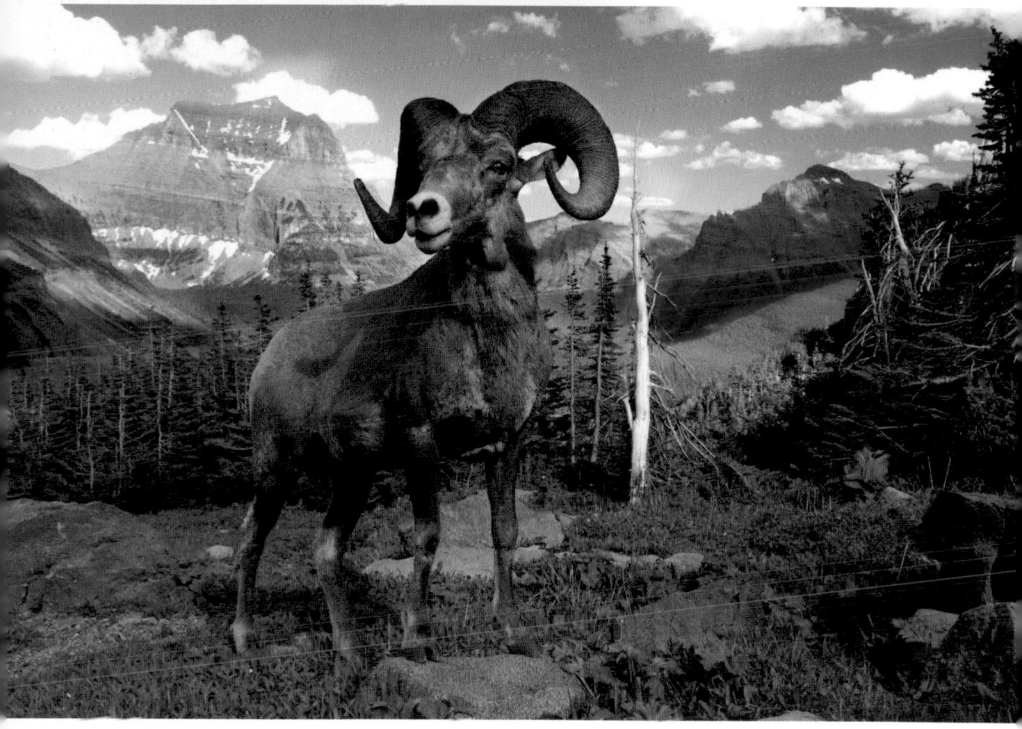

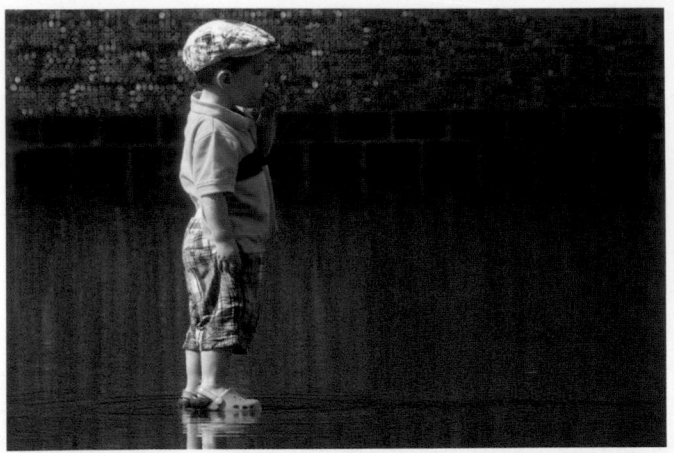

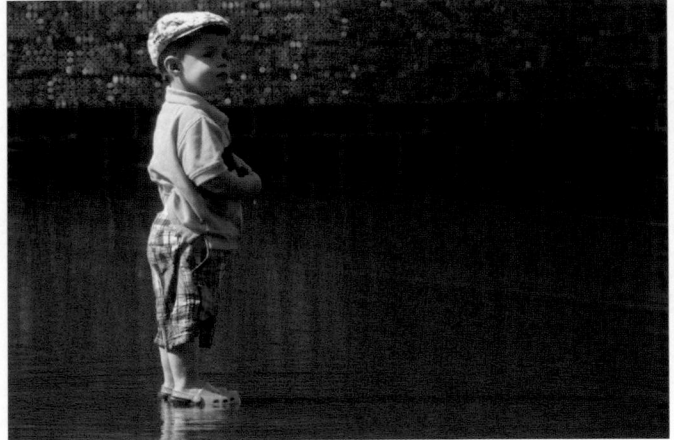

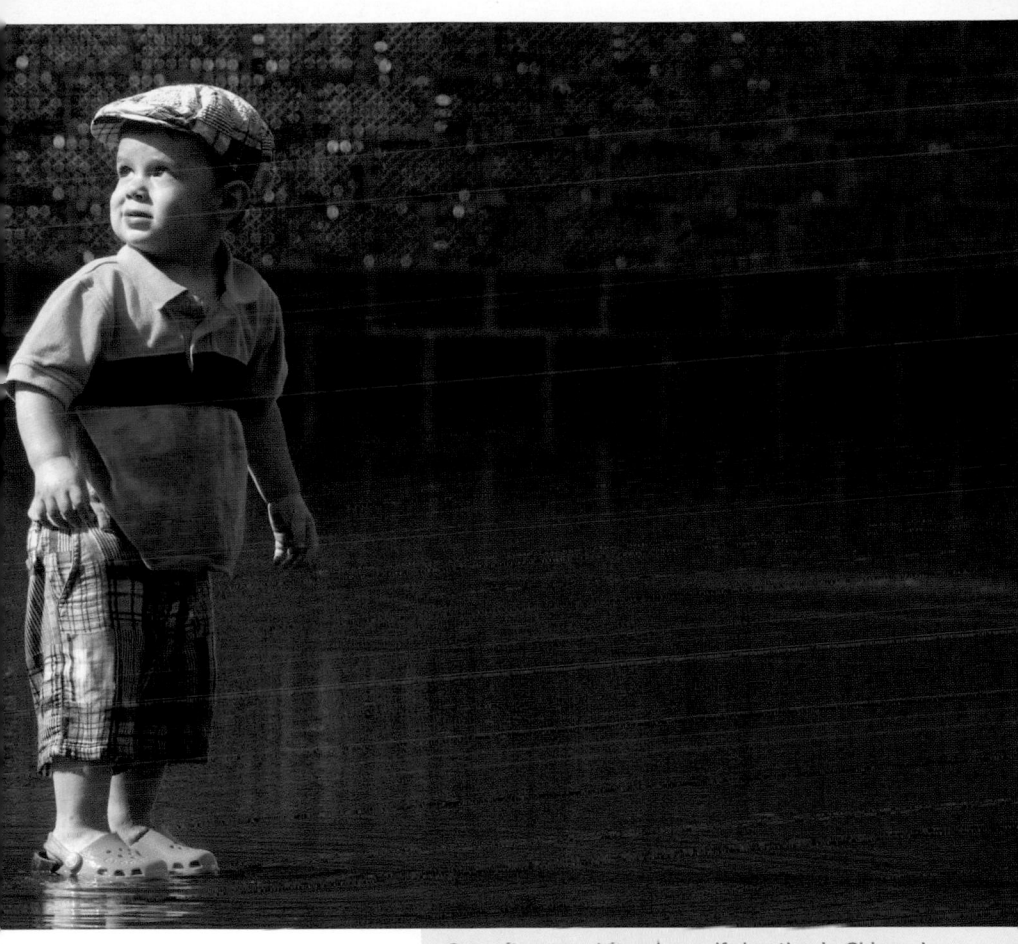

One afternoon, I found myself shooting in Chicago's Millennium Park, photographing around the fountain where kids congregate to cool off on a hot summer day. I spotted a young boy whose bright-green clothing caught my attention. Using my Nikkor 70–300mm lens at 300mm, I was able to compose a pleasing horizontal composition that showcased him against the red glass brick background. In the first shot (opposite top), he is looking straight ahead at some other kids playing nearby. Soon someone, most likely his dad, called out to him and the boy slowly turned his head toward the sound—and there it was, the very brief yet decisive moment!

All images: Nikon D3X with Nikkor 70–300mm lens at 300mm, f/8 for 1/400 sec., ISO 100

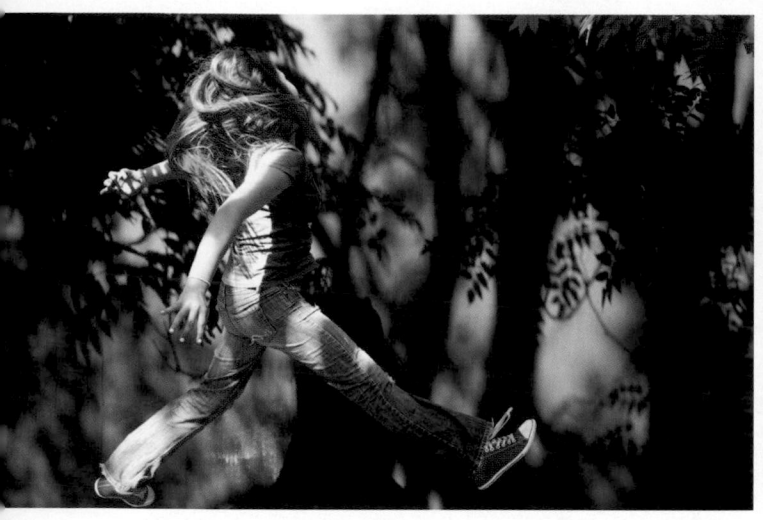

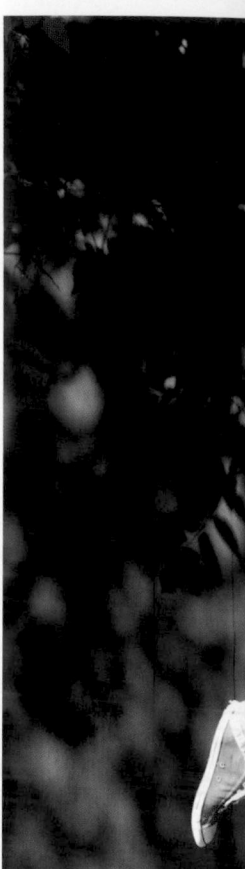

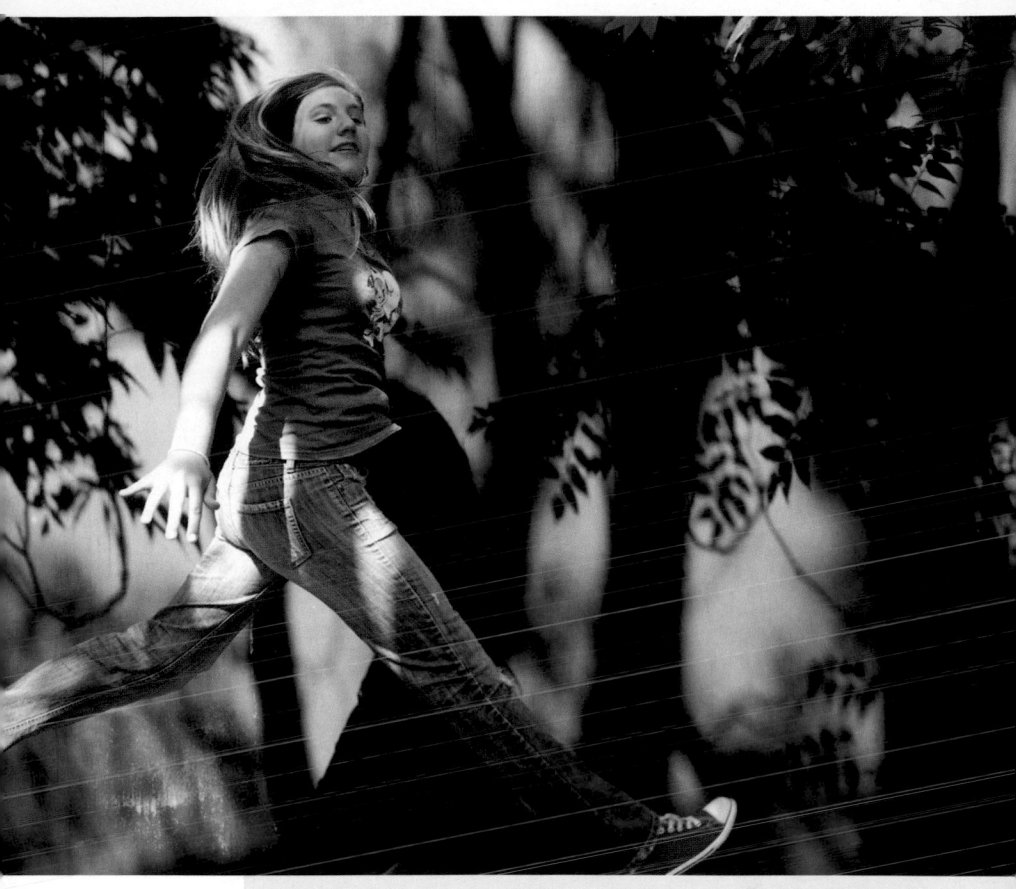

Sophie and I were in London for a workshop, and I asked her to run and jump in front of a blue wall covered in dappled sunlight. I wasn't thrilled with her clothing, but I was quite thrilled with the light on the wall, so perhaps the jump, combined with the dappled light, would be enough to carry this hoped-for decisive moment. I set my exposure and frame-filling composition, and on the count of three, Sophie ran and jumped! Clearly the first image (left) missed the moment. In the second image, however, Sophie's eyes and face are visible, and we even see a smile.

Unlike in the days of Cartier-Bresson, we now have a decided advantage when seeking out decisive moments: cameras with a built-in winder or motor drive. Don't apologize for it—embrace it! Realize first and foremost that if you don't *see* the possibilities for decisive moments, a camera with a motor drive is not much help anyway. Rather than divorcing yourself from the supersonic technology and using a manual camera that relies on a quick trigger finger, embrace the technology and invest your time training your eye to see and anticipate these moments. And, of course, always have your camera at the ready!

Both images: Nikon D3X with Nikkor 24–85mm lens at 35mm, f/8 for 1/500 sec., ISO 100

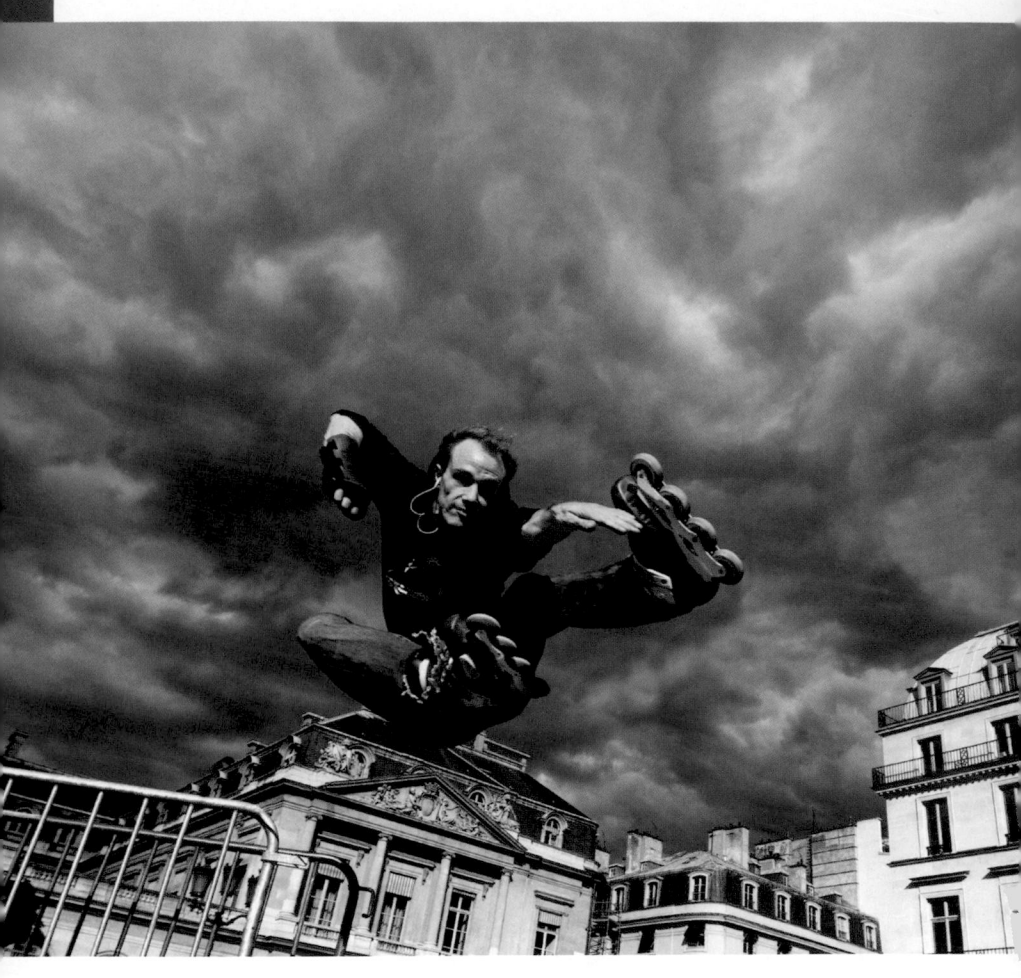

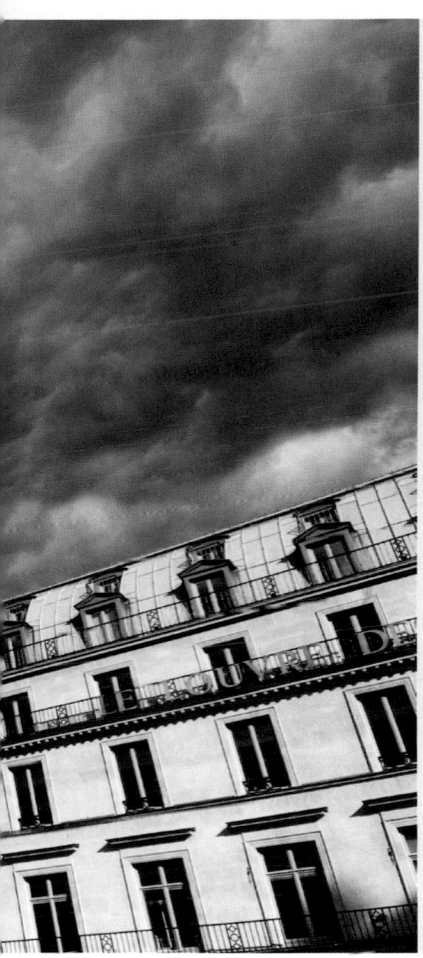

I am not a sports photographer, but I absolutely love shooting sports. If I stumble into a park and a football game is going on, or I actually make a plan to shoot motocross racing in Oregon or surfers hanging ten in Hawaii, my level of anxiety increases tenfold. It is not an anxiety associated with lack of confidence but more of knowing that any number of "decisive moments" may reveal themselves on my camera's digital monitor.

One day, my students and I found ourselves lying on the hard concrete right near the entrance to the Louvre stop of the Paris Metro. Why were we lying on the concrete? We had just come up the stairs from the subway and spotted a young physics professor in Rollerblades, launching himself over a metal barricade. The skies to the east were dark and foreboding, and to the west it looked like the skies might soon open up. I approached the young man and asked if he planned to skate much longer, and his promising response was that he would stay and do whatever we wanted as long as we sent him some prints! For the next 40 minutes, he jumped and jumped. The sun popped out from behind the clouds to the west, blanketing the buildings to the east and our skating enthusiast in warm light. Many shots were taken during those 40 minutes—but none more decisive than the one you see here.

Nikon D3X with Nikkor 16–35mm lens at 20mm, f/8 for 1/800 sec., ISO 200

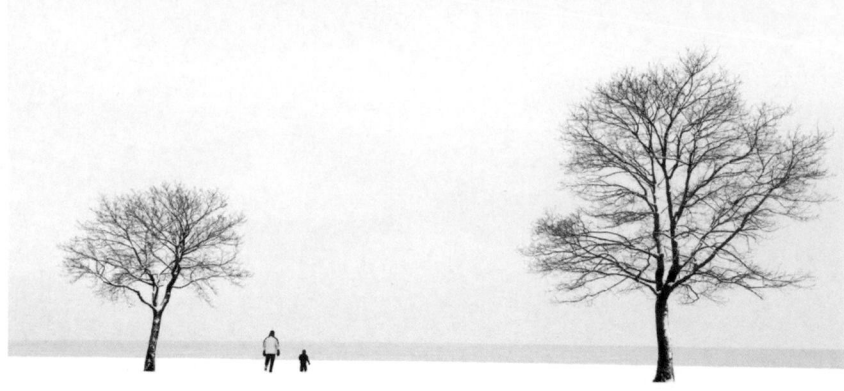

Following one of Chicago's worst blizzards in eighty-eight years, I stepped out, headed for a nearby park along Chicago's Lakeshore Drive. I did not expect to see a lot of activity in the park, other than the occasional dog owner hurriedly walking a dog. About an hour after I arrived, I spotted, at some distance away, an adult and a small child getting out of their car and suiting up for a walk in the park. I ventured in their direction with my camera and 16-35mm lens and was fortunate, very fortunate, to take a number of frames of father and son walking toward the lake, framed between "father and son" trees.

This in itself was enormously gratifying—the symbolism of father and son between the two trees—but something told me to keep shooting, and I was never so happy as when, a few seconds later, the father reached out to touch his son on the head for a very brief moment, as if to say, "I am here, close, and will keep you safe from harm." The moment was gone in an instant, but I was ready.

Both images: Nikon D3X with 16-35mm lens at 22mm, f/11 for 1/60 sec., ISO 200

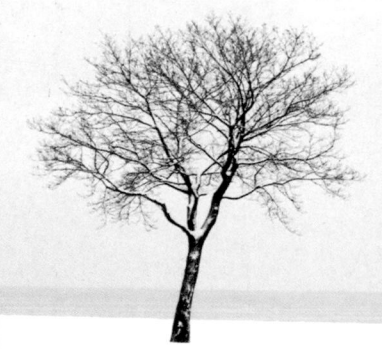

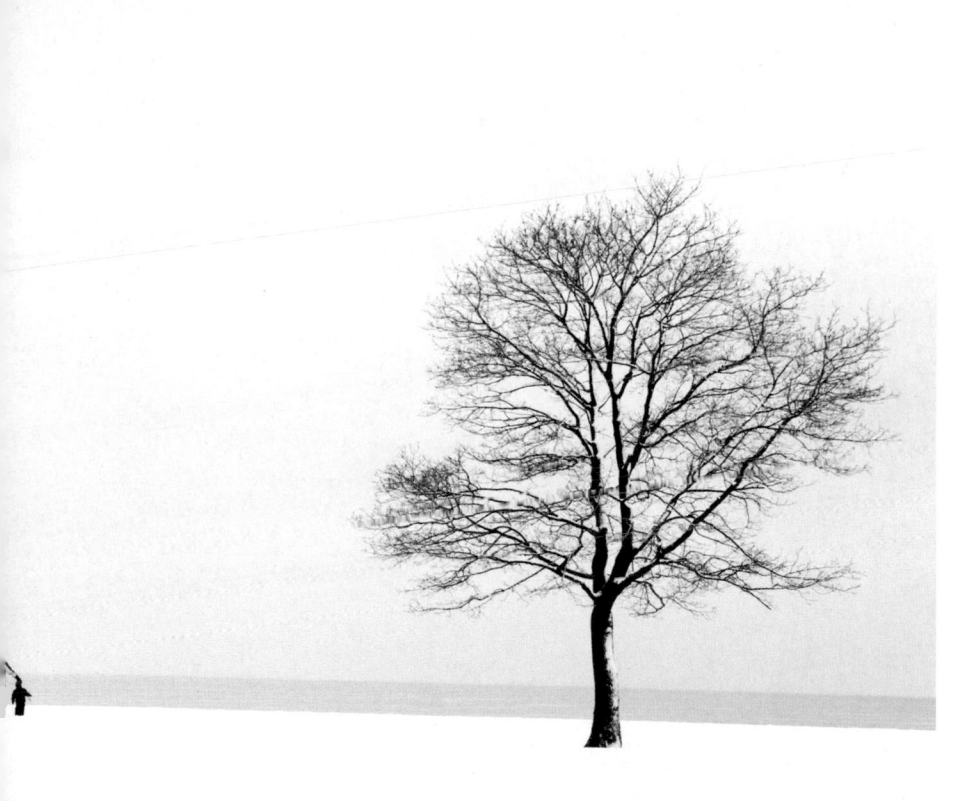

CAPTURING THE
DECISIVE MOMENT

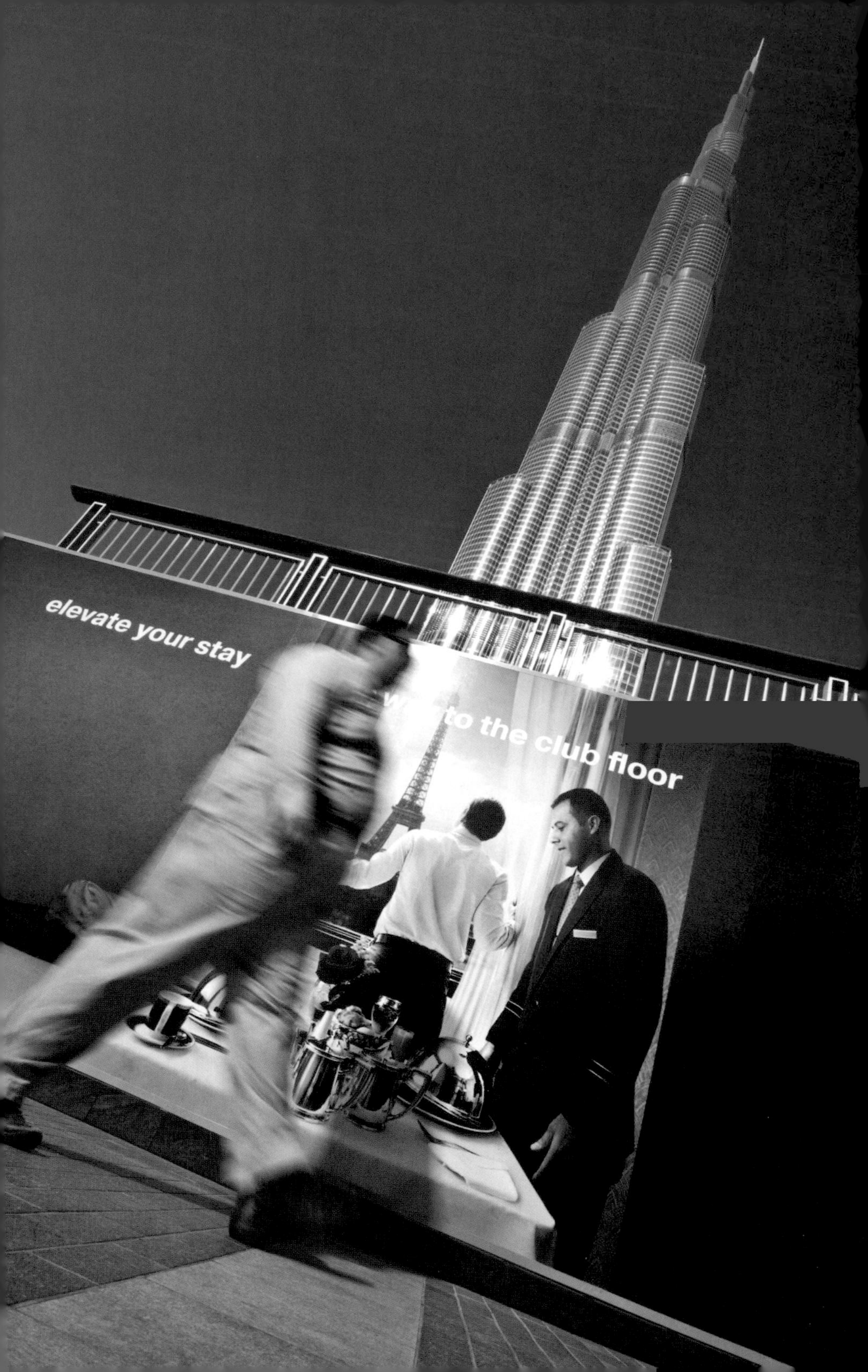
elevate your stay
to the club floor

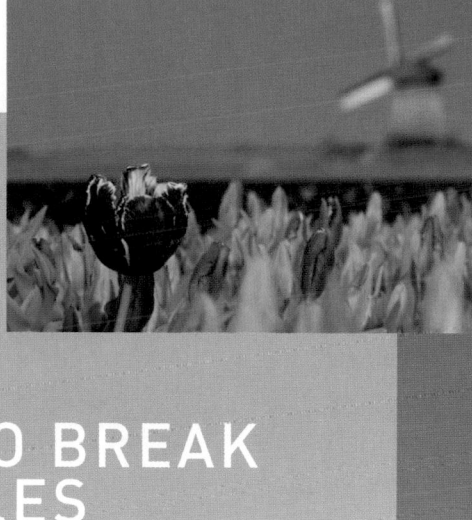

14

WHEN TO BREAK
THE RULES

Where would we be in this world without revolutions, protests, and strikes? Depending on which side of the argument you find yourself, it is safe to say that some revolutions, protests, and strikes have been good for society and some maybe not so good, but one thing is certain: humans were meant to revolt, to protest, and to speak out. So if you have issues with the rules and suggestions in this book, I fully understand. Actually, I agree with you! You and I are artists, and history has shown that artists have effected great change over time. As evidence, just look at the social change wrought by the iconic images of Robert Capa, Larry Burrows, and Eddie Adams.

Most of us do recognize "rules" of photography, yet as artists, we may also march to the sound of a different drummer. Yes, at times you will place the horizon line in the middle and deliberately center your subject. You may make it a point to create mergers, and even shoot exposures that are way too dark or light. Welcome to the world of anarchy!

Nikon D3X with Nikkor 16–35mm lens, f/11 for 1/400 sec., ISO 200

CENTERING YOUR SUBJECT

Although it may not happen often, there are some competitions—whether in the arts, sports, or business—where no *one* clear winner can be chosen. In effect, the performance of two actors, athletes, or salespeople can be so similar that both deserve a first-place award.

Similarly, when you come upon a mirrored landscape, such as a snow-capped mountain reflected in an alpine lake, there are clearly two "winners": the mountain and its reflection. In cases like these, placing the horizon line right through the middle of the frame gives both subjects equal importance, breaking the rules but somehow making perfect sense at the same time.

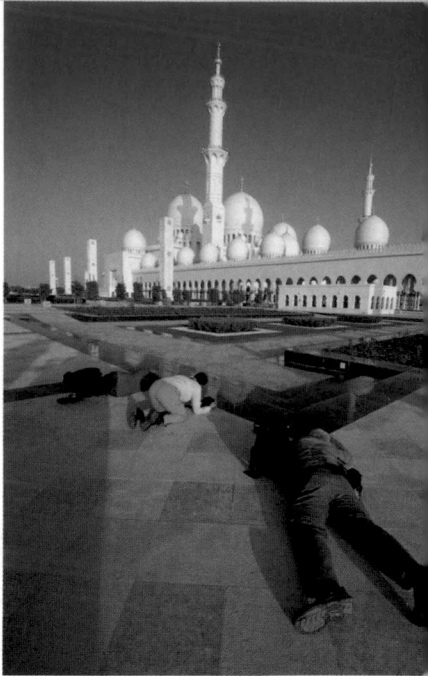

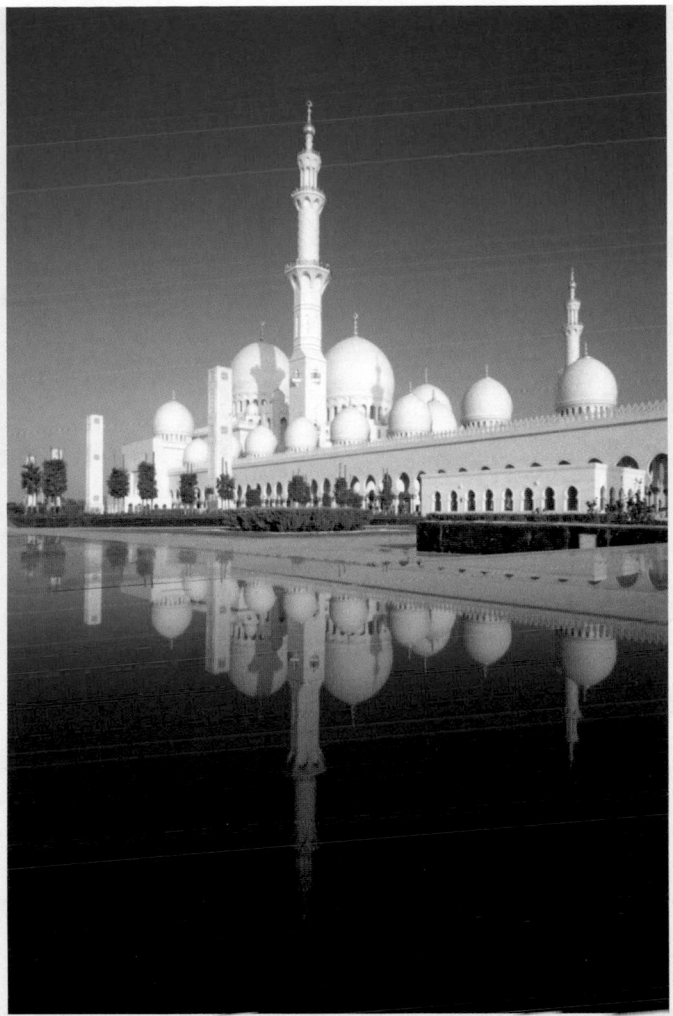

I am often surprised when asked where the horizon line should go when shooting a mirrored reflection. More often than not, these compositions insist on a horizon line running right through the middle of the frame. Despite the obvious 50/50 composition that this creates, you can end up with "two" images of the Golden Section at work, doubling the impact of the overall arrangement.

When I suggested to my students that they lie down at the edge of this highly polished black marble with their wide-angle lenses, they discovered a wonderful reflection of the Sheikh Zayed Mosque. Notice how the Golden Section is alive and well in both halves of this image. As such, it is anything but a static 50/50 composition.

Nikon D3X with Nikkor 16–35mm lens at 16mm, f/22 for 1/60 sec., ISO 100

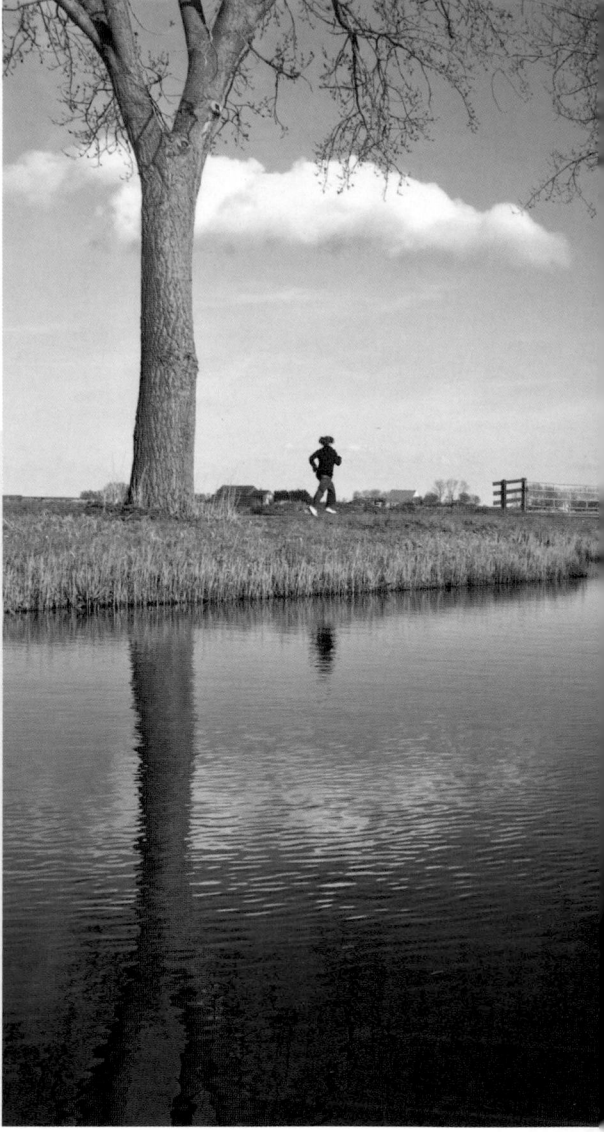

Water is a great source for mirrored reflections, and when the wind dies down, Holland gets my vote for offering the most mirrored reflection possibilities. It was during a break in one of my Holland workshops, when my assistant, Jill, and I ventured out to shoot runners in the landscape, with Jill standing in as the runner, red sweater already in her bag.

The resulting composition is split 50/50, but notice how the Golden Section is again alive and well in both sections of the image. Notice, too, how the lines of trees form converging parallels between the image's two halves for about two-thirds of the frame. The sense of movement, caused both by Jill running and the converging parallels, keeps the image from being static despite its 50/50 composition.

Nikon D3X with Nikkor 16–35mm lens at 20mm, f/16 for 1/125 sec., ISO 100

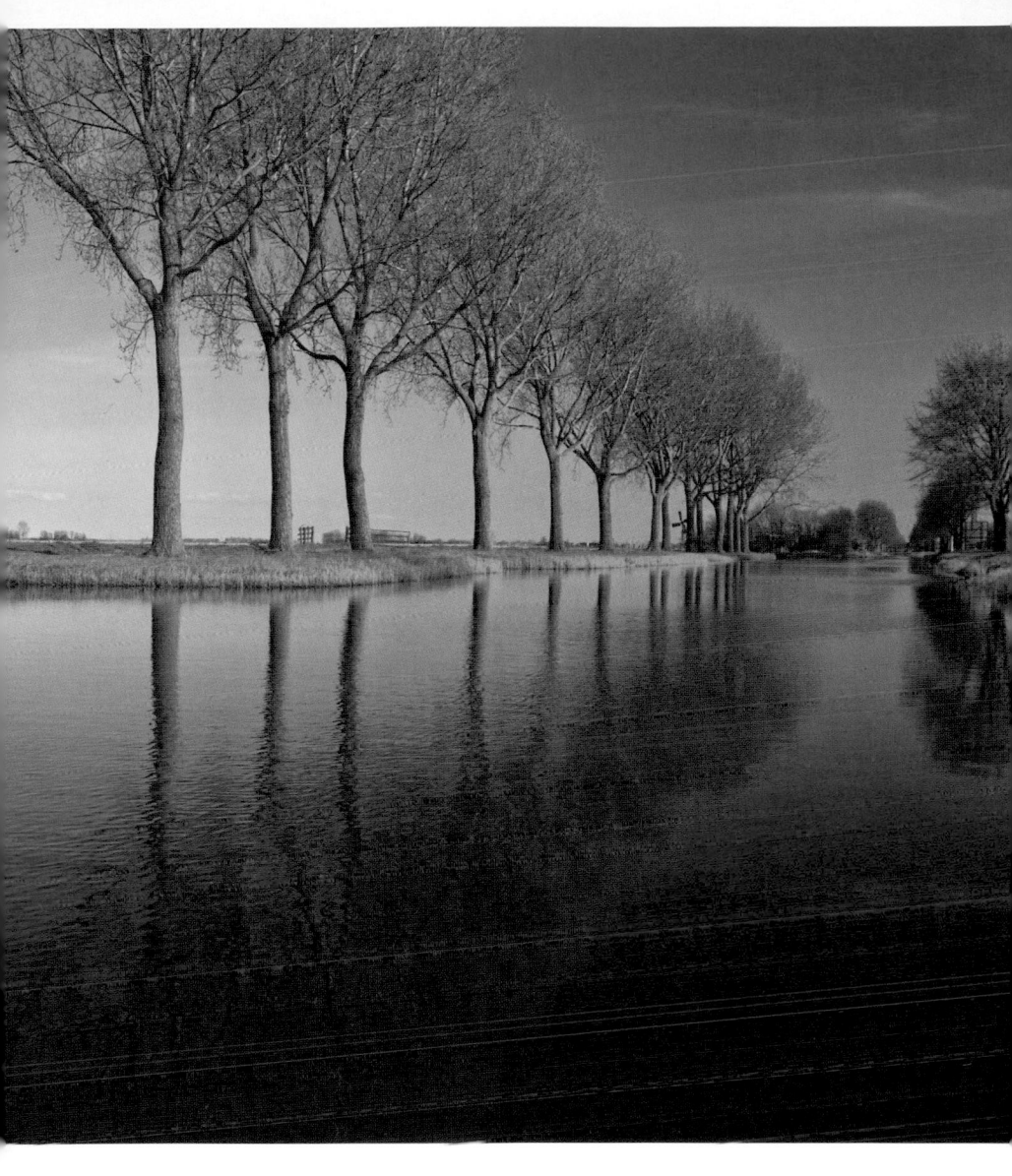

WHEN TO BREAK
THE RULES

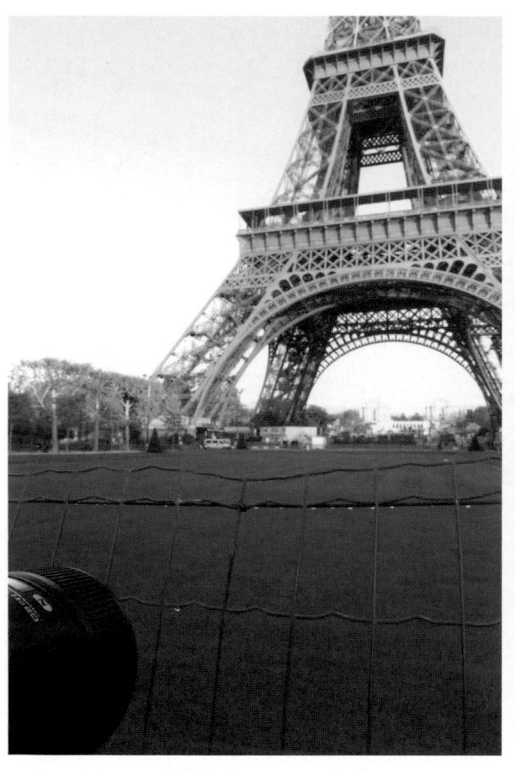

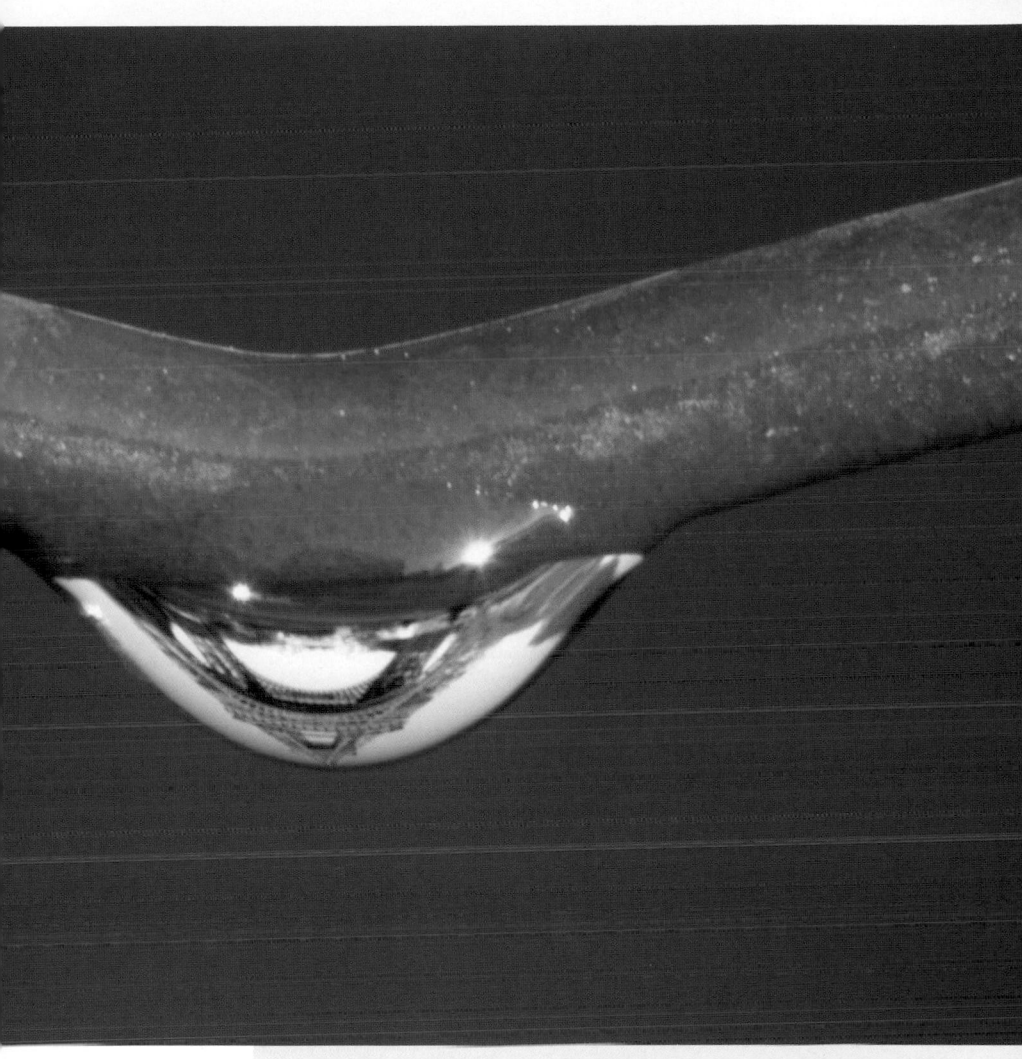

I was thrilled to discover some inexpensive fencing placed around the Eiffel Tower because it collected "dewdrops" from the previous evening's watering of the grass. On this particular sunny autumn morning, I reached for my Micro-Nikkor 105mm lens and got to work photographing these miniature "fish-eye lenses." Upon close inspection, dewdrops always record a fish-eye image of whatever is behind them—in this case, the Eiffel Tower. As you can see, the Eiffel Tower is there inside the dewdrop. And even though it is centered, it works! Why? In large part because of the strong curvilinear line, with its soothing, calming message. It just wouldn't work placed anywhere else but in the middle.

Nikon D3X with Micro-Nikkor 105mm lens, f/32 for 1/8 sec., tripod, ISO 100

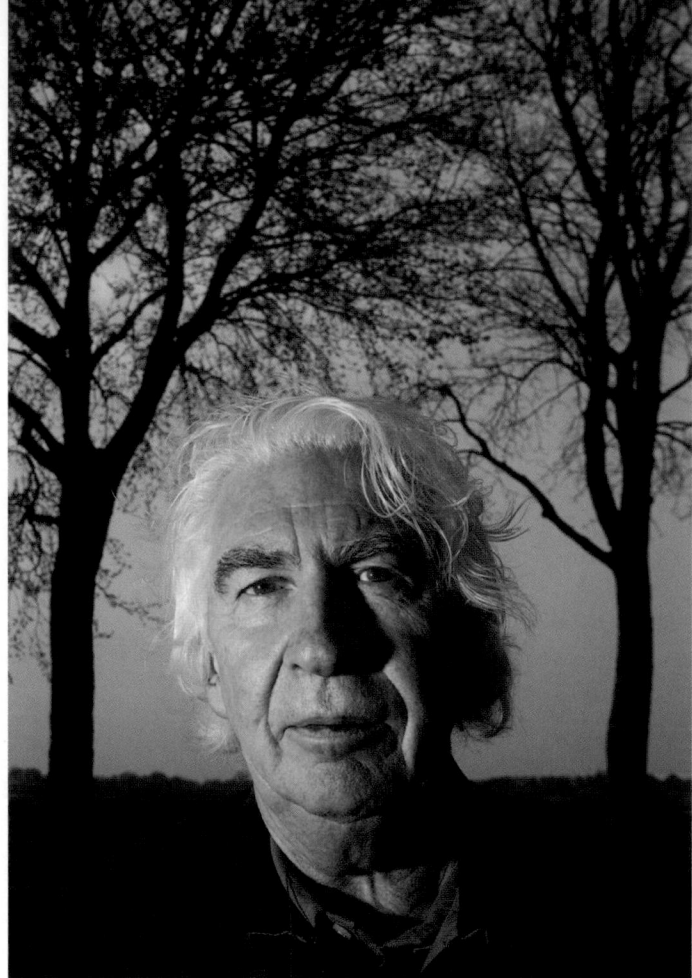

My student Dennis Bennett has the "Einstein look," and I have been photographing him since the first workshop he attended. You might recognize him if you own my book *Understanding Flash Photography*, since he is featured in that book several times. On this particular occasion, I was explaining the flash exposure technique of controlling the ambient light exposure with shutter speed, and Dennis agreed to be the model.

The resulting photo, shown here, was quick to stir up a dialog on why I had placed Dennis in the middle of the frame. On closer inspection, notice how the "background layer" of the two trees subtly frames Dennis. Notice also the placement of the horizon line, near the bottom third of the image. In effect, this image owes its balance and tension to the background layer. Even though Dennis comprises no more than 50 percent of this secondary layer, we are not troubled by it at all because of the background layer.

Nikion D3X with Nikkor 24–85mm lens at 35mm, f/16 for 1/125 sec., ISO 200

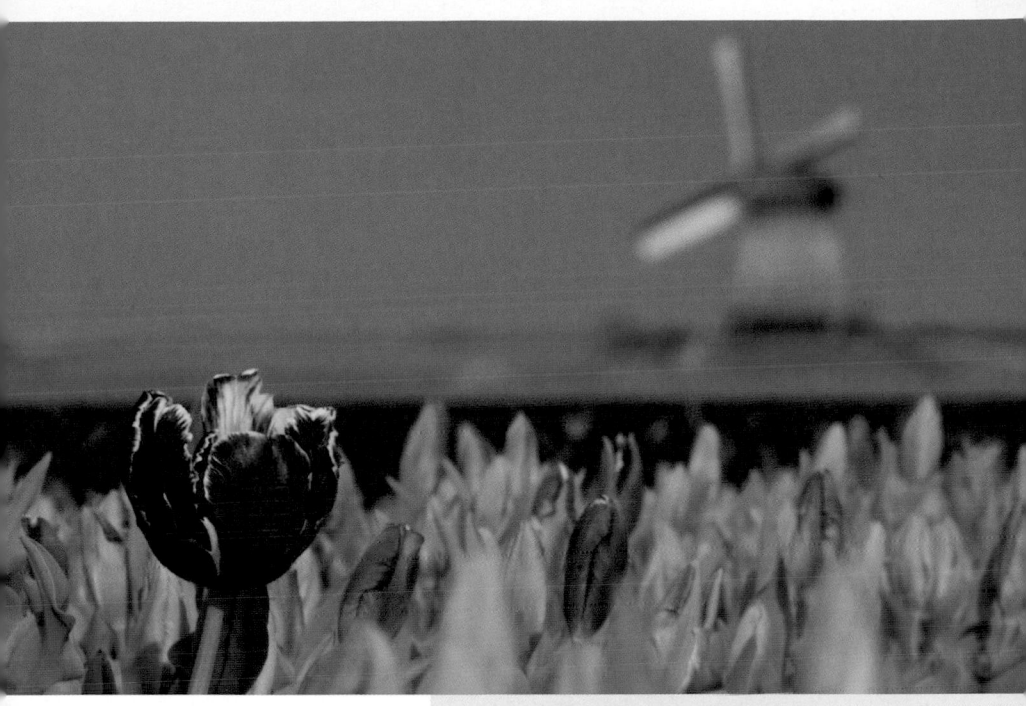

In this image, the horizon line runs right through the middle of the frame, yet it is hard to argue that this image does not work. Why? For one thing the visual weight of the in-focus flower keeps the eye from getting hung up on the 50/50 split of the landscape. The brain always assumes that whatever is in focus is the most important. Additionally, the tulip in the lower left and the windmill in the upper right combine to create a sort of diagonal line, which suggests movement and keeps the eye/brain from getting tripped up on the normally static feeling you would get from a 50/50 horizon line.

Nikon D300S with Nikkor 70–300mm lens at 300mm, f/6.3 for 1/500 sec., ISO 200

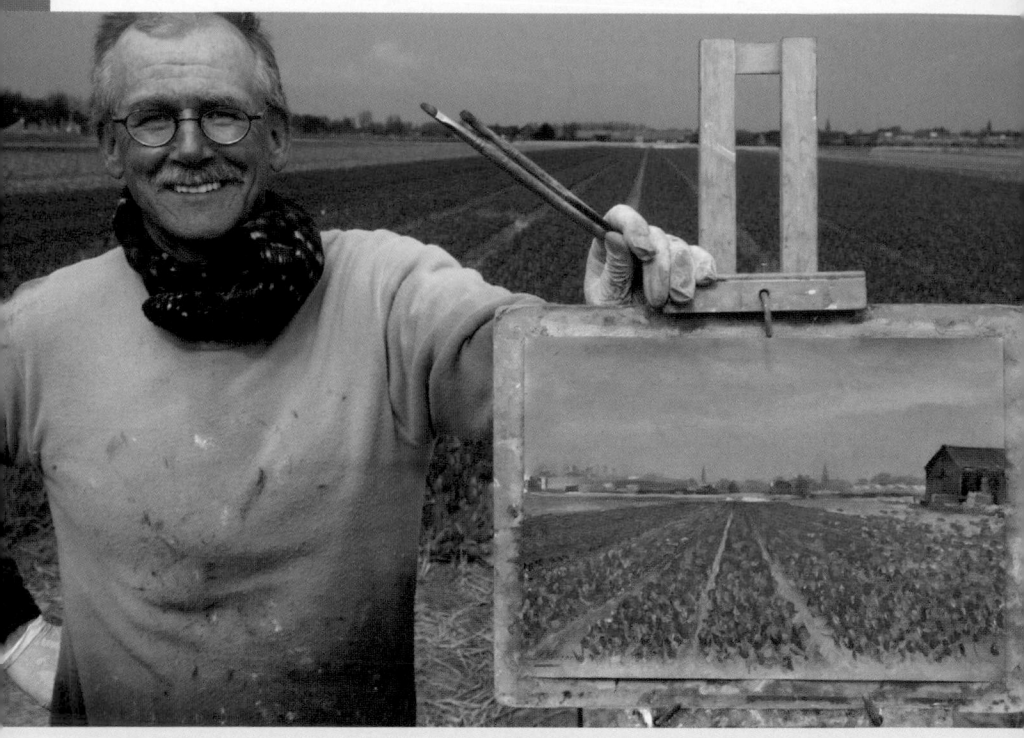

Above: This next image is a bit tricky. Clearly, I chose to place my horizon line near the top third of the image, yet it can be argued that the portrait of the artist and his painting divide the frame into two equal vertical halves. On closer inspection, however, notice how the painter's face, in the upper-left third, plays off his painting, found in the lower-right third. Again, the diagonal line between the two suggests movement, keeping the image from feeling static. (I might add that at no time did I discuss with the artist why he chose to place *his* horizon line in the middle of his painting, but I will say that the movement suggested by the converging lines of tulips eliminates any static sense and keeps the eye/brain from feeling bored.)

Nikon D3X with Nikkor 24–85mm lens at 35mm, f/22 for 1/60 sec., ISO 200

Opposite: When I shot the kayak racer shown here, the roar of the water was so loud that my students and I had to yell to speak to each other. The day had been all about superfast shutter speeds for razor-sharp, action-filled images. During a break, I suggested that we all consider panning or zooming the lens while handholding the camera and using abnormally slow exposures. Yes, this would result in blurry images but, oh my, would they ever be images of high energy! Funny thing about high-energy images: They don't have to be sharp to get the eye and the brain's attention.

Nikon D2X with Nikkor 70–200mm lens, f/22 with a 3-stop ND filter for 1/2 sec., ISO 200

EMBRACING BLUR

I was once sitting in a fairly large hall listening to a photographer talk, when the speaker shouted, "Sharpness is *king!*" It really got my attention. It also got under my skin when it became clear he was suggesting that at *no* time should *any* kind of blurring be allowed—other than from a "cascading waterfall." Needless to say, I would not be too popular in this man's photographic circle. I wrote a whole book about shutter speed, much of it dedicated to the idea of motion.

I still recall with great fondness an accidental image I shot years ago while visiting New York City for the first time. I was in Times Square and I accidentally tripped the shutter release on my Nikkormat FTn camera, which just happened to have the shutter speed set at 1/2 sec. Since this was during the era of film, I did not see the result of this mistake for several days. In fact, I forgot all about it, and not until I returned home and began editing the twenty-plus rolls of processed slide film did I stumble across that mistake and immediately exclaimed, "Wow!" Since that memorable day, I have made it a point to experiment with slow shutter speeds. Many of my experiments have been miserable failures, but as the saying goes, each failure has also brought me that much closer to success.

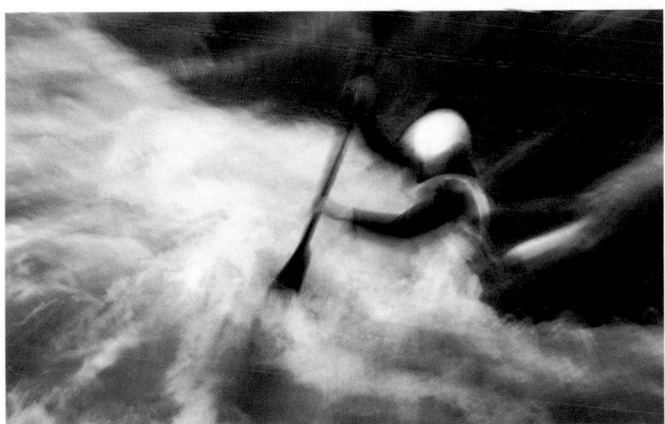

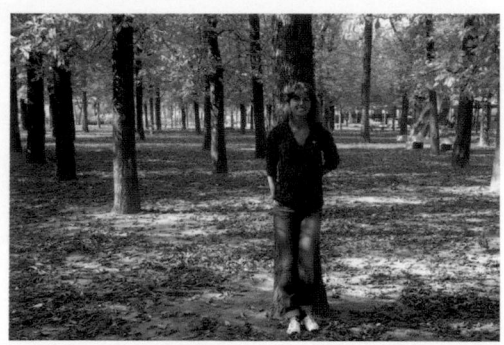

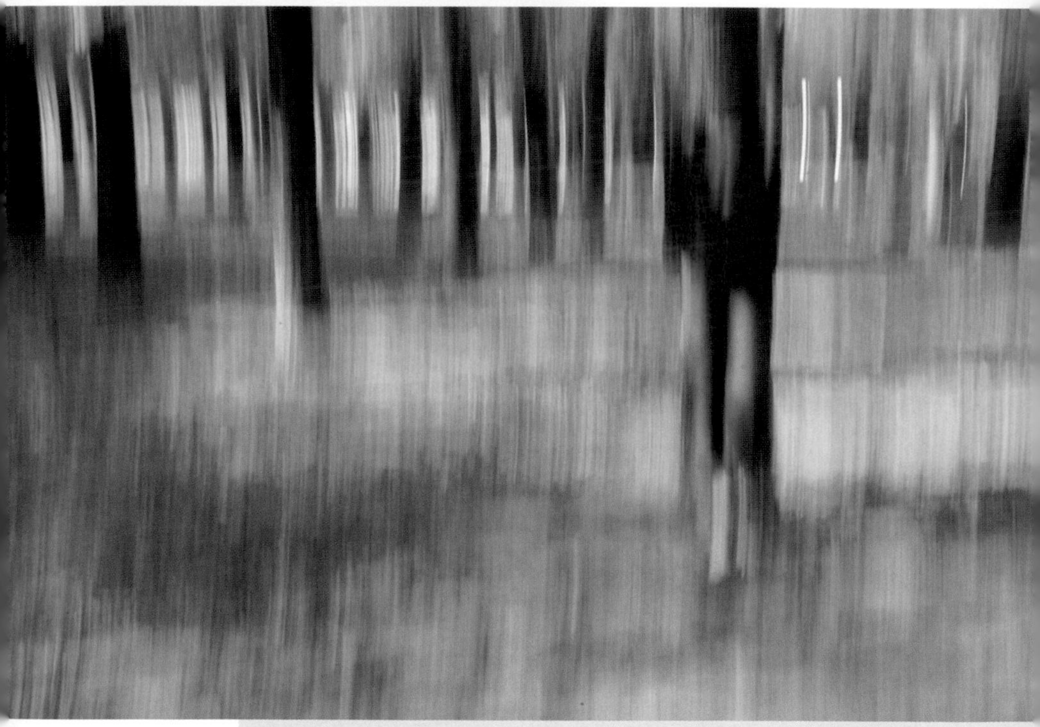

During my Paris workshop, the girlfriend of one of my students agreed to model for another "blurry" idea. As you can see, the first photograph (top) is a pleasing image of a young woman standing against a tree in a park. But when we take that same composition with a slower shutter speed, moving the camera in an upward manner, we get a blurry, sweeping, brushstroke effect and a much more active image. It isn't that the first image is bad, but this second image is another option on the road of creative expression.

Top: Nikon D3X with Nikkor 24–85mm lens, f/8 for 1/250 sec., ISO 100; Bottom: Nikon D3X with Nikkor 24–85mm lens, f/22 for 1/8 sec., 2-stop ND filter, ISO 100

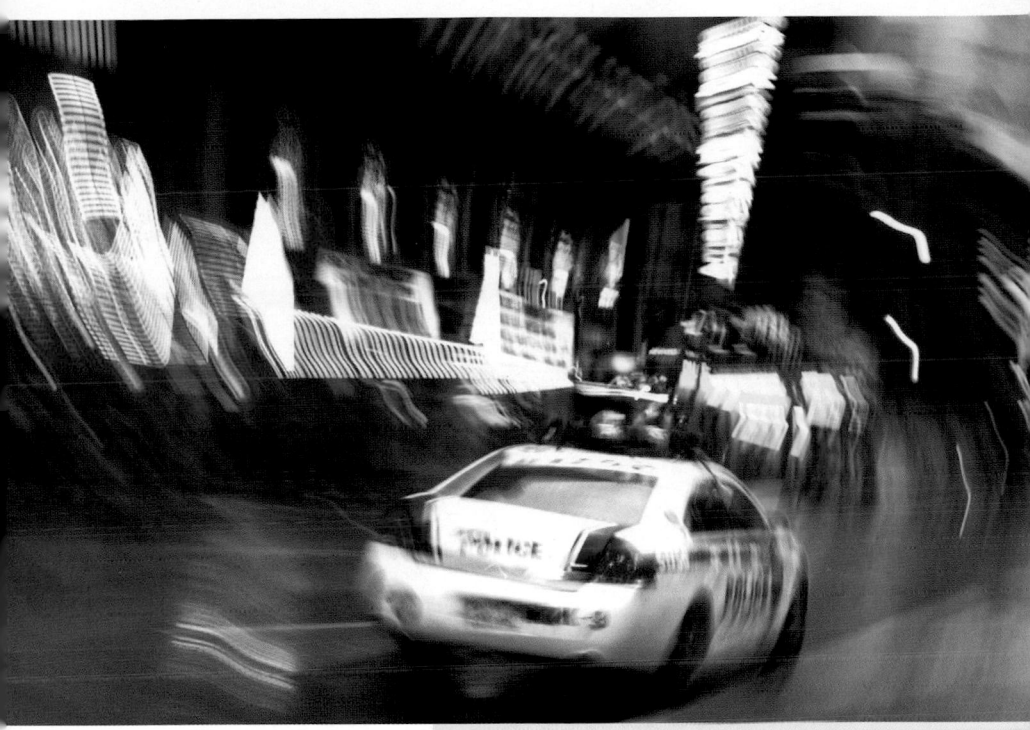

Consider the following the next time it rains and you find yourself out and about in a city. Stop your lens all the way down to f/22, and with the ISO at 200, chances are good that you will be able to get a correct exposure at or near 1/8 sec. (Add a polarizing filter to your lens if necessary.) Leaving your tripod at home, walk the streets and frame any number of colorful scenes, zooming, twisting, and spinning your street zoom lens as you shoot at 1/8 sec. (or, if you can, 1/4 sec.). Think of it as painting; the slow shutter speed combined with your moving of the camera creates the "brushstrokes." Don't worry about the rules of composition—just shoot! You could argue that in the image shown, the police car is too centered, and I would agree, at least for a second or two. But then I am quickly whisked away from any such concern by the simple energy of this overall composition.

Nikon D3X with Nikkor 24–85mm lens, f/22 for 1/8 sec., ISO 100

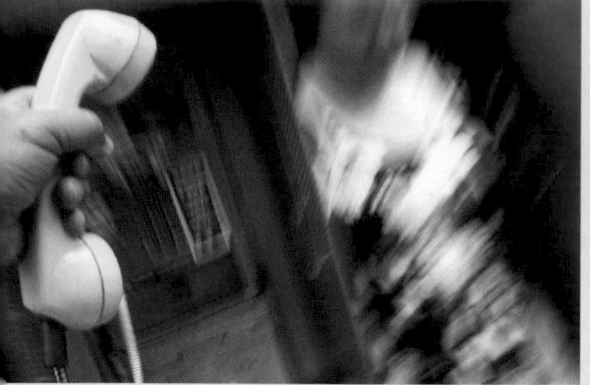

When was the last time you photographed your own hand? The possibilities are endless with this idea, considering the many things most of us can do with just a single hand. Here are just two examples: carrying my cup of coffee to a table at an outdoor café in Christchurch, New Zealand, and hanging up a phone on the Bowery in Manhattan. Both images are high energy, their blurred "brushstroke," as I call it, creating a wonderful and welcome tension as it surrounds and circles the somewhat sharp hand and coffee cup/phone.

Above: Nikon D3X with Nikkor 16–35mm lens at 20mm, f/22 for 1/15 sec., ISO 100; Right: Nikon D300S with Nikkor 12–24mm lens at 18mm, f/22 for 1/15 sec., ISO 200

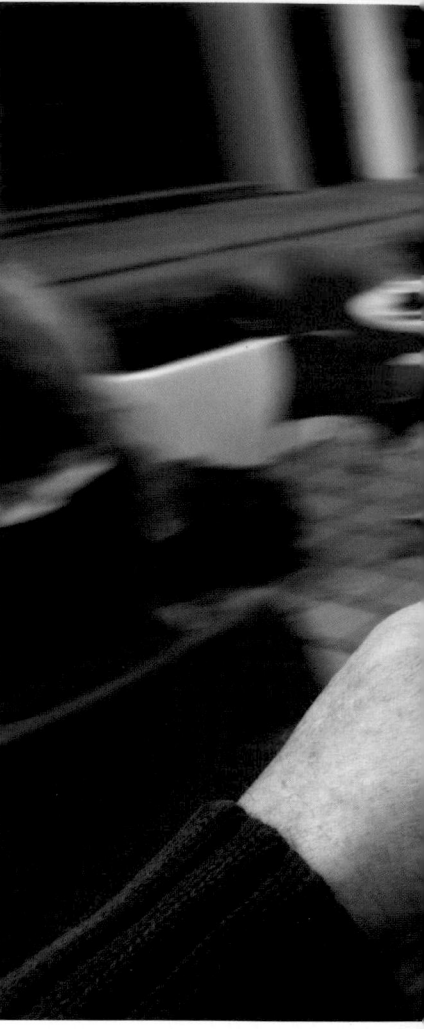

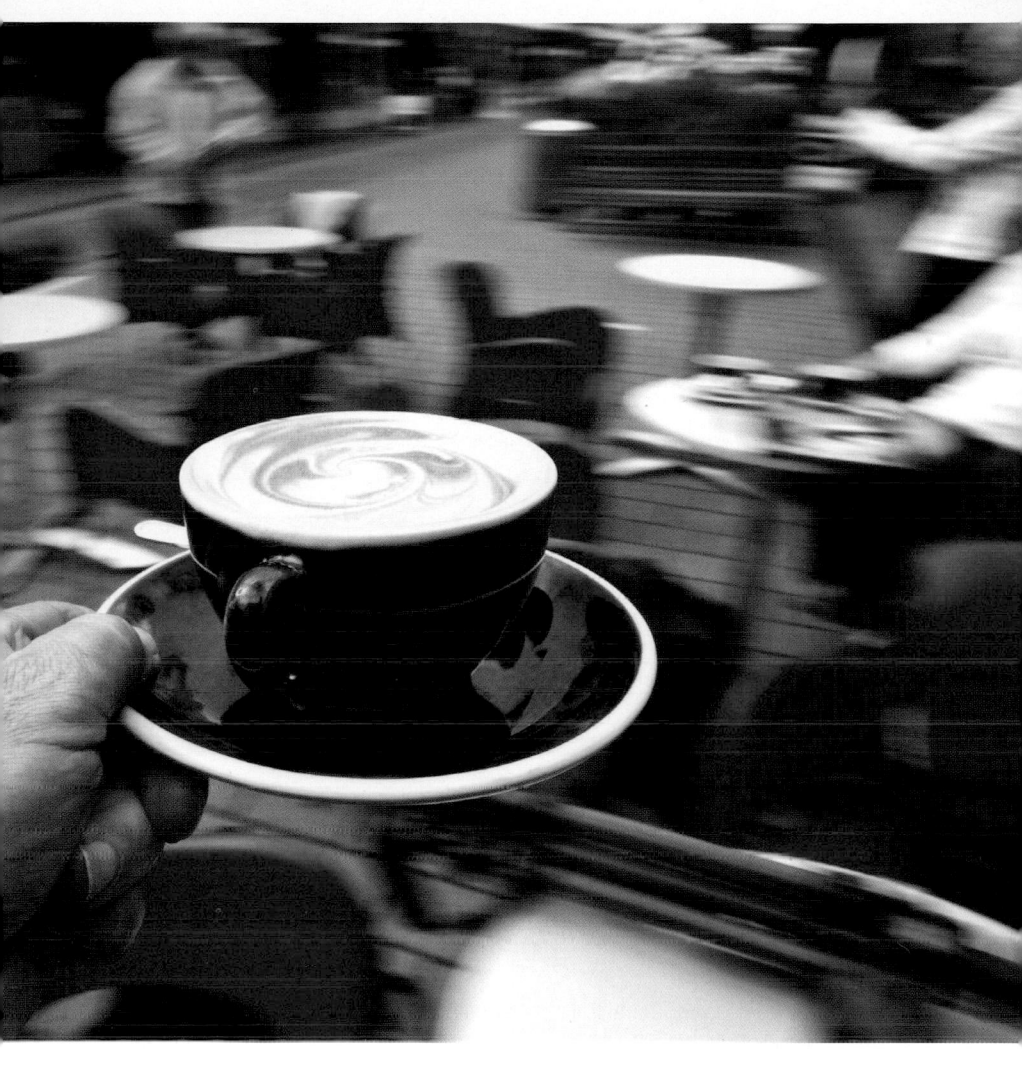

271
WHEN TO BREAK
THE RULES

TILTING THE HORIZON LINE

As I began editing my slides following a trip to the Mojave Desert some years ago, I felt great disappointment. Many of my slides of the very pristine desert scene, beautifully lit by early morning sidelight, were "off" because the horizon lines were crooked. Today there are accessories, namely bubble levels, which sit atop the camera's hot shoe to help you eliminate crooked horizons. Some cameras, Nikons specifically, also help you do this with a feature called the Virtual Horizon. Indeed, when it comes to the "picture-perfect postcard," a level horizon line is the norm. Yet I must add that crooked horizons—those made *deliberately*, mind you—do have their place.

I have a confession to make. It was at least ten years before I deliberately composed a scene with a crooked horizon, and it was one of the hardest things I've ever done. But even though my first one was ten years in the making, I haven't stopped since. A crooked horizon, especially when combined with motion, serves to accentuate the drama and the energy that motion-filled compositions inherently convey. The only decision you need to make, other than tilting your camera at an angle close to 45 degrees, is whether to suggest that your subject is going uphill or downhill!

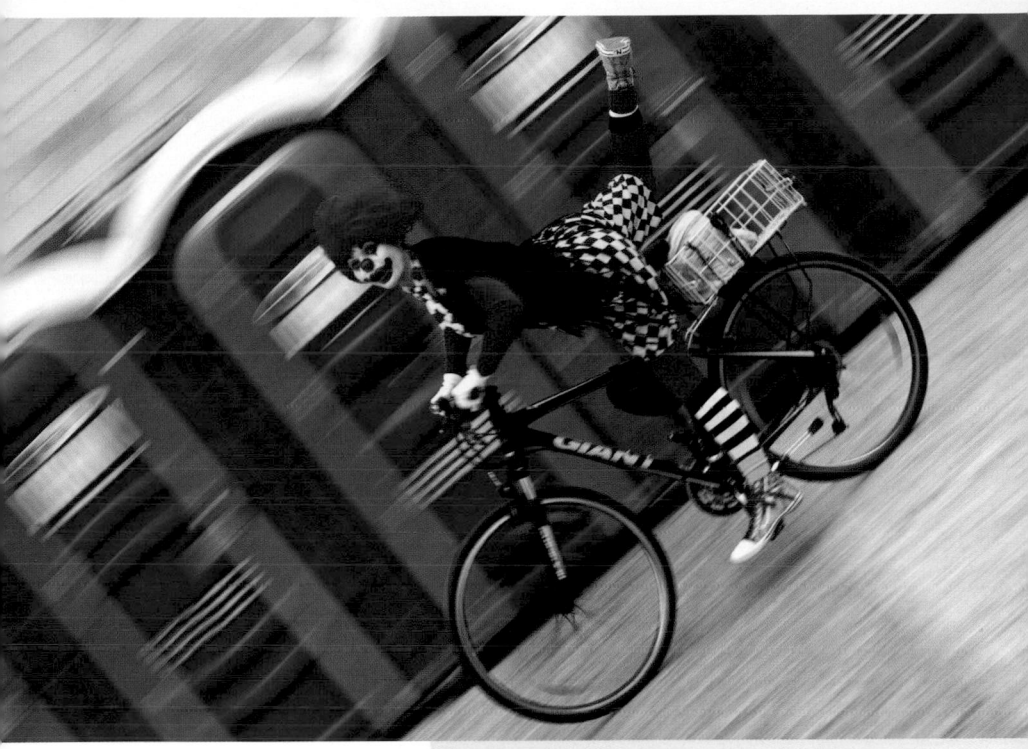

As this clown rode on her bike, I had the option of composing her going "uphill" or "downhill," and it's clear which one I chose. Why did I choose downhill? Look at the relaxed position of her leg. Rare is the bicycle rider who goes uphill with one leg in a restful position like this. By combining a slow shutter speed with "panning" the moving subject (moving the camera at the same rate of speed and direction of the subject), I created a motion-filled image. And with the added camera tilt and crooked horizon, I've heightened the speed and urgency of the clown on the bike even further.

Nikon D3X with Nikkor 24–85mm lens, f/22 for 1/20 sec., ISO 100

BUBBLE LEVELS

On top of your camera's hot shoe you can place a bubble level (available for purchase in most camera stores) that will help guarantee a level horizon. Other cameras have a Virtual Horizon feature, and many cameras today have a Rule of Thirds grid as well—all great tools for ensuring a clean composition.

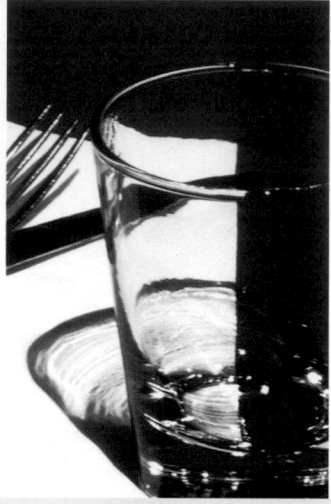

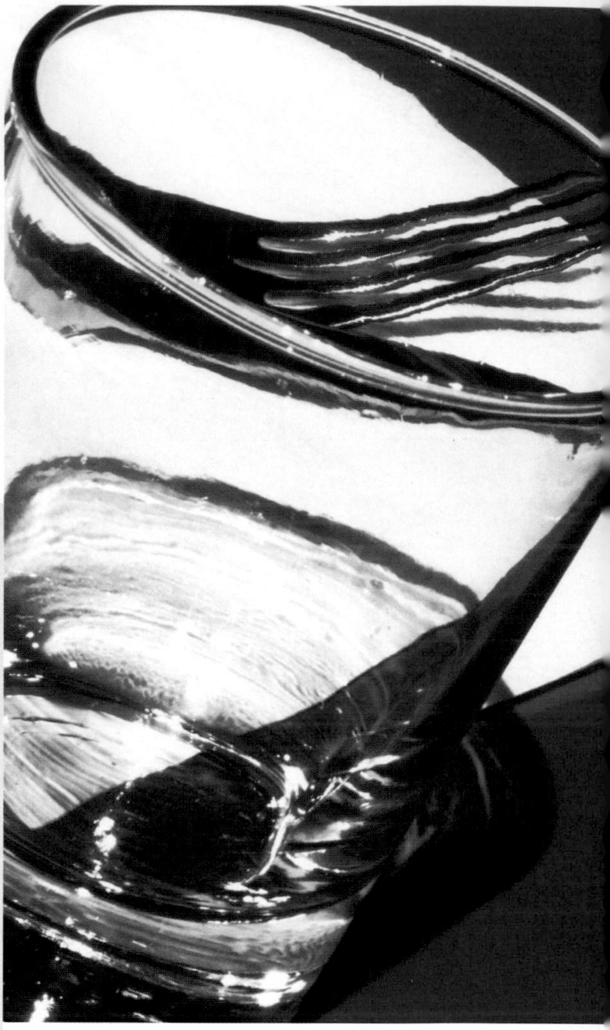

It's entirely possible that if I were a child today, I would be diagnosed as having a slight case of attention deficit/hyperactivity disorder. I have a hard time sitting still for any length of time; it seems no more than a minute or two goes by before I find myself reaching for my Leica D-Lux 5 or Nikon D3X with the Micro-Nikkor lens and looking at the silverware, glassware, or the salt and pepper shakers in front of me on the restaurant table. I guess I'm just curious, and that curiosity has led me to record some unlikely images over the years—images that do get people's attention.

On this particular day, at an outdoor café in Cassis, France, I was playing with the Leica D-Lux 5, shooting close-ups of the water glass and silverware against a colorful paper tablecloth. Quite honestly, it was not all that interesting until I started tilting the camera. As you can see here, even something as simple as line, shape, and color can benefit from a crooked horizon.

Leica D-Lux 5 with 24mm lens, f/5.5 for 1/250 sec., ISO 100

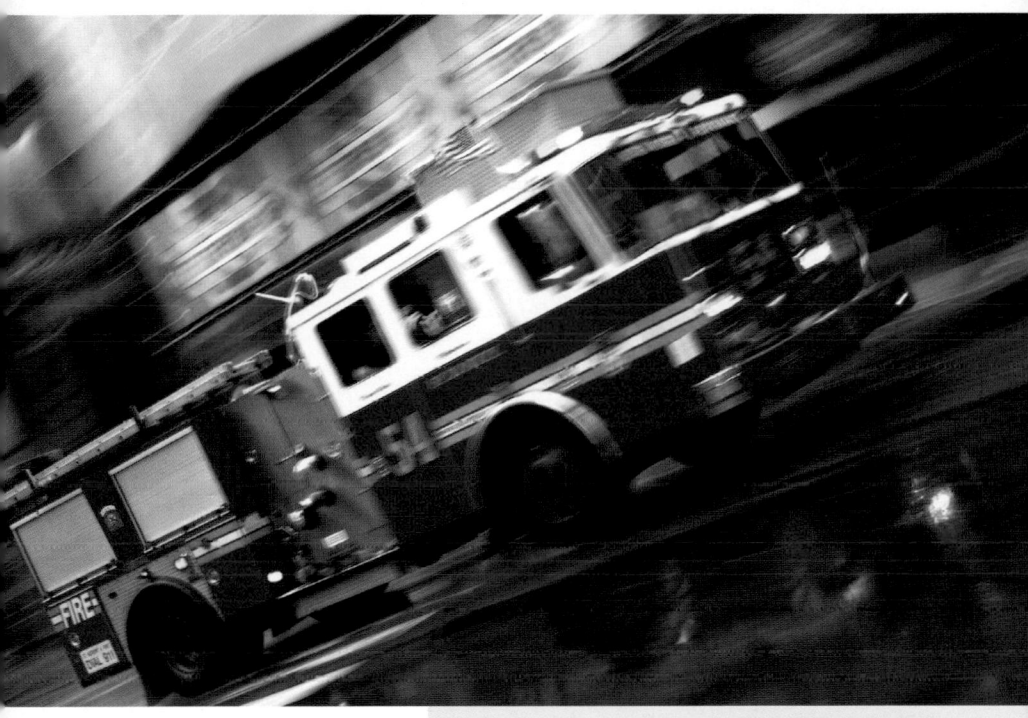

Putting out fires is hard work, so all the more reason to create the impression that this fire truck is waging an "uphill battle." Here the blurred background of New York City's Times Square serves up a healthy dose of streaked color.

Nikon D3X with Nikkor 24–85mm lens, f/16 for 1/15 sec., ISO 100

MERGING
ELEMENTS

In some situations, you'll want to delib-erately merge separate elements—sometimes for humor, other times for abstraction. The goal of a success-ful "merger" is to cause the viewer a momentary sense of disorientation.

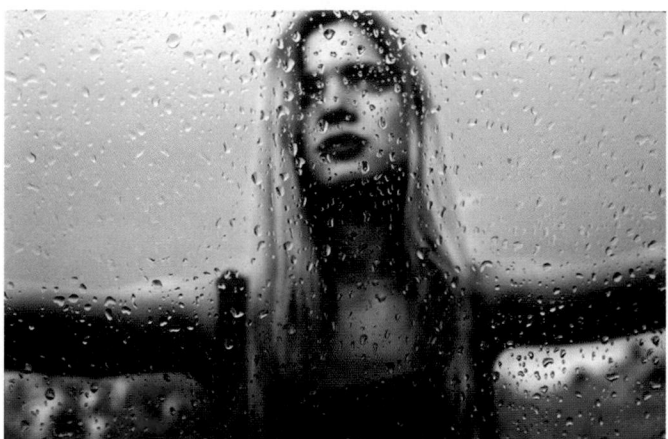
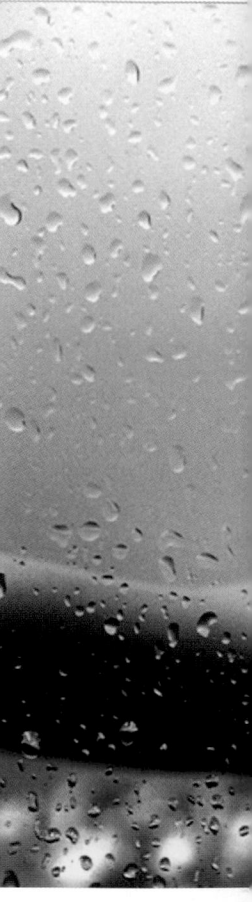

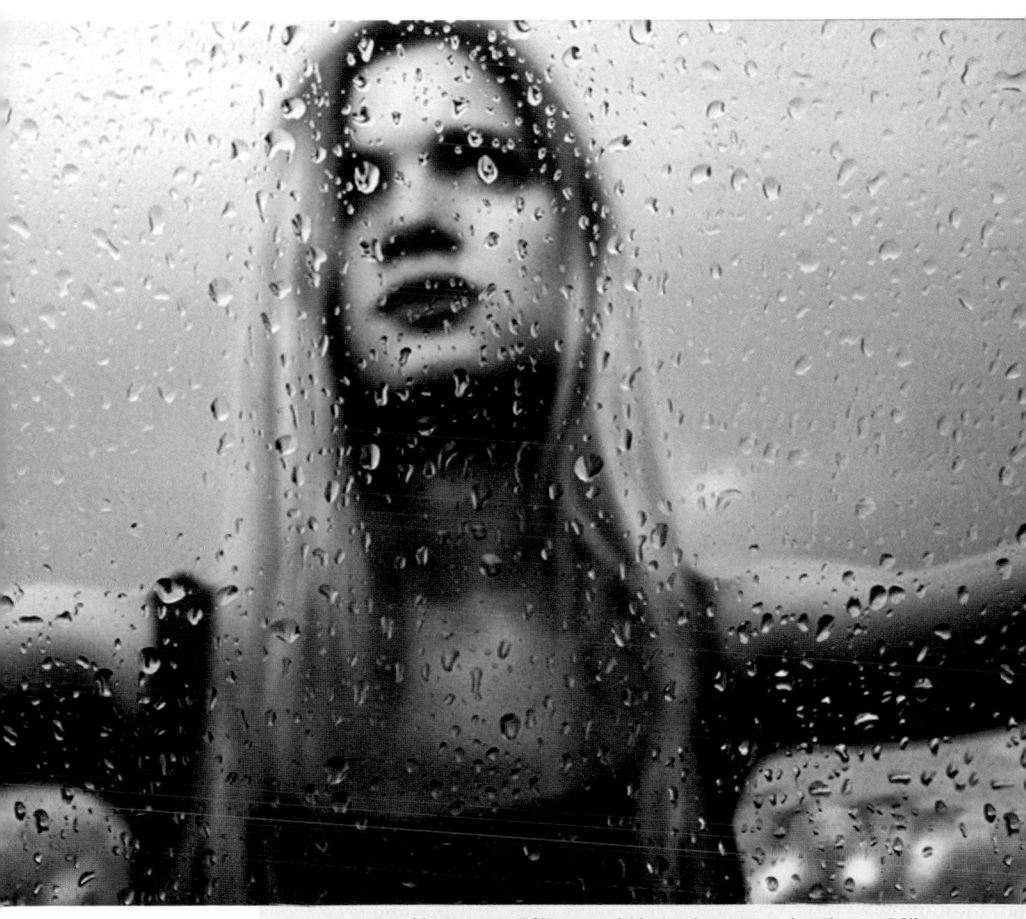

When we lived in France, Céline would babysit our two daughters. Céline was also interested in modeling, but on our first outing together it did nothing but rain most of the afternoon. So I asked Céline to stand with her arms outstretched, touching the car's roof, and shot a rather abstract image of her through the rain-soaked glass. After taking several shots, one of which you see at left, the idea came to me: What if Céline moved a wee bit to her left? I might be able to deliberately merge drops of rain over her eyes—and, as luck would have it, I was able to do just that. As the second image above shows, my daughters' babysitter was indeed someone you wouldn't want to mess with!

Nikkor 35–70mm lens at 35mm, f/8 for 1/30 sec., ISO 100

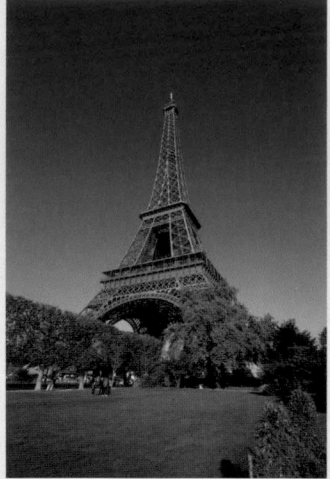

In truth, the Eiffel Tower is actually quite small. In fact, it is not much bigger than a small garden ornament that an ordinary garden vine can easily cling to. In all seriousness, one of the great things about a wide-angle lens is that it can contain a great deal of "stuff," due to its wide angle of view, plus it can focus very close. This gives us the opportunity to merge distant subjects with extreme close-ups to create some wonderful illusions. By walking up to the blooming vine you see above and shooting it up close while angling the camera upward, I created the impression that the vine is growing from the base of a very small Eiffel Tower.

Nikon D3X with Nikkor 16–35mm lens at 16mm, f/22 for 1/60 sec., ISO 100

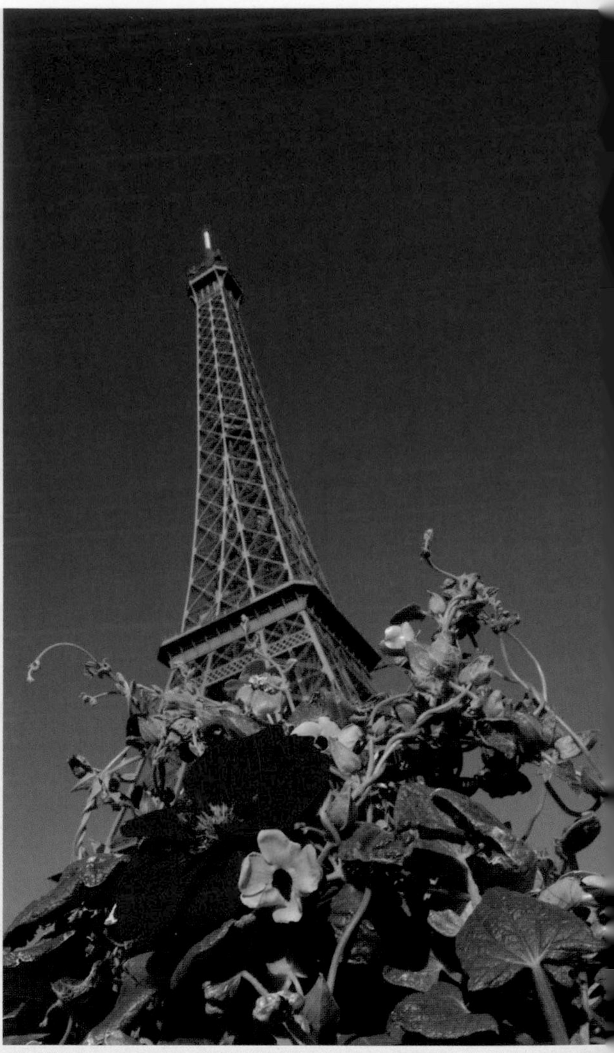

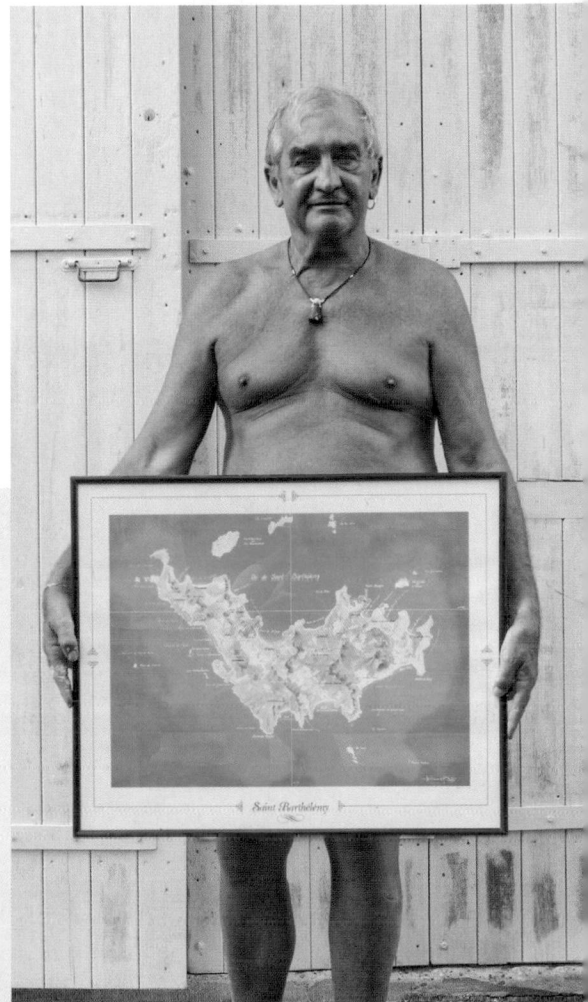

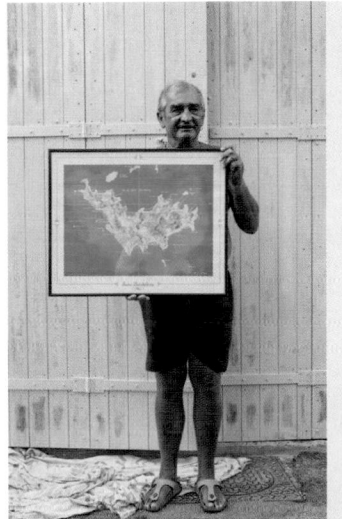

In the small town of Riez, near the Valensole Plain in Provence, France, I met a nice Frenchman who was anxious to share with me that he also owned a home in the French Caribbean. So important was it to him that during our brief conversation he rushed inside his small home and returned almost as quickly, holding a framed map of the Caribbean island where his home was located. He asked if I would take a picture of him holding the map, and although I thought his request was a bit odd, I obliged, initially capturing a perfectly pleasant snapshot of a guy holding a framed map. Almost immediately after taking the shot, I was struck with the idea of having him hold the picture frame in front of his shorts, and sure enough, it created the illusion that he wasn't wearing any clothes. Because I was shooting digitally, I was able to share the illusion with him and we both had a good laugh.

Nikon D300S with Nikkor 24–85mm lens at 24mm, f/11 for 1/200 sec., ISO 200

WHEN TO BREAK
THE RULES

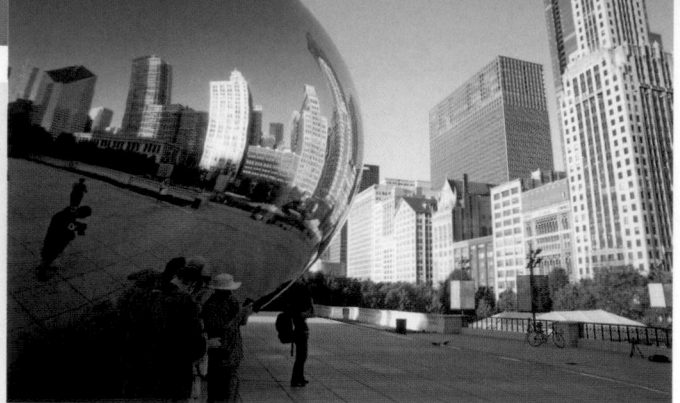

One of Chicago's most famous landmarks, artist Anish Kapoor's *Cloud Gate*, or the "Bean," as it is affectionately called by locals, offers numerous photo ops as the cityscape and its ever-changing light and weather is reflected in the Bean's highly polished surface. Handholding my camera and wide-angle lens, I moved close to the Bean and looked up, initially capturing part of the Chicago skyline along with its reflection in the Bean (above). After moving a bit closer to the Bean while still looking through the camera, I was able to merge a portion of the reflection in the Bean with the actual skyline, resulting in an unusual abstract (right).

Nikon D3X with Nikkor 16–35mm lens at 20mm, f/22 for 1/50 sec., ISO 100

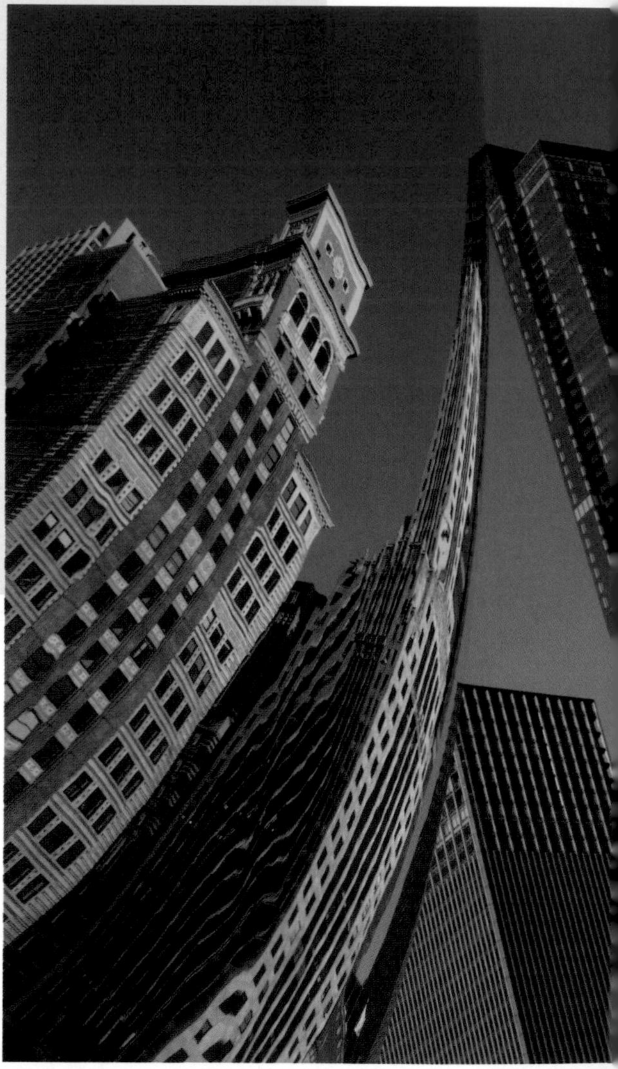

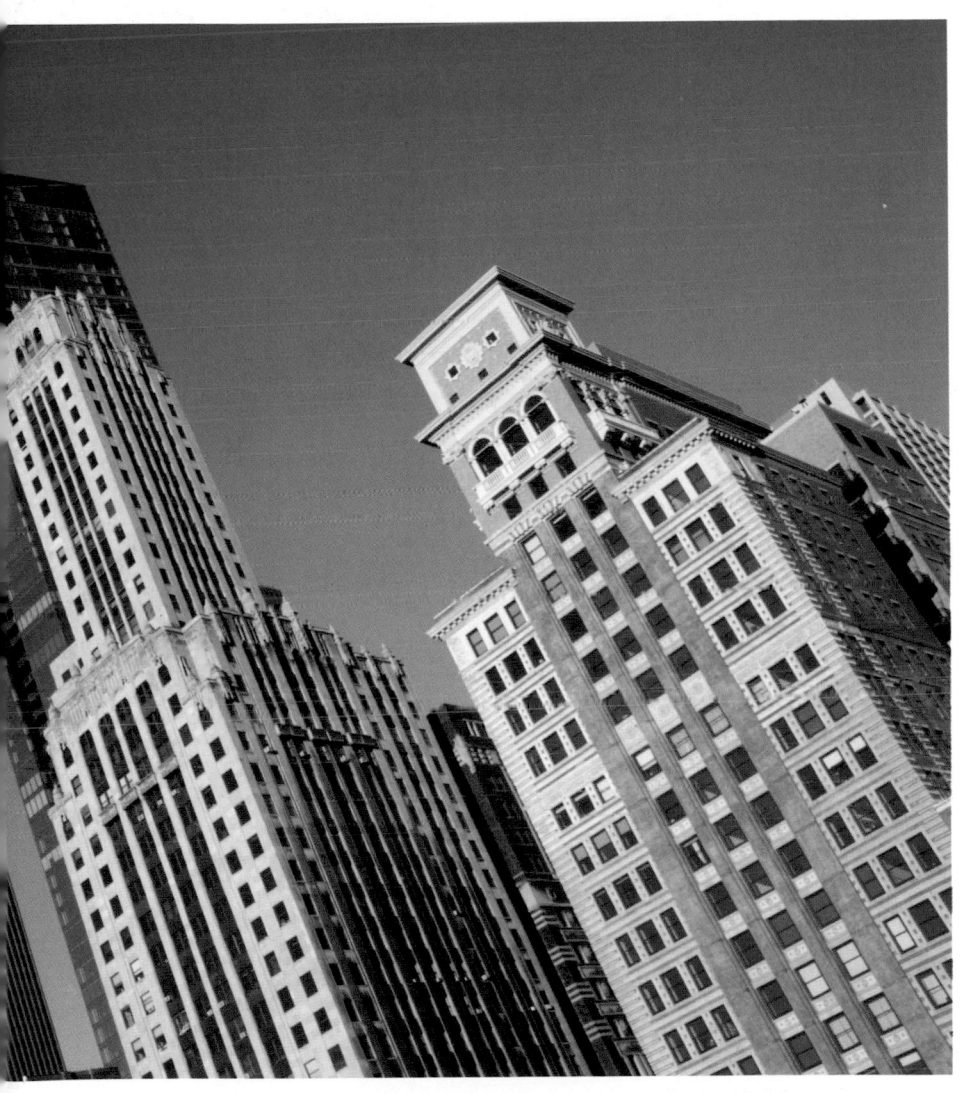

WHEN TO BREAK
THE RULES

NOT FILLING
THE FRAME

Many photographers would readily agree that filling the frame with their subject made all the difference in creating a composition with impact, and I would concur. Filling the frame, as I discussed earlier in this book, is one of the first and easiest compositional hurdles that every photographer needs to overcome.

Yet as a typical "artist"—aka rule breaker—this idea of "filling the frame" should not be considered ironclad. Whether you find yourself taking a number of steps back, or choosing a lens that deliberately "pushes" a subject farther away (such as the wide-angle lens), you will one day make the discovery that sometimes "small and distant" can create the biggest impact.

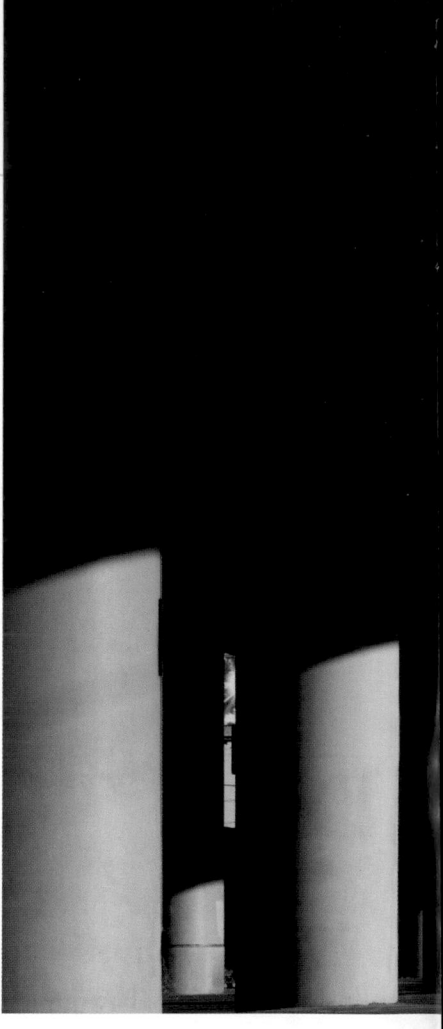

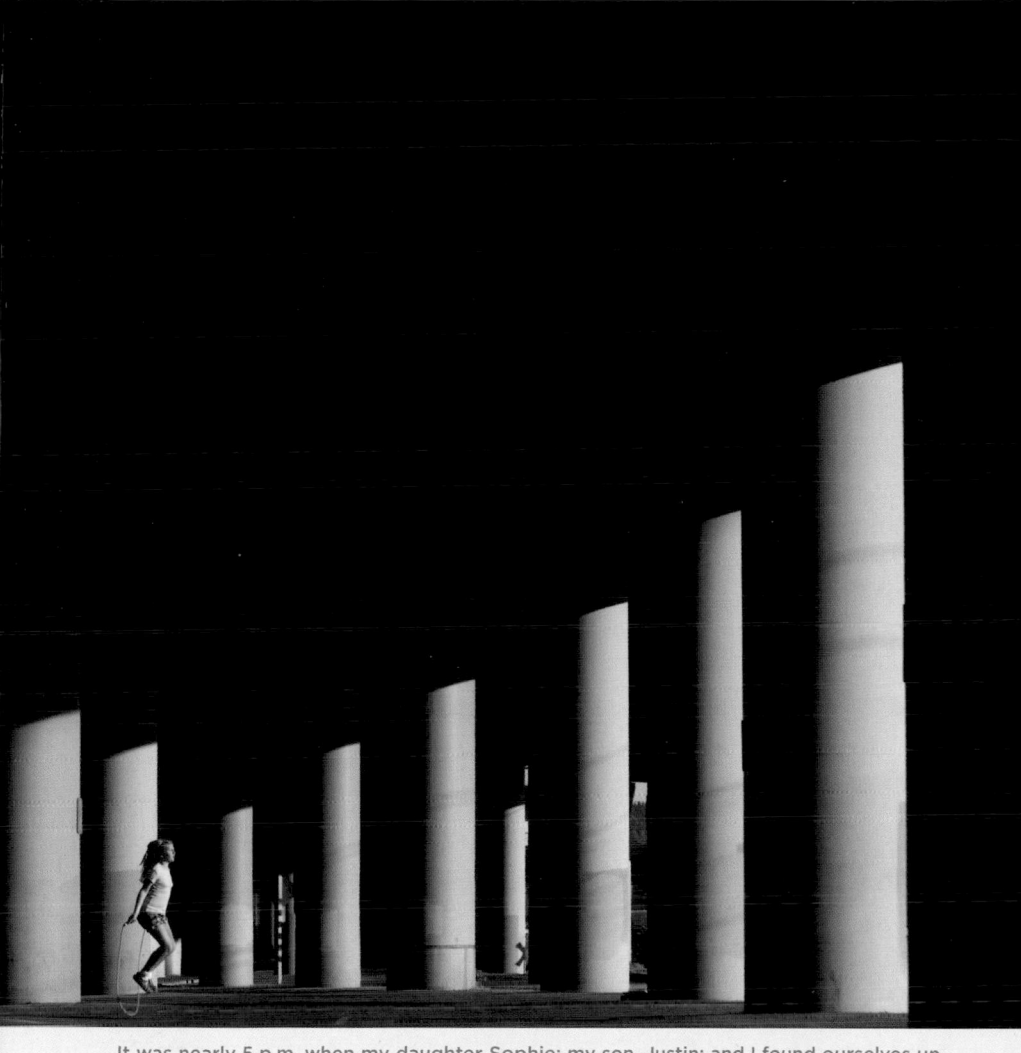

It was nearly 5 p.m. when my daughter Sophie; my son, Justin; and I found ourselves underneath the West Seattle Bridge near downtown Seattle. When I spotted Sophie jumping rope, I quickly got my camera and 70–300mm lens and framed the large pillar supports of the bridge, "filling the frame" with Sophie. You might argue that, in fact, the frame is not filled with Sophie, and I agree that the frame is not "physically" filled by her image. But psychologically, she does indeed fill the frame, and the reason is due to an optical law. When a pattern exists (as it does here with the repeating shapes of the pillars), any object or subject that breaks or upsets that pattern carries the greatest visual weight. Sophie looks nothing like the pillars so she clearly breaks the pattern and, in turn, gets all our attention. In addition, because we know the size and shape of the human form, we can also assume that the pillars are quite large. Finally, note how the low-angled light and resulting shadows create converging parallels of shadow, which lead the eye to Sophie and frame her, too.

Nikon D300S with Nikkor 70–300mm lens at 200mm, f/8 for 1/500 sec., ISO 200

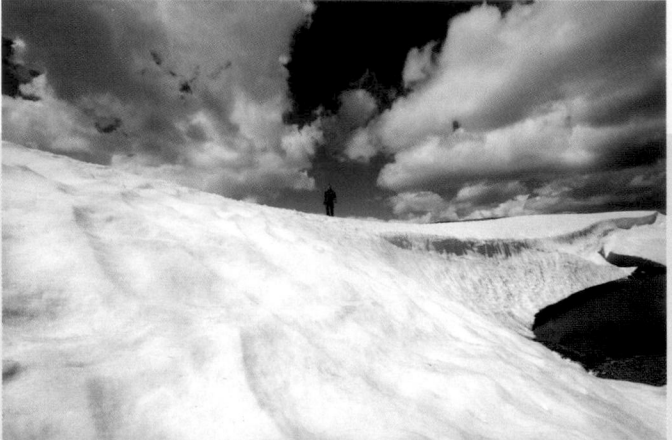

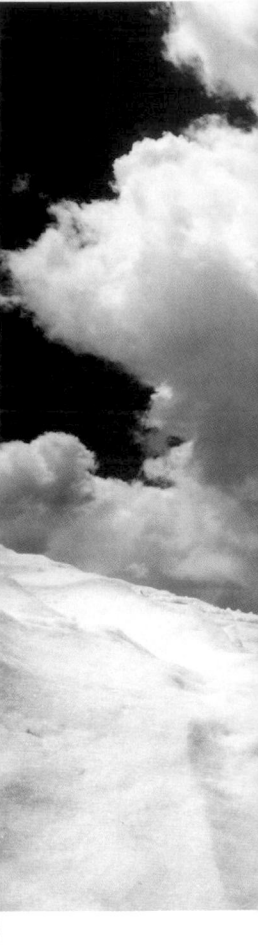

One of the least understood lenses by many amateur photographers is the wide-angle lens. At each and every workshop I teach, I hear several students say that they don't like the wide-angle because it makes everything look small and distant. I would be the first to agree with that statement, as well as the first to call on the wide-angle lens for that very reason—*if* I am photographing a "vast" landscape and can incorporate a person into the frame.

While hiking in the Bugaboo Mountains of Canada last summer with a group of students, we came across a small snowfield that, when shot from below, gave the impression of being far more vast than it really was. I asked one of my students, David, if he would walk across the snowfield, since he happened to be wearing a red jacket, the best color to contrast with all that white. Although David and the snowfield were no more than a hundred feet in front of me, the 16mm lens creates the impression that David is much farther away, and the snowfield appears much larger and more expansive (above). However, the inclusion of the exposed rock and small pool of water on the far right takes away from the illusion of a vast field of snow. Additionally, the horizon line is running through the middle of the frame and David is centered.

By moving a few feet closer and pointing the camera a bit upward, I was able to clean up the composition (right). Rather than fill the foreground with a portrait of David against a backdrop of a field of snow, I chose to place him in the scene as a very small, yet quite distinguishable subject. David's small size conveys immediately that the field of snow is "vast and huge." Although David is indeed small, his role in the overall composition is actually huge!

Both images: Nikon D3X with Nikkor 16–35mm lens at 16mm f/11 for 1/250 sec., ISO 100

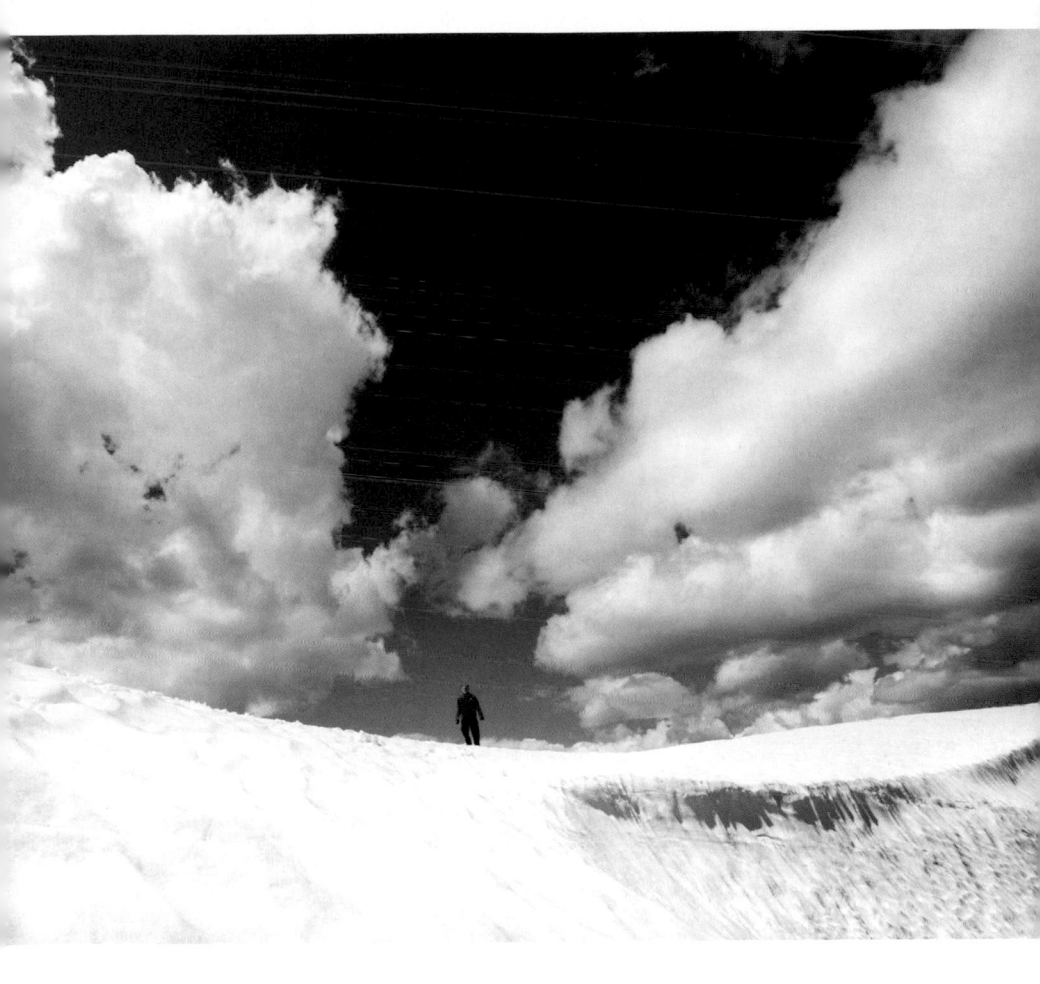

INDEX